T0224084

Lecture Notes in Computer Science 6299

Commenced Publication in 1973
Founding and Former Series Editors:
Gerhard Goos, Juris Hartmanis, and Jan van Leeuwen

Zoltán Horváth   Rinus Plasmeijer
Viktória Zsók (Eds.)

Central European Functional Programming School

Third Summer School, CEFP 2009
Budapest, Hungary, May 21-23, 2009
and Komárno, Slovakia, May 25-30, 2009
Revised Selected Lectures

 Springer

Volume Editors

Zoltán Horváth
Eötvös Loránd University, Faculty of Informatics
Department of Programming Languages and Compilers
Pázmány Péter Sétány 1/C, 1117 Budapest, Hungary
E-mail: hz@inf.elte.hu

Rinus Plasmeijer
Radboud University, Computer and Information Sciences Institute
Heyendaalseweg 135, 6525 AJ Nijmegen, The Netherlands
E-mail: rinus@cs.ru.nl

Viktória Zsók
Eötvös Loránd University, Faculty of Informatics
Department of Programming Languages and Compilers
Pázmány Péter Sétány 1/C, 1117 Budapest, Hungary
E-mail: zsv@inf.elte.hu

Library of Congress Control Number: 2010940290

CR Subject Classification (1998): D.1.1, D.3.2, F.3.3, D.1-2, D.1.5, C.2, F.4

LNCS Sublibrary: SL 1 – Theoretical Computer Science and General Issues

ISSN   0302-9743
ISBN   978-3-642-17684-5 Springer Berlin Heidelberg New York

springer.com

© Springer-Verlag Berlin Heidelberg 2010

Typesetting: Camera-ready by author, data conversion by Scientific Publishing Services, Chennai, India
Printed on acid-free paper   06/3180

Preface

This volume presents the revised lecture notes of selected talks given at the third Central European Functional Programming School, CEFP 2009, held during 25–30 May in Komárno (Slovakia) at Selye János University. It was co-organized with the TFP 2009 conference. The summer school included a three-day warm-up session organized at Eötvös Loránd University, Budapest, Hungary during 21–23 May, 2009.

The summer school was organized in the spirit of the advanced programming schools. CEFP focuses on involving an ever-growing number of students, researchers, and teachers from Central- and Eastern-European countries. The intensive program offered a creative and inspiring environment and a great opportunity to present and exchange ideas on new topics of functional programming.

The lectures covered a wide range of subjects like design patterns, semantics, types, and advanced programming in various functional programming languages.

We are very grateful to the lecturers and researchers for the time and the effort they devoted to the talks and the revised lecture notes. The lecture notes were each carefully checked by reviewers selected from experts on functional programming. Afterwards the papers were revised once more by the lecturers. This revision process guaranteed that only high-quality papers were accepted for the volume.

The last two papers of the volume are selected papers from the PhD workshop of the summer school.

We would like to express our gratitude for the work of all the members of the Program Committee and the Organizing Committee.

The web-page for the summer school can be found at
http://www.inf.elte.hu/english/conf/tfp_cefp_2009/

August 2010

Zoltán Horváth
Rinus Plasmeijer
Viktória Zsók

Organization

CEFP 2010 was co-organized by the Selye János University, Komárno (Slovakia) and Eötvös Loránd University, Budapest, Hungary.

Sponsoring Institutions

The summer school was supported by the CEEPUS program (via the CEEPUS CII-HU-19 Network) and by the two organizing universities.

Table of Contents

Rapid Prototyping of DSLs with F# 1
  Adam Granicz

Erlang Behaviours: Programming with Process Design Patterns 19
  Francesco Cesarini and Simon Thompson

Reasoning about Codata 42
  Ralf Hinze

Programming in Manticore, a Heterogenous Parallel Functional
Language 94
  Matthew Fluet, Lars Bergstrom, Nic Ford, Mike Rainey,
  John Reppy, Adam Shaw, and Yingqi Xiao

Non-monadic Models of Mutable References 146
  Péter Diviánszky

Software Testing with QuickCheck 183
  John Hughes

An Effective Methodology for Defining Consistent Semantics of
Complex Systems 224
  Pieter Koopman, Rinus Plasmeijer, and Peter Achten

Types for Units-of-Measure: Theory and Practice 268
  Andrew Kennedy

Functional Programming with C++ Template Metaprograms 306
  Zoltán Porkoláb

Embedding a Proof System in Haskell 354
  Gergely Dévai

Impact Analysis of Erlang Programs Using Behaviour Dependency
Graphs 372
  Melinda Tóth, István Bozó, Zoltán Horváth, László Lövei,
  Máté Tejfel, and Tamás Kozsik

Author Index 391

Rapid Prototyping of DSLs with F#

Adam Granicz

IntelliFactory, Budapest, Hungary
adam.granicz@intellifactory.com
http://www.intellifactory.com

Abstract. In these lecture notes we present the F# implementation of a small programming language we call Simply. We give the parser implementation using active patterns, F#'s unique feature for extensible pattern matching, which as we demonstrate provide an elegant and type-safe mechanism to embed parsers as an alternative approach to parser generators. We also build an evaluator, and extend the core Simply language with Logo-like primitives and build a graphical shell environment around it.

As a warm-up, we give a rudimentary survey of some notable F# features, including sequence expressions and active patterns. For a treatment of units of measure, used briefly in the Simply shell environment, the reader is encouraged to study [AK-09] and [AK-CEFP-09].

1 F#

F# is a statically type-checked, type-inferred, script-like functional programming language for the .NET framework. It supports object-oriented and imperative programming, and comes with built-in language features for asynchronous and metaprogramming [DS-06]. For more information about F# refer to [DS-09].

1.1 Getting Started with F#

Most of the examples in this warm-up section and the later sections on DSL development can be typed in directly into F# Interactive, and in fact, this is the easiest way to get acquainted with F#. F# Interactive can be run in two modes: directly as a command-line tool by invoking fsi.exe, or inside Visual Studio as a plug-in - which is installed by default with the F# Visual Studio extensions (part of the main F# installer). As the lecture goes on, it is suggested to try the examples with Visual Studio, by opening an F# sandbox project and adding F# source files to this project. Therefore, it is easy to interact with F# Interactive either by typing code into the F# Interactive window, or highlighting some code in the editor window and pressing Alt+Enter. This Visual Studio command sends the highlighted text into F# Interactive, adding any new definitions into the currently running session.

An F# Interactive session can be exited and restarted any time by typing "exit 1;;" into the F# Interactive window.

Z. Horváth, R. Plasmeijer, and V. Zsók (Eds.): CEFP 2009, LNCS 6299, pp. 1–18, 2010.

1.2 Sequences and Sequence Expressions

Sequences are data that can be enumerated on demand - they are a lazy data structure. The F# data type `seq<'T>` is an alias for the .NET interface type `IEnumerable<'T>`, and effectively all of the .NET and F# collections are sequences.

Sequences are a powerful abstraction in F# programming, and in fact they are used to wrap all kinds of data sources besides ordinary collections, including databases, LINQ queries for XML and relational data, and so on.

F# provides rich support for sequences. Ordinary *sequences* of integers and real numbers can easily be constructed using the sequence notation:

```
{ 1 .. 100 }       // All integers between 1 and 100.
{ 1.0 .. 100.0 }  // All integers between 1 and 100 as doubles.
{ 1 .. 2 .. 100 } // All odd numbers between 1 and 100.
```

Sequence comprehensions are a formalism to construct a sequence of values using a generator function:

```
seq { for i in 1 .. 100 -> i*i }  // The first 100 squares.
```

This code is equivalent to

```
seq { 1 .. 100 } |> Seq.map (fun i -> i*i)
```

Sequence expressions are a form of *computation expressions* or *workflows*, F#'s unique feature that adds *monadic syntax* over F# code.

Consider the example in Figure 1 that yields all the files in a given folder including those in all the subfolders.

Note that subfolders are not searched until the sequence is enumerated, e.g. until the file names are actually consumed. In this expression, `yield` is used to return a single new element in the sequence, and `yield!` to return a sequence of elements.

```
open System.IO

let rec AllFiles dir =
    seq { for file in dir |> Directory.GetFiles do
              yield file
          for subdir in dir |> Directory.GetDirectories do
              yield! subdir |> AllFiles }
```

Fig. 1. Returning all files in a given folder as a sequence

1.3 Pattern Matching and Active Patterns

Pattern matching is a fundamental concept in functional programming. Take a look at the following code snippet:

```
type Expr =
    | Integer of int
    | Binop   of (int -> int -> int) * Expr * Expr

let rec Eval = function
    | Integer i ->
        i
    | Binop (f, e1, e2) ->
        f (Eval e1) (Eval e2)
```

Here, the type `Expr` is defined to be an algebraic data type (a variant or discriminated union type) with two shapes, each carrying different values. These values can be extracted using pattern matching, and an example is given in the `Eval` function above.

Active patterns [DS-07] are special functions that are applied on the value being matched *before* pattern matching actually takes place. As with ordinary pattern matching, active patterns are statically checked for exhaustiveness. Their main advantage is that different conceptual views can be erected on any value, at any time, preserving encapsulation.

Active patterns are defined inside pipes (and a surrounding set of parentheses). Pattern cases can be closed or open (partial). Closed active patterns are made up of one or more pattern cases that collectively completely describe their input, whereas partial active patterns only attempt to describe parts of the input value space.

Converting Values. Single-case active patterns can be used to convert values. Consider the following:

```
open System

let (|NiceString|) s =
    if s |> String.IsNullOrEmpty then
        NiceString ""
    else
        NiceString (s.Trim())
```

Here, `NiceString` is the only pattern case and thus it always matches in a pattern match:

```
let _ =
    let (NiceString str) = "  with whitespace "
    str |> printf "Result = [%s]\n"
```

Partitioning Values. A more typical use of active patterns is to decompose or partition the input value:

```
let (|Empty|Number|String|) (s: string) =
    let res = ref 0
    if s |> String.IsNullOrEmpty && s.Trim() = "" then
        Empty
    elif Int32.TryParse(s, res) then
        Number !res
    else
        String s

let _ =
    match "123a" with
    | Number i -> printf "Number: %d\n" i
    | String s -> printf "String: %s\n" s
    | Empty    -> printf "empty\n"

let (|Even|Odd|) i = if i % 2 = 0 then Even else Odd

let _ =
    match 154321 with
    | Even -> printf "something strange happened"
    | Odd  -> printf "everything ok"
```

Describing Values. Partial active patterns work slightly differently from complete active patterns in that they must indicate whether a pattern match is made or not by returning an option value as opposed to one of the pattern cases. One example of using active patterns for describing values is checking for primeness:

```
let (|Prime|_|) (n: int) =
    { 2 .. n |> float |> Math.Sqrt |> Math.Floor |> int }
    |> Seq.exists (fun i -> n % i = 0)
    |> function
        | true -> None | false -> Some n

let _ =
    match 13 with
    | Prime _ -> printf "Prime\n"
    | _       -> printf "Not prime\n"
```

Active patterns can be parameterized like any ordinary function. Consider the following:

```
let (|DivisibleBy|_|) div num =
    if num % div = 0 then Some () else None
```

```
let _ =
    match 154323 with
    | DivisibleBy 13 _ -> printf "divisible by 13\n"
    | _                -> printf "not divisible\n"
```

2 Developing DSLs

Table 1 summarizes the grammar of the small programming language we call Simply, for its simple but elegant syntax. In the subsequent sections we will describe the steps necessary to implement an interpreter for Simply.

Table 1. The grammar of the Simply language

Symbol	Definition	Comment
$f ::=$	i	Numbers
	$v(e_1...e_n)$	Function application
	v	Variables
	(e)	
$t ::=$	$f * t$	Multiplication
	f/t	Division
	f	
$e ::=$	$t + e$	Addition
	$t - e$	Subtraction
	t	
$command ::=$	$[e_1...e_n]$	Sequencing
	repeat e as v $command$	Repeat blocks
	fun v ($v_1...v_n$) = $command$	Function definition
	e	Yielding an expression
$prog ::=$	$command_1...command_n$	

A short Simply program in Figure 2 gives a feeling of its syntax:

```
canvas(500 600)

fun oneStep(i) = [ pendown() go(i) penup() turn(15) go(5) ]

repeat 50 as i [ oneStep(i) ]
```

Fig. 2. A short Simply example program

2.1 Defining the Language Primitives

Take a look at the following module definition. It is added to an explicit namespace, this is the namespace we will be using for this tutorial and all subsequent modules will be added to it.

This Ast module defines three inner types. var and num are simply aliases and define the types we are using to represent variables and numbers, respectively.

The Expr type defines the various shapes that Simply expressions can take. There are four elementary shapes: numbers, variables, function applications, and binary operations - all expressions in the language are built from them. These are expressed as a discriminated union type, with the pipe character preceding each union label, followed by the type of the value it carries. Note how additional static members have been augmented to this expression type, each providing shortcuts to the corresponding arithmetic operations.

F# function types are defined using the arrow (->), which has left associativity. For instance, num -> num -> num is the type of a curried function that takes two numeric values and returns another.

```
namespace IntelliFactory.CEFP2009.Simply

module Ast =
    type var = string

    type num = float

    type Expr =
        | Number   of num
        | Var      of var
        | FunApply of var * Expr list
        | BinOp    of (num -> num -> num) * Expr * Expr
    with
        static member Sum (e1, e2)  = Expr.BinOp (( + ), e1, e2)
        static member Diff (e1, e2) = Expr.BinOp (( - ), e1, e2)
        static member Prod (e1, e2) = Expr.BinOp (( * ), e1, e2)
        static member Div  (e1, e2) = Expr.BinOp (( / ), e1, e2)
```

Simply programs are made up of a sequence of commands, which we represent as a list. Commands themselves are either repeat-blocks, function definitions, ordinary expressions, or sequences of further commands.

```
    type Command =
        | Repeat   of Expr * var * Command
        | FunDef   of var * var list * Command
        | Yield    of Expr
        | Sequence of Command list

    type Prog = Program of Command list
```

2.2   Building the Parser Using Active Patterns

The following module implements the parser for Simply using active patterns. The heart of the parser is the `matchToken` function - this takes a regular expression pattern and an input string to match against and returns a pair option, where the first value in the tuple is the matched string and the second is the remaining string.

```
namespace IntelliFactory.CEFP2009.Simply

module Language =
    open System
    open System.Text.RegularExpressions

    let matchToken pattern s =
        Regex.Match(s, "\A(" + pattern + ")((?s).*)",
            RegexOptions.Multiline)
        |> fun m ->
            if m.Success then
                (m.Groups.[1].Value, m.Groups.[2].Value) |> Some
            else
                None
```

We can use `matchToken` to build active pattern recognizers for various terminal (all capital-case) and non-terminal symbols. We start by implementing the discarding of whitespace and comments, and the star operator (as a higher-order active pattern, matching zero or many occurrences of a given recognizer).

```
    let (|WS|_|) = matchToken "[ |\t|\n|\n\r]+"
    let (|COMMENT|_|) = matchToken "#.*[\n|\r\n]"

    let (|DISCARDED|_|) s =
        match s with
        | WS rest
        | COMMENT rest ->
            rest |> Some
        | _ ->
            None

    let rec (|Star|_|) f acc s =
        match f s with
        | Some (res, rest) ->
            (|Star|_|) f (res :: acc) rest
        | None ->
            (acc |> List.rev , s) |> Some
```

We can use these active patterns to implement a basic lexer that is able to tokenize some input by splitting at whitespaces and matching against a given pattern.

```
let (|Ignored|_|) s = (|Star|_|) (|DISCARDED|_|) [] s

let rec MatchTokenNoWS s pattern =
    match (|Ignored|_|) s with
    | Some (_, rest) ->
        rest |> matchToken pattern
    | None ->
        s |> matchToken pattern

let MatchToken s f pattern =
    pattern |> MatchTokenNoWS s |> Option.bind f

let MatchSymbol s pattern =
    pattern |> MatchToken s (fun (_, rest) -> rest |> Some)
```

At this point, writing the active pattern recognizers for various terminal symbols becomes straightforward:

```
let (|NUMBER|_|) s =
    "[0-9]+\.?[0-9]*" |> MatchToken s
        (fun (n, rest) -> (n |> Double.Parse, rest) |> Some)

let (|ID|_|) s =
    "[a-zA-Z]+" |> MatchToken s (fun res -> res |> Some)

let (|PLUS|_|)   s = "\+" |> MatchSymbol s
let (|MINUS|_|)  s = "-"  |> MatchSymbol s
let (|MUL|_|)    s = "\*" |> MatchSymbol s
let (|DIV|_|)    s = "/"  |> MatchSymbol s
let (|LPAREN|_|) s = "\(" |> MatchSymbol s
let (|RPAREN|_|) s = "\)" |> MatchSymbol s

let (|LBRACK|_|) s = "\[" |> MatchSymbol s
let (|RBRACK|_|) s = "\]" |> MatchSymbol s
let (|EQ|_|)     s = "="  |> MatchSymbol s

let (|FUN|_|)    s = "fun"    |> MatchSymbol s
let (|REPEAT|_|) s = "repeat" |> MatchSymbol s
let (|AS|_|)     s = "as"     |> MatchSymbol s
```

Note that (|ID|_|) parses identifiers containing alphabetic characters only. Note also how (|NUMBER|_|) extracts the number matched as a `double` value. This kind of pattern is heavily used in the subsequent grammar rules, making the building up of the parser type-safe. Any error in the parsing logic should now surface as a compiler error, and as a result, building up more complex grammars becomes significantly easier than using parser generators.

Now we get to implementing the parser for the grammar in Table 1. A transliteration is as follows:

```
let rec (|Factor|_|) = function
    | NUMBER (n, rest) ->
        (Ast.Expr.Number n, rest) |> Some
    | ID (f, LPAREN (Star (|Expression|_|) []
                          (args, RPAREN rest))) ->
        (Ast.Expr.FunApply (f, args), rest) |> Some
    | ID (v, rest) ->
        (Ast.Expr.Var v, rest) |> Some
    | LPAREN (Expression (e, RPAREN rest)) ->
        (e, rest) |> Some
    | _ ->
        None

and (|Term|_|) = function
    | Factor (e1, MUL (Term (e2, rest))) ->
        (Ast.Expr.Prod (e1, e2), rest) |> Some
    | Factor (e1, DIV (Term (e2, rest))) ->
        (Ast.Expr.Div (e1, e2), rest) |> Some
    | Factor (e, rest) ->
        (e, rest) |> Some
    | _ ->
        None

and (|Expression|_|) = function
    | Term (e1, PLUS (Expression (e2, rest))) ->
        (Ast.Expr.Sum (e1, e2), rest) |> Some
    | Term (e1, MINUS (Expression (e2, rest))) ->
        (Ast.Expr.Diff (e1, e2), rest) |> Some
    | Term (e, rest) ->
        (e, rest) |> Some
    | _ ->
        None

let rec (|Command|_|) = function
    | LBRACK (Star (|Command|_|) [] (commands,
                                      RBRACK rest)) ->
        (Ast.Command.Sequence commands, rest) |> Some
    | REPEAT (Expression (i, AS (
                          ID (v, Command (body,
```

```
                                       rest))))) ->
                (Ast.Command.Repeat (i, v, body), rest) |> Some
          | FUN (ID (f, LPAREN (Star (|ID|_|) []
                                   (pars, RPAREN
                                       (EQ (Command (body,
                                                    rest))))))) ->
                (Ast.Command.FunDef (f, pars, body), rest) |> Some
          | Expression (e, rest) ->
                (Ast.Command.Yield e, rest) |> Some
          | _ ->
              None
```

Finally, programs are simply a sequence of commands:

```
let (|Prog|_|) = function
    | Star (|Command|_|) [] (commands, rest) ->
        (Ast.Prog.Program commands, rest) |> Some
    | _ ->
        None
```

It is also useful to provide an active pattern recognizer that can recognize the end of the input string, we will be using this in the user interface code to check against badly formed input.

```
let (|Eof|_|) s =
    if s |> String.IsNullOrEmpty then
        () |> Some
    else
        match s with
        | Ignored (_, rest)
            when rest |> String.IsNullOrEmpty ->
            () |> Some
        | _ ->
            None
```

2.3   Writing the Evaluator

The evaluator is implemented as a new module and uses a custom record type Env to keep track of the variables/bindings and functions (these are treated separately for simplicity reasons) encountered during evaluation. This environment can also be instantiated with various pre-defined, built-in functions as we will see later.

```
module Evaluator =
    type Env = {
        Variables: Map<Ast.var, Ast.num>
```

```
    Functions: Map<Ast.var, (Ast.var list * Ast.Command)>
    BuiltInFunctions: Map<Ast.var, Ast.num list -> Ast.num>
}
with
    member self.AddVar v i =
        { self with Variables = Map.add v i self.Variables }

    static member BuiltIns =
        { Variables = Map.empty
          Functions = Map.empty
          BuiltInFunctions = Map.empty }

    member self.AddFun f pars body =
        { self with
            Functions =
                Map.add f (pars, body) self.Functions }

    member self.AddBuiltInFun fname f =
        { self with
            BuiltInFunctions =
                Map.add fname f self.BuiltInFunctions }
```

The evaluator is a set of mutually-recursive functions: `EvalProg` evaluates an entire program, `EvalCommand` evaluates a command, and `EvalExpr` evaluates an expression.

```
let rec EvalProg env (Ast.Prog.Program prog) =
    List.fold (fun (env, _) command ->
        EvalCommand env command) (env, 0.) prog
and EvalCommand (env: Env) = function
    | Ast.Command.Repeat (e, v, body) ->
        { 1 .. e |> EvalExpr env |> snd |> int}
        |> Seq.fold (fun ((env: Env), _) i ->
            body
            |> EvalCommand (env.AddVar v (float i))) (env, 0.)
        |> fun (_, res) ->
            env, res
    | Ast.Command.FunDef (f, pars, body) ->
        env.AddFun f pars body, 0.
    | Ast.Command.Yield e ->
        EvalExpr env e
    | Ast.Command.Sequence commands ->
        commands
        |> Seq.fold (fun (env, acc) e ->
            EvalCommand env e) (env, 0.)
and CombineExpr env e1 e2 f =
```

```
        let _, r1 = EvalExpr env e1
        let _, r2 = EvalExpr env e2
        env, f r1 r2
    and EvalExpr (env: Env) = function
        | Ast.Expr.Number n ->
            env, n
        | Ast.Expr.BinOp (f, e1, e2) ->
            CombineExpr env e1 e2 f
        | Ast.Expr.Var v ->
            match Map.tryFind v env.Variables with
            | None ->
                v |> sprintf "Unbound '%s'" |> failwith
            | Some i ->
                env, i
        | Ast.Expr.FunApply (f, args) ->
            match Map.tryFind f env.Functions with
            | None ->
                match Map.tryFind f env.BuiltInFunctions with
                | None ->
                    f
                    |> sprintf "Unbound function '%s'"
                    |> failwith
                | Some ff ->
                    env, args
                        |> List.map (EvalExpr env >> snd)
                        |> ff
            | Some (pars, body) ->
                List.fold2 (fun (env: Env) param arg ->
                    arg
                    |> EvalExpr env
                    |> snd
                    |> env.AddVar param) env pars args
                |> fun env2 ->
                    EvalCommand env2 body
                    |> fun (_, res) ->
                        env, res
```

3   The Programming Shell around Simply

Figure 3 depicts a possible embedding of Simply into a shell environment. This has two main parts: the shell environment itself and the language extensions for the Simply-based DSL's initial vocabulary. We will cover both in this section, however the UI build-up of the shell environment is left as an exercise to the reader, and here we assume that this is supplied by another project in the same Visual Studio solution. This UI project is expected to implement the main UI

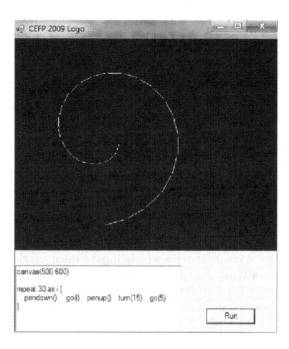

Fig. 3. The Simply language instantiated with a Logo-like shell

window as depicted in Figure 3, with the main form type `LogoUI` in the same namespace as the previous modules, and expose (e.g. make public) certain controls by the names we use in the consuming shell client (implemented in the `FrontEnd` module) in this section.

The shell client uses a global state, encapsulated by the `State` type, to store the position and direction of the Logo turtle, the state of the drawing pen (whether it is on or off), and the reference to the canvas we are drawing on.

```
namespace IntelliFactory.CEFP2009.Simply

module FrontEnd =
    open System
    open System.Windows.Forms
    open System.Drawing
    open IntelliFactory.CEFP2009.Simply.Language
    open IntelliFactory.CEFP2009.Simply.Evaluator

    [<Measure>]
    type deg

    [<Measure>]
    type rad
```

```
let (|Radian|) (i: float<deg>) = i / 180.<deg> * Math.PI
let deg (f: float) = f * 1.<deg>

type Position = {
    mutable X: float
    mutable Y: float
}
type State = {
    mutable Position: Position
    mutable Direction: float<deg>
    mutable PenOn: bool
    mutable Canvas: Graphics
}
```

At this point, we can create shorthand bindings to the main shell UI form (this is to be assembled as a WinForms project separately by the reader - dragging and dropping the appropriate controls as seen in Figure 3, and setting their visibility to public in the code behind file), the canvas on the form (this is assumed to be a PictureBox object), and a simple white pen object that we are going to be using for drawing.

```
let form = new LogoUI.MainForm()
let canvas = form.PictureBox
let pen = new Pen(Color.White)
```

We create the initial state of the shell: the turtle at $(0, 0)$ facing upward.

```
let state = ref {
    Position = { X=0.; Y=0. }
    Direction = 90.<deg>
    PenOn = true
    Canvas = null
}
```

Simply can easily be extended with built-in functions by adding them to the environment that is used during evaluation. Below we take the initial empty environment and add a handful of functions as follows:

- **canvas** (width height) - creates a new canvas of the given size. This function must be called before any drawing operation.
- **turn** (deg) - turns the turtle *deg* degrees counter-clockwise. Note the clever use of units of measure to ensure that degrees are used.
- **penup** () - turns the pen off, causing any drawing operation to leave no mark.
- **pendown** () - turns the pen on, causing any drawing operation to show up.

– **go** (length) - moves the turtle *length* pixels. Once again, note the use of the
(|Radian|) active pattern to convert degrees to radians to work with the
standard math functions.

```
let builtins =
    Env.BuiltIns
    |> fun env ->
        env.AddBuiltInFun "canvas" (fun [f1; f2] ->
            let bmp =
                new Bitmap(
                    f1 |> int,
                    f2 |> int,
                    Imaging.PixelFormat.Format16bppRgb555)
            let gra = System.Drawing.Graphics.FromImage bmp
            canvas.Image <- bmp
            canvas.Width <- bmp.Width
            canvas.Height <- bmp.Height
            (!state).Canvas <- gra
            (!state).Direction <- 90.<deg>
            (!state).PenOn <- true
            (!state).Position <-
                { X = canvas.Height / 2 |> float
                  Y = canvas.Height / 2 |> float }
            0.)
    |> fun env ->
        env.AddBuiltInFun "turn" (fun [f] ->
            (!state).Direction <- (!state).Direction+deg f
            0.)
    |> fun env ->
        env.AddBuiltInFun "penup" (fun [] ->
            (!state).PenOn <- false
            0.)
    |> fun env ->
        env.AddBuiltInFun "pendown" (fun [] ->
            (!state).PenOn <- true
            0.)
    |> fun env ->
        env.AddBuiltInFun "go" (fun [f] ->
            let (Radian rad) = (!state).Direction
            let dx = Math.Cos rad |> (*) f
            let dy = Math.Sin rad |> (*) f
            if (!state).PenOn then
                (!state).Canvas.DrawLine(pen,
                    (!state).Position.X |> int,
                    (!state).Position.Y |> int,
                    (!state).Position.X + dx |> int,
```

```
                    (!state).Position.Y + dy |> int)
            (!state).Position <-
                { X = (!state).Position.X + dx
                  Y = (!state).Position.Y + dy }
        0.)
```

Next is adding an event handler for the Run button (which is to be exposed as btnRun by the UI project added by the reader). This takes the text from the code input control (tbInput), tries to parse it as a valid program ending with Eof, and if succeeds evaluates it with the environment we just assembled, or otherwise signals a syntax error.

```
form.btnRun.Click.Add (fun _ ->
    match form.tbInput.Text with
    | Prog (e, Eof) ->
        try
            e
            |> EvalProg builtins |> snd
            |> printf "Result=%f"
        with
        | e ->
            e.Message
            |> sprintf "Execution Error\n%s"
            |> MessageBox.Show |> ignore
    | Prog (e, rest) ->
        rest
        |> sprintf "Syntax Error\nRemaining text=%s"
        |> MessageBox.Show |> ignore
    | _ ->
        sprintf "Syntax error" |> MessageBox.Show |> ignore)
form |> Application.Run
```

4   Further Considerations

The evaluator presented here comes with a number of simplifications. Some of these include:

- **Limited language features**. There are no variable assignments, conditionals, types other than real numbers, higher-order functions, etc. Simply in the implementation presented here only supports defining and calling functions, a simple looping construct (repeat <e> as <v> <body>), and basic arithmetic.
- **Lacking proper semantic checking**. Parameter shadowing in nested functions, multiple types, and type checking is missing. This is addressed in [AG-09].

- **Efficient parsing**. The active pattern-based implementation presented here has the obvious advantage of being a straightforward transliteration of the corresponding BNF grammar, being type-safe, and being unambiguous. Unambiguity is achieved automatically by the pattern matching semantics: once a successful match is made, all other possibilities are ignored. This requires the parser writer to list rules in a well-defined order, but this in most real-life situations is easy to derive.

  However, the highly nested nature of the grammar causes a great number of token derivations and this makes the parser's performance sub-standard. There are at least two different ways to address this:

  - Memoizing tokens read at a particular position in the source string. This is not difficult but its memory consumption can be large.
  - Restructuring/left-factoring the grammar rules to avoid backtracking. For instance,

    ```
    and (|Term|_|) = function
        | Factor (e1, MUL (Term (e2, rest))) ->
            (Ast.Expr.Prod (e1, e2), rest) |> Some
        | Factor (e1, DIV (Term (e2, rest))) ->
            (Ast.Expr.Div (e1, e2), rest) |> Some
        | Factor (e, rest) ->
            (e, rest) |> Some
        | _ ->
            None
    ```

    becomes this:

    ```
    and (|Term|_|) = function
        | Factor (e1, rest) ->
            match rest with
            | MUL (Term (e2, rest)) ->
                (Ast.Expr.Prod (e1, e2), rest) |> Some
            | DIV (Term (e2, rest)) ->
                (Ast.Expr.Div (e1, e2), rest) |> Some
            | _ ->
                (e1, rest) |> Some
        | _ ->
            None
    ```

5   Conclusions

F# active patterns provide a quick and type-safe mechanism to prototype parsers in near-BNF style. This allows language implementers to describe their grammars and the subsequent phases in their interpreters or compilers in F#, without having to resort to external tools such as parser generators.

The implementation of Simply as given in these lecture notes follows the standard interpreter pattern. F# provides easy access to various .NET libraries, and even our rudimentary graphics implementation shows the strengths associated with this coupling.

References

[AG-09]   Granicz, A.: Prototyping DSLs in F#: Parsing and Semantic Check-
               ing (August 24, 2009),
               http://www.devx.com/dotnet/Article/42552, DevX.com
[IF-09]   Granicz, A., Tayanovskyy, A., Björnson, J., Echeverri, D., et al.: In-
               telliFactory blogs (2009), http://www.intellifactory.com/blogs
[DS-07]   Syme, D., Neverov, G., Margetson, J.: Extensible Pattern Matching
               Via a Lightweight Language Extension. In: The Proceedings of the
               International Conference on Functional Programming, vol. 42(9), pp.
               29–42 (2007)
[DS-06]   Syme, D.: Leveraging.NET Meta-Programming Components from F#
               - Integrated Queries and Interoperable Heterogeneous Execution. In:
               The Proceedings of the ACM SIGPLAN Workshop on ML and its
               Applications, pp. 43–54 (2006)
[DS-09]   Syme, D., et al.: The F# Web Site (2009), http://fsharp.net
[AK-09]   Kennedy, A.: Blog Site (2009),
               http://blogs.msdn.com/andrewkennedy
[AK-CEFP-09]   Kennedy, A.: Types for Units-of-Measure: Theory and Practice
               (2009),
               http://research.microsoft.com/en-us/um/people/akenn/units/
               CEFP09RevisedNotes.pdf

Erlang Behaviours:
Programming with Process Design Patterns

Francesco Cesarini[1] and Simon Thompson[2]

[1] Erlang Solutions Ltd., London, United Kingdom
francesco@erlang-solutions.com
http://www.erlang-solutions.com
[2] School of Computing, University of Kent, Canterbury, United Kingdom
s.j.thompson@kent.ac.uk
http://www.cs.kent.ac.uk/~sjt/

Abstract. Erlang processes run independently of each other, each using separate memory and communicating with each other by message passing. These processes, while executing different code, do so following a number of common patterns. By examining different examples of Erlang-style concurrency in client/server architectures, we identify the generic and specific parts of the code and extract the generic code to form a process skeleton. In Erlang, the most commonly used patterns have been implemented in library modules, commonly referred to as OTP behaviours. They contain the generic code framework for concurrency and error handling, simplifying the complexity of concurrent programming and protecting the developer from many common pitfalls.

Keywords: Erlang, OTP, behaviour, generic, client/server, process, message passing, design pattern, concurrency, fault-tolerance.

1 Introduction

Processes in Erlang systems run concurrently in separate memory, and communicate with each other by message passing. Processes can be used for a wealth of applications, including as gateways to databases, as handlers for protocol stacks, and to manage the logging of trace messages from other processes. Although these processes handle different requests, there will be similarities in how these requests are handled. We call these similarities design patterns.

In these lecture notes, we will look at the particular example of the client/server process design pattern, abstracting out generic principles from specific examples. An experienced Erlang programmer will recognize these patterns in the design phase of the project, and so will use libraries and templates that are part of the OTP framework. Section 1 gives a brief introduction to Erlang, providing the necessary background to the rest of the chapter. Section 2 of these lecture notes introduces the concept of an Erlang process skeleton, a pattern followed by most processes irrespective of their behaviour or function. Section 3 introduces client/server behaviours in Erlang processes, using an example taken from

Z. Horváth, R. Plasmeijer, and V. Zsók (Eds.): CEFP 2009, LNCS 6299, pp. 19–41, 2010.

mobile telephony. Section 4 takes this example, and re-implements it using the
gen_server OTP behaviour library. These lecture notes are based on the authors' book *Erlang Programming*, ISBN: 978-0-596-51818-9 published in 2009 by
O'Reilly Media.

2   Erlang

This section gives a brief overview of those aspects of Erlang covered in these
notes; more details of these and other aspects of Erlang and the OTP library can
be found in the online documentation for the language as well as in our book.

Erlang is at basis a functional language, with no side-effects due to assignment
since Erlang contains single assignment: each (instance of a) variable can only
be assigned to once, so that variables assignments play the role of definitions in
other languages. An example module is given now

```
-module(factorial).
-export([fac/1]).

fac(0) -> 1;
fac(N) when N>0 ->
    Prev = fac(N-1),
    n*Prev.
```

This contains an assignment to Prev, as well as a simple case of definition by
pattern matching. The clauses of the function definition are separated by semi-
colons, and the first head matching the argument is used. In this example, the
first clause gives the factorial of zero, the second factorials of positive numbers.
The body of each clause is a sequence of expressions, and the result of that clause
is the final expression in the body.

Within the module functions are called in the usual way; outside, the name
of the module is prepended as in factorial:fac(3). It is possible to define
functions with the same name but different numbers of arguments this is called
their "arity". In the export directive in the factorial module the fac function
of arity one is denoted by fac/1.

Erlang contains tuples (or product types) and lists. Tuples are enclosed in
curly brackets, as in {ok,37}; lists in square brackets [23,34]. The notation
[X|Xs] matches a non empty list with head X and tail Xs. Identifiers beginning
with a lower case letter denote atoms, which simply stand for themselves; the
'ok' in the tuple {ok,37} is an example of an atom. Atoms used in this way are
often used to distinguish between different kinds of function result: as well as
'ok' results, there might be results of the form {error, ``Error string''}.

Erlang concurrency is by message passing between processes, each executing
in a separate memory space. Processes are identified by process identifiers, called
'Pid's, but processes can also be registered under a name; this should only be
used for long-lived, "static" processes. A message Msg is sent to a process with
process id Pid thus: Pid ! Msg. A process can find out its pid by calling the

built-in function (BIF) `self/0`, and this can then be sent to other processes for them to use to communicate with the original process.

Suppose that a process expects to receive messages of the form {ok, N} and {error, St}. To process these it uses a `receive` statement

```
receive
    {ok, N} ->
        N+1;
    {error, _} ->
        0
end
```

The result of this is a number, with the particular result determined by pattern matching. When the value of a variable is not needed, the wild-card '_' can be used, as shown.

Message passing between processes is asynchronous, and the messages received by a process are placed in the process's mailbox in the order in which they arrive. Suppose that now the `receive` statement above is to be executed: if the first element in the mailbox is either {ok, N} or {error, St}: the corresponding result will be returned. If the first message in the mailbox is not of this form, it is retained in the mailbox, and the second is processed in a similar way. If no messages match, then the `receive` will wait for a matching message to be received.

The remainder of these notes give many examples of concurrent Erlang processes, and we move to looking at those now.

3   Process Skeletons

There is a common pattern to the behaviour of processes, regardless of the particular purpose for which the process was created. To start with, a processes has to be spawned and then, optionally, have its alias registered. The first action of the newly spawned process is to initialize the process loop data. The loop data is often the result of arguments passed to the spawn built-in function (BIF) at the initialization of the process. Its loop data is stored in a variable we refer to as the process state. The state is passed to a receive-evaluate function, running a loop which receives a message, handles it, updates the state, and passes it back as an argument to a tail-recursive call. If one of the messages it handles is a 'stop' message, the receiving process will clean up after itself and then terminate.

This is a recurring design among processes that we usually refer to as a design pattern, and it will occur regardless of the task the process has been assigned to perform in the body of the loop. Figure 1 shows an example skeleton.

Let's now look at the differences between the particular processes which conform to this pattern:

- The arguments passed to the spawn BIF calls will differ from one process to another.

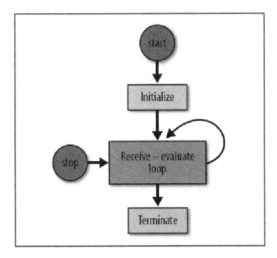

Fig. 1. Process skeleton

- You have to decide whether you should register a process under an alias, and, if you do register it, what alias should be used.
- In the function that initializes the process state, the actions taken will differ based on the tasks the process will perform.
- The state of the system is represented by the loop data in every case, but the contents of the loop data will vary among processes.
- When in the body of the receive-evaluate loop, processes will receive different messages and handle them in different ways.
- Finally, on termination, the cleanup will vary from process to process.

So, even if a skeleton of generic actions exists, these actions are complemented by specific ones that are directly related to the specific tasks assigned to the process. Using this skeleton as a template, one can create processes which act as servers, as finite state machines, as event handlers and as supervisors. In the following sections, we will concentrate on client/server models.

4   Client/Server Models

Erlang processes can be used to implement client/server solutions, where both clients and servers are represented as Erlang processes. A server could be a FIFO queue to a printer, a window manager, or a file server. The resources it handles could be a database, calendar, or finite list of items such as rooms, books, or radio frequencies. Clients access these resources by sending the server a request to print a file, to update a window, to book a room, or to use a frequency. The server receives the request, handles it, and responds with an acknowledgment and a return value if the request was successful, or with an error if the request did not succeed.

When implementing client/server behaviour, clients and servers are represented as Erlang processes. Interaction between them takes place through the sending and receiving of messages. Message passing is often hidden in functional interfaces, so that instead of calling:

```
printerserver ! {print, File}
```

a client would call a print function, as in:

```
printerserver:print(File)
```

This is a form of information hiding, where we do not make the client aware that the server is a process, that it could be registered, and that it might reside on a remote computer. Nor do we expose the message protocol being used between the client and the server, keeping the interface between them safe and simple. All the client needs to do is call a function and use with the return value of the fucntion.

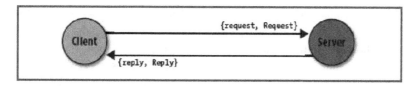

Fig. 2. Synchronous message passing

If a client using the service or resource handled by the server expects a reply to the request, the implementation of the call to the server has to be synchronous, as in Figure 2. If the client does not need a reply, the call to the server can be asynchronous. When you encapsulate synchronous and asynchronous calls in a function call, the function commonly returns the atom `ok`, indicating that the request was sent to the server. Functions encapsulating synchronous calls will return the value expected by the client. These return values usually follow the format `ok`, `{ok, Result}`, when the result is successful or `{error, Reason}` when it is unsuccessful. In the latter case the `Reason` encapsulates why the request has failed.

4.1   A Client/Server Example

So that you understand what we are talking about, let's walk through a client/ server example and test it in the shell. This server is responsible for managing radio frequencies on behalf of its clients, the mobile phones connected to the network. The phone requests a frequency whenever a call needs to be connected, and releases it once the call has terminated (see Fig. 3 below).

When a mobile phone has to set up a connection to another subscriber, it calls the client function `frequency:allocate/0`. This call has the effect of generating

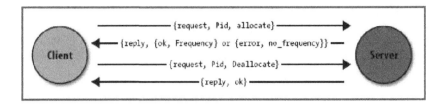

Fig. 3. Synchronous message passing

a synchronous message which is sent to the server. The server handles it and responds with either a message containing an available frequency or an error if all frequencies are being used. The result of the `allocate/0` call will therefore be either {ok, Frequency} or {error, no_frequencies}.

Through a functional interface, we hide the message-passing mechanism, the format of these messages, and the fact that the frequency server is implemented as a registered Erlang process. If we were to move the server to a remote host, we could do so without having to change the client interface.

When the client has completed its phone call and releases the connection, it needs to deallocate the frequency so that other clients can reuse it. It does so by calling the client function `frequency:deallocate(Frequency)`. The call results in a message being sent to the server. The server can then make the frequency available to other clients and responds with the atom `ok`. The atom is sent back to the client and becomes the return value of the `deallocate/1` call. Figure 3 above shows the message sequence diagram of this example.

The code for the server is in the `frequency` module. Here is the first part:

```
-module(frequency).
-export([start/0, stop/0, allocate/0, deallocate/1]).
-export([init/0]).

%% These are the start functions used to create and
%% initialize the server.

start() ->
    register(frequency, spawn(frequency, init, [])).

init() ->
    Frequencies = {get_frequencies(), []},
    loop(Frequencies).
```

When spawning a process, you have to export the `init/0` function because it is used by the `spawn/3` BIF. We have put this function in a separate `export` clause to distinguish it from the client functions, which are supposed to be called from other modules. On the other hand, calling `frequency:init()` explicitly anywhere in your code is considered to be very bad practice.

The newly spawned process starts executing in the `init/0` function. It creates a tuple consisting of the available frequencies, retrieved through the `get_frequencies/0` call, and a list of the allocated frequencies – initially given by the empty list – as the server has just been started. The tuple, which forms the state or loop data, is bound to the `Frequencies` variable and passed as an argument to the receive-evaluate function, which in this example we've called `loop/1`.

In the `init/0` function, we use the variable `Frequencies` for readability reasons, but nothing is stopping us from creating the tuple directly in the call thus `loop({get_frequencies(), []})`.

Here is how the client functions are implemented:

```
%% The client Functions
stop()            -> call(stop).
allocate()        -> call(allocate).
deallocate(Freq) -> call({deallocate, Freq}).

%% We hide all message passing and the message
%% protocol in a functional interface.

call(Message) ->
    frequency ! {request, self(), Message},
    receive
        {reply, Reply} -> Reply
    end.
```

Client and supervisor processes can interact with the frequency server using what we refer to as client functions. These exported functions include `start`, `stop`, `allocate`, and `deallocate`. They call the `call/1` function, passing the message to be sent to the server as an argument. This function will encapsulate the message protocol between the server and its clients, sending a message of the format {request, Pid, Message}. The atom `request` is a tag in the tuple, `Pid` is the process identifier of the calling process (returned by calling the `self/0` BIF in the calling process), and `Message` is the argument originally passed to the `call/1` function.

When the message has been sent to the process, the client is suspended in the `receive` clause waiting for a response of the format {reply, Reply}, where the atom `reply` is a tag and the variable `Reply` is the actual response. The server response is pattern-matched, and the contents of the variable `Reply` become the return value of the client functions.

Pay special attention to how message passing and the message protocol have been abstracted to a format independent of the action relating to the message itself; this is a form of information hiding, that allows the details of the protocol and the message structure to be modified without affecting any of the client code. Now that we have covered the code to start and interact with the frequency server, let's take a look at its receive-evaluate loop:

```erlang
%% The Main Loop
loop(Frequencies) ->
    receive
        {request, Pid, allocate} ->
            {NewFrequencies, Reply} = allocate(Frequencies, Pid),
            reply(Pid, Reply),
            loop(NewFrequencies);
        {request, Pid , {deallocate, Freq}} ->
            NewFrequencies = deallocate(Frequencies, Freq),
            reply(Pid, ok),
            loop(NewFrequencies);
        {request, Pid, stop} ->
            reply(Pid, ok)
    end.

reply(Pid, Reply) ->
    Pid ! {reply, Reply}.
```

The receive clause will accept three kinds of requests originating from the client functions, namely allocate, deallocate, and stop. These requests follow the format defined in the call/1 function, that is, {request, Pid, Message}. The Message is pattern-matched in the expression and used to determine which clause is executed. This, in turn, determines the internal functions that are called. These internal functions will return the new loop data, which in our example consists of the pair of lists of available and allocated frequencies, and where needed, a reply to send back to the client. The client Pid, sent as part of the request, is used to identify the calling process and is used in the reply/2 call.

Assume a client wants to initiate a call. To do so, it would request a frequency by calling the frequency:allocate/0 function. This function sends a message of the format {request, Pid, allocate} to the frequency server, pattern matching in the first clause of the receive statement. This message will result in the server function allocate(Frequencies, Pid) being called, where Frequencies is the loop data containing a tuple of allocated and available frequencies. The allocate function will check whether there are any available frequencies:

```erlang
allocate({[], Allocated}, _Pid) ->
    {{[], Allocated}, {error, no_frequencies}};
allocate({[Freq|Frequencies], Allocated}, Pid) ->
    link(Pid),
    {{Frequencies,[{Freq,Pid}|Allocated]},{ok,Freq}}.
```

If there are frequencies available, it will return the updated loop data, where the newly allocated frequency has been moved from the available list and stored together with the Pid in the list of allocated frequencies. The reply sent to the client is of the format {ok, Frequency}.

If no frequencies are available, the loop data is unchanged and the {error, no_frequency} message is returned as a reply.

After calling the `allocate` function, the reply is sent to the client by calling `reply(Pid, Message)`, which formats the message according to the internal client/server message format and sends it back to the client. Finally, the function `loop/1` is called recursively, passing the new loop data as an argument.

Deallocation works in a similar way. The client function call results in the message `{request, Pid, {deallocate, Frequency}}` being sent and matched in the second clause of the receive statement. This makes a call to `deallocate(Frequencies, Frequency)` and the `deallocate` function moves the `Frequency` from the allocated list to the deallocated one, returning the updated loop data. The atom `ok` is sent back to the client, and the `loop/1` function is called recursively with the updated loop data.

If the `stop` request is received, `ok` is returned to the calling process and the server terminates, as there is no more code to execute. In the previous two clauses, `loop/1` was called in the final expression of the `receive` clause, but not in this case.

We complete this system by implementing the deallocation function, which assumes that it is only called when the frequency to be deallocated is indeed allocated:

```
deallocate({Free, Allocated}, Freq) ->
    NewAllocated=lists:keydelete(Freq, 1, Allocated),
    {[Freq|Free], NewAllocated}.
```

The `allocate/2` and `deallocate/2` functions are local to the `frequency` module, and are what we refer to as internal help functions. You can see an example of the frequency allocator in action now:

```
1> c(frequency).
{ok,frequency}
2> frequency:start().
true
3> frequency:allocate().
{ok,10}
4> frequency:allocate().
{ok,11}
5> frequency:allocate().
{ok,12}
6> frequency:allocate().
{ok,13}
7> frequency:allocate().
{ok,14}
8> frequency:allocate().
{ok,15}
9> frequency:allocate().
{error,no_frequency}
10> frequency:deallocate(11).
ok
```

```
11> frequency:allocate().
{ok,11}
12> frequency:stop().
ok
```

4.2 A Process Pattern Example

In this section we look at two other client-server examples, and when doing so, we compare and contrast them to the frequency server we described in the previous section. Picture an application, either a web browser or a word processor, which handles many simultaneously open windows centrally controlled by a window manager. As we aim to have a process for each truly concurrent activity, spawning a process for every window is the way to go. These processes would probably not be registered, as many windows of the same type could be running concurrently, so communication to them is by means of their Pid.

After being spawned, each process would call the initialize function, which draws and displays the window and its contents. The return value of the initialize function contains references to the widgets displayed in the window. These references are stored in the state variable and are used whenever the window needs updating. The state variable is passed as an argument to a tail-recursive function that implements the receive-evaluate loop.

In this loop function, the process waits for events originating in or relating to the window it is managing. It could be a user typing in a form or choosing a menu entry, or an external process pushing data that needs to be displayed. Every event relating to this window is translated to an Erlang message and sent to the process. The process, upon receiving the message, calls the handle function, passing the message and state as arguments. If the event were the result of a few keystrokes typed in a form, the handle function might want to display them. If the user picked an entry in one of the menus, the handle function would take appropriate actions in executing that menu choice. Or, if the event was caused by an external process pushing data, possibly an image from a webcam or an alert message, the appropriate widget would be updated. The receipt of these events in Erlang would be seen as a generic pattern in all processes. What would be considered specific and change from process to process is how these events are handled.

Finally, what if the process receives a stop message? This message might have originated from a user picking the Exit menu entry or clicking the Destroy button, or from the window manager broadcasting a notification that the application is being shut down. Regardless of the reason, a stop message is sent to the process. Upon receiving it, the process calls a terminate function, which destroys all of the widgets, ensuring that they are no longer displayed. After the window has been shut down, the process terminates because there is no more code to execute.

Look at the following process skeleton. Could you not fit all of the specific code into the `initialize/1`, `handle_msg/2`, and `terminate/1` functions for not only the window example, but also the frequency server?

```erlang
-module(server).
-export([start/2, stop/1, call/2]).
-export([init/1]).

start(Name, Data) ->
    Pid = spawn(server, init,[Data]),
    register(Name, Pid),
    ok.

stop(Name) ->
    Name ! {stop, self()},
    receive {reply, Reply} -> Reply end.

call(Name, Msg) ->
    Name ! {request, self(), Msg},
    receive {reply, Reply} -> Reply end.

reply(To, Msg) ->
    To ! {reply, Msg}.

init(Data) ->
    loop(initialize(Data)).

loop(State) ->
    receive
        {request, From, Msg} ->
            {Reply,NewState} = handle_msg(Msg, State),
            reply(From, Reply),
            loop(NewState);
        {stop, From} ->
            reply(From, terminate(State))
    end.

initialize(...)      -> ...
handle_msg(...,...) -> ...
terminate(...)       -> ...
```

Using the generic code in the preceding skeleton, let's go through the GUI example one last time:

- The `initialize/1` function draws the window and displays it, returning a reference to the widget that gets bound to the state variable.
- Every time an event arrives in the form of an Erlang message, the event is taken care of in the `handle_msg` function. The call takes the message and the state as arguments and returns an updated `State` variable. This variable is passed to the recursive loop call, ensuring that the process is kept alive. Any reply is also sent back to the process where the request originated.

– If the `stop` message is received, `terminate/1` is called, destroying the window and all the widgets associated with it. The `loop` function is not called, allowing the process to terminate normally.

This server skeleton example actually exists for client/servers, finite state machines, event handlers and supervisor processes as library modules which come as part as the OTP middleware. In the next section, we describe the clientserver behaviour, often referred to as the `gen_server`.

5 OTP Behaviours

In previous section, we introduced patterns that recur when you program using the Erlang concurrency model. We discussed functionality common to concurrent systems, and you saw that processes will handle very different tasks in a similar way. We also emphasized special cases and potential problems that have to be handled when dealing with concurrency.

Picture a project with 50 developers spread across several geographic locations. If the project is not properly coordinated and no templates are provided, how many different client/server implementations might the project end up with? Even more dangerous, how many of these implementations will handle special borderline cases and concurrency-related errors correctly, if at all? Without a code review, can you be sure there is a uniform way across the system to handle server crashes that occur after clients have sent a request to the server? Or guarantee that the response from a request is indeed the response, and not just any message that conforms to the internal message protocol?

OTP behaviours address all of these issues by providing library modules that implement the most common concurrent design patterns. Behind the scenes, without the programmer having to be aware of it, the library modules ensure that errors and special cases are handled in a consistent way. As a result, OTP behaviours provide a set of standardized building blocks used in designing and building industrial-grade systems. The subject of OTP behaviours and their related middleware is vast. In this section, we provide the overview you need to get started.

5.1 Introduction

OTP behaviours are a formalization of process design patterns. They are implemented in library modules that are provided with the standard Erlang distribution. These library modules do all of the generic process work and error handling. The specific code, written by the programmer, is placed in a separate module and called through a set of predefined callback functions.

OTP behaviours include worker processes, which do the actual processing, and supervisors, whose task is to monitor workers and other supervisors. Worker behaviours, often denoted in diagrams as circles, include servers, event handlers, and finite state machines. Supervisors, denoted in illustrations as squares, monitor their children, both workers and other supervisors, creating what is called a supervision tree.

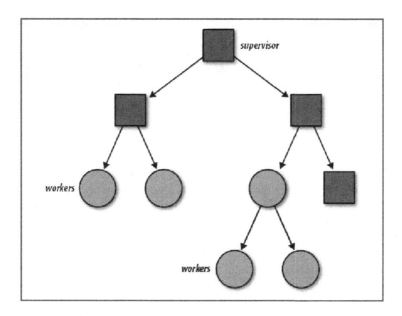

Fig. 4. OTP Supervision Tree

Supervision trees are packaged into a behaviour called an application. OTP applications not only are the building blocks of Erlang systems, but also are a way to package reusable components. Industrial-grade systems consist of a set of loosely-coupled, possibly distributed applications. These applications are part of the standard Erlang distribution or are specific applications developed by you, the programmer.

Do not confuse OTP applications with the more general concept of an application, which usually refers to a more complete system that solves a high-level task. Examples of OTP applications include the Mnesia database or the Simple Network Management Protocol (SNMP) agent. An OTP application is a reusable component that packages library modules together with supervisor and worker processes. From now on, when we refer to an application, we will mean an OTP application.

The behaviour module contains all of the generic code. Although it is possible to implement your own behaviour module, doing so is rare because the behaviour modules that come as part of the Erlang/OTP distribution will cater to most of the design patterns you would use in your code. The generic functionality provided in a behaviour module includes operations such as the following:

- Spawning and possibly registering the process
- Sending and receiving client messages as synchronous or asynchronous calls, including defining the internal message protocol
- Storing the loop data and managing the process loop
- Stopping the process

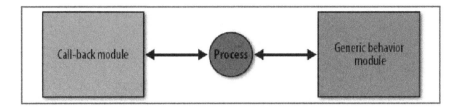

Fig. 5. Splitting the code in generic and specific modules

Although the behaviour module is provided, the programmer has to develop the callback module. A callback module contains all of the specific code required to deliver the desired functionality. The specific code is invoked through a callback interface that is standardized for each behaviour.

The loop data is a variable that will contain the data the behaviour needs to store in between calls. After the call, an updated variant of the loop data is returned. This updated loop data, often referred to as the new loop data, is passed as an argument in the next call. Loop data is also often referred to as the behaviour state.

The functionality to be included in the callback module for the generic server application to deliver the specific required behaviour includes the following:

– Initializing the process loop data, and, if the process is registered, the process name.
– Handling the specific client requests, and, if synchronous, the replies sent back to the client.
– Handling and updating the process loop data in between the process requests.
– Cleaning up the process loop data upon termination.

There are many advantages to splitting the code into generic behaviour libraries and specific callback modules:

– Because many of the special cases and errors that might occur are already handled in the solid, well-tested behaviour library, you can expect fewer bugs in your product.
– For this reason, and also because so much of the code is already written for you, you can expect to have a shorter time to market.
– It forces the programmer to write code in a way that avoids errors typically found in concurrent applications.
– Finally, your whole team will come to share a common programming style.

When reading someone else's code while armed with a basic comprehension of the existing behaviours, no effort is required to understand the client/server protocol, looking for where and how processes are started or terminated, or how the loop data is handled. All of it is managed by the generic behaviour library. Instead of having to focus on how everything is done, you can focus on what is being done specifically in this case, as coded in the callback module.

5.2 Generic Servers

Generic servers that implement client/server behaviours are defined in the
gen_server behaviour that comes as part of the standard library application.
In explaining generic servers, we will use the frequency server example from the
client server section.

We will rewrite the frequency.erl module, migrating it from an Erlang
process to a gen_server behaviour. In doing so, we will not touch the client
interface, keeping the API as it is. When working your way through the example,
if you are interested in the details, have the online Erlang manual pages for the
gen_server module to hand.

5.3 Starting Your Server

With the gen_server behaviour, instead of using the spawn and spawn_link
BIFs, you will use the gen_server:start/4 and gen_server:start_link/4
functions.

The main difference between spawn and start is the synchronous nature of
the call. Using start instead of spawn makes starting the worker process more
deterministic and prevents unforeseen race conditions, as the call will not return
the pid of the worker until it has been initialized. You call the functions as follows
(we show two variants for each of the functions):

```
gen_server:start_link(ServerName,CallBackModule,Arguments,Options)
gen_server:start(ServerName, CallBackModule, Arguments, Options)

gen_server:start_link(CallBackModule, Arguments, Options)
gen_server:start(CallBackModule, Arguments, Options)
```

In the preceding calls:

- ServerName is a tuple of the format {local, Name} or {global, Name},
  denoting a local or global. Name for the process if it is to be registered. If
  you do not want to register the process and instead reference it using its pid,
  you omit the argument and use a start_link/3 or start/3 function call
  instead.
- CallbackModule is the name of the module in which the specific callback
  functions are placed.
- Arguments is a valid Erlang term that is passed to the init/1 callback function. You can choose what type of term to pass: if you have many arguments
  to pass, use a list or a tuple; if you have none, pass an atom or an empty
  list, ignoring it in the callback function.
- Options is a list that allows you to set the memory management flags
  fullsweep_after and heapsize, as well as tracing and debugging flags.
  Most behaviour implementations just pass the empty list.

The start functions will spawn a new process that calls the init(Arguments)
callback function in the CallbackModule, with the Arguments supplied.

The init function must initialize the LoopData of the server and has to return a tuple of the format {ok, LoopData}. LoopData contains the first instance of the loop data that will be passed between the callback functions. If you want to store some of the arguments you passed to the init function, you would do so in the LoopData variable.

The obvious difference between the start_link and start functions is that start_link links to its parent and start doesn't. This needs a special mention, however, as it is an OTP behaviour's responsibility to link itself to the supervisor. The start functions are often used when testing behaviours from the shell, as a typing error causing the shell process to crash would not affect the behaviour. All variants of the start and start_link functions return {ok, Pid}.

Before going ahead with the example, let's quickly review what we have discussed so far. You start a gen_server behaviour using the gen_server:start_link call. This results in a new process that calls the init/1 callback function. This function initializes the LoopData and returns the tuple {ok, LoopData}.

In our example, we call start_link/4, registering the process with the same name as the callback module, using the ?MODULE macro call. We don't pass any arguments, and as a result, just send the empty list. The options list is kept empty:

```
start() ->
    gen_server:start_link({local, ?MODULE}, ?MODULE, [], []).

init(_Args) ->
    {ok, {get_frequencies(), []}}.

get_frequencies() -> [10,11,12,13,14,15].
```

Although the supervisor process might call the start_link/4 function, the init/1 callback is called by a different process: the one that was just spawned. Our LoopData contains the tuple of available and allocated frequencies. If the server LoopData does not need to be passed inbetween calls, a value still has to be included when returning the {ok, LoopData} structure. We get around it by returning the atom null.

Do only what is necessary and minimize the operations in your init function, as the call to init is a synchronous call that prevents all of the other serialized processes from starting until it returns.

5.4 Passing Messages

If you want to send a message to your server, you use the following calls:

```
gen_server:cast(Name, Message)
gen_server:call(Name, Message)
```

In the preceding calls:

- Name is either the local registered name of the server or the tuple {global, Name}. It could also be the process identifier of the server.
- Message is a valid Erlang term containing a message passed on to the server. For asynchronous message requests, you use cast/2. If you're using a pid, the call will immediately return the atom ok, regardless of whether the gen_server to which you are sending the message is alive. These semantics are no different from the standard Name! Message construct, where if the registered process Name does not exist, the calling process terminates.

Upon receiving the message, gen_server will call the function handle_cast(Message, LoopData) in the callback module. Message is the argument passed to the cast/2 function, and LoopData is the argument originally returned by the init/1 callback function. The handle_cast/2 callback function handles the specifics of the message, and upon finishing, it has to return the tuple {noreply, NewLoopData}. In future calls to the server, the NewLoopData value most recently returned will be passed as an argument when a message is sent to the server.

If you want to send a synchronous message to the server, you use the call/2 function. Upon receiving this message, the process uses the handle_call(Message, From, LoopData) function in the callback module. It contains specific code for the particular server, and having completed, it returns the tuple {reply, Reply, NewLoopData}. Only now does the call/3 function synchronously return the value Reply. If the process to which you are sending a message does not exist, regardless of whether it is registered, the process invoking the call function terminates.

Let's start by taking two functions from our service API; we will provide the whole program later. They are called by the client process and result in a synchronous message being sent to the server process registered with the same name as the callback module. Note that validating the data sent to the server should occur on the client side. If the client sends incorrect information, the server should terminate.

```
allocate()       ->
    gen_server:call(?MODULE, {allocate, self()}).
deallocate(Freq) ->
    gen_server:call(?MODULE, {deallocate, Freq}).
```

Upon receiving the messages, the gen_server process calls the handle_call/3 callback function dealing with the messages in the same order in which they were sent:

```
handle_call({allocate, Pid}, _From, Frequencies) ->
    {NewFrequencies, Reply} = allocate(Frequencies, Pid),
    {reply, Reply, NewFrequencies};
handle_call({deallocate, Freq}, _From, Frequencies) ->
    NewFrequencies=deallocate(Frequencies, Freq),
    {reply, ok, NewFrequencies}.
```

Note the return value of the callback function. The tuple contains the control atom `reply`, telling the `gen_server` generic code that the second element of the tuple is the `Reply` to be sent back to the client. The third element of the tuple is the new `LoopData`, which, in a new iteration of the server, is passed as the third argument to the `handle_call/3` function; in both cases here it is unchanged. The argument `_From` is a tuple containing a unique message reference and the client process identifier. The tuple as a whole is used in library functions that we will not be discussing in this article. In the majority of cases, you will not need it.

The `gen_server` library module has a number of mechanisms and safeguards built in that function behind the scenes. If your client sends a synchronous message to your server and you do not get a response within five seconds, the process executing the `call/2` function is terminated. You can override this by using the following code:

```
gen_server:call(Name, Message, Timeout)
```

where `Timeout` is a value in milliseconds or the atom `infinity`. The timeout mechanism was originally put in place for deadlock prevention purposes, ensuring that servers that accidentally call each other are terminated after the default timeout. The crash report would be logged, and hopefully would result in a patch. Most applications will function appropriately with a timeout of five seconds, but under very heavy loads, you might have to fine-tune the value and possibly even use `infinity`; this choice is very application-dependent. All of the critical code in Erlang/OTP uses `infinity`.

Other safeguards when using the `gen_server:call/2` function include the case of sending a message to a non-existing server as well as the case that a server that crashes before sending its reply. In both cases, the calling process will terminate. In raw Erlang, sending a message that is never pattern-matched in a receive clause is a bug that can cause a memory leak.

What do you think happens if you do a `call` or a `cast` to your server, but do not handle the message in the `handle_call/3` and `handle_cast/2` calls, respectively? In OTP, when a `call` or a `cast` is called, the message will always be extracted from the process mailbox and the respective callback functions are invoked. If none of the callback functions pattern-matches the message passed as the first argument, the process will crash with a function clause error. As a result, such issues will be caught in the early stages of the testing phase and dealt with accordingly.

5.5   Stopping the Server

How do you stop the server? In your `handle_call/3` and `handle_cast/2` callback functions, instead of returning `{reply, Reply, NewLoopData}` or `{noreply, NewLoopData}`, you can return `{stop, Reason, Reply, NewLoopData}` or `{stop, Reason, NewLoopData}`, respectively. Something has to trigger this return value, often a stop message sent to the server. Upon receiving the stop tuple containing the `Reason` and `LoopData`, the generic code executes the `terminate(Reason, LoopData)` callback.

The `terminate` function is the natural place to insert the code needed to clean up the `LoopData` of the server and any other persistent data used by the system. The `stop` call does not have to occur within a synchronous call, so let's use `cast` when implementing it:

```erlang
stop() ->
    gen_server:cast(?MODULE, stop).

handle_cast(stop, Frequencies) ->
    {stop, normal, Frequencies}.

terminate(_Reason, _Frequencies) ->
    ok.
```

Remember that `stop/0` will be called by the client process, while the `handle_cast/2` and `handle_call/2` functions are called by the behaviour process. In the `handle_cast/2` callback, we return the reason normal in the `stop` construct. Any reason other than normal will result in an error report being generated.

With thousands of generic servers potentially being spawned and terminated every second, generating error reports for every one of them is not the way to go. You should return a non-normal value only if something that should not have happened occurs and you have no way to recover. A socket being closed or a corrupt message from an external source should not promot a non-normal exit reason.

Use of the behaviour callbacks as library functions and invoking them from other parts of your program is an extremely bad practice. For example, you should never call `frequency:init(FileName)` from another module to retrieve the initial loop data. Calls to behaviour callback functions should originate only from the behaviour library modules as a result of an event occurring in the system, and never directly by the user.

The Example in Full

Here is the `frequency.erl` module in full, rewritten as a `gen_server` behaviour:

```erlang
% File: frequency.erl
%% Purpose gen_server call back module for the frequency
%% allocator

-module(frequency2).
-export([start/0, stop/0, allocate/0, deallocate/1]).
-export([init/1, terminate/2, handle_cast/2, handle_call/3]).
```

```erlang
%% The start and stop Functions
start() ->
    gen_server:start_link({local, ?MODULE}, ?MODULE, [], []).

stop() ->
    gen_server:cast(?MODULE, stop).

%%  The client Functions
allocate()       ->
    gen_server:call(?MODULE, {allocate, self()}).
deallocate(Freq) ->
    gen_server:call(?MODULE, {deallocate, Freq}).

%% Callback functions
handle_call({allocate, Pid}, _From, Frequencies) ->
    {NewFrequencies, Reply} = allocate(Frequencies, Pid),
    {reply, Reply, NewFrequencies};

handle_call({deallocate, Freq}, _From, Frequencies) ->
    NewFrequencies=deallocate(Frequencies, Freq),
    {reply, ok, NewFrequencies}.

handle_cast(stop, Frequencies) ->
    {stop, normal, Frequencies}.

init(_Args) ->
    {ok, {get_frequencies(), []}}.

terminate(_Reason, _Frequencies) ->
    ok.

%% Local Functions
get_frequencies() -> [10,11,12,13,14,15].

allocate({[], Allocated}, _Pid) ->
    {{[], Allocated}, {error, no_frequencies}};
allocate({[Freq|Frequencies], Allocated}, Pid) ->
    {{Frequencies,[{Freq,Pid}|Allocated]},{ok,Freq}}.

deallocate({Free, Allocated}, Freq) ->
    {value,{Freq, _Pid}}= lists:keysearch(Freq,1,Allocated),
    NewAllocated=lists:keydelete(Freq,1,Allocated),
    {[Freq|Free],  NewAllocated}.
```

Running the gen_server

When testing the `gen_server` instance in the shell, you get exactly the same behaviour as when you used the server process that you coded yourself. However, the code is more solid, as deadlocks, server crashes, timeouts, and other errors related to concurrent programming are handled behind the scenes. The following calls:

```
start(Name, Mod, Arguments, Opts)
start_link(Name, Mod, Arguments, Opts),
```

where `Name` is an optional argument, spawn a new process. The process will result in the callback function `init(Arguments)` being called, which should return one of the values {ok, LoopData} or {stop, Reason}. If `init/1` returns {stop, Reason} the `terminate/2` "cleanup" function will not be called.

Synchronous communication

Use `call(Name, Msg)` to send a synchronous message to your server. It will result in the callback function `handle_call(Msg, From, LoopData)` being called by the server process. The expected return values include {reply, Reply, NewLoopData} and {stop, Reason, Reply, NewLoopData}.

Asynchronous communication

If you want to send an asynchronous message, use `cast(Name, Msg)`. It will be handled in the `handle_cast(Msg, LoopData)` callback function, returning either {noreply, NewLoopData} or {stop, Reason, NewLoopData}.

Non-OTP-compliant messages

Upon receiving non-OTP-compliant messages, `gen_server` will execute the `handle_info(Msg, LoopData)` callback function. The function should return either {noreply, NewLoopData} or {stop, Reason, NewLoopData}.

Termination

Upon receiving a `stop` construct from one of the callback functions (except for `init`), the `terminate(Reason, LoopData)` callback is invoked. In `terminate/2`, you would typically undo things you did in `init/1`. Its return value is ignored.

6   Other Behaviours

Finite state machines are a crucial component of telecom systems. The `gen_fsm` module provides you with a behaviour that you can use to implement processes acting as finite state machines. States are defined as callback functions that return a tuple containing the next State and the updated loop data. You can send events to these states synchronously and asynchronously. The finite state machine callback module should also export the standard callback functions such as `init`, `terminate`, and `handle_info`. Examples of processes acting as finite state machines include protocol stacks, communication layers, mutex semaphores as well as high level control flow in telephony systems.

Event handlers and managers are another behaviour implemented in the gen_event library module. The idea is to create a centralized point that receives events of a specific kind. Events can be sent synchronously and asynchronously with a predefined set of actions being applied when they are received. Possible responses to events include logging them to file, sending off an alarm in the form of an SMS, or collecting statistics. Each of these actions is defined in a separate callback module with its own loop data, preserved in between calls. Handlers can be added, removed, or updated for every specific event manager. So, in practice, for every event manager, there could be many callback modules, and different instances of these callback modules could exist in different managers. Event handlers include processes receiving alarms, live trace data, equipment related events or simple logs.

The supervisor behaviour's task is to monitor its children and, based on some preconfigured rules, take action when they terminate. The children that make up the supervision tree include both supervisors and worker processes. Worker processes are OTP behaviours including gen_server and gen_event.

Worker processes have to link themselves to the supervisor behaviour and handle specific system messages that are not exposed to the programmer. This is different from the way in which one process links to another in raw Erlang, and because of this, we cannot mix the two mechanisms.

The application behaviour is used to package Erlang modules into reusable components. An Erlang system will consist of a set of loosely-coupled applications. Some are developed by the programmer or the open source community, and others will be part of the OTP distribution. The Erlang runtime system and its tools will treat all applications equally, regardless of whether they are part of the Erlang distribution or not.

There are two kinds of applications. The most common form of applications, called normal applications, will start the supervision tree and all of the relevant static workers. Library applications such as the Standard Library, which come as part of the Erlang distribution, contain library modules but do not start the supervision tree. This is not to say that the code may not contain processes or supervision trees. It just means they are started as part of a supervision tree belonging to another application.

For more information on behaviours not covered in this paper, we recommend the OTP Design Principles User's Guide, available in the documentation section of the http://erlang.org website.

7   Conclusions

The generic servers described in these lecture notes give an example of how OTP behaviours work. Behaviours we have not covered but which we briefly introduced in this chapter include finite state machines, event handlers, supervisors and special processes. All of these behaviour library modules have manual pages that you can reference. In addition, the Erlang documentation has a section on OTP design principles that provides more detailed explanations and examples.

Workers and supervisors create supervision trees which when packaged in applications give software architects a generic and powerful approach to packaging and deployment of software. The benefits are reduced code sizes, generic error handling and reuse of components, ensuring that you don't "reinvent the wheel" in writing Erlang solutions.

Reasoning about Codata

Ralf Hinze

Computing Laboratory, University of Oxford
Wolfson Building, Parks Road, Oxford, OX1 3QD, England
ralf.hinze@comlab.ox.ac.uk
http://www.comlab.ox.ac.uk/ralf.hinze/

Abstract. Programmers happily use induction to prove properties of recursive programs. To show properties of corecursive programs they employ coinduction, but perhaps less enthusiastically. Coinduction is often considered a rather low-level proof method, in particular, as it departs quite radically from equational reasoning. Corecursive programs are conveniently defined using recursion equations. Suitably restricted, these equations possess *unique solutions*. Uniqueness gives rise to a simple and attractive proof technique, which essentially brings equational reasoning to the coworld. We illustrate the approach using two major examples: streams and infinite binary trees. Both coinductive types exhibit a rich structure: they are applicative functors or idioms, and they can be seen as memo-tables or tabulations. We show that definitions and calculations benefit immensely from this additional structure.

1 Introduction

These lecture notes show how to use codata in modelling and programming and how to reason about codata, with the main focus on the latter. Codata is the dual of data, with an emphasis on observation rather than construction, and the indefinite rather than the finite.

Data is captured by inductive datatypes, whose elements can be constructed in a finite number of steps. Functional programming has been characterised as data-oriented programming: new datatypes are introduced with ease; elements of those types are analysed by recursive functions, conveniently defined by recursion equations; data constructors can be used on the right-hand side of equations to synthesise data and on the left-hand side to analyse data. Programmers happily use equational reasoning and induction to prove properties of recursive programs.

Dually, codata is captured by coinductive datatypes, whose elements can be deconstructed in a finite number of steps. Codata is synthesised using corecursive programs. To show properties of corecursive programs, programmers employ coinduction, but perhaps less enthusiastically. Coinduction is often considered a rather low-level proof method, especially, as it departs quite radically from equational reasoning. In these notes we introduce an alternative proof technique, based on unique fixed points, that remedies these problems. But we are skipping ahead.

Z. Horváth, R. Plasmeijer, and V. Zsók (Eds.): CEFP 2009, LNCS 6299, pp. 42–93, 2010.

Though data is dual to codata, it is not equally appreciated. For instance, in the seminal textbook on the "Algebra of Programming" [3] the authors devote a single paragraph to codata, remarking "We shall not have any use for such infinite data structures, however, and their discussion is therefore omitted." We hope to convince the reader that the notion of codata is equally valuable and that it has a lot to offer, both for the working programmer and for the working mathematician. For the programmer, it promises

- more elegant programs through a holistic or wholemeal approach,
- avoidance of case analysis,
- increased compositionality through separation of concerns.

For the mathematician, it promises

- more elegant proofs through a holistic or wholemeal approach,
- avoidance of index variables and subscripts,
- avoidance of case analysis and induction.

The simplest example of a coinductive type is the type of streams, where a stream is an infinite sequence of elements. In a lazy functional language, such as Haskell [31], streams are easy to define and many textbooks on Haskell reproduce the folklore examples of Fibonacci or Hamming numbers defined by recursion equations over streams. One has to be a bit careful in formulating a recursion equation, basically avoiding that the sequence defined swallows its own tail. However, if this care is exercised, the equation possesses a *unique solution*. Uniqueness can be exploited to prove that two streams are equal: if they satisfy the same recursion equation, then they are!

Let us illustrate the proof technique using a concrete example. Consider Figure 1, which displays a proof concerning a simple property of the Fibonacci numbers. The setting is very conventional, using a recurrence to define the Fibonacci numbers and an inductive proof to establish the property. The formalisation makes intensive use of the delimited Σ-notation. (Fourier introduced the notation in 1820, and it is reported to have taken the mathematical world by storm [14].) Summation is a binder introducing an index variable that ranges over some set. More often than not, the index variable then appears as a subscript referring to an element of some other set or sequence. In Figure 1, summation introduces the variable i, which is then used to index the Fibonacci sequence. Now, for comparison, let us re-develop the proof in a coinductive setting.

The Fibonacci sequence is defined by a set of recursion equations.

$$
\begin{aligned}
\mathit{fib} &= 0 \prec \mathit{fib}' \\
\mathit{fib}' &= 1 \prec \mathit{fib}'' \\
\mathit{fib}'' &= \mathit{fib} + \mathit{fib}'
\end{aligned}
$$

The definitions that make this work are introduced in Section 3. For the moment, it suffices to know that $\prec$ prepends an element to a stream and that the arithmetic operations are lifted point-wise to streams. Quite noticeable, index variables and subscripts are avoided by treating the sequence of Fibonacci numbers as a single entity.

The Fibonacci numbers are defined by the recurrence

$$
\begin{aligned}
\mathcal{F}_0 &= 0 \\
\mathcal{F}_1 &= 1 \\
\mathcal{F}_{n+2} &= \mathcal{F}_n + \mathcal{F}_{n+1} \ .
\end{aligned}
$$

The numbers satisfy a myriad of properties. For instance, if we add the first k Fibonacci numbers, we obtain $\mathcal{F}_{k+1} - 1$. Let us prove this simple fact. We show $\forall n \in \mathbb{N} \, . \, P(n)$, where P is given by

$$
P(k) \quad :\Longleftrightarrow \quad \sum_{i=0}^{k-1} \mathcal{F}_i = \mathcal{F}_{k+1} - 1 \ .
$$

The proof proceeds by induction. *Basis:* $P(0)$.

$$
\sum_{i=0}^{-1} \mathcal{F}_i
$$

$=$ { empty sum }

$\quad 0$

$=$ { arithmetic }

$\quad 1 - 1$

$=$ { definition of $\mathcal{F}_1$ }

$\quad \mathcal{F}_1 - 1$

Inductive step: $\forall n \in \mathbb{N} \, . \, P(n) \Longrightarrow P(n+1)$. Assume $P(n)$, then

$$
\sum_{i=0}^{n} \mathcal{F}_i
$$

$=$ { split sum }

$\quad \left(\sum_{i=0}^{n-1} \mathcal{F}_i \right) + \mathcal{F}_n$

$=$ { ex hypothesi $P(n)$ }

$\quad \mathcal{F}_{n+1} - 1 + \mathcal{F}_n$

$=$ { arithmetic and definition of $\mathcal{F}_{n+2}$ }

$\quad \mathcal{F}_{n+2} - 1 \ .$

Fig. 1. A famous recurrence and an inductive proof

In the same spirit, summation is defined as a stream transformer or operator: it takes an input stream to the stream of its partial sums. Summation Σ is characterised by the following property.

$$\Sigma\, s = t \quad \Longleftrightarrow \quad t = 0 \prec s + t$$

The equivalence captures the fact that summation is the *unique solution* of the equation on the right-hand side.

The property of the Fibonacci numbers, adding the first k numbers yields $\mathcal{F}_{k+1} - 1$, is then captured by a simple stream equation: $\Sigma\, fib = fib' - 1$. Again, neither binders nor index variables are required. (By contrast, the corresponding statement in Figure 1 involves three binders: the universal quantifier introduces n, the abstraction defining the predicate P introduces k, and the delimited sum introduces i.) The proof is fairly straightforward. The characterisation of Σ leaves us with the task of showing $fib' - 1 = 0 \prec fib + fib' - 1$. We reason

$$\begin{aligned}
& fib' - 1 \\
= \quad & \{ \text{ definition of } fib' \text{ and } fib'' \} \\
& (1 \prec fib + fib') - 1 \\
= \quad & \{ \text{ arithmetic } \} \\
& 0 \prec fib + fib' - 1 \ .
\end{aligned}$$

The fairly voluminous, inductive argument in Figure 1 is replaced by a simple two-step calculation. It is the fact that summation is the *unique solution* of $\Sigma\, s = 0 \prec s + \Sigma\, s$ that makes the proof fly. In a nutshell, the proof method of unique fixed points brings equational reasoning to the coworld. Of course, it is by no means restricted to streams and can be used equally well to prove properties of infinite trees or the observational equivalence of instances of an abstract datatype.

Objectives. The primary goal of these lecture notes is to familiarise you with the notion of codata. We shall make the ideas hinted above concrete using two major running examples: streams and infinite binary trees. At the end of the course, you should be able to capture sequences, iterative algorithms, infinite processes etc using recursion equations, and you should be able to prove properties using the unique fixed-point principle. Streams and infinite trees exhibit a rich structure: they are idioms and tabulations. We investigate these notions in considerable depth as they enable us to structure calculations more clearly.

Prerequisites. We assume a basic knowledge of the functional programming language Haskell [31] — we shall make use of kinds, datatypes, type classes and lazy evaluation. Some knowledge of category theory is helpful, but not required.

Outline. The rest of these notes are structured as follows. Section 2 reviews the notion of an applicative functor or idiom. Section 3 introduces the type of streams, our prime example of a coinductive datatype. Section 4 illustrates capturing recurrences using streams and investigates the relationship between streams and functions from the natural numbers. Section 5 applies the framework to finite calculus, the discrete counterpart of infinite calculus, where finite difference replaces the derivative and summation replaces integration. Section 6 introduces infinite trees, our second example of an inductive datatype, and discusses some applications. Both streams and infinite trees can be seen as tabulations or memo-tables. Section 7 investigates the notion of tabulation in more detail. Finally, Section 8 concludes. Related work is discussed at the end of each section, where appropriate.

2   Background: Idioms

Most definitions we encounter later on make use of operations lifted to streams or infinite trees. We obtain these liftings almost for free, as these datatypes are so-called *applicative functors* or *idioms* [27].

> **infixl** 9 $\diamond$
> **class** *Idiom* ϕ **where**
> $pure :: \alpha \to \phi\, \alpha$
> $(\diamond)\ \ :: \phi\,(\alpha \to \beta) \to (\phi\, \alpha \to \phi\, \beta)$

The constructor class introduces an operation for embedding a value into an idiomatic structure, and an application operator that takes a structure of functions to a function between structures. Consider as a simple example the *dual-core idiom*, which executes two programs in parallel.

> **data** *Pair* $\alpha = Pair\ \{\, outl :: \alpha, outr :: \alpha\,\}$

> **instance** *Idiom Pair* **where**
> $pure\ a =\ Pair\ a\ a$
> $u \diamond v\ \ =\ Pair\ ((outl\ u)\ (outl\ v))\ ((outr\ u)\ (outr\ v))$

The method *pure* duplicates its argument; idiomatic apply takes a pair of functions and a pair of arguments to a pair of results.

The type *Pair* can be seen as a very simple *container type*, which can accommodate exactly two elements. An alternative representation of a two-element container is a function from the Booleans: $Pair\ \alpha \cong Bool \to \alpha$. Generalising from *Bool*, we obtain the environment idiom '$\alpha \to$' — the type '$\alpha \to$' is actually a monad, but we shall not make use of the additional structure.

> **instance** *Idiom* $(\alpha \to)$ **where**
> $pure\ a = \lambda x \to a$
> $f \diamond g\ \ = \lambda x \to (f\ x)\ (g\ x)$

The idiom threads an environment, the argument x, through an idiomatic structure: *pure* discards the environment and $\diamond$ distributes it to its two arguments. Interestingly, *pure* is the combinator K and '$\diamond$' is the combinator S from combinatory logic [7]. The combinators were re-discovered in the 1970s to form the basis of an implementation technique for lazy functional languages [37].

Idioms abound, here are further examples of idioms and idiom transformers.

- The constant type constructor *Const A* with

$$Const\ \alpha\ \beta = \alpha$$

is an idiom if *A* is a monoid.
- The identity type constructor is an idiom.

$$Id\ \alpha = \alpha$$

- Idioms are closed under type composition.

$$(\phi \cdot \psi)\ \alpha = \phi\ (\psi\ \alpha)$$

- Idioms are closed under type pairing.

$$(\phi \mathbin{\dot{\times}} \psi)\ \alpha = (\phi\ \alpha, \psi\ \alpha)$$

The type constructor $\dot{\times}$ lifts pairing to parametric datatypes, type constructors of kind $\star \to \star$. The type *Pair* is isomorphic to $Id \mathbin{\dot{\times}} Id$.
- Every monad is an idiom — but not the other way round.

Exercise 1. Define suitable datatypes to represent the idioms and idiom transformers listed above. Then turn the types into instances of the *Idiom* class.

> **instance** $(Monoid\ \alpha) \Rightarrow Idiom\ (Const\ \alpha)$
> **instance** *Idiom Id*
> **instance** $(Idiom\ \phi, Idiom\ \psi) \Rightarrow Idiom\ (\phi \cdot \psi)$
> **instance** $(Idiom\ \phi, Idiom\ \psi) \Rightarrow Idiom\ (\phi \mathbin{\dot{\times}} \psi)$

(Section 6.2 defines the *Monoid* type class.) □

Using nested idiomatic applications, we can lift an arbitrary function pointwise to an idiomatic structure. Here are generic combinators for lifting unary and binary operations.

> map :: $(Idiom\ \phi) \Rightarrow (\alpha \to \beta) \to (\phi\ \alpha \to \phi\ \beta)$
> $map\ f\ u = pure\ f \diamond u$
> zip :: $(Idiom\ \phi) \Rightarrow (\alpha \to \beta \to \gamma) \to (\phi\ \alpha \to \phi\ \beta \to \phi\ \gamma)$
> $zip\ g\ u\ v = pure\ g \diamond u \diamond v$

Using *zip* we can, for instance, lift pairing to idioms.

> **infixl** 6 $\star$
> $(\star)$ :: $(Idiom\ \phi) \Rightarrow \phi\ \alpha \to \phi\ \beta \to \phi\ (\alpha, \beta)$
> $(\star) = zip\ (,)$

The quizzical '(,)' is Haskell's pairing constructor.

For convenience and conciseness of notation, we lift the arithmetic operations to idioms. In Haskell, this is easily accomplished using the numeric type classes. Here is an excerpt of the code.[1]

```
instance (Idiom φ, Num α) ⇒ Num (φ α) where
  (+)            = zip (+)
  (−)            = zip (−)
  (∗)            = zip (∗)
  negate         = map negate    -- unary minus
  fromInteger i  = pure (fromInteger i)
```

We shall make intensive use of overloading, going beyond Haskell's predefined numeric classes. For instance, we also lift exponentiation u^v to idioms.

In these lecture notes, we mainly consider two idioms, streams and infinite trees. In both cases, the familiar arithmetic laws also hold for the lifted operators.

Speaking of laws, every instance of *Idiom* must satisfy four laws:

$$pure\ id \diamond u \qquad\qquad = u \qquad\qquad\qquad\qquad\qquad\text{(identity)}$$
$$pure\ (\cdot) \diamond u \diamond v \diamond w = u \diamond (v \diamond w) \qquad\qquad\qquad\text{(composition)}$$
$$pure\ f \diamond pure\ x \quad = pure\ (f\ x) \qquad\qquad\qquad\text{(homomorphism)}$$
$$u \diamond pure\ x \qquad\quad = pure\ (\lambda f \rightarrow f\ x) \diamond u \qquad\qquad\text{(interchange)}$$

The first two laws imply the well-known *functor laws*: *map* preserves identity and composition (hence the names of the idiom laws).

$$map\ id \quad\ = id$$
$$map\ (f \cdot g) = map\ f \cdot map\ g$$

Every instance of Haskell's *Functor* class should satisfy these two laws (*map* is called *fmap* in *Functor*).

The interchange law allows us to swap pure and impure computations. This move possibly brings together pure computations, which can subsequently be merged using the homomorphism law. In fact, the idiom laws imply a normal form: every idiomatic expression can be rewritten into the form $pure\ f \diamond u_1 \diamond \cdots \diamond u_n$, a pure function applied to impure arguments. Put differently, applicative functors or idioms capture the notion of lifting: $\lambda u_1 \cdots u_n \rightarrow pure\ f \diamond u_1 \diamond \cdots \diamond u_n$ is the lifted version of the $n$ary function f (assuming that f is curried). For instance, the environment idiom '$\alpha \rightarrow$' captures lifting operators to function spaces: $zip\ (+)\ f\ g = pure\ (+) \diamond f \diamond g = S\ (S\ (K\ (+))\ f)\ g = \lambda x \rightarrow f\ x + g\ x$.

Every structure comes equipped with structure-preserving maps; so do idioms: a polymorphic function $h :: \forall \alpha . \phi\ \alpha \rightarrow \psi\ \alpha$ is called an *idiom homomorphism* if and only if it preserves the idiomatic structure:

$$h\ (pure\ a) = pure\ a \qquad\qquad\qquad\qquad\qquad\qquad\qquad (1)$$
$$h\ (x \diamond y) \quad = h\ x \diamond h\ y\ . \qquad\qquad\qquad\qquad\qquad\quad (2)$$

---

[1] Unfortunately, this does not quite work with the Standard Haskell libraries, as *Num* has two super-classes, *Eq* and *Show*, which cannot sensibly be defined generically.

The function $pure :: \forall \alpha \,.\, \alpha \rightarrow \phi\,\alpha$ itself is a homomorphism from the identity idiom Id to the idiom ϕ. Condition (2) for $pure$ is equivalent to the homomorphism law, hence its name.

2.1   Summary and Related Work

Idioms capture the notion of lifting. Using $pure$ and $\diamond$ we can, in particular, lift arithmetic operations point-wise to structures. The environment functor is the paradigmatic example of an idiom; it captures lifting operations point-wise to functions.

Categorically, idioms are *lax monoidal functors* [26] with strength. Programmatically, idioms arose as an interface for parsing combinators [34]. McBride and Paterson [27] introduced the notion to a wider audience. For the idioms we consider in these notes, the lifted operators satisfy the same properties as the 'unlifted' ones. This does, however, not hold in general [21].

3   Streams

A stream is an infinite sequence of elements. Here are some examples of (initial segments of) streams of natural numbers.

$$\langle 0, 1, 8, 27, 64, 125, 216, 343, 512, 729, 1000, 1331, \ldots \rangle$$
$$\langle 1, 3, 9, 27, 81, 243, 729, 2187, 6561, 19683, 59049, \ldots \rangle$$
$$\langle 0, 0, 1, 1, 2, 4, 3, 9, 4, 16, 5, 25, 6, 36, 7, 49, \ldots \rangle$$
$$\langle 0, 0, 2, 4, 8, 14, 24, 40, 66, 108, 176, 286, 464, 752, \ldots \rangle$$
$$\langle 0, 1, 2, 6, 15, 40, 104, 273, 714, 1870, 4895, 12816, \ldots \rangle$$

Exercise 2. Describe the streams using natural language.   □

Since Haskell is a lazy language, we can capture the type of streams as a datatype: *Stream* α is like Haskell's list data type $[\alpha]$, except that there is no base constructor so we cannot construct a finite stream. The *Stream* type is not an inductive type, but a *coinductive type*, whose semantics is given by a *final coalgebra* [1].

> **data** *Stream* $\alpha = Cons\ \{\,head :: \alpha, tail :: Stream\ \alpha\,\}$
>
> **infixr** 5 $\prec$
> $(\prec)$ $:: \forall \alpha \,.\, \alpha \rightarrow Stream\ \alpha \rightarrow Stream\ \alpha$
> $a \prec s = Cons\ a\ s$

Streams are constructed using $\prec$, which prepends an element to a stream. They are destructed using *head*, which yields the first element, and *tail*, which returns the stream without the first element.

Streams are an idiom, which means that we can effortlessly lift functions to streams:

> **instance** *Idiom Stream* **where**
> $pure\ a = s$ **where** $s = a \prec s$
> $s \diamond t\ \ = (head\ s)\ (head\ t) \prec (tail\ s) \diamond (tail\ t)\ .$

Using this vocabulary we are already able to define the usual suspects: the natural numbers ($A001477^2$), the factorial numbers ($A000142$), and the Fibonacci numbers ($A000045$).

$$nat = 0 \prec nat + 1$$
$$fac = 1 \prec (nat + 1) * fac$$
$$fib = 0 \prec fib'$$
$$fib' = 1 \prec fib + fib'$$

Note that $\prec$ binds less tightly than $+$. For instance, $0 \prec nat + 1$ is grouped $0 \prec (nat + 1)$. The definitions capture invariants. For instance, incrementing the naturals by 1 and then prepending 0 yields again the naturals. Here is an attempt to visualise the invariant:

0	1	2	3	4	5	6	7	8	9	$\cdots$		nat
+	+	+	+	+	+	+	+	+	+	$\cdots$		+
0	1	1	1	1	1	1	1	1	1	1	$\cdots$	$0 \prec 1$
‖	‖	‖	‖	‖	‖	‖	‖	‖	‖	‖	$\cdots$	‖
0	1	2	3	4	5	6	7	8	9	10	$\cdots$	nat .

The table makes explicit that 1 in $nat + 1$ is actually an infinite sequence of ones and that '$+$' zips two streams using addition.

The four sequences are given by recursion equations adhering to a strict scheme: each equation defines the head and the tail of the sequence, the latter possibly in terms of the entire sequence. As an aside, we will use the convention that the identifier x' denotes the tail of x, and x'' the tail of x'. The Fibonacci numbers provide an example of mutual recursion: fib' refers to fib and vice versa. Actually, in this case mutual recursion is not necessary, as a quick calculation shows: $fib' = 1 \prec fib + fib' = (1 \prec fib) + (0 \prec fib') = (1 \prec fib) + fib$. So, an alternative definition is

$$fib = 0 \prec fib + (1 \prec fib) .$$

The table below visualises the definition.

0	1	1	2	3	5	8	13	21	34	$\cdots$		fib
+	+	+	+	+	+	+	+	+	+	$\cdots$		+
0	1	0	1	1	2	3	5	8	13	21	$\cdots$	$0 \prec 1 \prec fib$
‖	‖	‖	‖	‖	‖	‖	‖	‖	‖	‖	$\cdots$	‖
0	1	1	2	3	5	8	13	21	34	55	$\cdots$	fib

The Fibonacci function is the folklore example of a function whose straightforward definition leads to a very inefficient program, see Exercise 9. By contrast, the stream definition, fib, does not suffer from this problem: to determine the nth element only $max\,\{n - 1, 0\}$ additions are required.

---

[2] Most if not all integer sequences defined in these lecture notes are recorded in Sloane's On-Line Encyclopedia of Integer Sequences [35]. Keys of the form $Annnnnn$ refer to entries in that database.

It is fun to play with the sequences. Here is a short interactive session.

> $\gg$ *fib*
> $\langle 0, 1, 1, 2, 3, 5, 8, 13, 21, 34, 55, 89, 144, 233, 377, ..\rangle$
> $\gg$ *nat* $*$ *nat*
> $\langle 0, 1, 4, 9, 16, 25, 36, 49, 64, 81, 100, 121, 144, 169, 196, ..\rangle$
> $\gg$ *fib*$'^2$ $-$ *fib* $*$ *fib*$''$
> $\langle 1, -1, 1, -1, 1, -1, 1, -1, 1, -1, 1, -1, 1, -1, 1, ..\rangle$
> $\gg$ *fib*$'^2$ $-$ *fib* $*$ *fib*$''$ == $(-1)^{nat}$
> *True*

The part after the prompt, $\gg$, is the user's input. The result of each submission is shown in the subsequent line. This document has been produced using lhs2TEX [22]. The session displays the actual output of the Haskell interpreter, generated automatically with lhs2TEX's active features.

Obviously, we cannot print out a sequence in full. The *Show* instance for *Stream* only displays the first n elements. Likewise, we cannot test two streams for equality: == only checks whether the first n elements are equal. So, 'equality' is most useful for falsifying conjectures. For the purposes of these notes, n equals 15.

In Haskell, the same function can be defined in at least three different ways[3]. The same is true of sequences: here are three different variants of the stream of natural numbers — and there are more to come.

$$nat = 0 \prec nat + 1$$
$$nat = 0 \prec pure\ (+) \diamond nat \diamond pure\ 1$$
$$nat = 0 \prec map\ (1+)\ nat$$

The definitions can be shown equivalent using the idiom laws. As an example, the following calculation proves $nat + 1 = map\ (1+)\ nat$ — the most difficult part has been relegated to an exercise.

$$nat + 1$$
$$= \quad \{\ \text{definition of} + \text{and}\ fromInteger\ \}$$
$$zip\ (+)\ nat\ (pure\ 1)$$
$$= \quad \{\ \text{definition of}\ zip\ \}$$
$$pure\ (+) \diamond nat \diamond pure\ 1$$
$$= \quad \{\ \text{Exercise 3}\ \}$$
$$pure\ (+) \diamond pure\ 1 \diamond nat$$
$$= \quad \{\ \text{homomorphism law}\ \}$$
$$pure\ (1+) \diamond nat$$
$$= \quad \{\ \text{definition of}\ map\ \}$$
$$map\ (1+)\ nat$$

---

[3] See http://www.willamette.edu/~fruehr/haskell/evolution.html for an amusing illustration of this fact using the factorial function as an example.

The proof exemplifies the typical style of reasoning: we transform the left-hand side into the right-hand side by repeatedly replacing equals by equals. The comments in curly braces justify the individual steps.

Exercise 3. Show $s + 1 = 1 + s$ using solely the idiom laws. (First, make sure that your understand why the laws are baptised 'identity', 'composition', 'homomorphism' and 'interchange'. The text explains why.) Does lifted commutativity $s + t = t + s$ hold in every idiom? Conversely, what base-level identities can be lifted through any idiom? The paper "Lifting Operators and Laws" [21] answers these questions.   □

3.1   Interleaving

Another important operator is *interleaving* of two streams.

> **infixr** 5 ⋎
> (⋎)   :: ∀α . *Stream* α → *Stream* α → *Stream* α
> $s ⋎ t = head\ s ≺ t ⋎ tail\ s$

Though the symbol is symmetric, ⋎ is not commutative. Neither is it associative. Let us consider an example application. The above definition of the naturals is based on the unary number system. Using interleaving, we can alternatively base the sequence on the binary number system.

$$bin = 0 ≺ 2 * bin + 1 ⋎ 2 * bin + 2$$

Since ⋎ has lower precedence than the arithmetic operators, the right-hand side of the equation above is grouped $0 ≺ ((2 * bin + 1) ⋎ (2 * bin + 2))$.

Now that we have two, quite different definitions of the natural numbers, the question naturally arises as to whether they are actually equal. Reassuringly, the answer is yes. Proving the equality of streams or of stream operators is one of our main activities in these lecture notes. However, we postpone a proof of $nat = bin$, until we have the prerequisites at hand.

Many numeric sequences are actually interleavings in disguise: for instance, $(-1)^{nat} = 1 ⋎ -1$, $nat\ \textbf{div}\ 2 = nat ⋎ nat$, and $nat\ \textbf{mod}\ 2 = 0 ⋎ 1$.

The interleaving operator interacts nicely with lifting.

$$pure\ a ⋎ pure\ a \quad = pure\ a$$
$$(s_1 ◇ s_2) ⋎ (t_1 ◇ t_2) = (s_1 ⋎ t_1) ◇ (s_2 ⋎ t_2)$$

A simple consequence is $(s ⋎ t) + 1 = s + 1 ⋎ t + 1$ or, more generally, $map\ f\ (s ⋎ t) = map\ f\ s ⋎ map\ g\ t$. The two laws show, in fact, that interleaving is a homomorphism (from *Pair · Stream* to *Stream*). Interleaving is even an isomorphism; the reader is encouraged to work out the details.

Property (3) is also called *abide law* because of the following two-dimensional way of writing the law, in which the two operators are written either *above* or bes*ide* each other.

s_1 ◇ s_2	s_1	s_2		s_1 | s_2	s_1	s_2
⋎	=	⋎ ◇ ⋎		———	=	—|—
t_1 ◇ t_2	t_1	t_2		t_1 | t_2	t_1 | t_2

The two-dimensional arrangement is originally due to Hoare, the catchy name is due to Bird [4]. The geometrical interpretation can be further emphasised by writing the two operators | and −, like on the right-hand side [11].

Exercise 4. Try to capture the sequences listed in the introduction to Section 3 using stream equations. For the latter two puzzles experiment a little with the Fibonacci sequences *fib* and *fib'*. *Hint:* Sloane's On-Line Encyclopedia of Integer Sequences lists most integer sequences one can think of.   □

Exercise 5. Turn the following verbal descriptions into streams.

1. The sequence of natural numbers divisible by 3.
2. The sequence of natural numbers *not* divisible by 3.
3. The sequence of cubes.
4. The sequence of all finite binary strings:

$$\langle [\,], [0], [1], [0,0], [1,0], [0,1], [1,1], [0,0,0], [1,0,0], [0,1,0], ..\rangle \ .$$

5. The bit-reversed positive numbers:

$$\langle 1, 2, 3, 4, 6, 5, 7, 8, 12, 10, 14, 9, 13, 11, 15, ..\rangle \ .$$

The order of all bits, except the most significant one, in the binary expansion of n is reversed.   □

3.2   Definitions and Proofs

Not every legal Haskell definition of type *Stream* τ actually defines a stream. Two simple counterexamples are $s_1 = tail\ s_1$ and $s_2 = head\ s_2 \prec tail\ s_2$. Both of them loop in Haskell; when viewed as stream equations they are ambiguous.[4] In fact, they admit infinitely many solutions: every constant stream is a solution of the first equation, every stream is a solution of the second one. This situation is undesirable from both a practical and a theoretical standpoint. Fortunately, it is not hard to restrict the *syntactic* form of equations so that they possess *unique solutions*. We insist that equations adhere to the following form:

$$x = h \prec t \ ,$$

where x is an identifier of type *Stream* τ, h is a constant expression of type τ, and t is an expression of type *Stream* τ possibly referring to x or some other stream identifier in the case of mutual recursion. However, neither h nor t may contain *head* or *tail*.

If x is a parametrised stream or a stream operator,

$$x\ x_1\ \ldots\ x_n = h \prec t$$

---

[4] There is a slight mismatch between the theoretical framework of streams and the Haskell implementation of streams. Since products are lifted in Haskell, *Stream* τ additionally contains partial streams such as $\bot$, $a_0 \prec \bot$, $a_0 \prec a_1 \prec \bot$ and so forth. We simply ignore this extra complication here.

then h and t may use *head* x_i or *tail* x_i provided x_i is of the right type. Apart from that, no other uses of *head* or *tail* are permitted. Equations of this form are called *admissible*.

For a formal account of these requirements, we refer the interested reader to the paper "Streams and Unique Fixed Points" [18], which contains a constructive proof that admissible equations indeed have unique solutions. Looking back, we find that the definitions we have encountered so far, including those of *pure*, $\diamond$ and $\curlyvee$, are admissible.

If $x = \varphi\, x$ is an admissible equation, we denote its unique solution by *fix* φ. (The equation implicitly defines a function in x. A solution of the equation is a fixed point of this function and vice versa.) The fact that the solution is unique is captured by the following property.

$$\textit{fix } \varphi = s \Longleftrightarrow \varphi\, s = s$$

Read from left to right it states that *fix* φ is indeed a solution of $x = \varphi\, x$. Read from right to left it asserts that any solution is equal to *fix* φ. Now, if we want to prove $s = t$ where $s = \textit{fix } \varphi$, then it suffices to show that $\varphi\, t = t$.

As a first example, let us prove the *idiom homomorphism law*.

$$\begin{aligned}
&\textit{pure } f \diamond \textit{pure } a \\
=\ &\{\text{ definition of } \diamond \} \\
&(\textit{head } (\textit{pure } f))\ (\textit{head } (\textit{pure } a)) \prec \textit{tail } (\textit{pure } f) \diamond \textit{tail } (\textit{pure } a) \\
=\ &\{\text{ definition of } \textit{pure } \} \\
&f\ a \prec \textit{pure } f \diamond \textit{pure } a
\end{aligned}$$

Consequently, *pure* $f \diamond$ *pure* a equals the unique solution of $x = f\ a \prec x$, which by definition is *pure* $(f\ a)$.

That was easy. The next proof is not much harder. We show that the natural numbers are even and odd numbers interleaved: $nat = 2 * nat \curlyvee 2 * nat + 1$.

$$\begin{aligned}
&2 * nat \curlyvee 2 * nat + 1 \\
=\ &\{\text{ definition of } nat \} \\
&2 * (0 \prec nat + 1) \curlyvee 2 * nat + 1 \\
=\ &\{\text{ arithmetic } \} \\
&(0 \prec 2 * nat + 2) \curlyvee 2 * nat + 1 \\
=\ &\{\text{ definition of } \curlyvee \} \\
&0 \prec 2 * nat + 1 \curlyvee 2 * nat + 2 \\
=\ &\{\text{ arithmetic } \} \\
&0 \prec (2 * nat \curlyvee 2 * nat + 1) + 1
\end{aligned}$$

Inspecting the second but last term, we note that the result furthermore implies $nat = 0 \prec 2 * nat + 1 \curlyvee 2 * nat + 2$, which in turn proves $nat = bin$.

Now, if both s and t are given as fixed points, $s = \textit{fix } \varphi$ and $t = \textit{fix } \psi$, then there are at least four possibilities to prove $s = t$:

$$\varphi\,(\psi\,s) = \psi\,s \quad \Longrightarrow \quad \psi\,s = s \quad \Longrightarrow \quad s = t$$
$$\psi\,(\varphi\,t) = \varphi\,t \quad \Longrightarrow \quad \varphi\,t = t \quad \Longrightarrow \quad s = t\;.$$

We may be lucky and establish one of the equations. Unfortunately, there is no success guarantee. The following approach is often more promising. We show $s = \chi\,s$ and $\chi\,t = t$. If χ has a unique fixed point, then $s = t$. The important point is that we discover the function χ on the fly during the calculation. Proofs in this style are laid out as follows.

$$s$$
$$= \quad \{\text{ why? }\}$$
$$\chi\,s$$
$$\sqsubset \quad \{\,x = \chi\,x \text{ has a unique solution }\}$$
$$\chi\,t$$
$$= \quad \{\text{ why? }\} \quad.$$
$$t$$

The symbol $\sqsubset$ is meant to suggest a link connecting the upper and the lower part. Overall, the proof establishes that $s = t$.

Let us illustrate the technique by proving *Cassini's identity*: $\textit{fib}'^2 - \textit{fib} * \textit{fib}'' = (-1)^{\textit{nat}}$.

$$\textit{fib}'^2 - \textit{fib} * \textit{fib}''$$
$$= \quad \{\text{ definition of } \textit{fib}'' \text{ and arithmetic }\}$$
$$\textit{fib}'^2 - (\textit{fib}^2 + \textit{fib} * \textit{fib}')$$
$$= \quad \{\text{ definition of } \textit{fib} \text{ and definition of } \textit{fib}' \}$$
$$1 \prec (\textit{fib}''^2 - (\textit{fib}'^2 + \textit{fib}' * \textit{fib}''))$$
$$= \quad \{\text{ arithmetic }\}$$
$$1 \prec (-1) * (\textit{fib}'^2 - (\textit{fib}'' - \textit{fib}') * \textit{fib}'')$$
$$= \quad \{\,\textit{fib}'' - \textit{fib}' = \textit{fib}\,\}$$
$$1 \prec (-1) * (\textit{fib}'^2 - \textit{fib} * \textit{fib}'')$$
$$\sqsubset \quad \{\,x = 1 \prec (-1) * x \text{ has a unique solution }\}$$
$$1 \prec (-1) * (-1)^{\textit{nat}}$$
$$= \quad \{\text{ definition of } \textit{nat} \text{ and arithmetic }\}$$
$$(-1)^{\textit{nat}}$$

When reading $\sqsubset$-proofs, it is easiest to start at both ends working towards the link. Each part follows a typical pattern, which we will see time and time again: starting with e we unfold the definitions obtaining $e_1 \prec e_2$; then we try to express e_2 in terms of e.

So far, we have been concerned with proofs about streams. However, the proof techniques apply equally well to parametric streams or stream operators! As an example, let us prove the abide law by showing $f = g$ where

$$f\ s_1\ s_2\ t_1\ t_2 = (s_1 \diamond s_2) \curlyvee (t_1 \diamond t_2) \quad \text{and} \quad g\ s_1\ s_2\ t_1\ t_2 = (s_1 \curlyvee t_1) \diamond (s_2 \curlyvee t_2) \, .$$

The proof is straightforward involving only bureaucratic steps.

$\quad f\ a\ b\ c\ d$
$= \quad \{ \text{definition of } f \}$
$\quad (a \diamond b) \curlyvee (c \diamond d)$
$= \quad \{ \text{definition of } \diamond \text{ and definition of } \curlyvee \}$
$\quad head\ a \diamond head\ b \prec (c \diamond d) \curlyvee (tail\ a \diamond tail\ b)$
$= \quad \{ \text{definition of } f \}$
$\quad head\ a \diamond head\ b \prec f\ c\ d\ (tail\ a)\ (tail\ b)$
$\sqsubset \quad \{ x\ s_1\ s_2\ t_1\ t_2 = head\ s_1 \diamond head\ s_2 \prec x\ t_1\ t_2\ (tail\ s_1)\ (tail\ s_2) \}$
$\quad head\ a \diamond head\ b \prec g\ c\ d\ (tail\ a)\ (tail\ b)$
$= \quad \{ \text{definition of } g \}$
$\quad head\ a \diamond head\ b \prec (c \curlyvee tail\ a) \diamond (d \curlyvee tail\ b)$
$= \quad \{ \text{definition of } \diamond \text{ and definition of } \curlyvee \}$
$\quad (a \curlyvee c) \diamond (b \curlyvee d)$
$= \quad \{ \text{definition of } g \}$
$\quad g\ a\ b\ c\ d$

Henceforth, we leave the two functions implicit sparing ourselves two rolling and two unrolling steps. On the downside, this makes the common pattern around the link more difficult to spot.

Exercise 6. The parametric stream *from* is given by

$$from \quad :: Nat \to Stream\ Nat$$
$$from\ n = n \prec from\ (n + 1) \, .$$

Show that $from\ n + pure\ k = from\ (n + k)$ in at least two different ways.   □

Exercise 7. Prove the other idiom laws using the unique fixed-point principle.   □

3.3   Recursion and Iteration

The stream *nat* is constructed by repeatedly mapping a function over a stream. We can capture this recursion scheme using a combinator, which implements *recursive* or *top-down* constructions.

$$recurse :: \forall \alpha \, . \, (\alpha \to \alpha) \to (\alpha \to Stream\ \alpha)$$
$$recurse\ f\ a = s$$
$$\textbf{where}\ s = a \prec map\ f\ s$$

So, $nat = recurse\ (+1)\ 0$.

Alternatively, we can build a stream by repeatedly applying a given function to a given initial seed. The combinator *iterate* captures this *iterative* or *bottom-up* construction.

$$iterate :: \forall \alpha . (\alpha \rightarrow \alpha) \rightarrow (\alpha \rightarrow Stream\ \alpha)$$
$$iterate\ f\ a \quad = loop\ a$$
$$\textbf{where}\ loop\ x = x \prec loop\ (f\ x)$$

So, *iterate* $(+1)$ 0 is yet another definition of the naturals. The type α can be seen as a type of states and the resulting stream as an enumeration of the state space. One could argue that *iterate* is more natural than *recurse*. This intuition is backed up by the fact that *map* $g \cdot$ *iterate* f is the *unfold* or *anamorphism* of the *Stream* codatatype. Very briefly, the unfold is characterised by the following *universal property*.

$$h = unfold\ g\ f \quad \Longleftrightarrow \quad head \cdot h = g \quad \text{and} \quad tail \cdot h = h \cdot f$$

Read from left to right it states that *unfold* $g\ f$ is a solution of the equations *head* $\cdot h = g$ and *tail* $\cdot h = h \cdot f$. Read from right to left the property asserts that *unfold* $g\ f$ is the unique solution.

The functions *iterate* and *recurse* satisfy an important fusion law, which amounts to the free theorem of $\forall \alpha . (\alpha \rightarrow \alpha) \rightarrow (\alpha \rightarrow Stream\ \alpha)$.

$$map\ h \cdot recurse\ f_1 = recurse\ f_2 \cdot h$$
$$\Uparrow$$
$$h \cdot f_1 = f_2 \cdot h$$
$$\Downarrow$$
$$map\ h \cdot iterate\ f_1 = iterate\ f_2 \cdot h$$

Here is a unique fixed-point proof of the first fusion law.

$$map\ h\ (iterate\ f_1\ a)$$
$$= \quad \{ \text{ definition of } iterate \text{ and } map \}$$
$$h\ a \prec map\ h\ (iterate\ f_1\ (f_1\ a))$$
$$\sqsubset \quad \{ x\ a = h\ a \prec x\ (f_1\ a) \text{ has a unique solution} \}$$
$$h\ a \prec iterate\ f_2\ (h\ (f_1\ a))$$
$$= \quad \{ \text{ assumption: } h \cdot f_1 = f_2 \cdot h \}$$
$$h\ a \prec iterate\ f_2\ (f_2\ (h\ a))$$
$$= \quad \{ \text{ definition of } iterate \}$$
$$iterate\ f_2\ (h\ a)$$

The linking equation $g\ a = h\ a \prec g\ (f_1\ a)$ corresponds to the unfold for *Stream*, which as we have noted can be defined in terms of *map* and *iterate*.

The fusion law implies *map* $f \cdot$ *iterate* f = *iterate* $f \cdot f$, which is the key for proving *nat* = *iterate* $(+1)$ 0, or, more generally,

$$recurse\ f\ a = iterate\ f\ a \quad .$$

We show that *iterate f a* is the unique solution of $x = a \prec map\ f\ x$.

$$iterate\ f\ a$$
$$= \quad \{\ \text{definition of } iterate\ \}$$
$$a \prec iterate\ f\ (f\ a)$$
$$= \quad \{\ \text{iterate fusion law: } h = f_1 = f_2 = f\ \}$$
$$a \prec map\ f\ (iterate\ f\ a)$$

Exercise 8. When are *iterate f a* and *iterate g b* equal? As a simple example, consider *iterate* (["hi"]++) [] and *iterate* (++["hi"]) []. Can you find sufficient and necessary conditions? □

3.4   Summary and Related Work

The type of streams is a simple example of a coinductive datatype. The type has the structure of an idiom, which allows us to lift arbitrary functions to streams. Streams can be conveniently defined using recursion equations. Admissible equations have unique solutions, which is the basis of the unique fixed-point principle. For streams, recursive and iterative constructions coincide.

This section is based on the paper "Streams and Unique Fixed Points" [18], which in turns draws from Rutten's work on stream calculus [32,33]. Rutten introduces streams and stream operators using coinductive definitions, which he calls *behavioural differential equations*. As an example, the Haskell definition of lifted addition

$$s + t = head\ s + head\ t \prec tail\ s + tail\ t$$

translates to

$$(s + t)(0) = s(0) + t(0) \quad \text{and} \quad (s + t)' = s' + t'\ ,$$

where $s(0)$ denotes the head of s, its initial value, and s' the tail of s, its stream derivative. (The notation goes back to Hoare.) However, Rutten relies on coinduction as the main proof technique.

Various proof methods for corecursive programs are discussed by Gibbons and Hutton [13]. Interestingly, the technique of unique fixed points is not among them. Unique fixed-point proofs are closely related to the principle of *guarded induction* [6], which goes back to the work on process algebra [30]. Loosely speaking, the guarded condition ensures that functions are productive by restricting the context of a recursive call to one ore more constructors. For instance,

$$nat = 1 \prec nat + 1$$

is not guarded as $+$ is not a constructor. However, *nat* can be defined by *iterate* $(+1)$ 0 as *iterate* is guarded. The proof method then allows us to show that *iterate* $(+1)$ 0 is the unique solution of $x = x \prec x + 1$ by constructing a suitable proof transformer using guarded equations. Indeed, the central idea underlying guarded induction is to express proofs as lazy functional programs.

4 Application: Recurrences

A *recurrence* or recurrence relation is a set of equations that defines a sequence, a function from the natural numbers. It typically provides a boundary value and an equation for the general value in terms of earlier ones, see Figure 1 for an example. Using $\prec$ and $\curlyvee$ we can often capture a function from the natural numbers by a single equation. Though functions from the naturals and streams are in a one-to-one correspondence, a stream is usually easier to manipulate. Before we consider concrete examples, we first explore tabulation in more depth.

4.1 Tabulation

In Section 2 we have noted in passing by that *Pairs* are in a one-to-one correspondence to functions from the Booleans. Streams enjoy an analogous property, they are in a one-to-one correspondence to functions from the natural numbers:

$$Stream\ \alpha \cong Nat \to \alpha\ ,$$

where the inductive datatype *Nat* is given by the Pseudo-Haskell definition

data $Nat = 0 \mid Nat + 1$.

(Strictly speaking, this defines the unary numbers or Peano numerals, which *represent* the natural numbers.) A stream can be seen as the tabulation of a function from the natural numbers. Conversely, a function of type $Nat \to \alpha$ can be implemented by looking up a memo-table. Here are the functions that witness the isomorphism.

$$
\begin{aligned}
&tabulate \quad :: \forall \alpha\ .\ (Nat \to \alpha) \to Stream\ \alpha \\
&tabulate\ f = f\ 0 \prec tabulate\ (f \cdot (+1)) \\[4pt]
&lookup \qquad\quad :: \forall \alpha\ .\ Stream\ \alpha \to (Nat \to \alpha) \\
&lookup\ s\ 0 \qquad = head\ s \\
&lookup\ s\ (n+1) = lookup\ (tail\ s)\ n
\end{aligned}
$$

The functions *lookup* and *tabulate* are mutually inverse

$$
\begin{aligned}
lookup \cdot tabulate &= id \\
tabulate \cdot lookup &= id\ ,
\end{aligned}
$$

and they satisfy the following naturality properties.

$$
\begin{aligned}
map\ f \cdot tabulate &= tabulate \cdot (f\ \cdot) \\
(f\ \cdot) \cdot lookup &= lookup \cdot map\ f
\end{aligned}
$$

Note that post-composition $(f\ \cdot)$ is the mapping function for the environment idiom $\tau \to$. The laws are somewhat easier to memorise, if we write them in a point-wise style.

$$
\begin{aligned}
map\ f\ (tabulate\ g) &= tabulate\ (f \cdot g) \\
f \cdot lookup\ t &= lookup\ (map\ f\ t)
\end{aligned}
$$

A simple consequence of the first law is $tabulate\ f = map\ f\ (tabulate\ id)$. Hence, $tabulate$ is fully determined by the image of the identity, which is the stream of natural numbers (see below). So, one way of tabulating an arbitrary function is to map the function over the stream of natural numbers.

The simplest recurrences are of the form $a_0 = k$ and $a_{n+1} = f(a_n)$, for some natural number k and some function f on the naturals. As an example, the recurrence below defines $\mathcal{T}_n$, the minimum number of moves to solve the Tower of Hanoï problem for n discs.

$$\mathcal{T}_0 = 0$$
$$\mathcal{T}_{n+1} = 2 * \mathcal{T}_n + 1$$

It is not hard to see that the stream defined

$$tower = 0 \prec 2 * tower + 1$$

implements the same sequence. In general, the recurrence $a_0 = k$ and $a_{n+1} = f(a_n)$ is captured by the stream equation $s = k \prec map\ f\ s$, or more succinctly by $recurse\ f\ k$. Though fairly obvious, the relation is worth exploring.

On the face of it, the linear recurrence corresponds to the $fold$ or $catamorphism$ of the inductive type Nat.

$$fold \qquad\qquad :: \forall \alpha\ .\ (\alpha \to \alpha) \to \alpha \to (Nat \to \alpha)$$
$$fold\ s\ z\ 0 \qquad = z$$
$$fold\ s\ z\ (n+1) = s\ (fold\ s\ z\ n)$$

Catamorphisms are dual to anamorphisms, enjoying a dual characterisation.

$$h = fold\ s\ z \quad \Longleftrightarrow \quad h\ 0 = z \quad \text{and} \quad h \cdot (+1) = s \cdot h$$

Some consequences of the universal property are the $reflection\ law$, $fold\ (+1)\ 0 = id$, and the $computation\ laws$, $fold\ s\ z\ 0 = z$ and $fold\ s\ z \cdot (+1) = s \cdot fold\ s\ z$.

Now, tabulating $fold\ s\ z$ gives $recurse\ s\ z$ (hence the name of the combinator). The proof of this fact makes crucial use of $tabulate$'s naturality property.

$$tabulate\ (fold\ s\ z)$$
$$= \quad \{\ \text{definition of } tabulate\ \}$$
$$fold\ s\ z\ 0 \prec tabulate\ (fold\ s\ z \cdot (+1))$$
$$= \quad \{\ \text{computation laws}\ \}$$
$$z \prec tabulate\ (s \cdot fold\ s\ z)$$
$$= \quad \{\ \text{naturality of } tabulate\ \}$$
$$z \prec map\ s\ (tabulate\ (fold\ s\ z))$$

Consequently, there are, at least, three equivalent ways of expressing the linear recurrence $a_0 = k$ and $a_{n+1} = f(a_n)$.

$$tabulate\ (fold\ f\ k) = recurse\ f\ k = iterate\ f\ k$$

Using the reflection law, this furthermore implies that *nat* is the tabulation of the identity function:

$$tabulate\ id$$
$$=\quad \{\text{ reflection law: } fold\ (+1)\ 0 = id\ \}$$
$$tabulate\ (fold\ (+1)\ 0)$$
$$=\quad \{\text{ see above }\}$$
$$recurse\ (+1)\ 0\ .$$

Exercise 9. The naîve implementation of the Fibonacci numbers is horribly inefficient.

$$\mathcal{F}_0 \quad = 0$$
$$\mathcal{F}_1 \quad = 1$$
$$\mathcal{F}_{n+2} = \mathcal{F}_n + \mathcal{F}_{n+1}$$

But, can you make this more precise? For instance, how many additions are performed in order to compute $\mathcal{F}_n$, or, how many recursive calls are made? Express your findings as stream equations. Then try to relate the two streams to examples we have encountered so far.   □

Exercise 10. Determine the number of binary strings of some given length that do not contain adjacent zeros. Again, first try to come up with a system of recursion equations and then try to relate the streams to known examples.   □

We already know that *fib* tabulates the Fibonacci function $\mathcal{F}$. To sharpen our calculational skills let us try to derive the stream definition from the recurrence given in Exercise 9. The recurrence does not fit the simple scheme discussed above, so we have to start afresh. The calculations are effortless if we make use of the fact that *tabulate* is an idiom homomorphism between the environment idiom $Nat \rightarrow$ and *Stream*.

$$tabulate\ (pure\ a) = pure\ a$$
$$tabulate\ (x \diamond y)\ = tabulate\ x \diamond tabulate\ y$$

Since tabulation and look-up are inverses, this implies that *lookup* is an idiom homomorphism, as well.

$$lookup\ (pure\ a) = pure\ a$$
$$lookup\ (x \diamond y)\ = lookup\ x \diamond lookup\ y$$

Returning to the problem of tabulating $\mathcal{F}$, it is useful to rewrite the last equation of $\mathcal{F}$ in a point-free style: $\mathcal{F} \cdot (+2) = \mathcal{F} + \mathcal{F} \cdot (+1)$. The right-hand side makes use of addition lifted to the environment idiom.

$$tabulate\ \mathcal{F}$$
$$=\quad \{\text{ definition of } tabulate\ \}$$
$$\mathcal{F}_0 \prec tabulate\ (\mathcal{F} \cdot (+1))$$

$=$ { definition of *tabulate* and arithmetic }

$\quad \mathcal{F}_0 \prec \mathcal{F}_1 \prec tabulate \ (\mathcal{F} \cdot (+2))$

$=$ { definition of $\mathcal{F}$ }

$\quad 0 \prec 1 \prec tabulate \ (\mathcal{F} + \mathcal{F} \cdot (+1))$

$=$ { *tabulate* is an idiom homomorphism }

$\quad 0 \prec 1 \prec tabulate \ \mathcal{F} + tabulate \ (\mathcal{F} \cdot (+1))$

$=$ { definition of *tabulate* }

$\quad 0 \prec 1 \prec tabulate \ \mathcal{F} + tail \ (tabulate \ \mathcal{F})$

The only non-trivial step is the second but last one, which uses $tabulate \ (f + g) = tabulate \ f + tabulate \ g$, which in turn is syntactic sugar for $tabulate \ (pure \ (+) \diamond f \diamond g) = pure \ (+) \diamond tabulate \ f \diamond tabulate \ g$. Since *tabulate* preserves the idiomatic structure, the derivation goes through nicely. The resulting equation

$$fib = 0 \prec 1 \prec fib + tail \ fib$$

is equivalent to the definitions given in Section 3.

Tabulation and look-up allow us to switch swiftly between functions from the naturals and streams. So, even if coinductive structures are not available in your language of choice, you can still use stream calculus for program transformations. The next exercise aims to illustrate this point by deriving an efficient *iterative* implementation of $\mathcal{F}$.

Exercise 11. Turn the Fibonacci sequence

$$fib = 0 \prec fib + (1 \prec fib)$$

into an iterative form: $map \ g \ (iterate \ f \ a) = unfold \ g \ f$. There are, at least, two approaches:

– Pair *fib* and *fib'*

$\quad fib \star fib'$,

where $(\star) = zip \ (,)$ turns a pair of streams into a stream of pairs, see Section 2.
– Use the fact that the tails of *fib* are linear combinations of *fib* and *fib'*.

$\quad i * fib + j * fib'$

Hint: Express the tail of $i * fib + j * fib'$ as a linear combination of *fib* and *fib'* and then capture the corecursion using *unfold*.

Try to relate the two approaches.   □

Exercise 12. Turn the equation

$$x = (a \prec map \ f \ x) + s$$

into an iterative form. *Hint:* You may find the function $tails = iterate \ tail$ useful. Try pairing x with $tails \ s$. As an aside, *tails* is the comultiplication of the comonad *Stream*.   □

Exercise 13. Complete the proof that $tabulate \ f = map \ f \ nat$.   □

4.2   Bit-Fiddling

Now, let us tackle a slightly more involved class of recurrences. The sequence given by the 'binary' recurrence $a_0 = k$, $a_{2n+1} = f(a_n)$ and $a_{2n+2} = g(a_n)$ corresponds to the stream $s = k \prec map\ f\ s \curlyvee map\ g\ s$. We have already seen an instance of this scheme in Section 3.

$$bin = 0 \prec 2 * bin + 1 \curlyvee 2 * bin + 2$$

Here, the parameters of the general scheme are instantiated by $k = 0$, $f\ n = 2 * n + 1$ and $g\ n = 2 * n + 2$. In other words, a is the identity and bin is its tabulation: $bin = tabulate\ id = nat$. For the positive numbers, we can derive a similar equation.

$$bin + 1$$
$$=\quad \{\ \text{definition of } bin\ \}$$
$$(0 \prec 2 * bin + 1 \curlyvee 2 * bin + 2) + 1$$
$$=\quad \{\ \text{abide law and arithmetic}\ \}$$
$$1 \prec 2 * (bin + 1) \curlyvee 2 * (bin + 1) + 1$$

We have calculated the definition below.

$$bin' = 1 \prec 2 * bin' \curlyvee 2 * bin' + 1$$

Since the equation has a unique solution, we know that $bin' = bin + 1 = nat + 1 = nat'$. The definition of bin' captures a well-known recipe for generating the positive numbers in binary: start with 1, then repeatedly shift the bits to the right (lsb first), placing a 0 or a 1 in the left-most, least significant position.

Using a similar approach we can characterise the most significant bit of a positive number ($0 \prec msb$ is $A053644$).

$$msb = 1 \prec 2 * msb \curlyvee 2 * msb$$

The most significant bit of 1 is 1, the most significant bit of both $2 * bin'$ and $2 * bin' + 1$ is $2 * msb$.

Another example along these lines is the 1s-counting sequence ($A000120$), also known as the *binary weight*. The binary representation of the even number $2*nat$ has the same number of 1s as nat; the odd number $2 * nat + 1$ has one 1 more. Hence, the sequence satisfies $ones = ones \curlyvee ones + 1$. Adding two initial values, we can turn the property into a definition.

$$ones\ = 0 \prec ones'$$
$$ones' = 1 \prec ones' \curlyvee ones' + 1$$

It is important to note that $x = x \curlyvee x + 1$ does not have a unique solution. However, all solutions are of the form $ones + c$.

Exercise 14. Prove this claim. *Hint:* Let s be a solution of $x = x \curlyvee x + 1$. Show that $s - pure\ (head\ s)$ satisfies the definition of $ones$.   □

Let us inspect the sequences.

$\gg$ msb
$\langle 1, 2, 2, 4, 4, 4, 4, 8, 8, 8, 8, 8, 8, 8, 8, \ldots \rangle$
$\gg$ $bin' - msb$
$\langle 0, 0, 1, 0, 1, 2, 3, 0, 1, 2, 3, 4, 5, 6, 7, \ldots \rangle$
$\gg$ $ones$
$\langle 0, 1, 1, 2, 1, 2, 2, 3, 1, 2, 2, 3, 2, 3, 3, \ldots \rangle$

The sequence $bin' - msb$ ($A053645$) exhibits a nice pattern; it describes the distance to the largest power of two at most bin'. In binary, this amounts to removing the most significant bit.

Here is a sequence that every computer scientist should know: the *binary carry sequence* or *ruler function* ($A007814$).

$$carry = 0 \curlyvee carry + 1$$

(The form of the equation does not quite meet the requirements. We allow ourselves some liberty, as a simple unfolding turns it into an admissible form: $carry = 0 \prec carry + 1 \curlyvee 0$. The unfolding works as long as the first argument of $\curlyvee$ is a sequence defined elsewhere.) Let us peek at some values.

$\gg$ $carry$
$\langle 0, 1, 0, 2, 0, 1, 0, 3, 0, 1, 0, 2, 0, 1, 0, \ldots \rangle$

The sequence gives the exponent of the largest power of two dividing bin', that is, the number of leading zeros in the binary representation (lsb first). In other words, it specifies the running time of the binary increment. The table below illustrates the relationship.

```
1
0 1
‾1 1
0 0 1
‾1 0 1
0 1 1
‾1 1 1
0 0 0 1
‾1 0 0 1
0 1 0 1
‾1 1 0 1
0 0 1 1
‾1 0 1 1
0 1 1 1
‾1 1 1 1
0 0 0 0 1
```

For emphasis, prefixes of zeros are underlined. There is also an intriguing connection to infinite binary trees. If we turn the table by 90° to the left, we can see the correspondence more clearly.

```
                                            1
              1  1  1  1  1  0   0  0  0  0  0   1
        1  1  0  0  1  1  0  1  1  1  0  0  1  1  1  1
     1  0  1  0  1  0  1  0  1  0  1  0  1  0  1  0  0  1
                                               0  0  0  1
```

The lines correspond to the marks on a (binary) ruler; this is why *carry* is also called the ruler function. If we connect each 0-prefix of length n with the nearest 0-prefix of length $n+1$, we obtain the so-called *sideways tree*, an infinite tree, which has no root, but extends infinitely upwards.

Exercise 15. Prove that the sequence given by $a_0 = k$, $a_{2n+1} = f(a_n)$ and $a_{2n+2} = g(a_n)$ corresponds to the stream $s = k \prec map\ f\ s \curlyvee map\ g\ s$. *Hint:* Use $nat = bin$ and Exercise 13.   □

4.3   Summary and Related Work

A stream tabulates a function from the naturals. Tabulation and look-up are idiom isomorphisms between the environment idiom $Nat \rightarrow$ and $Stream$. Using $\prec$ and $\curlyvee$ we can capture 'unary' and 'binary' recurrences.

The section is also based on "Streams and Unique Fixed Points" [18].

5   Application: Finite Calculus

Let us move on to another application of streams: *finite calculus*. Finite calculus is the discrete counterpart of infinite calculus, where finite difference replaces the derivative and summation replaces integration. We shall see that difference and summation can be easily recast as stream operators. The resulting calculus is elegant and fun to use.

5.1   Finite Difference

A common type of puzzle asks the reader to continue a given sequence of numbers. A first routine step towards solving the puzzle is to calculate the difference of subsequent elements. This stream operator, *finite difference* or *forward difference*, enjoys a simple, non-recursive definition.

$$\Delta \quad :: (Num\ \alpha) \Rightarrow Stream\ \alpha \rightarrow Stream\ \alpha$$
$$\Delta\ s = tail\ s - s$$

Here are some examples ($A000079$, $A094267$, $A003215$, $A033428$).

> $\Delta\ 2^{nat}$
$\langle 1, 2, 4, 8, 16, 32, 64, 128, 256, 512, 1024, 2048, 4096, 8192, ..\rangle$
> $\Delta\ carry$
$\langle 1, -1, 2, -2, 1, -1, 3, -3, 1, -1, 2, -2, 1, -1, 4, ..\rangle$
> $\Delta\ nat^3$
$\langle 1, 7, 19, 37, 61, 91, 127, 169, 217, 271, 331, 397, 469, 547, ..\rangle$
> $3 * nat^2$
$\langle 0, 3, 12, 27, 48, 75, 108, 147, 192, 243, 300, 363, 432, 507, 588, ..\rangle$

Infinite calculus has an attractive rule for the derivative of a power: $(x^{n+1})\frac{d}{dx} = (n+1)x^n$. Unfortunately, the last two examples show that finite difference does not interact well with ordinary powers: $\Delta\ nat^3$ is by no means $3 * nat^2$. An alternative power that blends nicely with Δ is the *falling factorial power* defined

$$x^{\underline{0}} = 1$$
$$x^{\underline{n+1}} = x * (x-1)^{\underline{n}}\ .$$

As usual, we lift the operator to streams: $s^{\underline{n}} = map\ (\lambda x \to x^{\underline{n}})\ s$. The new power satisfies $s * (s-1)^{\underline{n}} = s^{\underline{n+1}} = s^{\underline{n}} * (s-n)$. Hence, finite calculus has a handy rule to match the one for the derivative of a power.

$$\Delta\ (nat^{\underline{n+1}}) = (pure\ n + 1) * nat^{\underline{n}}$$

The proof is entirely straightforward.

$$\Delta\ (nat^{\underline{n+1}})$$
$=$ { definition of Δ }
$$tail\ (nat^{\underline{n+1}}) - nat^{\underline{n+1}}$$
$=$ { definition of nat }
$$(nat + 1)^{\underline{n+1}} - nat^{\underline{n+1}}$$
$=$ { $s * (s-1)^{\underline{n}} = s^{\underline{n+1}} = s^{\underline{n}} * (s-n)$ }
$$(nat + 1) * nat^{\underline{n}} - nat^{\underline{n}} * (nat - pure\ n)$$
$=$ { arithmetic }
$$(pure\ n + 1) * nat^{\underline{n}}$$

The following session shows that falling factorial powers behave as expected.

> $nat^{\underline{3}}$
$\langle 0, 0, 0, 6, 24, 60, 120, 210, 336, 504, 720, 990, 1320, 1716, 2184, ..\rangle$
> $\Delta\ (nat^{\underline{3}})$
$\langle 0, 0, 6, 18, 36, 60, 90, 126, 168, 216, 270, 330, 396, 468, 546, ..\rangle$
> $3 * nat^{\underline{2}}$
$\langle 0, 0, 6, 18, 36, 60, 90, 126, 168, 216, 270, 330, 396, 468, 546, ..\rangle$

Table 1. Converting between powers and falling factorial powers

$$x^0 = x^{\underline{0}}$$
$$x^1 = x^{\underline{1}}$$
$$x^2 = x^{\underline{2}} + x^{\underline{1}}$$
$$x^3 = x^{\underline{3}} + 3 * x^{\underline{2}} + x^{\underline{1}}$$
$$x^4 = x^{\underline{4}} + 6 * x^{\underline{3}} + 7 * x^{\underline{2}} + x^{\underline{1}}$$

$$x^{\underline{0}} = x^0$$
$$x^{\underline{1}} = x^1$$
$$x^{\underline{2}} = x^2 - x^1$$
$$x^{\underline{3}} = x^3 - 3 * x^2 + 2 * x^1$$
$$x^{\underline{4}} = x^4 - 6 * x^3 + 11 * x^2 - 6 * x^1$$

Table 2. Laws for finite difference (c and n are constant streams)

$$\Delta \, (tail \; s) \; = \; tail \, (\Delta \, s)$$
$$\Delta \, (a \prec s) \; = \; head \; s - a \prec \Delta \, s$$
$$\Delta \, (s \curlyvee t) \; = \; (t - s) \curlyvee (tail \; s - t)$$
$$\Delta \, n \qquad\;\; = \; 0$$
$$\Delta \, (n * s) \;\; = \; n * \Delta \, s$$

$$\Delta \, (s + t) \quad = \Delta \, s + \Delta \, t$$
$$\Delta \, (s * t) \quad\; = \; s * \Delta \, t + \Delta \, s * tail \; t$$
$$\Delta \, c^{nat} \qquad = \; (c - 1) * c^{nat}$$
$$\Delta \, (nat^{\underline{n+1}}) = (n + 1) * nat^{\underline{n}}$$

One can convert mechanically between powers and falling factorial powers using Stirling numbers [14]. The details are beyond the scope of these lecture notes. For reference, Table 1 displays the correspondence up to the fourth power.

Table 2 lists the rules for finite differences. First of all, Δ is a *linear operator*: it distributes over sums. The stream 2^{nat} is the discrete analogue of e^x as $\Delta \, 2^{nat} = 2^{nat}$. The product rule is similar to the product rule of infinite calculus except for an occurrence of *tail* on the right-hand side.

$$\Delta \, (s * t)$$
$$= \quad \{ \text{ definition of } \Delta \text{ and definition of } * \}$$
$$tail \; s * tail \; t - s * t$$
$$= \quad \{ \text{ arithmetic } \}$$
$$s * tail \; t - s * t + tail \; s * tail \; t - s * tail \; t$$
$$= \quad \{ \text{ distributivity } \}$$
$$s * (tail \; t - t) + (tail \; s - s) * tail \; t$$
$$= \quad \{ \text{ definition of } \Delta \}$$
$$s * \Delta \, t + \Delta \, s * tail \; t$$

Exercise 16. The product rule $\Delta \, (s * t) = s * \Delta \, t + \Delta \, s * tail \; t$ is somewhat asymmetric. Can you find a symmetric variant? Prove it correct.   □

5.2   Summation

Finite difference Δ has a right-inverse: the *anti-difference* or *summation* operator Σ. We can easily derive its definition.

$$\Delta \, (\Sigma \, s) = s$$

$$\Longleftrightarrow \quad \{ \text{ definition of } \Delta \,\}$$
$$tail\ (\Sigma\ s) - \Sigma\ s = s$$
$$\Longleftrightarrow \quad \{ \text{ arithmetic }\}$$
$$tail\ (\Sigma\ s) = s + \Sigma\ s$$

Setting $head\ (\Sigma\ s) = 0$, we obtain

$$\Sigma \quad :: (Num\ \alpha) \Rightarrow Stream\ \alpha \rightarrow Stream\ \alpha$$
$$\Sigma\ s = t \ \textbf{where}\ t = 0 \prec s + t \ .$$

We have additionally applied λ-dropping [8], turning the higher-order equation $\Sigma\ s = 0 \prec s + \Sigma\ s$ defining Σ into a first-order equation $t = 0 \prec s + t$ defining $t = \Sigma\ s$ with s fixed. The firstification of the definition enables sharing of computations as illustrated below.

$$
\begin{array}{cccccccccccccc}
t_0 & t_1 & t_2 & t_3 & t_4 & t_5 & t_6 & t_7 & t_8 & t_9 & t_{10} & \cdots & & t \\
\| & \| & \| & \| & \| & \| & \| & \| & \| & \| & \| & \cdots & & \| \\
0 & s_0 & s_1 & s_2 & s_3 & s_4 & s_5 & s_6 & s_7 & s_8 & s_9 & \cdots & & 0 \prec s \\
& + & + & + & + & + & + & + & + & + & + & \cdots & & + \\
& t_0 & t_1 & t_2 & t_3 & t_4 & t_5 & t_6 & t_7 & t_8 & t_9 & \cdots & & t
\end{array}
$$

Here are some applications of summation ($A004520$, $A000290$, $A011371$, $0 \prec A000330$ and $0 \prec A036799$).

$\gg \ \Sigma\ (0 \curlyvee 1)$
$\langle 0, 0, 1, 1, 2, 2, 3, 3, 4, 4, 5, 5, 6, 6, 7, ..\rangle$
$\gg \ \Sigma\ (2 * nat + 1)$
$\langle 0, 1, 4, 9, 16, 25, 36, 49, 64, 81, 100, 121, 144, 169, 196, ..\rangle$
$\gg \ \Sigma\ carry$
$\langle 0, 0, 1, 1, 3, 3, 4, 4, 7, 7, 8, 8, 10, 10, 11, ..\rangle$
$\gg \ \Sigma\ nat^2$
$\langle 0, 0, 1, 5, 14, 30, 55, 91, 140, 204, 285, 385, 506, 650, 819, ..\rangle$
$\gg \ \Sigma\ (nat * 2^{nat})$
$\langle 0, 0, 2, 10, 34, 98, 258, 642, 1538, 3586, 8194, 18434, 40962, 90114, ..\rangle$

The definition of Σ suggests an unusual approach for determining the sum of a sequence: if we observe that a stream satisfies $t = 0 \prec s + t$, then we may conclude that $\Sigma\ s = t$. The step makes use of the fact that $\Sigma\ s$ is the unique solution of its defining equation. For example, $\Sigma\ 1 = nat$ as $nat = 0 \prec nat + 1$, $\Sigma\ (2 * nat + 1) = nat^2$ as $nat^2 = 0 \prec nat^2 + 2 * nat + 1$, and $\Sigma\ (1 \prec fib) = fib$ as $fib = 0 \prec (1 \prec fib) + fib$. This is *summation by happenstance*.

Of course, if we already know the sum, we can use the definition to verify our conjecture. As an example, let us prove $\Sigma\ fib'^2 = fib * fib'$ — the elements of this sequence are known as the *golden rectangle numbers* ($A001654$).

$$fib * fib'$$
$$= \quad \{ \text{ definition of } fib \text{ and definition of } fib' \,\}$$

$$(0 \prec \mathit{fib}') * (1 \prec \mathit{fib} + \mathit{fib}')$$
$$= \quad \{ \text{ arithmetic } \}$$
$$0 \prec \mathit{fib}'^2 + \mathit{fib} * \mathit{fib}'$$

The unique fixed-point proof avoids the inelegant case analysis of a traditional inductive proof.

The *Fundamental Theorem of finite calculus* relates Δ and Σ.

$$t = \Delta \, s \iff \Sigma \, t = s - \mathit{pure} \, (\mathit{head} \, s)$$

The implication from right to left is easy to show using $\Delta \, (\Sigma \, t) = t$ and $\Delta \, c = 0$. For the reverse direction, we reason

$$\Sigma \, (\Delta \, s)$$
$$= \quad \{ \text{ definition of } \Sigma \}$$
$$0 \prec \Sigma \, (\Delta \, s) + \Delta \, s$$
$$\sqsubset \quad \{ \, x = 0 \prec x + \Delta \, s \text{ has a unique solution } \}$$
$$0 \prec s - \mathit{pure} \, (\mathit{head} \, s) + \Delta \, s$$
$$= \quad \{ \text{ definition of } \Delta \text{ and arithmetic } \}$$
$$(\mathit{head} \, s \prec \mathit{tail} \, s) - \mathit{pure} \, (\mathit{head} \, s)$$
$$= \quad \{ \text{ extensionality: } s = \mathit{head} \, s \prec \mathit{tail} \, s \, \}$$
$$s - \mathit{pure} \, (\mathit{head} \, s) \ .$$

For instance, $\Sigma \, 2^{nat} = 2^{nat} - 1$, since $2^{nat} = \Delta \, 2^{nat}$ and $\mathit{head} \, (2^{nat}) = 1$.

Using the Fundamental Theorem we can transform the rules in Table 2 into rules for summation, see Table 3. As an example, the rule for products, *summation by parts*, can be derived from the product rule of Δ. Let $c = \mathit{pure} \, (\mathit{head} \, (s * t))$, then

$$s * \Delta \, t + \Delta \, s * \mathit{tail} \, t = \Delta \, (s * t)$$
$$\iff \quad \{ \text{ Fundamental Theorem } \}$$
$$\Sigma \, (s * \Delta \, t + \Delta \, s * \mathit{tail} \, t) = s * t - c$$
$$\iff \quad \{ \Sigma \text{ is linear } \}$$
$$\Sigma \, (s * \Delta \, t) + \Sigma \, (\Delta \, s * \mathit{tail} \, t) = s * t - c$$
$$\iff \quad \{ \text{ arithmetic } \}$$
$$\Sigma \, (s * \Delta \, t) = s * t - \Sigma \, (\Delta \, s * \mathit{tail} \, t) - c \ .$$

Unlike the others, this law is not compositional: $\Sigma \, (s * t)$ is not given in terms of $\Sigma \, s$ and $\Sigma \, t$, a situation familiar from infinite calculus.

Here is an alternative proof of $\Sigma \, \mathit{fib} = \mathit{fib}' - 1$ that uses some of the laws in Table 3.

$$\mathit{fib} = 0 \prec \mathit{fib} + (1 \prec \mathit{fib})$$
$$\iff \quad \{ \text{ summation by happenstance } \}$$

Table 3. Laws for summation (c and n are constant streams)

$$\Sigma\,(tail\ s)\ = tail\,(\Sigma\ s) - pure\,(head\ s)$$
$$\Sigma\,(a \prec s)\ = 0 \prec pure\ a + \Sigma\ s$$
$$\Sigma\,(s \curlyvee t)\ = u \curlyvee (s + u)$$
$$\textbf{where}\ u = \Sigma\ s + \Sigma\ t$$
$$\Sigma\,(s * \Delta\ t) = s * t - \Sigma\,(\Delta\ s * tail\ t)$$
$$- pure\,(head\,(s * t))$$

$$\Sigma\ n\quad\ = n * nat$$
$$\Sigma\,(n * s) = n * \Sigma\ s$$
$$\Sigma\,(s + t) = \Sigma\ s + \Sigma\ t$$
$$\Sigma\ c^{nat}\quad = (c^{nat} - 1)\,/\,(c - 1)$$
$$\Sigma\,(nat^{\underline{n}}) = nat^{\underline{n+1}}\,/\,(n + 1)$$

$$\Sigma\,(1 \prec fib) = fib$$
$$\Longleftrightarrow\quad \{\ \text{summation law}\ \}$$
$$0 \prec 1 + \Sigma\ fib = fib$$
$$\Longrightarrow\quad \{\ s_1 = s_2 \Longrightarrow tail\ s_1 = tail\ s_2\ \}$$
$$1 + \Sigma\ fib = fib'$$
$$\Longleftrightarrow\quad \{\ \text{arithmetic}\ \}$$
$$\Sigma\ fib = fib' - 1$$

Using the rules we can mechanically calculate summations of polynomials. The main effort goes into converting between ordinary and falling factorial powers. Here is a formula for the sum of the first n squares, the *square pyramidal numbers* ($0 \prec A000330$).

$$\Sigma\ nat^2$$
$$=\quad \{\ \text{converting to falling factorial powers}\ \}$$
$$\Sigma\,(nat^{\underline{2}} + nat^{\underline{1}})$$
$$=\quad \{\ \text{summation laws}\ \}$$
$$\tfrac{1}{3} * nat^{\underline{3}} + \tfrac{1}{2} * nat^{\underline{2}}$$
$$=\quad \{\ \text{converting to ordinary powers}\ \}$$
$$\tfrac{1}{3} * (nat^3 - 3 * nat^2 + 2 * nat) + \tfrac{1}{2} * (nat^2 - nat)$$
$$=\quad \{\ \text{arithmetic}\ \}$$
$$\tfrac{1}{6} * (nat - 1) * nat * (2 * nat - 1)$$

Calculating the summation of a product, say, $\Sigma\,(nat * 2^{nat})$ is often more involved. Recall that the rule for products, *summation by parts*, is imperfect: to be able to apply it, we have to spot a difference among the factors. In the expression above, there is an obvious candidate: c^{nat}. Let us see how it goes.

$$\Sigma\,(nat * 2^{nat})$$
$$=\quad \{\ \Delta\,2^{nat} = 2^{nat}\ \}$$
$$\Sigma\,(nat * \Delta\,2^{nat})$$
$$=\quad \{\ \text{summation by parts}\ \}$$
$$nat * 2^{nat} - \Sigma\,(\Delta\ nat * tail\ 2^{nat})$$

$$= \quad \{ \Delta \; nat = 1, \text{ and definition of } nat \}$$
$$nat * 2^{nat} - 2 * \Sigma \, 2^{nat}$$
$$= \quad \{ \text{ summation law } \}$$
$$nat * 2^{nat} - 2 * (2^{nat} - 1)$$
$$= \quad \{ \text{ arithmetic } \}$$
$$(nat - 2) * 2^{nat} + 2$$

As a final example, let us tackle a sum that involves the interleaving operator: $\Sigma \; carry$ ($A011371$). The sum is important, as it determines the amortised running time of the binary increment. Let us experiment ($A011371$, $A000120$).

$$\gg \; \Sigma \; carry$$
$$\langle 0, 0, 1, 1, 3, 3, 4, 4, 7, 7, 8, 8, 10, 10, 11, .. \rangle$$
$$\gg \; nat - \Sigma \; carry$$
$$\langle 0, 1, 1, 2, 1, 2, 2, 3, 1, 2, 2, 3, 2, 3, 3, .. \rangle$$
$$\gg \; nat \geqslant \Sigma \; carry$$
$$True$$

We observe that the sum is always at most nat, which would imply that the amortised running time, $\Sigma \; carry \; / \; nat$, is constant. This is nice, but can we actually quantify the difference? Let us approach the problem from a different angle. The binary increment changes the number of 1s, so we might hope to relate $carry$ to $ones$. The increment flips the leading 1s to 0s and flips the first 0 to 1. Since $carry$ defines the number of leading 0s, we obtain the following alternative definition of $ones$.

$$ones = 0 \prec ones + 1 - carry$$

We omit the proof that both definitions are indeed equal. (If you want to try, use a $\sqsubset$-proof.) Now, we can invoke the *summation by happenstance* rule.

$$ones = 0 \prec ones + (1 - carry)$$
$$\Longleftrightarrow \quad \{ \text{ summation by happenstance } \}$$
$$\Sigma \, (1 - carry) = ones$$
$$\Longleftrightarrow \quad \{ \text{ arithmetic } \}$$
$$\Sigma \; carry = nat - ones$$

Voilà. We have found a closed form for $\Sigma \; carry$.

Exercise 17. Derive the sum rule $\Sigma \, (s + t) = \Sigma \, s + \Sigma \, t$ from the sum rule $\Delta \, (s + t) = \Delta \, s + \Delta \, t$ using the Fundamental Theorem. □

Exercise 18. Work out $\Sigma \; nat^3$ using the summation laws and the correspondence between powers and falling factorial powers. □

Exercise 19. Here is an alternative definition of Σ

$$\Sigma \; s = 0 \prec pure \; (head \; s) + \Sigma \; (tail \; s) \; ,$$

which uses a second-order fixed point. The code implements the naïve way of summing: the ith element is computed using i additions not reusing any previous results. Prove that the two definitions of Σ are equivalent.   □

Exercise 20. Generalise the derivation of $\Sigma\ (nat * 2^{nat})$ to $\Sigma\ (nat * c^{nat})$, where c is a constant stream.   □

5.3   Summary and Related Work

Finite calculus serves as an elegant application of corecursive definitions and the unique fixed-point principle. Index variables and subscripts are avoided by taking a holistic view treating sequences as a single entity.

Again, most of the material has been taken from "Streams and Unique Fixed Points" [18]. Two further corecursion schemes for stream-generating functions, scans and convolutions, are introduced in a recent paper [20]. The paper also presents a novel proof of Moessner's theorem. Scans generalise summation, convolution generalises the product of power series. Very briefly, a sequence of numbers, $a_0, a_1, a_2 \ldots$, can be used to represent a power series, $a_0 + a_1 z + a_2 z^2 + a_3 z^3 + \cdots$, in some formal variable z. In fact, many papers on streams emphasise the 'power series' view of streams, most notably, [24,28,29]. Interestingly, the papers use lazy lists to represent streams, resulting in additional code to cover the empty list.

6   Infinite Trees

Streams are a lovely example of a coinductive datatype, but there is, of course, the danger of overspecialisation. To counteract this danger, we look at a second example in this section: infinite binary trees (trees for short). Trees are in many respects similar to streams, but, as we shall see, there are also some important differences. In a nutshell, streams relate to trees in the same way as unary numbers (Peano numerals) relate to binary numbers (bit strings).

Figure 2 displays the first five levels of an infinite binary tree that contains all the naturals. It is a *fractal* object, in the sense that parts of it are similar to the whole. The tree can be transformed into its left subtree by first doubling and then incrementing the elements (which is why the subtree contains exactly the odd numbers). To obtain the right subtree, we have to interchange the order of the two steps: the elements are first incremented and then doubled (which explains why the subtree contains exactly the even numbers greater than 0). This description can be nicely captured by a *corecursive* definition:

$$nat = Node\ 0\ ((2 * nat) + 1)\ (2 * (nat + 1))\ .$$

(We re-use some of the identifiers introduced in the previous sections to denote infinite trees. In case of ambiguity, we employ qualified names.) As to be expected, the operations are lifted point-wise to trees. Like streams, trees are an idiom. But we are skipping ahead.

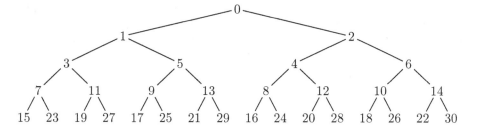

Fig. 2. The tree of natural numbers

The type *Tree* α is a *coinductive datatype*. Its definition is similar to the standard textbook definition of binary trees, except that there is no base constructor, so we cannot build a finite tree.

> **data** *Tree* α = *Node* { *root* :: α, *left* :: *Tree* α, *right* :: *Tree* α }

Trees are constructed using *Node*. They are destructed using *root*, which yields the label of the root node, and *left* and *right*, which return the left and the right subtree, respectively.

As mentioned above, trees are an idiom, which means that we can effortlessly lift functions to trees:

> **instance** *Idiom Tree* **where**
> *pure a = t* **where** *t = Node a t t*
> *t ◇ u = Node* ((*root t*) (*root u*)) (*left t ◇ left u*) (*right t ◇ right u*) .

Recall that *pure*, *map* and *zip* and the arithmetic operations are overloaded to work with an arbitrary idiom. By virtue of the above instance declaration we can use them for infinite trees, as well. Here is variation of *nat* that captures a well-known recipe for generating the positive numbers: start with 1, then repeatedly double the number, adding 0 or 1 to the result.

> *pos = Node* 1 (2 ∗ *pos* + 0) (2 ∗ *pos* + 1)

6.1 Definitions and Proofs

As for streams, we can restrict the *syntactic* form of equations so that they possess *unique solutions*. As *admissible* equation is of the form

> $x\ x_1\ \ldots\ x_n = Node\ a\ l\ r$,

where x is an identifier of type $\tau_1 \to \cdots \to \tau_n \to Tree\ \tau$, a is a constant expression of type τ, and l and r are expressions of type *Tree* τ possibly referring to x or some other tree operator in the case of mutual recursion. The expressions may use *root* x_i, *left* x_i or *right* x_i provided x_i is of the right type. Apart from that, no other uses of the projection functions are permitted.

Admissible equations have unique solutions. Hence we can adopt the unique fixed-point principle to prove that two infinite trees are equal: if they satisfy the same recursion equation, then they are. The proof of $nat + 1 = pos$ below illustrates the principle: we show that $nat + 1$ satisfies the recursion equation of pos.

$$nat + 1$$
$$= \quad \{ \text{ definition of } nat \}$$
$$(Node\ 0\ ((2 * nat) + 1)\ (2 * (nat + 1))) + 1$$
$$= \quad \{ \text{ arithmetic } \}$$
$$Node\ 1\ (2 * (nat + 1) + 0)\ (2 * (nat + 1) + 1)$$

Like for streams, the familiar arithmetic laws also hold for the lifted operators.

Exercise 21. There are essentially two ways of generating an infinite tree that contains all bit strings (lists of zeros and ones).

$$lbits = Node\ []\ (map\ ([0]\mathbin{+\!\!+})\ lbits)\ (map\ ([1]\mathbin{+\!\!+})\ lbits)$$
$$rbits = Node\ []\ (map\ (\mathbin{+\!\!+}[0])\ rbits)\ (map\ (\mathbin{+\!\!+}[1])\ rbits)$$

Show that $map\ reverse\ lbits = rbits$ using the unique fixed-point principle. How are *lbits* and *rbits* related to *nat* and *pos*?   □

6.2   Recursion and Iteration

The combinator *recurse* captures *recursive* or *top-down* tree constructions; the functions f and g are repeatedly mapped over the whole tree:

$$recurse :: \forall \alpha\ .\ (\alpha \to \alpha) \to (\alpha \to \alpha) \to (\alpha \to Tree\ \alpha)$$
$$recurse\ f\ g\ a = t$$
$$\mathbf{where}\ t \quad = Node\ a\ (map\ f\ t)\ (map\ g\ t)\ .$$

Thus, an alternative definition of *nat* is $recurse\ (\lambda n \to 2*n+1)\ (\lambda n \to 2*n+2)\ 0$.

We can also construct a tree in an *iterative* or *bottom-up* fashion; the functions f and g are repeatedly applied to the given initial seed a:

$$iterate :: \forall \alpha\ .\ (\alpha \to \alpha) \to (\alpha \to \alpha) \to (\alpha \to Tree\ \alpha)$$
$$iterate\ f\ g\ a = loop\ a$$
$$\mathbf{where}\ loop\ x = Node\ x\ (loop\ (f\ x))\ (loop\ (g\ x))\ .$$

The type α can be seen as a type of states and the infinite tree as an enumeration of the state space.

We have overloaded the names *recurse* and *iterate* to denote operations both on streams and on trees. The abuse of language is justified as both sets of operations satisfy similar laws. For instance, $map\ h \cdot iterate\ f\ g$ is the *unfold* of the *Tree* codatatype. Furthermore, both *recurse* and *iterate* satisfy a *fusion* law:

$$map\ h \cdot recurse\ f_1\ g_1 = recurse\ f_2\ g_2 \cdot h$$

$$\Uparrow$$

$$h \cdot f_1 = f_2 \cdot h \wedge h \cdot g_1 = g_2 \cdot h$$

$$\Downarrow$$

$$map\ h \cdot iterate\ f_1\ g_1 = iterate\ f_2\ g_2 \cdot h \ .$$

Exercise 22. Prove the fusion laws, and then use fusion to give an alternative proof of *map reverse lbits = rbits*. □

How are *recurse f g a* and *iterate f g a* related? Contrary to the situation for streams, they are certainly not equal. Consider Figure 3, which displays the trees *recurse* ([0]⧺) ([1]⧺) [] and *iterate* ([0]⧺) ([1]⧺) []. Since f and g are applied in different orders — inside out and outside in — each level of *recurse f g a* is the *bit-reversal permutation* of the corresponding level of *iterate f g a*. For brevity's sake, one tree is called the *bit-reversal permutation* tree of the other. Exercises 21 and 22 explain the term bit-reversal permutation: a bit string can be seen as a path into an infinite tree — this is the central theme of Section 6.3 — following the reversed path leads to the permuted element.

Now, can we transform an instance of *recurse* into an instance of *iterate*? Yes, if the two functions are pre- or post-multiplications of elements of some given *monoid*. Let us introduce a suitable type class:

infixr 5 ∘
class *Monoid* α **where**
$\quad \epsilon \quad :: \alpha$
$\quad (\circ) :: \alpha \to \alpha \to \alpha \ .$

The *recursion-iteration lemma* then states

$$recurse\ (a\circ)\ (b\circ)\ \epsilon = iterate\ (\circ a)\ (\circ b)\ \epsilon \ , \tag{3}$$

where a and b are elements of some monoid $(M, \circ, \epsilon)$. To establish the lemma, we show that *iterate* (∘a) (∘b) ϵ satisfies the defining equation of *recurse* (a∘) (b∘) ϵ, that is $t = Node\ \epsilon\ (map\ (a\circ)\ t)\ (map\ (b\circ)\ t)$:

$\qquad iterate\ (\circ a)\ (\circ b)\ \epsilon$
$= \quad \{$ definition of *iterate* $\}$
$\qquad Node\ \epsilon\ (iterate\ (\circ a)\ (\circ b)\ (\epsilon \circ a))\ (iterate\ (\circ a)\ (\circ b)\ (\epsilon \circ b))$
$= \quad \{\ \epsilon \circ x = x = x \circ \epsilon\ \}$
$\qquad Node\ \epsilon\ (iterate\ (\circ a)\ (\circ b)\ (a \circ \epsilon))\ (iterate\ (\circ a)\ (\circ b)\ (b \circ \epsilon))$
$= \quad \{$ fusion: $(x\circ) \cdot (\circ y) = (\circ y) \cdot (x\circ)\ \}$
$\qquad Node\ \epsilon\ (map\ (a\circ)\ (iterate\ (\circ a)\ (\circ b)\ \epsilon))\ (map\ (b\circ)\ (iterate\ (\circ a)\ (\circ b)\ \epsilon))\ .$

As an example, *recurse* ([0]⧺) ([1]⧺) [] = *iterate* (⧺[0]) (⧺[1]) []; both expressions construct the infinite tree of all bit strings, shown in Figure 3 (a).

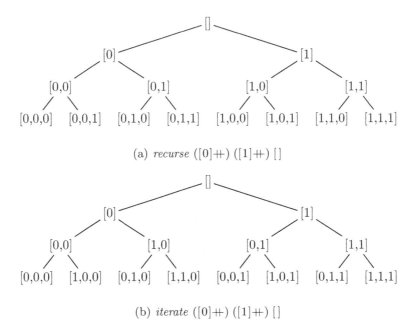

(a) *recurse* (([0]⧺) (([1]⧺) []

(b) *iterate* (([0]⧺) (([1]⧺) []

Fig. 3. A tree that contains all bit strings and its bit-reversal permutation tree

At first sight, it seems that the applicability of the lemma is somewhat hampered by the requirement on the form of the two arguments. However, since *endomorphisms*, functions of type $\tau \to \tau$ for some τ, form a monoid, we can easily rewrite an arbitrary instance of *recurse* into the required form ($\diamond$ is function application below, the 'apply' of the identity idiom):

$$
\begin{aligned}
& recurse\ f\ g\ a \\
=\ & \{\ \text{identity}\ \} \\
& recurse\ f\ g\ ((\diamond a)\ id) \\
=\ & \{\ \text{fusion: } (\diamond x) \cdot (f\ \cdot) = f \cdot (\diamond x)\ \} \\
& map\ (\diamond a)\ (recurse\ (f\ \cdot)\ (g\ \cdot)\ id) \\
=\ & \{\ \text{definition of } map\ \} \\
& pure\ (\diamond a) \diamond recurse\ (f\ \cdot)\ (g\ \cdot)\ id \\
=\ & \{\ \text{interchange law}\ \} \\
& recurse\ (f\ \cdot)\ (g\ \cdot)\ id \diamond pure\ a \\
=\ & \{\ \text{recursion-iteration lemma}\ \} \\
& iterate\ (\cdot f)\ (\cdot g)\ id \diamond pure\ a\ .
\end{aligned}
$$

(Note that we cannot 'un-fuse' the final expression.) This transformation turns a recursive construction into an iterative one, where functions serve as the internal state. One could argue the resulting construction is not really iterative (after all, the functions involved create a chain of closures). However, often we can provide a concrete representation of these functions, for instance, as a matrix, see the paper "The Bird tree" [19] for an example along these lines.

6.3 Tabulation

Like streams, infinite trees are a tabulation: they are in a one-to-one correspondence to functions from the binary numbers:

$$Tree\ \alpha \cong Bin \to \alpha\ ,$$

where the datatype Bin is given by

data $Bin = Nil\ |\ One\ Bin\ |\ Two\ Bin$.

(The type is isomorphic to the type of lists of bits, that we have used in the previous section. For the purposes of this section, a tailor-made datatype is preferable.) A tree can be seen as the tabulation of a function from the binary numbers. Conversely, a function of type $Bin \to \alpha$ can be implemented by looking up a memo-table. Here are the functions that witness the isomorphism.

$$
\begin{aligned}
&tabulate \quad :: \forall \alpha\ .\ (Bin \to \alpha) \to Tree\ \alpha \\
&tabulate\ f = Node\ (f\ Nil)\ (tabulate\ (f \cdot One))\ (tabulate\ (f \cdot Two)) \\
&lookup \qquad\quad :: \forall \alpha\ .\ Tree\ \alpha \to (Bin \to \alpha) \\
&lookup\ t\ Nil \quad\ = root\ t \\
&lookup\ t\ (One\ b) = lookup\ (left \quad t)\ b \\
&lookup\ t\ (Two\ b) = lookup\ (right\ t)\ b
\end{aligned}
$$

Again, we have overloaded the names to also denote operations on trees. (Exercise 24 asks you to capture the overloading using type classes.) This is justified as the new functions satisfy exactly the same properties as the old ones: they are mutually inverse and they are natural in the value type α. Tabulating the identity yields the infinite tree of binary numbers:

$$
\begin{aligned}
&\quad tabulate\ id \\
&= \quad \{\ \text{definition of } tabulate\ \} \\
&\quad Node\ Nil\ (tabulate\ One)\ (tabulate\ Two) \\
&= \quad \{\ \text{naturality of } tabulate\ \} \\
&\quad Node\ Nil\ (map\ One\ (tabulate\ id))\ (map\ Two\ (tabulate\ id))\ .
\end{aligned}
$$

Consequently, $tabulate\ id = bin$ where bin is given by

$$bin = Node\ Nil\ (map\ One\ bin)\ (map\ Two\ bin)\ .$$

Modulo the representation of binary numbers, bin is equivalent to nat, $lbits$ and $rbits$.

In Section 4.1 we have discussed at length how to tabulate functions. For variety, we consider the opposite problem here, namely, how to turn an infinite tree into a recursive or iterative algorithm. To this end, we require the *fold* or *catamorphism* for the inductive datatype *Bin*.

$$fold :: \forall \alpha . (\alpha \rightarrow \alpha) \rightarrow (\alpha \rightarrow \alpha) \rightarrow \alpha \rightarrow (Bin \rightarrow \alpha)$$
$$fold\ one\ two\ nil\ Nil\quad = nil$$
$$fold\ one\ two\ nil\ (One\ b) = one\ (fold\ one\ two\ nil\ b)$$
$$fold\ one\ two\ nil\ (Two\ b) = two\ (fold\ one\ two\ nil\ b)$$

The naming of identifiers makes explicit that a fold replaces constructors by functions. Like for streams, tabulation relates *fold* to *recurse*. Conversely, untabulating a recursive construction yields a fold.

$$tabulate\ (fold\ one\ two\ nil)\quad = recurse\ one\ two\ nil$$

$$lookup\ (recurse\ one\ two\ nil) = fold\ one\ two\ nil$$

As an example, let us derive a recursive algorithm for *fast exponentiation*. Let c be a constant. We seek an efficient implementation of $(pure\ c)^{nat}$. Let us calculate.

$$(pure\ c)^{nat}$$
$$= \quad \{ \text{ definition of } nat \ \}$$
$$Node\ c^0\ (pure\ c)^{(2*nat)+1}\ (pure\ c)^{2*(nat+1)}$$
$$= \quad \{ \text{ laws of exponentials } \}$$
$$Node\ 1\ (((pure\ c)^{nat})^2 * pure\ c)\ ((pure\ c)^{nat} * pure\ c)^2$$

Consequently, $(pure\ c)^{nat} = recurse\ (\lambda x \rightarrow x^2 * c)\ (\lambda x \rightarrow (x * c)^2)\ 1$ or equivalently $lookup\ (pure\ c)^{nat} = fold\ (\lambda x \rightarrow x^2 * c)\ (\lambda x \rightarrow (x * c)^2)\ 1$. The derivation can be readily generalised to an arbitrary monoid. For instance, 2×2 matrices with matrix multiplication form a monoid, so the program can be used to calculate the Fibonacci numbers in logarithmic time:

$$\begin{pmatrix} 0\ 1 \\ 1\ 1 \end{pmatrix}^n = \begin{pmatrix} \mathcal{F}_{n-1} & \mathcal{F}_n \\ \mathcal{F}_n & \mathcal{F}_{n+1} \end{pmatrix} ,$$

with $\mathcal{F}_{-1} = 1$.

Can we also derive an iterative algorithm for fast exponentiation? There are, at least, two choices: we can use the recursion-iteration lemma (see the previous section) and go higher-order, or we can use the bit-reversal permutation lemma (introduced below) and do some bit-fiddling.

Very briefly, the first approach yields

$$lookup\ (recurse\ f\ g\ a)\ n$$
$$= \quad \{ \text{ Section 6.2 } \}$$
$$lookup\ (iterate\ (\cdot\ f)\ (\cdot\ g)\ id \diamond pure\ a)\ n$$
$$= \quad \{ \ lookup \text{ is an idiom homomorphism } \}$$
$$(lookup\ (iterate\ (\cdot\ f)\ (\cdot\ g)\ id) \diamond lookup\ (pure\ a))\ n$$
$$= \quad \{ \text{ environment idiom } \}$$
$$lookup\ (iterate\ (\cdot\ f)\ (\cdot\ g)\ id)\ n\ a\ .$$

We build up an infinite tree of functions, look-up the function at position n and then apply it to a.

For the second approach, recall that *recurse f g a* is the bit-reversal permutation tree of *iterate f g a*. One way to formulate this relationship is via *lookup*:

$$lookup\ (recurse\ f\ g\ a) = lookup\ (iterate\ f\ g\ a) \cdot reverse\ , \qquad (4)$$

where *reverse* mirrors a binary number. The proof of Equation (4), dubbed the *bit-reversal permutation lemma*, proceeds smoothly if we turn *Bin* into an instance of *Num*, *Enum* and *Monoid*. Then *tabulate* can be written more perspicuously as

$$tabulate\ f = Node\ (f\ \epsilon)\ (tabulate\ (f \cdot (1\circ)))\ (tabulate\ (f \cdot (2\circ)))\ .$$

Equation (4) calls for an inductive proof. We can circumvent induction by applying *tabulate* to both sides of the equation. Let $h = lookup\ (iterate\ f\ g\ a)$, we show that *tabulate (h · reverse)* satisfies the recursion equation of *recurse f g a*.

$$tabulate\ (h \cdot reverse)$$
$=$ { definition of *tabulate* and $(h \cdot reverse)\ \epsilon = a$ }
$$Node\ a\ (tabulate\ (h \cdot reverse \cdot (1\circ)))\ (tabulate\ (h \cdot reverse \cdot (2\circ)))$$
$=$ { definition of *reverse* }
$$Node\ a\ (tabulate\ (h \cdot (\circ1) \cdot reverse))\ (tabulate\ (h \cdot (\circ2) \cdot reverse))$$
$=$ { proof obligation }
$$Node\ a\ (tabulate\ (f \cdot h \cdot reverse))\ (tabulate\ (g \cdot h \cdot reverse))$$
$=$ { naturality of tabulate }
$$Node\ a\ (map\ f\ (tabulate\ (h \cdot reverse)))\ (map\ g\ (tabulate\ (h \cdot reverse)))$$

It remains to discard the proof obligations $h \cdot (\circ1) = f \cdot h$ and $h \cdot (\circ2) = g \cdot h$, which capture the fact that the most significant bit determines the function applied in the last iteration. Again, to avoid an inductive proof we show the equivalent *tabulate (h · (∘1)) = map f (iterate f g a)*. Let $k = lookup \cdot iterate\ f\ g$, then

$$tabulate\ (k\ a \cdot (\circ1))$$
$=$ { definition of tabulate and $(k\ a \cdot (\circ1))\ \epsilon = f\ a$ }
$$Node\ (f\ a)\ (tabulate\ (k\ a \cdot (\circ1) \cdot (1\circ)))\ (tabulate\ (k\ a \cdot (\circ1) \cdot (2\circ)))$$
$=$ { monoids: $(x\circ) \cdot (\circ y) = (\circ y) \cdot (x\circ)$ }
$$Node\ (f\ a)\ \epsilon)\ (tabulate\ (k\ a \cdot (1\circ) \cdot (\circ1)))\ (tabulate\ (k\ a \cdot (2\circ) \cdot (\circ1)))$$
$=$ { definition of k }
$$Node\ (f\ a)\ (tabulate\ (k\ (f\ a) \cdot (\circ1)))\ (tabulate\ (k\ (g\ a) \cdot (\circ1)))$$
$\subset$ { $x\ a = Node\ (f\ a)\ (x\ (f\ a))\ (x\ (g\ a))$ has a unique solution }
$$Node\ (f\ a)\ (map\ f\ (iterate\ f\ g\ (f\ a)))\ (map\ f\ (iterate\ f\ g\ (g\ a)))$$

$=$ { definition of *map* and *iterate* }

   map f (*iterate f g a*) .

The proof of $h \cdot (\circ 2) = g \cdot h$ proceeds analogously.

It remains to deforest the intermediate data structure created by *iterate*. If we 'un-tabulate' *iterate*, setting *loop f g* $=$ *lookup* $\cdot$ *iterate f g*, we obtain an iterative or *tail-recursive* function, which can be seen as the counterpart of *foldl* for binary numbers.

loop   :: $\forall \alpha . (\alpha \to \alpha) \to (\alpha \to \alpha) \to \alpha \to (Bin \to \alpha)$
loop f g a Nil $= a$
loop f g a (*One b*) $=$ *loop f g* (*f a*) *b*
loop f g a (*Two b*) $=$ *loop f g* (*g a*) *b*

To summarise, we have derived two iterative algorithms for fast exponentiation:

power c n $=$ *loop* $(\cdot (\lambda x \to x^2 * c))$ $(\cdot (\lambda x \to (x * c)^2))$ *id n* 1
power c n $=$ *loop* $(\lambda x \to x^2 * c)$ $(\lambda x \to (x * c)^2)$ 1 (*reverse n*) .

The latter function is called the square-and-multiply algorithm or binary exponentiation. In fact, it corresponds to a variant known as the *Montgomery powering ladder.* (Exponentiation is used in most public-key crypto systems. The algorithm above is less vulnerable to attacks, since in each step a squaring and a multiplication is performed.)

Exercise 23. The datatype *Bin* implements the 1-2 *number system*, a variant of the binary system, which uses the digits $\{1, 2\}$, rather than $\{0, 1\}$. (A distinct advantage of this number system is that each natural number has a unique representation.) The functions

toNat :: *Bin* $\to$ *Nat*
toNat $=$ *fold* $(\lambda n \to 2 * n + 1)$ $(\lambda n \to 2 * n + 2)$ 0

toBin :: *Nat* $\to$ *Bin*
toBin $=$ *fold succ zero*

convert between unary numbers and these binary numbers. Implement *zero* :: *Bin* and *succ* :: *Bin* $\to$ *Bin*. Show that *toNat* and *toBin* are inverses.   □

Exercise 24. Capture *lookup* and *tabulate* using a type class. Since two types are involved, the type of keys and the type of tables, you need either multi-parameter type classes or type families.   □

6.4   Infinite Trees and Sequences

The type of natural numbers is isomorphic to the type of binary numbers: $Nat \cong Bin$. This implies that the type of streams is isomorphic to the type of infinite binary trees:

Stream $\alpha \cong$ *Tree* α .

We obtain the *canonical isomorphism* for converting a stream into a tree and vice versa by following the aforementioned chain of isomorphisms. Let $toNat :: Bin \to Nat$ and $toBin :: Nat \to Bin$ be the isomorphisms witnessing $Nat \cong Bin$, see Exercise 23. Then $stream :: Tree\ \alpha \to Stream\ \alpha$ and $tree :: Stream\ \alpha \to Tree\ \alpha$ are given by the following diagram.

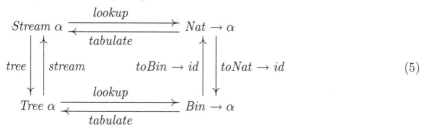

$$(5)$$

Here, $f \to g$ is the mapping function of the function space type constructor defined $(f \to g)\ h = g \cdot h \cdot f$.

The interactive session below shows that *stream* converts the tree of natural numbers, see Figure 2, into the stream of natural numbers.

> $\gg$ $stream\ (recurse\ (\lambda n \to 2 * n + 1)\ (\lambda n \to 2 * n + 2)\ 0)$
> $\langle 0, 1, 2, 3, 4, 5, 6, 7, 8, 9, 10, 11, 12, 13, 14, .. \rangle$
> $\gg$ $stream\ (iterate\ (\lambda n \to 2 * n + 1)\ (\lambda n \to 2 * n + 2)\ 0)$
> $\langle 0, 1, 2, 3, 5, 4, 6, 7, 11, 9, 13, 8, 12, 10, 14, .. \rangle$

It is important to note that *stream* does *not* list the elements level-wise from left to right, rather, it involves a bit-reversal permutation. Hence, streaming the iterative construction yields the permuted list of naturals $(0 \prec A081241)$.

For calculational purposes, it is useful to derive versions of *stream* and *tree* that do not involve number systems. For streaming, the idea is to define functions that mimic the projection functions *head* and *tail*. Clearly, *root* is the counterpart of *head*, the counterpart of *tail* is *chop* given by

$$chop\ :: \forall \alpha\ .\ Tree\ \alpha \to Tree\ \alpha$$
$$chop\ t = Node\ (root\ (left\ t))\ (right\ t)\ (chop\ (left\ t))\ .$$

The name indicates that it chops off the root of a given tree, interleaving the two subtrees. (The definition is reminiscent of Υ, this is not a coincidence, see below.) The projection functions are related by

$$root \qquad\quad = head \cdot stream \tag{6}$$
$$stream \cdot chop = tail \cdot stream\ . \tag{7}$$

In other words, *stream* is a so-called *representation changer* [23]. Given these prerequisites, it is a simple exercise to derive *stream*.

$$stream\ t$$
$$= \quad \{\ \text{extensionality:}\ s = head\ s \prec tail\ s\ \}$$
$$\quad head\ (stream\ t) \prec tail\ (stream\ s)$$
$$= \quad \{\ stream\ \text{is a representation changer: (6) and (7)}\ \}$$
$$\quad root\ t \prec stream\ (chop\ s)$$

We obtain

$$stream \quad :: \forall \alpha \,.\, Tree\ \alpha \to Stream\ \alpha$$
$$stream\ t = root\ t \prec stream\ (chop\ t)\ .$$

Conversely, for *tree* we define functions that mimic the projection functions *root*, *left* and *right*. The counterparts of *left* and *right* are *even · tail* and *odd · tail*, respectively, where *even* and *odd* are given by

$$even, odd :: \forall \alpha \,.\, Stream\ \alpha \to Stream\ \alpha$$
$$even\ s \quad = head\ s \prec odd\ (tail\ s)$$
$$odd\ s \quad = \qquad\qquad even\ (tail\ s)\ .$$

Exercise 25. Formulate laws that capture the fact that *head* is the counterpart of *root* etc. Use the laws to derive an implementation of *tree*. (The resulting equation is displayed below.) □

The isomorphism *tree* is then given by

$$tree \quad :: \forall \alpha \,.\, Stream\ \alpha \to Tree\ \alpha$$
$$tree\ s = Node\ (head\ s)\ (tree\ (even\ (tail\ s)))\ (tree\ (odd\ (tail\ s)))\ .$$

Exercise 26. Both *stream* and *tree* are given as unfolds or anamorphisms — they *construct* a stream from a tree and vice versa. In Haskell, inductive datatypes and coinductive types coincide [12]. For that reason, we can also define the isomorphisms as folds or catamorphisms — these variants *deconstruct* a tree to form a stream and vice versa.

$$stream'\ (\sim(Node\ a\ l\ r)) = node\ a\ (stream'\ l)\ (stream'\ r)$$
$$tree'\ (\sim(Cons\ a\ s)) \qquad = cons\ a\ (tree'\ s)$$

(The twiddles on the left-hand side delay pattern matching for increased laziness.) Define the helper functions *node* and *cons*. □

The two functions *stream* and *tree* satisfy a variety of properties: they are mutually inverse, they are natural in the element type and, most importantly, they are idiom homomorphisms. If you have solved Exercise 26, then you know that constructing a node corresponds roughly to interleaving two streams.

$$stream\ (Node\ a\ l\ r) = a \prec stream\ l\ \curlyvee\ stream\ r \qquad (8)$$
$$tree\ (a \prec l\ \curlyvee\ r) \quad = Node\ a\ (tree\ l)\ (tree\ r) \qquad (9)$$

Finally, the stream of natural numbers corresponds to the tree of natural numbers. The proof is straightforward: we show that *tree Stream.nat* satisfies the recursion equation of *Tree.nat*.

$$tree\ nat$$
$$= \quad \{\ property\ of\ nat\ and\ definition\ of\ \curlyvee\ \}$$
$$\quad tree\ (0 \prec 2 * nat + 1\ \curlyvee\ 2 * (nat + 1))$$
$$= \quad \{\ property\ of\ tree\ (9)\ \}$$
$$\quad Node\ 0\ (tree\ (2 * nat + 1))\ (tree\ (2 * (nat + 1)))$$
$$= \quad \{\ tree\ is\ an\ idiom\ homomorphism\ \}$$
$$\quad Node\ 0\ (2 * tree\ nat + 1)\ (2 * (tree\ nat + 1))$$

We have noted in the introduction to this section that streams relate to trees in the same way as unary numbers relate to binary numbers. A stream corresponds to a function from the natural numbers. Looking up the stream has, at best, a linear running time — if each element of the sequence is constructed in constant time. A tree corresponds to a function from the binary numbers. Looking up the tree has, at best, a logarithmic running time. Consequently, transforming a stream into a tree possibly transforms a linear into a logarithmic algorithm. In a sense, we have already seen an example along those lines: fast exponentiation. In the previous section we have derived an efficient implementation of $Tree.lookup\ ((pure\ c)^{Tree.nat})$. It remains to make the transition from streams to trees explicit.

$$
\begin{aligned}
& Stream.lookup\ ((pure\ c)^{Stream.nat}) \\
= \quad & \{\ \text{isomorphism: } stream \cdot tree = id\ \} \\
& Stream.lookup\ (stream\ (tree\ ((pure\ c)^{Stream.nat}))) \\
= \quad & \{\ Stream.lookup \cdot stream = (toBin \rightarrow id) \cdot Tree.lookup\ (5)\ \} \\
& Tree.lookup\ (tree\ ((pure\ c)^{Stream.nat})) \cdot toBin \\
= \quad & \{\ tree \text{ is an idiom homomorphism }\} \\
& Tree.lookup\ ((pure\ c)^{tree\ Stream.nat}) \cdot toBin \\
= \quad & \{\ tree\ Stream.nat = Tree.nat\ \} \\
& Tree.lookup\ ((pure\ c)^{Tree.nat}) \cdot toBin
\end{aligned}
$$

The example nicely demonstrates separation of concerns: a program is factored into a corecursive part that constructs codata and a recursive part that inspects the codata, taking care of termination.

The central step in the above derivation is the use of $tree$, which transforms a stream to a tree. Perhaps surprisingly, the opposite transformation is equally useful. If we view an infinite binary tree as a state space, then $stream$ enumerates this space. The next section considers such an example.

Exercise 27. Is $chop$ an idiom homomorphism?   □

6.5   Application: Enumerating the Positive Rationals

This section is organised as a set of exercises around a common theme: enumerating the positive rationals. The challenge is to set things up so that every positive rational occurs *exactly* once. This side condition rules out the naïve approach, generating all possible combinations of numerators and denominators, as the resulting enumeration will contain infinitely many copies of every positive rational.

There are, in fact, several ways to enumerate the positive rationals without duplicates. Probably the oldest method was discovered in the 1850s by the German mathematician Stern and independently a few years later by the French clockmaker Brocot. It is deceptively simple: Start with the two 'boundary

rationals' $^0/_1$ and $^1/_0$, which are not included in the enumeration, and then repeatedly insert the so-called *mediant* $^{a+b}/_{c+d}$ between two adjacent rationals $^a/_c$
and $^b/_d$.

Since the number of inserted rationals doubles with every step, the process
can be pictured by an infinite binary tree, the so-called Stern-Brocot tree, see
Figure 4. Its root is labelled with the first inserted mediant: $^{0+1}/_{1+0} = {}^1/_1$.

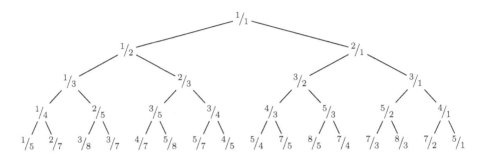

Fig. 4. Stern-Brocot tree

Exercise 28. (*Turn the informal description into a program*) If we represent an
inserted rational $^{a+b}/_{c+d}$ by the matrix $\left(\begin{smallmatrix} a & b \\ c & d \end{smallmatrix}\right)$, then its left and right descendant
can be determined as follows.

$$\begin{pmatrix} a & a+b \\ c & c+d \end{pmatrix} \longleftarrow \begin{pmatrix} a & b \\ c & d \end{pmatrix} \longmapsto \begin{pmatrix} a+b & b \\ c+d & d \end{pmatrix}$$

Phrase the transformations as matrix multiplications and then define the Stern-
Brocot tree as an *unfold*, a *map* after an *iterate*.   □

Exercise 29. (*Turn the iterative form into a recursive form*) Show that the iterative formulation is equivalent to the following recursive definition.

> *stern* :: *Tree Rational*
> *stern* = *Node* 1 (1 / (1 / *stern* + 1)) (*stern* + 1)

The definition makes explicit that the right subtree is the 'successor' of the entire
tree, see Figure 4. *Hint:* Use fusion and the recursion-iteration lemma.   □

Exercise 30. (*Relate the Stern-Brocot tree to Dijkstra's fusc sequence*) In one of
his EWDs [9], Dijkstra introduced the following function, also known as Stern's
diatomic sequence

$$\begin{aligned} \mathcal{S}_1 &= 1 \\ \mathcal{S}_{2*n} &= \mathcal{S}_n \\ \mathcal{S}_{2*n+1} &= \mathcal{S}_n + \mathcal{S}_{n+1} \ , \end{aligned}$$

which is a strange variant of *fib*.

Tabulate the function: *fusc* = *tabulate* $\mathcal{S}$. *Hint:* You may find it helpful to use
the function *chop* that serves as the counterpart of *tail*.

Show that $stern = fusc \div fusc'$, where $\div$ constructs a rational from two integers and $fusc' = chop\ fusc$.   □

Exercise 31. (*Turn the recursive form of fusc into an iterative one*) Turn the trees

$$num = Node\ 1\ num \qquad (num + den)$$
$$den\ = Node\ 1\ (num + den)\ den$$

into an iterative form (*num* and *den* are more telling names for *fusc* and *fusc'*). There are, at least, two approaches:

– Pair *num* and *den*

$$num \star den\ ,$$

where $(\star) = zip\ (,)$ turns a pair of trees into a tree of pairs.
– Use the fact that the subtrees of *num* are linear combinations of *num* and *den*.

$$i * num + j * den$$

(Dijkstra [10] uses a similar approach to show that $fusc + fusc' = brp\ (fusc + fusc')$, where *brp* transforms a tree to its bit-reversal permutation.)

Try to relate the two approaches, see also Exercise 11.   □

Exercise 32. (*Show that the rationals are in their lowest common form*) In Exercise 30 we have shown that $stern = num \div den$. This fact does *not*, however, imply that $map\ numerator\ stern = num$ and $map\ denominator\ stern = den$. (Why?) In order to prove the latter two equations, we have to show that the rationals $num \div den$ are in their lowest common form, that is, the greatest common divisor of *num* and *den* is 1:

$$num\ \triangledown\ den = 1\ ,$$

where $\triangledown$ denotes the greatest common divisor lifted to trees.   □

Exercise 33. (*Show that the Stern-Brocot tree contains every rational at most once*) Again, there are, at least, two approaches. One can show that *stern* is a search-tree using the following fact about mediants: if $a/c \leqslant b/d$, then

$$a/c \leqslant {a+b}/{c+d} \leqslant b/d\ .$$

Alternatively, one can show that *lookup stern* is injective by demonstrating that it has a left-inverse (*g* is the left-inverse of *f* iff $g \cdot f = id$). Rational numbers are in a one-to-one correspondence to bit strings. The following instrumented version of the greatest common divisor

$$a\ \blacktriangledown\ b = \textbf{case}\ compare\ a\ b\ \textbf{of}$$
$$LT\ \rightarrow 0 : (a\ \blacktriangledown\ (b - a))$$
$$EQ\ \rightarrow []$$
$$GT\ \rightarrow 1 : ((a - b)\ \blacktriangledown\ b)\ ,$$

maps two positive numbers to a bit string. We claim that this defines the required left-inverse. Establish the result by showing

$$num \ \blacktriangledown \ den = tabulate \ id \ .$$

Why is this sufficient?   □

Exercise 34. (*Show that the Stern-Brocot tree contains every rational at least once*) Show that *lookup stern* is surjective by demonstrating that it has a right-inverse (*g* is the right-inverse of *f* iff *f* · *g* = *id*).   □

Exercise 35. (*Linearise the Stern-Brocot tree*) Turn *stream stern* into an iterative form. In other words, enumerate the rationals!

1. As a first step, linearise *den*. You have to express *chop den* in terms of *den* and possibly *num*. To this end show that *chop den* = *num* + *den* − 2 ∗ *x* where *x* is the unique solution of *x* = *Node* 0 *num x*.
2. Show that the unique solution of *x* = *Node* 0 *num x* equals *num* **mod** *den*.
3. Using the results of the two previous items, linearise *num* and *den*, defining *snum* = *stream num* and *sden* = *stream den*.
4. Turn *snum* ⋆ *sden* into an iterative form.
5. *Polishing up:* Use the formula

$$1 \, / \, (\lfloor n \div d \rfloor + 1 - \{n \div d\}) = d \div (n + d - 2 \ast (n \bmod d))$$

to turn the result of the previous item into the following amazingly short program for enumerating the rationals.

$$rationals = iterate \ next \ 1$$
$$\mathbf{where} \ next \ r = 1 \, / \, (\lfloor r \rfloor + 1 - \{r\})$$

Here, ⌊*r*⌋ denotes the integral part of *r* and {*r*} its fractional part, such that *r* = ⌊*r*⌋ + {*r*}.   □

6.6 Summary and Related Work

The type of infinite binary trees is another example of a coinductive datatype. Like streams, infinite trees form an idiom. Trees can be defined using recursion equations; admissible equations have unique solutions. Unlike streams, recursive and iterative constructions do not coincide: one tree is the bit-reversal permutation tree of the other. A tree tabulates a function from the binary numbers. Tabulation and look-up are idiom isomorphisms between the environment idiom *Bin* → and *Tree*.

The section is loosely based on the paper "The Bird tree" [19], which introduces an alternative scheme for enumerating the positive rationals. It also develops an almost loopless algorithm for enumerating the elements of the infinite tree *recurse* (*a*∘) (*b*∘) *ε*, where *a* and *b* are elements of some given group.

7   Tabulation

We have repeatedly stressed the fact that a stream can be seen as a tabulation of a function from the unary numbers and that a tree tabulates a function from the binary numbers.

$$Nat \rightarrow \gamma \cong Stream\ \gamma$$
$$Bin \rightarrow \gamma \cong Tree\ \gamma$$

In this section we look at this relationship from a more principled perspective and show, among other things, that the two isomorphisms are based on the laws of exponentials.

As a warm-up exercise, consider tabulating a function from a non-recursive datatype. Probably every textbook on computer architecture includes truth tables for the logical connectives.

$$(\wedge) :: (Bool, Bool) \rightarrow Bool$$

False	False
False	True

A function from a pair of Booleans can be represented by a two-by-two table. Expressed in terms of type constructors we have

$$(Bool, Bool) \rightarrow Bool \cong ((Bool, Bool), (Bool, Bool))\ .$$

The relationship becomes more perspicuous, if we use mathematical notation for the types: $(Bool, Bool)$ corresponds to $(1+1) \times (1+1)$ where 1 is a one-element type, $+$ is disjoint union and $\times$ denotes the cartesian product — called $()$, *Either* and $(,)$ in Haskell. Rephrasing the above isomorphism in terms of the 'arithmetic types' we obtain

$$(1+1) \times (1+1) \rightarrow Bool \cong (Bool \times Bool) \times (Bool \times Bool)\ . \tag{10}$$

If we furthermore write the function space $K \rightarrow V$ as an exponential V^K — the type K is mnemonic for *key type* and V for *value type* — we realise that tabulation rests on the well-known *laws of exponentials*.

$$X^0 \cong 1 \qquad X^1 \cong X \qquad X^{A+B} \cong X^A \times X^B \qquad X^{A \times B} \cong (X^B)^A$$

A straightforward application of these laws proves the correspondence above, namely that we can tabulate a function from a pair of Booleans using a two-by-two table.

$$Bool^{(1+1) \times (1+1)}$$
$$= \quad \{\ X^{A \times B} \cong (X^B)^A\ \}$$
$$(Bool^{1+1})^{1+1}$$
$$= \quad \{\ X^{A+B} \cong X^A \times X^B\ \}$$
$$(Bool^1 \times Bool^1)^1 \times (Bool^1 \times Bool^1)^1$$
$$= \quad \{\ X^1 \cong X\ \}$$
$$(Bool \times Bool) \times (Bool \times Bool)$$

The derivation holds for every return type, so Equation (10) can, in fact, be generalised to an isomorphism between two type constructors

$$\Lambda \, V \, . \, (1+1) \times (1+1) \to V \cong \Lambda \, V \, . \, (V \times V) \times (V \times V) \ ,$$

or equivalently, in a 'point-free style',

$$(1+1) \times (1+1) \to \; \cong (Id \mathbin{\dot\times} Id) \mathbin{\dot\times} (Id \mathbin{\dot\times} Id) \ .$$

This is an isomorphism between two type constructors of kind $\star \to \star$. On the left-hand side, the two-argument type constructor '$\to$' is written without its second argument, so $Bool \times Bool \to$ has kind $\star \to \star$. On the right-hand side, we use the identity type constructor of kind $\star \to \star$ and the lifted product, which sends two type constructors of kind $\star \to \star$ to another type constructor of this kind. Using the types introduced in Section 2, the laws of exponentials can be rephrased as follows:

$0 \to \gamma$	$\cong 1$		$0 \to$	$\cong Const\ 1$
$1 \to \gamma$	$\cong \gamma$		$1 \to$	$\cong Id$
$(\alpha + \beta) \to \gamma \cong (\alpha \to \gamma) \times (\beta \to \gamma)$			$(\alpha + \beta) \to\ \cong (\alpha \to) \mathbin{\dot\times} (\beta \to)$	
$(\alpha \times \beta) \to \gamma \cong \alpha \to (\beta \to \gamma)$			$(\alpha \times \beta) \to\ \cong (\alpha \to) \cdot (\beta \to)$.	

The constructors on the right-hand side are container types. To represent a function from the empty type, we use an empty container; to represent a function from the one-element type, we use a one-element container; to represent a function from a disjoint union, we use a pair of containers; and finally, to represent a function from a pair, we use nested containers. The last law captures *currying*: a function of two arguments can be treated as a function of the first argument whose values are functions of the second argument. The law underlies, for instance, representations of two-dimensional arrays as arrays of arrays in the programming languages C or Java.

As an intermediate summary, tabulation is defined by induction on the structure of the key type; the construction is, however, parametric in the return type. Looking back at Section 2, we notice that all the container types involved have the structure of an idiom. Moreover, tabulation preserves the idiomatic structure of the environment idiom: one can show that datatype-generic versions of *tabulate* and *lookup* are idiom isomorphisms between the environment idiom and memo-tables. The proof is beyond the scope of these lecture notes.

Turning to recursive datatypes, we note that a function from a recursive type is tabulated by a recursive container type. Actually, we can be more precise than that: a function from an *inductive* type is tabulated by a *coinductive* container type. And indeed, both *Nat* and *Bin* are inductive types and both *Stream* and *Tree* are coinductive types. (In Haskell, inductive and coinductive types coincide, but it is useful to maintain the distinction.) Writing $\mu \, \alpha \, . \, \tau$ for an inductive type and $\nu \, \alpha \, . \, \tau$ for a coinductive type, the isomorphisms for streams and infinite trees can be written

$$(\mu \, \alpha \, . \, 1 + \alpha) \to \quad \cong \nu \, \beta \, . \, Id \mathbin{\dot\times} \beta$$
$$(\mu \, \alpha \, . \, 1 + \alpha + \alpha) \to\ \cong \nu \, \beta \, . \, Id \mathbin{\dot\times} \beta \mathbin{\dot\times} \beta \ .$$

The notation nicely makes the structure of the key and the corresponding container type explicit. In terms of constructors and destructors: 0 and $+1$ correspond to *head* and *tail*; *Nil*, *One* and *Two* correspond to *root*, *left* and *right*.

Table 4 extends the correspondence between key and container types to parametric types and types with embedded recursive types. To reduce clutter, we abbreviate $(\alpha_1, \ldots, \alpha_n)$ by $\boldsymbol{\alpha}$. It is understood that for each definition of K in the left column, T is defined by the corresponding entry in the right column.

Table 4. Tabulation: types of keys $K(\boldsymbol{\alpha})$ and tables $T(\boldsymbol{\beta})$

$$K(\boldsymbol{\alpha}) = \alpha_i \qquad\qquad\qquad T(\boldsymbol{\beta}) = \beta_i$$
$$K(\boldsymbol{\alpha}) = 0 \qquad\qquad\qquad T(\boldsymbol{\beta}) = Const\ 1$$
$$K(\boldsymbol{\alpha}) = 1 \qquad\qquad\qquad T(\boldsymbol{\beta}) = Id$$
$$K(\boldsymbol{\alpha}) = K_1(\boldsymbol{\alpha}) + K_2(\boldsymbol{\alpha}) \qquad T(\boldsymbol{\beta}) = T_1(\boldsymbol{\beta}) \mathbin{\dot\times} T_2(\boldsymbol{\beta})$$
$$K(\boldsymbol{\alpha}) = K_1(\boldsymbol{\alpha}) \times K_2(\boldsymbol{\alpha}) \qquad T(\boldsymbol{\beta}) = T_1(\boldsymbol{\beta}) \cdot T_2(\boldsymbol{\beta})$$
$$K(\boldsymbol{\alpha}) = \mu\,\alpha\,.\,K_1(\boldsymbol{\alpha}, \alpha) \qquad T(\boldsymbol{\beta}) = \nu\,\beta\,.\,T_1(\boldsymbol{\beta}, \beta)$$

Without proof we state the following

Theorem 1 (Tabulation). *Let* $K(\boldsymbol{\alpha})$ *and* $T(\boldsymbol{\beta})$ *be defined as in Table 4. Then*

$$K(\tau_1, \ldots, \tau_n) \to\ \cong\ T(\tau_1 \to, \ldots, \tau_n \to)\ .$$

for all types $\tau_1, \ldots, \tau_n$. □

Note that the type $T(\boldsymbol{\beta})$ of memo-tables contains only products, no sums, hence the terms table and tabulation. All the examples of tabulation we have seen before are instances of this scheme. For variety, let us discuss two further examples.

We have primarily considered functions from the natural numbers, what about the integers? Well, if integers are represented by

> **data** *Int = Neg Nat | Zero | Pos Nat* ,

then

> **data** *Tape* α = *Window* { *neg* :: *Stream* α, *zero* :: α, *pos* :: *Stream* α } .

is a suitable container type. A container of type *Tape* α can be seen as a tape that extends infinitely to the left and infinitely to the right, with the *zero* component marking the current position. Phrased in terms of the arithmetic type constructors, the two types are related by

$$Nat + 1 + Nat \to\ \cong\ Stream \mathbin{\dot\times} Id \mathbin{\dot\times} Stream\ .$$

If the key type involves products, then the container type is nested accordingly. For instance to represent a function from a pair of natural numbers, we use a stream of streams.

$$Nat \times Nat \to\ \cong\ Stream \cdot Stream$$

As we have noted before, the isomorphism above also underlies the usual encoding of two-dimensional arrays in C or Java — an array is a finite map of type $\{0, \ldots, n-1\} \to$ where n is the size.

Let us conclude the section with a brief discussion of proof techniques. If we want to establish a property of a function from the naturals, we have, at least, two choices. The standard approach is to use induction and case analysis, see Figure 1. A less conventional approach, favoured in these lecture notes, is to rephrase the function and the property in terms of streams and to use coinduction or, preferably, the unique fixed-point principle. Theorem 1 explains why the eschewed case-analysis disappears, it is replaced by a proof about pairs.

case analysis	$K_1(\alpha) + K_2(\alpha)$	$T_1(\beta) \,\dot\times\, T_2(\beta)$	pairs
pairs	$K_1(\alpha) \times K_2(\alpha)$	$T_1(\beta) \cdot T_2(\beta)$	nested proofs
induction	$\mu\,\alpha\,.\,K_1(\alpha, \alpha)$	$\nu\,\beta\,.\,T_1(\beta, \beta)$	coinduction

The laws of exponentials eliminate sums and consequently proofs by case analysis. This is why the unique fixed-point proof in Section 1 is so much more attractive than the inductive proof. To establish the equality of two pairs, we simply have to show that the corresponding elements are equal.

However, all that glitters is not gold. If the key type involves products, then we have to deal with a nested container type, which is often less manageable. Of course, tabulation establishes an isomorphism, which also allows us to transfer proofs from one setting to the other. So in principle, we can port an inductive proof to the coinductive setting. Conversely, even if we do not use streams or other coinductive types directly, we may profit from the widened perspective.

Overall, tabulation is a very valuable tool in the arsenal of techniques for program derivation and verification and it certainly deserves to be better known.

7.1   Summary and Related Work

Tabulation is based on the laws of exponentials. A function from an inductive type is tabulated by a coinductive type. Memo-tables are basically products, hence the name. In particular, they do not contain sums, which explains why the proofs in these lecture notes do without case analysis.

Finite versions of memo-tables are known as *tries* or *digital search trees*. Knuth [25] attributes the idea of a trie to Thue [36]. Connelly and Morris [5] formalised the concept of a trie in a categorical setting: they showed that a trie is a functor and that the corresponding look-up function is a natural transformation. The author gave a datatype-generic or polytypic definition of tries and memo-tables using type-indexed datatypes [16,17]. The insight that a function from an inductive type is tabulated by a coinductive type is due to Altenkirch [2]. If the trie structures are deforested, we obtain linear algorithms for sorting and grouping [15]. Like tries, these algorithms do not depend on an ordering relation, but use the structure of the elements to organise the working.

8   Conclusion

I hope you have enjoyed the journey. By and large, coinductive datatypes and corecursive programs are under-appreciated. We have demonstrated that they nicely support a holistic or wholemeal approach to programming and proving. A stream enables us to treat an infinite sequence of elements as a single entity. Likewise, a tree captures an infinite binary process.

Streams and trees can be conveniently defined using recursion equations. Admissible equations have unique solutions, which is the basis of the unique fixed-point principle. Both coinductive types have additional structure that can be put to good use. The idiomatic structure allows us to lift operations, which is a notational convenience not to be underestimated. Definitions and calculations benefit from the fact that streams and trees are memo-tables and that look-up and tabulation are idiom homomorphisms.

References

1. Aczel, P., Mendler, N.: A final coalgebra theorem. In: Dybjer, P., Pitts, A.M., Pitt, D.H., Poigné, A., Rydeheard, D.E. (eds.) Category Theory and Computer Science. LNCS, vol. 389, pp. 357–365. Springer, Heidelberg (1989)
2. Altenkirch, T.: Representations of first order function types as terminal coalgebras. In: Abramsky, S. (ed.) TLCA 2001. LNCS, vol. 2044, pp. 62–78. Springer, Heidelberg (2001)
3. Bird, R., de Moor, O.: Algebra of Programming. Prentice Hall Europe, London (1997)
4. Bird, R.: An introduction to the theory of lists. In: Broy, M. (ed.) Proceedings of the NATO Advanced Study Institute on Logic of programming and calculi of discrete design, Marktoberdorf, Germany, pp. 5–42. Springer, Heidelberg (1987)
5. Connelly, R.H., Morris, F.L.: A generalization of the trie data structure. Mathematical Structures in Computer Science 5(3), 381–418 (1995)
6. Coquand, T.: Infinite objects in type theory. In: Barendregt, H., Nipkow, T. (eds.) TYPES 1993. LNCS, vol. 806, pp. 62–78. Springer, Heidelberg (1994)
7. Curry, H., Feys, R.: Combinatory Logic, vol. 1. North-Holland, Amsterdam (1958)
8. Danvy, O.: An extensional characterization of lambda-lifting and lambda-dropping. In: Middeldorp, A. (ed.) FLOPS 1999. LNCS, vol. 1722, pp. 241–250. Springer, Heidelberg (1999)
9. Dijkstra, E.W.: EWD570: An exercise for Dr.R.M.Burstall (May 1976), the manuscript was published as Dijkstra, E.W.: Selected Writings on Computing: A Personal Perspective, pp. 215–216. Springer, Heidelberg (1982) ISBN 0-387-90652-5
10. Dijkstra, E.W.: EWD578: More about the function "fusc" (a sequel to EWD570) (May 1976), the manuscript was published as Dijkstra, E.W.: Selected Writings on Computing: A Personal Perspective, pp. 230–232. Springer, Heidelberg (1982)
11. Fokkinga, M.M.: Law and Order in Algorithmics. Ph.D. thesis, University of Twente (February 1992)
12. Fokkinga, M.M., Meijer, E.: Program calculation properties of continuous algebras. Tech. Rep. CS-R9104, Centre of Mathematics and Computer Science, CWI, Amsterdam (January 1991)

13. Gibbons, J., Hutton, G.: Proof methods for corecursive programs. Fundamenta Informaticae (XX), 1–14 (2005)
14. Graham, R.L., Knuth, D.E., Patashnik, O.: Concrete mathematics, 2nd edn. Addison-Wesley Publishing Company, Reading (1994)
15. Henglein, F.: Generic discrimination: Sorting and partitioning unshared data in linear time. In: Thiemann, P. (ed.) Proceedings of the 13th ACM Sigplan International Conference on Functional Programming (ICFP 2008), Victoria, BC, Canada, September 22–24, pp. 91–102. ACM, New York (2008)
16. Hinze, R.: Generalizing generalized tries. Journal of Functional Programming 10(4), 327–351 (2000)
17. Hinze, R.: Memo functions, polytypically! In: Jeuring, J. (ed.) Proceedings of the 2nd Workshop on Generic Programming, Ponte de Lima, Portugal, pp. 17–32 (July 2000), The proceedings appeared as a technical report of Universiteit Utrecht, UU-CS-2000-19
18. Hinze, R.: Functional Pearl: Streams and unique fixed points. In: Thiemann, P. (ed.) Proceedings of the 13th ACM SIGPLAN International Conference on Functional Programming (ICFP 2008), pp. 189–200. ACM Press, New York (2008)
19. Hinze, R.: Functional Pearl: The Bird tree. J. Functional Programming 19(5), 491–508 (2009)
20. Hinze, R.: Scans and convolutions—a calculational proof of Moessners theorem. In: Scholz, S.B. (ed.) Post-proceedings of the 20th International Symposium on the Implementation and Application of Functional Languages (IFL 2008), University of Hertfordshire, UK, September 10–12. LNCS, vol. 5836, Springer, Heidelberg (2009)
21. Hinze, R.: Lifting operators and laws (2010), http://www.comlab.ox.ac.uk/ralf.hinze/Lifting.pdf
22. Hinze, R., Löh, A.: Guide2lhs2tex (for version 1.13) (February 2008), http://people.cs.uu.nl/andres/lhs2tex/
23. Hutton, G., Meijer, E.: Functional Pearl:Back to basics: Deriving representation changers functionally. J. Functional Programming 6(1), 181–188 (1996)
24. Karczmarczuk, J.: Generating power of lazy semantics. Theoretical Computer Science 187, 203–219 (1997)
25. Knuth, D.E.: The Art of Computer Programming, Sorting and Searching, 2nd edn., vol. 3. Addison-Wesley Publishing Company, Reading (1998)
26. Mac Lane, S.: Categories for the Working Mathematician. Graduate Texts in Mathematics, 2nd edn. Springer, Heidelberg (1998)
27. McBride, C., Paterson, R.: Functional Pearl: Applicative programming with effects. Journal of Functional Programming 18(1), 1–13 (2008)
28. McIlroy, M.D.: Power series, power serious. J. Functional Programming 3(9), 325–337 (1999)
29. McIlroy, M.D.: The music of streams. Information Processing Letters 77, 189–195 (2001)
30. Milner, R.: Communication and Concurrency. International Series in Computer Science. Prentice Hall International, Englewood Cliffs (1989)
31. Peyton Jones, S.: Haskell 98 Language and Libraries. Cambridge University Press, Cambridge (2003)
32. Rutten, J.: Fundamental study: Behavioural differential equations: A coinductive calculus of streams, automata, and power series. Theoretical Computer Science 308, 1–53 (2003)
33. Rutten, J.: A coinductive calculus of streams. Math. Struct. in Comp. Science 15, 93–147 (2005)

34. Röjemo, N.: Garbage collection, and memory efficiency, in lazy functional languages. Ph.D. thesis, Chalmers University of Technology (1995)
35. Sloane, N.J.A.: The on-line encyclopedia of integer sequences (2009), http://www.research.att.com/~njas/sequences/
36. Thue, A.: Über die gegenseitige Lage gleicher Teile gewisser Zeichenreihen. Skrifter udgivne af Videnskaps-Selskabet i Christiania, Mathematisk-Naturvidenskabelig Klasse 1, 1–67 (1912), reprinted in Thue's Selected Mathematical Papers (Oslo: Universitetsforlaget), 413–477 (1977)
37. Turner, D.: A new implementation technique for applicative languages. Software - Practice and Experience 9, 31–49 (1979)

Programming in Manticore, a Heterogenous Parallel Functional Language

Matthew Fluet[1], Lars Bergstrom[2], Nic Ford[2], Mike Rainey[2], John Reppy[2], Adam Shaw[2], and Yingqi Xiao[2]

[1] Rochester Institute of Technology, Rochester NY 14623, USA
mtf@cs.rit.edu
[2] University of Chicago, Chicago IL 60637, USA
{larsberg,nford,mrainey,jhr,adamshaw,xiaoyq}@cs.uchicago.edu

Abstract. The Manticore project is an effort to design and implement a new functional language for parallel programming. Unlike many earlier parallel languages, Manticore is a *heterogeneous* language that supports parallelism at multiple levels. Specifically, the Manticore language combines Concurrent ML-style explicit concurrency with fine-grain, implicitly threaded, parallel constructs. These lectures will introduce the Manticore language and explore a variety of programs written to take advantage of heterogeneous parallelism.

At the explicit-concurrency level, Manticore supports the creation of distinct threads of control and the coordination of threads through first-class synchronous-message passing. Message-passing synchronization, in contrast to shared-memory synchronization, fits naturally with the functional-programming paradigm.

At the implicit-parallelism level, Manticore supports a diverse collection of parallel constructs for different granularities of work. Many of these constructs are inspired by common functional-programming idioms.

In addition to describing the basic mechanisms, we will present a number of useful programming techniques that are enabled by these mechanisms.

1 Introduction

Future improvements in microprocessor performance will largely come from increasing the *computational width* of processors, rather than increasing the clock frequency [33]. This trend is exhibited by multiple levels of hardware parallelism: single-instruction, multiple-data (SIMD) instructions; simultaneous-multithreading executions; multicore processors; multiprocessor systems. As a result, parallel computing is becoming widely available on commodity hardware. While these new designs solve the computer architect's problem of how to use an increasing number of transistors in a given power envelope, they create a problem for programmers and language implementors. Ideal applications for

Z. Horváth, R. Plasmeijer, and V. Zsók (Eds.): CEFP 2009, LNCS 6299, pp. 94–145, 2010.

this hardware, such as multimedia processing, computer games, and small-scale simulations, can themselves exhibit parallelism at multiple levels with different granularities, which means that a homogeneous language design will not take full advantage of the available hardware resources. For example, a language that provides data parallelism but not explicit concurrency will be inconvenient for the development of the networking and GUI components of a program. Similarly, a language that provides concurrency but not data parallelism will be ill-suited for the components of a program that demand fine-grain SIMD parallelism, such as image processing and particle systems.

Our thesis is that parallel programming languages must provide mechanisms for multiple levels of parallelism, both because applications exhibit parallelism at multiple levels and because hardware requires parallelism at multiple levels to maximize performance. For example, consider a networked flight simulator (Figure 1). This application might use SIMD instructions for physics simulation; data-parallel computations for particle systems [35] to model natural phenomena (*e.g.*, rain, fog, and clouds); light-weight parallel executions for preloading terrain and computing level-of-detail refinements; speculative search for artificial intelligence; concurrent threads for user interface and network components. Programming such an application will be challenging without language support for parallelism at multiple levels.

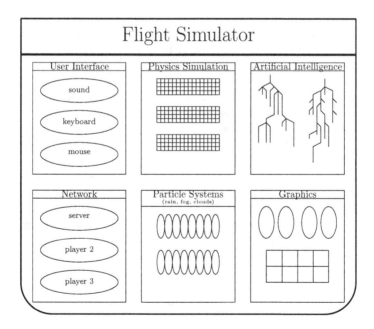

Fig. 1. An application with multiple levels of parallelism

Traditional imperative and object-oriented languages are poor choices for parallel applications. While they may support, or be extended with, concurrency constructs, their reliance on mutation of state as their core mechanism makes both writing correct programs and compiling efficient executables difficult. Existing parallel languages are also not a solution, since they have mostly been targeted at the narrow domain of high-performance scientific computing and large-scale parallelism. We need languages that can be used to write traditional commodity applications while exploiting the performance of tomorrow's multi-core hardware.

The Manticore project at the University of Chicago and the Rochester Institute of Technology[1] is an ambitious effort to lay the foundation for programming the commodity processors of the future, addressing the issues of *language design and implementation for multicore processors* [17,16]. As described above, our emphasis is on applications that might run on commodity multicore processors — applications that can exhibit parallelism at multiple levels with different granularities. To meet the demands of such applications, we propose a *heterogeneous* parallel language: a language that combines support for parallel computation at different levels into a common linguistic and execution framework.

We envision a high-level parallel programming language targeted at what we expect to be a typical commodity microprocessor in 2012. While predicting the future is always fraught with danger, we expect that these processors will have 8 or more general-purpose cores (*e.g.*, x86-64 processors) with SIMD instructions and 2–4 hardware thread contexts [33]. It is quite likely that these processors will also have special-purpose vector units, similar to those of the IBM Cell processor [23]. Furthermore, since it is unlikely that shared caches will scale to large numbers of cores, we expect a non-uniform or distributed-memory architecture inside the processor.

The problem posed by such processors is how to effectively exploit the different forms of parallelism provided by the hardware. We believe that mechanisms that are well integrated into a programming language are the best hope for achieving parallelism across a wide range of applications, which is why we are focusing on language design and implementation.

In the Manticore project, we are designing and implementing a parallel programming language that supports a range of parallel programming mechanisms. These include explicit threading with message passing to support both concurrent systems programming and coarse-grain parallelism, and nested-data parallelism mechanisms to support fine-grain computations.

The Manticore language is rooted in the family of statically-typed strict functional languages such as OCaml and SML. We make this choice because functional languages emphasize a value-oriented and mutation-free programming model, which avoids entanglements between separate concurrent computations [21,38,24,32]. We choose a strict language, rather than a lazy or lenient one, because we believe that strict languages are easier to implement efficiently

---

[1] Fluet was affiliated with the Toyota Technological Institute at Chicago for the first three years of this project.

and accessible to a larger community of potential users. On top of the sequential base language, Manticore provides the programmer with mechanisms for explicit concurrency and coarse-grain parallelism and mechanisms for fine-grain parallelism.

Manticore's concurrency mechanisms are based on Concurrent ML (CML) [39], which provides support for threads and synchronous message passing. Manticore's support for fine-grain parallelism is influenced by previous work on nested data-parallel languages, such as NESL [4,3,5] and Nepal [8,9,27].

In addition to language design, we are exploring a unified runtime framework, capable of handling the disparate demands of the various heterogeneous parallelism mechanisms exposed by a high-level language design and capable of supporting a diverse mix of scheduling policies. It is our belief that this runtime framework will provide a foundation for rapidly experimenting with both existing parallelism mechanisms and additional mechanisms not yet incorporated into high-level language designs for heterogeneous parallelism.

These lecture notes will introduce the Manticore language and selected programming techniques. Section 2 gives a brief overview of the Manticore language, setting the stage for more detailed treatment of specific language features. Section 3 describes the explicit-concurrency level of the Manticore language. Section 4 describes the implicit-parallelism level of the Manticore language.

2   Overview of the Manticore Language

Parallelism mechanisms can be roughly grouped into three categories:

- *implicit parallelism*, where the compiler and runtime system are exclusively responsible for partitioning the computation into parallel threads. Examples of this approach include Id [31], pH [32], and Sisal [20].
- *implicit threading*, where the programmer provides annotations (or hints) to the compiler as to which parts of the program are profitable for parallel evaluation, but mapping onto parallel threads is left to the compiler and runtime system. Examples of this approach include Nesl [3] and Nepal [9].
- *explicit threading*, where the programmer explicitly creates parallel threads. Examples of this approach include CML [39] and Erlang [1].

These different design points represent different trade-offs between programmer effort and programmer control. Automatic techniques for parallelization have proven effective for dense regular parallel computations (*e.g.*, dense matrix algorithms), but have been less successful for irregular problems. Manticore provides both implicit threading and explicit threading mechanisms. The former supports fine-grained parallel computation, while the latter supports coarse-grained parallel tasks and explicit concurrent programming. These parallelism mechanisms are built on top of a sequential functional language. In the sequel, we briefly discuss each of these in turn, starting with the sequential base language.

2.1   Sequential Programming

Manticore's sequential core language is based on the Standard ML (SML) language. The main differences are that Manticore does not have mutable data (*i.e.*, reference cells and arrays) and, in the present language implementation, Manticore has a simplified module system (omitting functors and sophisticated type sharing). Manticore does, however, have the functional elements of SML (datatypes, polymorphism, type inference, and higher-order functions) as well as exceptions. The inclusion of exceptions has interesting implications for the implicitly threaded mechanisms, but we believe that some form of exception mechanism is necessary for systems programming. As many researchers have observed, using a mutation-free computation language greatly simplifies the implementation and use of parallel features [21,38,24,32,13]. In essence, mutation-free functional programming reduces interference and data dependencies.

As the syntax and semantics of the sequential core language are largely orthogonal to (but potentially synergistic with) the parallel language mechanisms, we have resisted tinkering with the sequential SML core. The Manticore Basis, however, differs significantly from the SML Basis Library [19]. For example, we have a fixed set of numeric types — int, long, integer, float, and double — instead of SML's families of numeric modules.

2.2   Explicitly-Threaded Parallelism

The explicit concurrent programming mechanisms presented in Manticore serve two purposes: they support concurrent programming, which is an important feature for systems programming [22], and they support explicit parallel programming. Like CML, Manticore supports threads that are explicitly created using the **spawn** primitive. Threads do not share mutable state (as there is no mutable state in the sequential core language); rather they use synchronous message passing over typed channels to communicate and synchronize. Additionally, we use CML communication mechanisms to represent the interface to imperative features such as input/output. Section 3 explores this programming paradigm in more detail.

The main intellectual contribution of CML's design is an abstraction mechanism, called *first-class synchronous operations*, for building synchronization and communication abstractions. This mechanism allows programmers to encapsulate complicated communication and synchronization protocols as first-class abstractions, called *event values*, which encourages a modular style of programming where the actual underlying channels used to communicate with a given thread are hidden behind data and type abstraction. Events can range from simple message-passing operations to client-server protocols to protocols in a distributed system.

CML has been used successfully in a number of systems, including a multithreaded GUI toolkit [18], a distributed tuple-space implementation [39], a system for implementing partitioned applications in a distributed setting [44], and a higher-level library for software checkpointing [45]. The design of CML has inspired many implementations of CML-style concurrency primitives in other languages. These include other implementations of SML [29], other dialects of ML [25], other functional languages, such as HASKELL [40], SCHEME [15], and other high-level languages, such as JAVA [14]. We believe that this history demonstrates the effectiveness of CML's approach to concurrency.

2.3   Implicitly-Threaded Parallelism

Manticore provides implicitly-threaded parallel versions of a number of sequential forms. These constructs can be viewed as *hints* to the compiler about which computations are good candidates for parallel execution; the semantics of (most of) these constructs is sequential and the compiler and/or runtime system may choose to execute them in a single thread.[2]

Having a sequential semantics is useful in two ways: it provides the programmer with a deterministic programming model and it formalizes the expected behavior of the compiler. Specifically, the compiler must verify that the individual sub-computations in a parallel computation do not send or receive messages before executing the computation in parallel. Furthermore, if a sub-computation raises an exception, the runtime code must delay delivery of that exception until it has verified that all sequentially prior computations have terminated. Both of these restrictions require program analysis to implement efficiently. In some instances, a dynamic runtime check is used to guarantee the sequential semantics in a parallel execution.

Section 4 explores this programming paradigm in more detail. Here, we briefly introduce the implicitly parallel mechanisms:

Parallel arrays. Support for parallel computations over arrays and matrices is common in parallel languages. In Manticore, we support such computations using the nested parallel array mechanism inspired by NESL [4,3,5] and developed further by Nepal [8,9,27].

The key operations involving parallel arrays are *parallel comprehensions*, which allow the concise expressions of parallel loops that consume arrays and return a new array, and *parallel reductions*, which allow the concise expression of parallel loops that consume arrays and return scalars.

Parallel tuples. The parallel tuple expression form provides a hint to the compiler that the elements of the tuple may be evaluated in parallel. The basic form is

```
(| e1, ..., en |)
```

which describes a fork-join evaluation of the expressions e_i in parallel. The result is a normal tuple value.

Parallel bindings. Parallel arrays and tuples provide a fork-join pattern of computation, but in some cases more flexible scheduling is desirable.

---

[2] Shaw's Master's paper [42] provides a rigorous account of the semantics of a subset of these mechanisms.

In particular, we may wish to execute some computations speculatively. Manticore provides a parallel binding form

pval pat = exp

that launches the evaluation of the expression *exp* as a parallel thread. The sequential semantics of a parallel binding are similar to lazy evaluation: the binding is only evaluated (and only evaluated once) when one of its bound variables is demanded. In the parallel implementation, we use eager evaluation for parallel bindings, but such computations are canceled when the main thread of control reaches a point where their result is guaranteed never to be demanded.

Parallel cases. The parallel case expression form is a nondeterministic counterpart to SML's sequential case form. In a parallel case expression, the discriminants are evaluated in parallel and the match rules may include wildcard patterns that match even if their corresponding discriminants have not yet been fully evaluated. Thus, a parallel case expression nondeterministically takes any match rule that matches after sufficient discriminants have been evaluated.

Unlike the other implicitly-threaded mechanisms, parallel case is nondeterministic. We can still give a sequential semantics, but it requires including a source of non-determinism, such as McCarthy's **amb** [28], in the sequential language.

2.4   Future Directions

This section describes a first-cut design meant to give us a base for exploring multi-level parallel programming. Based on experience with this design, we plan to explore a number of different evolutionary paths for the language. First, we plan to explore other parallelism mechanisms, such as the use of futures with work stealing [30,7,6]. Such medium-grain parallelism would nicely complement the fine-grain parallelism (via parallel arrays) and the coarse-grain parallelism (via concurrent threads) present in Manticore. Second, there has been significant research on advanced type systems for tracking effects, which we may use to introduce imperative features into Manticore. As an alternative to traditional imperative variables, we will also examine synchronous memory (*i.e.*, I-variables and M-variables *à la* Id [31]) and *software transactional memory* (STM) [41].

3   Explicit Concurrency in Manticore

3.1   Introduction

The explicit-concurrency mechanisms of Manticore are based on Concurrent ML (CML) [39]. CML extends SML with synchronous message passing over typed channels and a powerful abstraction mechanism, called *first-class synchronous operations*, for building synchronization and communication abstractions. This mechanism allows programmers to encapsulate complicated communication and synchronization protocols as first-class abstractions, which encourages a modular style of programming where the actual underlying channels used to communicate with a given thread are hidden behind data and type abstraction.

Concurrent ML, as its name implies, emphasizes *concurrent* programming — programs consisting of multiple independent flows of sequential control, called processes. The execution of a concurrent program can be viewed as an interleaving of the sequential executions of its constituent processes. Although concurrent programming can be motivated by a desire to improve performance by exploiting multiprocessors, concurrency is a useful programming paradigm for certain application domains. For example, interactive systems (*e.g.*, graphical-user interfaces) have a naturally concurrent structure; similarly, distributed systems can often be viewed as concurrent programs.

As noted above, Manticore adopts Standard ML as its sequential core language, providing first-class functions, datatypes and pattern matching, exception handling, strong static typing, parametric polymorphism, *etc.* The explicit-concurrency mechanisms add the following features:

- dynamic creation of threads and typed channels.
- rendezvous communication via synchronous message passing.
- first-class synchronous operations, called events.
- automatic reclamation of threads and channels.
- pre-emptive scheduling of explicitly concurrent threads.
- efficient implementation — both on uniprocessors and multiprocessors.

3.2 Basic Concurrency Primitives

This section discusses the basic concurrency primitives provided by Manticore, including process creation and simple message passing via typed channels. Both processes and channels are created dynamically.

Threads. Processes (independent flows of sequential control) in Manticore are called *threads*. This choice of terminology emphasizes the fact that threads are lightweight and to distinguish them from other forms of process abstraction used in the Manticore runtime model. When a Manticore program begins executing, it consists of a single thread; this initial thread may create additional threads using the **spawn** e expression form. In the expression **spawn** e, the expression e is of type unit and the expression **spawn** e is of type tid (the type of a thread identifier). When the expression **spawn** e is evaluated, a new thread is created to evaluate the expression e. The newly created thread is called the *child* and its creator is called the *parent*. The child thread will execute until the evaluation of its initial expression is complete, at which time it terminates. In Manticore, the parent-child relationships between threads have no effect on the semantics of the program. For example, the termination of a parent thread does not affect child threads; each child thread is an independent flow of sequential control. Similarly, the termination of a child thread does not affect its parent thread; in particular, a parent thread does not wait for the termination of its children. Note that this means that the initial Manticore thread may terminate while other (children, grand-children, *etc.*) threads continue to execute. The whole program does not terminate until *all* threads have terminated or are blocked.

A thread may terminate in one of three ways. First, a thread may complete the evaluation of its initial expression. Second, a thread may explicitly terminate itself by calling the `exit` function, which has the signature:

val exit : unit -> 'a

Like a **raise** e expression, the result type of `exit` is 'a since it never returns. Third, a thread may raise an uncaught exception.[3] Note that such an exception is local to the thread in which it is raised; it is not propagated to its parent thread.

Because the number of threads in a Manticore program is unbounded and the number of (physical) processors is finite, the processors are multiplexed among the Manticore threads.[4] This is handled automatically by the Manticore run-time system, using periodic timer interrupts to provide preemptive scheduling of Manticore threads. Thus, the programmer is not required to ensure that each thread yields the processor at regular intervals (as is required by the so-called coroutine implementations of concurrency). This preemptive scheduling is important to support program modularity, because sequential code does not need to be modified to support explicit scheduling code. On the other hand, it places additional burden on the runtime system to efficiently manage the disparate demands of computation-bound and interactive threads.

In the concurrent-programming style promoted by Concurrent ML, threads are used very liberally. This style is supported by building threads upon first-class, heap-allocated continuations which yields threads are extremely cheap to create (on the order of 10 instruction) and impose very little space overhead (on the order of 100 bytes) [39,16,36]. Furthermore, the storage used to represent threads can be reclaimed by the garbage collector.

Channels. In order for multiple independent flows of sequential control to be useful, there must be some mechanism for communication and synchronization between the threads. In Manticore, the most important such mechanism is synchronous message passing on typed channels. The type constructor chan is used to generate the types of channels; a channel for communicating values of type t has the type t chan. There are two operations for channel communication, which have the signatures:

val recv : 'a chan -> 'a
val send : 'a chan * 'a -> unit

---

[3] In a sense, this is equivalent to the first manner in which a thread may terminate: the thread has completed the evaluation of its initial expression to an uncaught exception.

[4] The processors are further multiplexed to support the implicitly-threaded parallelism described in Section 4.

Message passing is synchronous, which means that both the sender and the receiver must be ready to communicate before either can proceed. When a thread executes a `recv` or `send` on a channel, we say that the thread is *offering* communication. The thread will block until some other thread offers a *matching* communication: the complementary operation on the same channel. When two threads offer matching communications, the message is passed from the sender to the receiver and both threads continue execution. Thus, message passing involves both communication of data and synchronization. Furthermore, message passing (specifically, the matching of senders and receivers) is a source of non-determinism. (In practice, a sender is matched with the receiver that has been blocked the longest or a receiver is matched with the sender that has been blocked the longest. However, the non-determinism in scheduling individual threads means that order in which threads become blocked on a message-passing operation is not deterministic.)

Note that channels are first-class values, created by the *channel* function, which has the signature:

```
val channel : unit -> 'a chan
```

Channels can be viewed as labels for *rendezvous* points — they do not name the sender or receiver, and they do not specify a direction of communication. Over the course of its lifetime, a channel may pass multiple values between multiple different threads. At any given time, there may be multiple threads offering to `recv` or `send` on the same channel. The nature of synchronous message passing ensures that each `recv` is matched with exactly one `send`.

Examples

Updatable storage cells. Although mutable state makes concurrent programming difficult, it is relatively easy to give an implementation of updatable storage cells on top of threads and channels. (Furthermore, updatable storage cells are a natural first example, since the desired behavior is well-known, placing the focus on the use of threads and channels.)

We define the following abstract interface to storage cells:

```
signature CELL = sig
  type 'a cell
  val cell : 'a -> 'a cell
  val get  : 'a cell -> 'a
  val put  : 'a cell * 'a -> unit
end
```

The operation `cell` creates a new cell initialized to the given value; the operations `get` and `put` are used to read and write a cell's value. Our approach is to represent the state of a cell by a thread, which we call the *server*, and to represent the `'a cell` type as a channel for communicating with the server. The complete implementation is as follows:

```
structure Cell : CELL = struct
  datatype 'a req = GET of 'a chan | PUT of 'a
  datatype 'a cell = CELL of 'a req chan

  fun get (CELL reqCh) =
    let
      val replyCh = channel ()
    in
      send (reqCh, GET replyCh) ;
      recv replyCh
    end

  fun put (CELL reqCh, y) =
    send (reqCh, PUT y)

  fun cell z =
    let
      val reqCh = channel ()
      fun loop x =
        case recv reqCh of
            GET replyCh => (send (replyCh, x) ; loop x)
          | PUT y = loop y
      val _ = spawn (loop z)
    in
      CELL reqCh
    end
end
```

The datatype 'a req defines the type of requests: either a GET to read the cell's value or a PUT to write the cell's value. The implementations of the get and put operations is straightforward. Each operation requires sending the appropriate request message to the server on the request channel. In the case of the get operation, the client first creates a reply channel, then the client sends the GET message (carrying the reply channel) to the server, and finally the client receives the cell's value on the reply channel. In the case of the put operation, the client sends the PUT message (carrying the new value for the cell).

The implementation of the cell operation is slightly more complicated. The cell operation creates a new cell, which involves allocating the request channel and spawning a new server thread to handle requests. Servers are typically implemented as infinite loops, with each iteration corresponding to a single client request. Since we are programming in a functional programming language, we use a tail recursive function to implement the loop.

The implementation of the CELL abstraction is a prototypical example of the *client-server* style of concurrent programming.

Sieve of Eratosthenes. Another important style of concurrent programming is the *dataflow network* style. In this style, computations are structured as networks of processes, where the data from one process flows to other processes in the network. Many of the processes in a dataflow network can be implemented as an infinitely looping thread that carries some local state from one iteration to the next. The forever function is useful for constructing such threads:

```
fun forever (init : 'a) (f: 'a -> 'a) : unit =
  let
    fun loop s = loop (f s)
    val _ = spawn (loop init)
  in
    ()
  end
```

The forever function takes two arguments, an initial state (of type 'a) and a function from states to states (of type 'a -> 'a), and it spawns a thread that repeatedly iterates the function.

A classic application of dataflow networks is for *stream processing*. A stream can be viewed as a possibly infinite sequence of values. For example, the succs function takes an initial integer and returns a channel on which a client may receive the stream of successors of the initial integer:

```
fun succs (i : int) : int chan =
  let
    val succsCh = channel ()
    fun succsFn j = (send (succsCh, j) ; j + 1)
    val () = forever i succsFn
  in
    succsCh
  end
```

Each application of the succs function creates a new instance of the stream of numbers; values are consumed from the stream by applying recv to the result channel.

This style of stream processing is similar to the notion of *lazy streams* as used in idiomatic functional programming. A principal difference is that these streams are stateful: once a value is read from a stream it cannot be read again.

A traditional example of stream programming is computing prime numbers using the *Sieve of Eratosthenes*. We start with the stream of integers beginning with 2 (the first prime number). To compute the primes, we filter out multiples of 2, which gives a stream beginning with 3 (the second prime number). We then filter out multiples of 3, yielding a stream beginning with 5 (the third prime number). At each step, we take the head of the stream (which is the next prime) and construct a new stream by filtering out multiples of the prime.

The filtering of a stream is provided by the following function, which takes a prime number p and an input stream inCh and returns a new stream outCh with multiples of p removed:

```
fun filter (p, inCh : int chan) : int chan =
  let
    val outCh = channel ()
    fun filterFn () =
      let
        val i = recv inCh
      in
        if (i mod p) <> 0 then send (outCh, i) else ()
      end
    val () = forever () filterFn
  in
    outCh
  end
```

The stream of primes is created by the following function:

```
fun primes () : int chan =
  let
    val primesCh = channel ()
    fun primesFn ch =
      let
        val p = recv ch
      in
        send (primesCh, p) ;
        filter (p, ch)
      end
    val _ = forever (succs 2) primesFn
  in
    primesCh
  end
```

The `primes` function creates a network of threads consisting of a `succFn` thread, which produces the stream of integers starting at 2, a chain of `filterFn` threads, which filter out multiples of primes that have been sent, and a `primeFn` thread, which sends primes on the `primesCh` channel and spawns new `filterFn` threads.

We can use the `primes` function (and associated dataflow network) to compute a list of the first n prime numbers:

```
fun firstPrimes n =
  let
    val primesCh = Primes.primes ()
  in
    List.tabulate (n, fn _ => recv primesCh)
  end
```

One may wonder what happens to the dataflow network after the list of the first n prime numbers has been returned. All of the threads created for the dataflow network are blocked sending to or receiving from channels in the network. None of these channels are used by non-blocked threads (in particular, the `primesCh` channel used in `firstPrimes` is unused once `firstPrimes` returns), and the whole network (threads and channels) is garbage collected. The key implementation strategy is that a channel maintain a reference to the threads that are blocked waiting to communicate on it (rather than a thread maintaining a reference to the channel on which it is blocked waiting to communicate). Thus, a blocked thread is automatically garbage collected when the channel on which it is blocked is garbage collected.

Fibonacci series. Another classic example of dataflow programming is the *Fibonacci series*, defined by the recurrence:

$$fib_1 = 1$$
$$fib_2 = 1$$
$$fib_{i+2} = fib_{i+1} + fib_i$$

Before implementing a Manticore program that generates the stream of Fibonacci numbers, it is worthwhile to consider the structure of the process network. Each element in the series is computed from the two previous elements. Thus, when the value fib_i is computed, it needs to be fed back into the network for the computation of fib_{i+1} and fib_{i+2}. Such a process network requires nodes that copy an input stream to two output streams and a node that provides a one-element delay in a stream. We also require a node that adds the values received from two streams. Figure 2 gives a pictorial representation of the process network for generating the Fibonacci series.

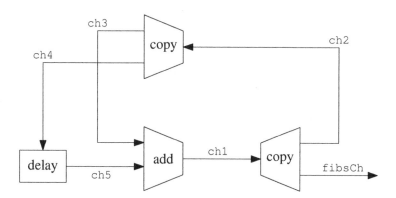

Fig. 2. The Fibonacci stream process network

As show in Figure 2, we can implement the Fibonacci stream using three general-purpose dataflow combinators: *add*, *copy*, and *delay*:

```
fun addStrms (inCh1, inCh2, outCh) =
  forever () (fn () =>
    send (outCh, (recv inCh1) + (recv inCh2)))

fun copyStrm (inCh, outCh1, outCh2) =
  forever () (fn () =>
    let val x = recv inCh
    in  send (outCh1, x) ; send (outCh2, x)
    end)

fun delayStrm first (inCh, outCh) =
  forever first (fn x =>
    (send (outCh, x) ; recv inCh))
```

Unlike the Sieve of Eratosthenes example, the process creation functions do not create their own channels. Because we need to construct a cyclic process network, we will pre-allocate the channels and supply them as arguments to the process creation functions. Note that the delayStrm combinator is similar to the copyStrm combinator, since it copies the elements from the inCh to the outCh; the difference is that the delayStrm first sends an initial value on the outCh, before copying the elements from the inCh to the outCh.

The implementation of the Fibonacci stream simply constructs the process network described in Figure 2:

```
fun fibs () : int chan =
  let
    val fibsCh = channel ()
    val ch1 = channel ()
    val ch2 = channel ()
    val ch3 = channel ()
    val ch4 = channel ()
    val ch5 = channel ()
  in
    copyStrm (ch1, ch2, fibsCh) ;
    copyStrm (ch2, ch3, ch4) ;
    delayStrm 0 (ch4, ch5) ;
    addStrms (ch3, ch5, ch1) ;
    send (ch1, 1) ;
    fibsCh
  end
```

As noted above, the channels for the network are allocated first and then the process nodes are created. A minor subtlety of the implementation is initializing the network: the delay node is initialized with the value 0 (one may think of this as $fib_0 = 0$) and the value 1 (fib_1) is sent on the channel ch1. This value is fed back into the network (via ch2 and ch3) to be added to 0 to produce the value 1 (fib_2).

3.3   First-Class Synchronous Operations

Basic First-class Synchronous Operations. Thus far, we have seen simple synchronous message passing examples using recv and send. While these operations permit the implementation of interesting concurrent programs, there are limits to the kinds of concurrent programs that can be expressed with just these operations.

A key programming mechanism in message-passing concurrency programming is *selective communication.* The basic idea is to allow a thread to block on a nondeterministic choice of several blocking communications — the first communication that becomes *enabled* is chosen. If two or more communications are simultaneously enabled, then one is chosen nondeterministically.[5] For example, note that there is a subtlety in the implementation of the Fibonacci network. The correctness of the implementation depends on the order in which the copyStrm combinator sends messages on its two output channels and on the order in which the addStrms combinator receives messages on its two input channels. If one were to reverse the order of the sends on ch3 and ch4, then the network would deadlock: the addStrms node would be attempting to receive a value on ch3, while the copyStrm node would be attempting to send a value on ch4, and the delayStrm node would be attempting to send a value on ch5.

Although we were able to carefully construct the Fibonacci network to avoid this problem, a more robust solution is to eliminate the dependence on the order of the blocking operations. For example, the addStrms combinator should block on reading a value from either inCh1 or inCh2; if it receives a value on inCh1 first, then it must block to receive a value on inCh2 (and vice versa). Similarly, the copyStrm combinator should block on sending a value to either outCh1 or outCh2; if it sends a value on outCh2 first, then it must block to send a value on outCh2 (and vice versa). Most concurrent languages with message passing provide a mechanism for selecting from a choice of several blocking communications.

However, there is a fundamental conflict between the desire for abstraction and the need for selective communication. In most concurrent languages with message passing, in order to formulate the selection from a choice of several blocking communications, one must explicitly list the blocking communications (*i.e.*, the individual recvs and sends with their arguments). This makes it difficult to construct abstract synchronous operations, because the constituent recvs and sends must be revealed (breaking the abstraction) in order for the synchronous operation to be used in selective communication.

---

[5] In practice, this nondeterminism is tempered by imposing priorities and/or fairness mechanisms on selective communication [39, Chapter 10].

Concurrent ML solves this problem by introducing *first-class synchronous operations*. The basic idea is to decouple the description of a synchronous operation (*e.g.*, "send the message m on the channel c") from the actual act of synchronizing on the operation. To do so, we introduce a new kind of abstract value, called an *event*, which represents a potential synchronous operation. (This is analogous to the way in which a function value represents a potential computation.) The type constructor event is used to generate the types of abstract synchronous operations; the type t event is the type of a synchronous operation that returns a value of type t when it is synchronized upon.

The basic event operations have the following signature:

```
val sync : 'a event -> 'a

val recvEvt : 'a chan -> 'a event
val sendEvt : 'a chan * 'a -> unit event

val choose : 'a event * 'a event -> 'a event
val wrap  : 'a event * ('a -> 'b) -> 'b event
val guard : (unit -> 'a event) -> 'a event
```

The sync operator forces synchronization on an event value. (This is analogous to the way in which a function application forces the potential computation represented by a function value.)

The recvEvt and sendEvt operators represent channel communication. The recvEvt and sendEvt operators are called *base-event constructors*, because they create event values that describe a single primitive synchronous operation. We can define recv and send as follows:

```
val recv = fn ch => sync (recvEvt ch)
val send = fn (ch, x) => sync (sendEvt (ch, x))
```

Later, we will see a small number of other base-event constructors.

The power of first-class synchronous operations comes from *event combinators*, which can be used to build more complicated event values from the base-event values. The choose combinator provides a generalized selective communication mechanism; the wrap combinator augments an event with a post-synchronization action (called the wrapper function); the guard combinator creates an event from a pre-synchronous action (called the guard function). Note that it is important that both the wrapper function and the guard function may spawn threads and may perform synchronizations.

It is worth considering (informally) the semantics of event synchronization. An event value can be viewed as a tree, where the leaves correspond to the base events (*e.g.*, recvEvt and sendEvt) and applications of guard, and the internal nodes correspond to applications of choose and wrap. For example, consider the event value constructed by:

```
val g2 = fn () => (spawn e2 ; wrap (bev2, w2))
val g3 = fn () => (spawn e3 ; bev3)
val ev = choose (
            wrap (bev1, w1),
            wrap (choose (
                    guard g2,
                    wrap (guard g3, w3)
                ), w4)
        )
```

where the bev_i are base events, the g_i are guard functions, and the w_i are wrapper functions. The leftmost portion of Figure 3 gives a pictorial representation of this event value, where choose nodes are labeled with ⊕, and wrap nodes are labeled with the wrapper functions, and guard nodes are labeled with the guard functions. When a thread evaluates sync ev, each of the guard functions at the leaves is evaluated to an event value, which replaces the guard node; if the resulting event value has additional guard functions at the leaves, then they are evaluated and replaced, until the final event value has only base events at the leaves. The rightmost portion of Figure 3 gives a pictorial representation of this final event value. The thread blocks until one of the bev_i is enabled by some other thread offering a matching communication. If multiple bev_i are enabled by matching communications, then one is chosen nondeterministically. Once a pair of matching communications are chosen, the sender's base event returns () and the receiver's base event returns the message. The wrapper functions on the path from the selected base event to the root are applied to the result, producing the result of the synchronization. For example, if bev2 is selected, with result v, then the result of sync ev is w4(w2(v)).

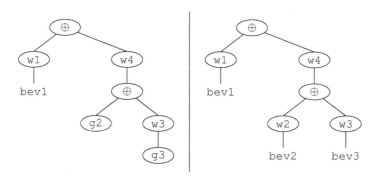

Fig. 3. An event value

We can use the choose and wrap combinators to give more robust implementations of the addStrms and copyStrm combinators:

```
fun addStrms (inCh1, inCh2, outCh) =
  forever () (fn () =>
    let
      val (a, b) =
        sync (choose (
          wrap (recvEvt inCh1, fn a => (a, recv inCh2)),
          wrap (recvEvt inCh2, fn b => (recv inCh1, b))
        ))
    in
      send (outCh, a + b)
    end)

fun copyStrm (inCh, outCh1, outCh2) =
  forever () (fn () =>
    let
      val x = recv inCh
    in
      sync (choose (
        wrap (sendEvt (outCh1, x),
              fn () => send (outCh2, x)),
        wrap (sendEvt (outCh2, x),
              fn () => send (outCh1, x))
      ))
    end)
```

In the revised addStrms combinator, we are choosing between the operation of receiving a message on inCh1 and the operation of receiving a message on inCh2; in each case, we use the wrap combinator to associate the action of receiving a message on the other channel. Similarly, in the revised copyStrm combinator, we are choosing between the operation of sending a message on outCh1 and the operation of sending a message on outCh2; in each case, we use the wrap combinator to associate the action of sending the value on the other channel. Using these revised combinators in the implementation of the Fibonacci network avoids the subtle correctness issue; more importantly, it frees clients that use the revised addStrms and copyStrm combinators from needing to know their specific behavior (*i.e.*, the revised addStrms and copyStrm combinators are more abstract).

Example — Swap channels. A simple example of a communication abstraction that uses all of the event combinators in its implementation is the *swap channel*. This is a new type of channel that allows two processes to swap values when they rendezvous. We define the following abstract interface to swap channels:

```
signature SWAP_CHANNEL = sig
  type 'a swap_chan
  val swapChannel : unit -> 'a swap_chan
  val swapEvt : 'a swap_chan * 'a -> 'a event
end
```

The operation swapChannel creates a new swap channel; the operation swapEvt is used to create an event that, when synchronized, simultaneously sends and receives a value on a swap channel. When two processes communicate on a swap channel, each sends a value and each receives a value; it is important that exactly two processes swap values.

Because swap channels provide symmetric message passing and the implementation is based on the asymmetric message-passing operations, each thread in a swap must offer to send a message and to receive a message on the same channel. The choose combinator suffices for this purpose. Once one thread has sent a value (and the other thread has received the value), a value must be sent in the other direction to complete the swap. We cannot use the channel on which the first value was sent, because other threads synchronizing on a swapEvt are trying to send and receive on that channel. We also cannot use another (dedicated) channel to complete the swap. For example, Figure 4 shows a swap mismatch. Threads P_1 and P_2 are matched (by sending and receiving on ch) and thread Q_1 and Q_2 are matched (by also sending and receiving on ch), but the values sent to complete the swap are mismatched: the value sent by P_2 on ch' (meant for P_1) is received by Q_1 and the value sent by Q_2 also on ch' (meant for Q_2) is received by P_1.

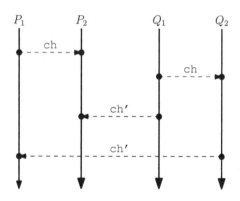

Fig. 4. A swap mismatch

To avoid this problem, we allocate a fresh channel to complete the second phase of the swap operation each time the swap operation is executed. The implementation is as follows:

```
structure SwapChannel : SWAP_CHANNEL = struct
  datatype 'a swap_chan = SC of ('a * 'a chan) chan

  fun swapChannel () = SC (channel ())

  fun swapEvt (SC ch, msgOut) =
    guard (fn () =>
      let
        val inCh = channel ()
      in
        choose (
          wrap (recvEvt ch,
                fn (msgIn, outCh) =>
                (send (outCh, msgOut) ; msgIn)),
            wrap (sendEvt (ch, (msgIn, inCh)),
                fn () => recv inCh)
        )
      end)
end
```

A swap channel is represented by a single channel on which is sent a pair consisting of both the value communicated in the first phase and a (private) channel on which is sent the value communicated in the second phase. Making the channel for the second phase private to each instance of the swap operation ensures that there is never a mismatch when sending the value in the second phase. However, this channel for the second phase must be allocated after the synchronization begins (because it must be private to this instance of the swap operation) and before the communication of the first value. This is precisely the behavior of the guard combinator.

The swap-channel abstraction illustrates several important programming techniques. The use of dynamically allocating a new channel to serve as the unique identifier for an operation is a common idiom. (Note that we used this technique in the implementation of updatable storage cells.) It is also an example that uses all of the event combinators: choose, wrap, and guard. Finally, it is a example that shows the utility of the event abstraction: clients that use the SWAP_CELL abstraction may treat the swapEvt operation as though it were a base event — it may be used in choose, wrap, and guard combinators.

3.4 Additional First-Class Synchronous Operations

We can extend the set of primitive first-class synchronous operations discussed above with additional combinators, base-event constructors, and various miscellaneous operations.

Simple Base-event Constructors. Recall that the recvEvt and sendEvt base-event constructors are enabled when there is a matching communication being offered by another synchronizing thread. One can imagine two extreme cases of recvEvt — one in which there is *always* another thread offering the matching communication and one in which there is *never* another thread offering the matching communication.

It is useful to realize these two extremes as (primitive) base-event constructors:

```
val alwaysEvt : 'a -> 'a event
val neverEvt  : 'a event
```

The alwaysEvt constructor is used to build an event value that is always enabled for synchronization. The neverEvt constructor is used to build an event value that is never enabled for synchronization. Because a neverEvt can never be chosen for synchronization, it is the identity for the choose combinator; hence, it is useful for choosing from a list of event values:

```
val chooseList : 'a event list -> 'a event =
  fn l => List.foldl choose neverEvt l
```

(Note that the nondeterminism in choose makes it an associative and symmetric operator; the choice of fold direction is arbitrary.)

Note that one cannot implement a reliable polling mechanism by combining alwaysEvt and choose. For example, the following function does not accurately poll a channel for input:

```
fun recvPoll (ch : 'a chan) : 'a option =
  sync (choose (
    alwaysEvt NONE,
    wrap (recvEvt ch, fn x => SOME x)
  ))
```

Although it will never block, it may return NONE even when there is a matching communication available on ch. This is because the choice of enabled events to be returned by the synchronization is nondeterministic — the alwaysEvt may be chosen over the recvEvt.

Negative Acknowledgements. When programming in the client-server style, we can characterize servers as either idempotent or not idempotent. A server that is idempotent is one such that the handling of a given request is independent of other requests. A server that is not idempotent may be servicing multiple requests at once (having accepted multiple requests), where each client is blocking on the receive of a reply from the server. If a client receives the reply, then (due to the synchronous nature of message passing) the server knows that the client has completed the request-reply protocol. However, if the client uses the receive of the reply in a choose combinator and another event is chosen for synchronization, then the server cannot know that the client will never complete the request-reply protocol.

To ensure the correct semantics in this kind of situation, we need a mechanism for *negative acknowledgements*. The following event combinator provides such a mechanism:

val withNack : (unit event -> 'a event) -> 'a event

This combinator behaves like the guard combinator — it takes a function (which we continue to call the guard function) whose evaluation is delayed until synchronization time. The difference is that the function is applied to an *abort event*, which is enabled only if the event returned by the guard function is *not* chosen in the synchronization.

External Synchronous Events. As noted earlier, concurrent programming is a useful programming paradigm for interactive systems (*e.g.*, graphical-user interfaces). An interactive system must deal with multiple (asynchronous) input streams (*e.g.*, keyboard, mouse, network) and multiple (asynchronous) output streams (*e.g.*, display, audio, network). Similarly, an interactive system often provides multiple services, where each service is largely independent, having its own internal state and control-flow. In sequential languages, these issues are often dealt with through complex event loops and callback functions.

Here, we describe the interface to various kinds of external synchronous events. By using first-class synchronous events, we can treat these external events using the same framework as internal synchronization.

Intput/Output. An important form of external event is the availability of user input. A very simplistic account of input/output for a console application would be to take the standard input, output, and error streams to be character channels:

val stdInCh : char channel
val stdOutCh : char channel
val stdErrCh : char channel

Of course, it is not sensible to send on stdInCh or to receive on stdOutCh or stdErrCh. A better interface is to expose the streams as events:

val stdInEvt : char event
val stdOutEvt : char -> unit event
val stdErrEvt : char -> unit event

We can naturally extend this style of interface to accommodate events for reading from and writing to files, sending and receiving on a network socket, *etc.*

In practice, one builds a higher-level I/O library above these primitive operations, much as the Standard ML Basis Library [19] builds imperative I/O and stream I/O levels above the primitive I/O level, which provides abstractions of the underlying operating system's unbuffered I/O operations.

Timeouts. Timeouts are another important example of external synchronous events. Most concurrent languages provide special mechanisms for "timing out" on a blocking operation. Using the framework of events, one can give base-event constructors for synchronizing on time events:

```
val timeOutEvt : time -> unit event
val atTimeEvt  : time -> unit event
```

The time type represents both absolute time and durations of time intervals. The timeOutEvt constructor takes a time value t (representing a time interval) and returns an event that becomes enabled at a time t units *relative* to the time at which the synchronization is performed. For example, a thread that evaluates the following expression will be delayed for one second:

```
sync (timeOutEvt (timeFromSeconds 1))
```

The atTimeEvt constructor takes a time value t (representing an absolute time) and returns an event that becomes enabled at time t.

Note that synchronization on time values is, by necessity, approximate. The granularity of the underlying system clock, scheduling delays in both the underlying operating system and the Manticore scheduler tend to delay synchronization on a time value slightly.

The fact that both input/output and timeouts are represented by events allows threads to combine them with other synchronous operations. For example, suppose that the program has prompted the user to enter Y or N, but wishes to proceed as though the user had entered N after a 10 second delay. This could be expressed by the following event:

```
choose (
  wrap (timeOutEvt (timeFromSeconds 10), fn () => #"N"),
  stdInEvt
)
```

3.5   Examples

We conclude with a few more examples of useful abstractions built atop the first-class synchronous operations.

Buffered Channels. The send and recv operations provide synchronous communication — both sender and receiver block until there is a matching communication. It is sometimes useful to support asynchronous communication — a sender does not block (its message is buffered in the channel) and a receiver blocks until there is an available message. This buffering of communication can be useful when a cyclic communication pattern is required (as in the Fibonacci process network).

We define the following abstract interface to buffered channels:

```
signature BUFFERED_CHAN = sig
  type 'a buffered_chan
  val bufferedChan : unit -> 'a buffered_chan
  val bufferedSend     : 'a buffered_chan * 'a -> unit
  val bufferedRecvEvt : 'a buffered_chan -> 'a event
end
```

As described above, a buffered channel consists of a queue of messages. The send operation adds a message to the queue without blocking the sender. The recvEvt operations attempts to take a message from the queue; if the queue is empty, it blocks until some other thread sends a message.

The implementation of buffered channels is similar to the implementation of the updatable storage cells: each time a buffered channel is created, a server thread is spawned to service requests to send on and receive on the channel.

```
structure BufferedChan : BUFFERED_CHAN = struct
  datatype 'a buffered_chan =
    BC of {inCh: 'a chan, outCh: 'a chan}

  fun bufferedSend (BC {outCh, ...}, x) = send (outCh, x)
  fun bufferedRecvEvt (BC {inCh, ...}) = recvEvt inCh

  fun bufferedChan () =
    let
      val (inCh, outCh) = (channel (), channel ())
      fun loop ([], []) = loop ([recv inCh], [])
        | loop ([], rear) = loop (rev rear, [])
        | loop (front as frontHd::frontTl, rear) =
          let
            val (front', rear') =
              sync (choose (
                      wrap (recvEvt inCh,
                            fn y => (front, y::rear)),
                      wrap (sendEvt (outCh, frontHd),
                            fn () => (frontTl, rear))
                  ))
          in
            loop (front', rear')
          end
      val _ = spawn (loop ([], []))
    in
      BC {inCh = inCh, outCh = outCh}
    end
end
```

Futures. Futures are a common mechanism for specifying parallel computation. (Indeed, many of the mechanisms in Section 4 can be seen as special cases of futures.) The future construct takes a computation, creates a (logically) separate thread and returns a placeholder (called a *future cell*) for the computation's result. The act of reading a value from a future cell is called *touching*. If a thread attempts to touch a future, before the computation of its value is completed, then the thread blocks.

Implementing futures is straightforward. Since touching a future is a synchronous operation, we represent a future cell as an event value and we use sync to touch a value. We define the following abstract interface to futures:

```
signature FUTURE = sig
  datatype 'a result = VAL of 'a | EXN of exn
  val future : ('a -> 'b) -> 'a -> 'b result event
end
```

Because the evaluation of a future might result in a raised exception, we introduce the result type constructor to distinguish evaluation to a value (VAL) from evaluation to a raised exception (EXN). The implementation is quite simple:

```
structure Future : FUTURE = struct
  datatype 'a result = VAL of 'a | EXN of exn
  fun future f x =
    let
      val ch = channel ()
      val _ = spawn (
        let
          val r = (VAL (f x)) handle exn => EXN exn
        in
          forever () (fn () => send (ch, r))
        end)
    in
      recvEvt ch
    end
end
```

To create a future, we create a channel on which to communicate the future result and spawn a thread to evaluate the computation and then repeatedly send the result on the channel. The future cell is represented by the event that receives the result on the channel.

Note that this is not a particularly efficient implementation of futures. A more efficient implementation can be build using synchronizing shared-memory (*e.g.*, *M-variables* and *I-variables* [31]), which themselves fit naturally into the framework of first-class synchronous events.

3.6   Conclusion

This section has discussed the explicit-concurrency mechanisms of Manticore, based upon those of Concurrent ML (CML). A much longer exposition, including detailed descriptions of non-trivial applications (a software build system; a concurrent window system; a distributed tuple-space), can be found in the book-length treatment of CML [39]. Two recent papers describe the parallel implementation of the Concurrent ML operations provided by Manticore [37,36].

4   Implicit Parallelism in Manticore

4.1   Introduction

Manticore provides implicitly-threaded parallel versions of a number of sequential forms. These constructs can be viewed as *hints* to the compiler about which computations are good candidates for parallel execution; the semantics of (most of) these constructs is sequential and the compiler and/or runtime system may choose to execute them in a single thread.

There are number of distinct reasons for introducing implicitly-threaded parallel constructs into a language (in addition to the explicitly-threaded concurrency constructs of Section 3). As noted in Section 1, parallel programming languages must provide mechanisms at multiple levels of parallelism, both because applications exhibit parallelism at multiple levels and because hardware requires parallelism at multiple levels to maximize performance. The implicitly-threaded parallel constructs are much better suited for expressing fine-grained parallelism (as might be executed using SIMD instructions). In a sense, the implicitly-threaded parallel constructs ease the burden for both the programmer and the compiler: the programmer is able to utilize simple parallel constructs, which efficiently (in terms of program text) express the desired parallelism, and the compiler is able to analyze and optimize these constructs, yielding programs that efficiently (in terms of time and computational resources) execute. Although the implicitly-threaded parallel constructs are necessarily more specific (and therefore less expressive) than the explicitly-threaded parallel constructs, this does not diminish their utility. Rather, they express common idioms of parallel computation and their limited expressiveness allows the compiler and runtime system to better manage the parallel computation.

Manticore introduces a number of implicitly-threaded parallel constructs:

- parallel arrays
- parallel tuples
- parallel bindings
- parallel cases

In addition to these implicitly-threaded parallel constructs visible in the source language, there is a general-purpose cancellation mechanism that is used to stop the (parallel) execution of computations when their results are guaranteed never to be demanded. (Note that this cancellation only applies to the implicitly-parallel constructs of Manticore, not to the explicitly-parallel constructs described in the previous section.)

As noted above, the implicitly-threaded parallel constructs provide a parallel execution of a sequential semantics. Having a sequential semantics is useful in two ways: it provides the programmer with a deterministic programming model and it formalizes the expected behavior of the compiler. Specifically, the compiler must verify that the individual sub-computations in a parallel computation do not send or receive messages before executing the computation in parallel. Furthermore, if a sub-computation raises an exception, the runtime code must delay delivery of that exception until it has verified that all sequentially prior computations have terminated. Both of these restrictions require program analysis to implement efficiently.

4.2   Parallel Arrays

Support for parallel computations on arrays and matrices is common in parallel languages. The reason for this is that operations on arrays and matrices naturally express *data parallelism*, in which a single computation is performed in parallel across a large number of data elements. In Manticore, we support such computations using the nested parallel array mechanism inspired by NESL [4,3,5] and developed further by Nepal [8,9,27] and Data Parallel Haskell (DPH) [11,10].

As might be expected, the type constructor `'a parray` is used to generate the types of parallel arrays, which are immutable sequences that can be computed in parallel. An important feature of parallel arrays is that they may be nested (*i.e.*, one can construct a parallel array of parallel arrays); multi-dimensional arrays need not be rectangular, which means that many irregular data structures can be represented. Furthermore, Manticore (like Nepal and DPH, but unlike NESL) supports parallel arrays of arbitrary types, admitting arrays of floating-point numbers, user-defined datatypes (*e.g.*, polymorphic lists or trees), functions, *etc.* Based on the parallel array element type and the parallel array operations, the compiler will map parallel array operations onto the appropriate parallel hardware (*e.g.*, operations on parallel arrays of floating-point numbers may be mapped onto SIMD instructions).

Parallel-Array Introduction. There are three basic expression forms that yield a parallel array. The simplest is an explicit enumeration of the expressions to be evaluated in parallel to yield the elements of the parallel array:

```
[| e1, ..., en |]
```

Thus, this parallel-array expression form constructs a parallel array of n elements, where the `[| |]` delimiters alert the compiler that the e_i may be evaluated in parallel.

Integer sequences are a common data structure in parallel algorithms. Manticore provides a parallel-array expression form for conveniently expressing integer sequences:

```
[| el to eh by es |]
```

This parallel-array expression form constructs a parallel array of integers, where the first element is `el`, the successive elements are `el + es`, `el + 2 * es`, ..., and the last element is `el + n * es` for the largest n such that `el + n * es <= eh`. For example, the expression

```
[| 1 to 31 by 10 |]
```

is equivalent to the expression

```
[| 1, 11, 21, 31 |]
```

If the step expression ("**by** es") is omitted, then it naturally defaults to 1.

The final expression form that creates a parallel array is a *parallel-array comprehension*, which provides a concise description of a parallel loop. In its full generality, a parallel-array comprehension has the form:

[| e | x1 **in** ea1, ..., xn **in** ean **where** ep |]

where e is an expression that computes the elements of the array, the ea_i are parallel-array expressions that provide inputs to e, and ep is a boolean expression that filters the input. (If the filter expression ("**where** ep" is omitted, then it naturally defaults to true.) If the input arrays ea_i have different lengths, all are truncated to the length of the shortest input, and they are processed, in parallel, in lock-step.[6]

Parallel-array comprehensions can be used to specify both SIMD parallelism that is mapped onto vector hardware (*e.g.*, Intel's SSE instructions) and SPMD parallelism where parallelism is mapped onto multiple cores. For example, to double each positive integer in a given parallel array of integers nums, one would use the following expression:

[| 2 * n | n **in** nums **where** n > 0 |]

This expression can evaluated efficiently in parallel using vector instructions. Two additional examples are the definitions of *parallel map* and *parallel filter* combinators; the former applies a function to each element of an array in parallel, while the latter discards elements of an array that do not satisfy a predicate:

fun mapP f xs = [| f x | x **in** xs |]
fun filterP p xs = [| x | x **in** xs **where** p x |]

Parallel-array comprehensions are first-class expressions; hence, the expressions defining the source parallel arrays of a comprehension can themselves be parallel-array comprehensions. For example, the main loop of a ray tracer generating an image of width w and height h can be written

[| [| trace(x,y) | x **in** [| 0 **to** w-1 |] |]
 | y **in** [| 0 **to** h-1 |] |]

This parallel comprehension within a parallel comprehension is an example of *nested data parallelism*.

The sequential semantics of expression forms that create (and eliminate) parallel arrays is defined by mapping them to lists (see [17] or [42] for details). The main subtlety in the parallel implementation is that if an exception is raised when computing its *i*th element, then we must wait until all preceding elements have been computed before propagating the exception.

---

[6] This behavior is known as *zip semantics*, since the comprehension loops over the zip of the inputs. Both NESL and Nepal have zip semantics, but Data Parallel Haskell [11] has *Cartesian-product semantics* where the iteration is over the product of the inputs.

Parallel-Array Elimination. There are a number of basic expression forms that consume a parallel array. The parallel-array comprehension described above is one such form. Another simple elimination form is the subscript operator that extracts a single element of a parallel array:

```
ea ! ei
```

where `ea` is a parallel-array expression and `ei` is an integer expression. Parallel arrays are indexed by zero; if the index is outside the range of the array, then the `Subscript` exception is raised.

An important expression form that consumes a parallel array is a *parallel-array reduction*, which provides a concise description of a parallel loop. This operation is available through a combinator with the signature:

```
val reduceP : ('a * 'a -> 'a) -> 'a -> 'a array -> 'a
```

The expression `reduceP f b ea` is similar to folding the function `f` over the elements of `ea` using the base value `b`. The difference is that the function is applied in parallel to the elements, using a tree-like decomposition of the array elements. Hence, it is important that the function `f` is an associative function with `b` as a left zero.

An obvious application of a parallel-array reduction is to sum all of the elements of a parallel array of integers:

```
fun sumP a = reduceP (fn (x, y) => x + y) 0 a
```

Note that `+` is an associative function with `0` as a (left and right) zero.

Additional Parallel-Array Operations. Before turning to some more examples, we describe a number of additional parallel-array operations. Although these operations can be implemented in terms of the expression forms and operations given above, most of them have direct implementations, for efficiency.

Since parallel arrays are finite data structures, it is often useful to query the number of elements in the parallel array. The `lengthP` operation has the signature:

```
val lengthP : 'a parray -> int
```

One possible implementation of `lengthP` is the following:

```
fun lengthP a = sumP (mapP (fn _ => 1) a)
```

Although parallel-array comprehensions may be used to express many computations, it is sometimes necessary to explicitly decompose a computation and explicitly combine the results. Hence, it is useful to be able to concatenate and flatten parallel arrays:

```
val concatP : 'a parray * 'a parray -> 'a parray
val flattenP : 'a parray parray -> 'a parray
```

Because `concatP` is an associative function with `[| |]` as a (left and right) zero, we can implement `flattenP` using `reduceP` and `concatP`:

```
fun flattenP a = reduceP concatP [| |] a
```

The concatenation of parallel arrays can be expressed as a comprehension:

```
fun concatP (a1, a2) =
  let
    val l1 = lengthP a1
    val l2 = lengthP a2
  in
    [| if i < l1 then a1 ! i else a2 ! (i - l1)
     | i in [| 0 to (l1 + l2 - 1) |] |]
  end
```

Examples. Parallel arrays are a natural representation for images:

```
type pixel = int * int * int
type img = pixel parray parray
```

We assume that a `pixel` represents the red, green, and blue components, each of which is in the range 0 to 255. Many image transformations can be expressed as a computation that is applied to each pixel of an image. For example, to convert a color image to a gray-scale image, we simply need to convert each color pixel to a gray-scale pixel:

```
fun rgbPixToGrayPix ((r, g, b) : pixel) : pixel =
  let
    val m = (r + g + b) / 3
  in
    (m, m, m)
  end
fun rgbImgToGrayImg (img : img) : img =
  [| [| rgbPixToGrayPix pix | pix in row |] | row in img |]
```

We can express the entire family of pixel-to-pixel transformations with a higher-order function:

```
fun xformImg (xformPix: pixel -> pixel) (img : img) : img =
  [| [| xformPix pix | pix in row |] | row in img |]
```

Although `xformImg` is simply a specialization of `mapP`, it serves as another example of conciseness of nested comprehensions.

Operations on vectors and matrices are classic motivating examples for nested data parallelism. A parallel array can be used to represent both dense and sparse vectors:

```
type vector = real parray
type sparse_vector = (int * real) parray
```

A sparse matrix can be can be represented naturally as an array of rows, where each row is a sparse vector:

```
type sparse_matrix = sparse_vector parray
```

To multiply a sparse matrix by a dense vector, we simply compute the dot product for each row:

```
fun dotp (sv: sparse_vector) (v: vector) : real =
   sumP [| x * (v!i) | (i,x) in sv |]
fun smvm (sm: sparse_matrix) (v: vector) : vector =
   [| dotp (row, v) | row in sm |]
```

Note that smvm expresses a nested parallel computation: dotp is applied to each row of the sparse matrix in parallel, while dotp is itself a parallel operation (comprised of both a parallel-array comprehension and a parallel-array reduction).

The quicksort algorithm is a common example in the nested data parallelism literature. We can implement quicksort in Manticore as follows:

```
fun quicksort (a: int parray) : int parray =
   if lengthP a < 2
      then a
      else let
             val pivot = ns ! 0
             val ss = [| filterP cmp a
                       | cmp in [| fn x => x < pivot,
                                   fn x => x = pivot,
                                   fn x => x > pivot |] |]
             val rs =
               [| quicksort a | a in [| ss!0, ss!2 |] |]
             val sorted_lt = rs!0
             val sorted_eq = ss!1
             val sorted_gt = rs!1
           in
             flattenP [| sorted_lt, sorted_eq, sorted_gt |]
           end
```

In this implementation, the argument parallel array a is partitioned into elements less than, equal to, and greater than the pivot element. Note the use of a parallel-array comprehension over an array of comparison functions, which is another example of nested data parallelism. The arrays of less-than and greater-than elements are recursively sorted in parallel by using another parallel comprehension. Finally, the sorted arrays of elements are flattened into a single array of sorted elements.

4.3   Parallel Tuples

The parallel arrays of the previous section provide a very regular form of parallelism. However, it is sometimes more convenient to express a less regular form of parallelism. Parallel tuples are similar in spirit to the explicit-enumeration parallel-array expression form. The parallel-tuple expression form provides a hint to the compiler that the elements of the tuple may be evaluated in parallel:

```
(| e1, ..., en |)
```

Thus, this parallel-tuple expression form constructs a tuple of n elements, where the $(|\ |)$ delimiters alert the compiler that the e_i may be evaluated in parallel.

A parallel tuple expresses a simple *fork/join* form of parallelism; each of the tuple components is evaluated in parallel and the computation of the tuple result blocks until all the sub-expressions are fully evaluated. Like parallel arrays, they enable the expression of computations with a high degree of parallelism in a very concise manner. Unlike parallel arrays, they support heterogeneous parallelism, because a tuple may be comprised of heterogeneous types and heterogeneous computations. Parallel tuples can thus avoid some awkwardness that can arise when using parallel arrays exclusively. For example, here is a revised quicksort implementation that uses both parallel arrays and parallel tuples to more naturally express the computation:

```
fun quicksort (a: int parray) : int parray =
  if lengthP a < 2
    then a
    else let
            val pivot = ns ! 0
            val (sorted_lt, sorted_eq, sorted_gt) =
              (| quicksort (filterP (fn x => x < pivot) a),
                 filterP (fn x => x = pivot),
                 quicksort (filterP (fn x => x > pivot) a) |)
         in
            flattenP [| sorted_lt, sorted_eq, sorted_gt |]
         end
```

The sequential semantics of parallel tuples is trivial: the expressions are evaluated in left-to-right order, just as they are for a (non-parallel) tuple. The implication for the parallel implementation is similar to that for parallel arrays: if an exception is raised when computing its ith element, then the implementation must wait until all preceding elements have been computed before propagating the exception.

Parallel tuples are convenient for expressing recursive functions, where the recursive calls can be evaluated in parallel. For example, here is a function to compute the binomial coefficient:

```
fun add (a, b) = a + b
fun choose (n, k) =
  if n = k then 1
  else if k = 0 then 1
  else add (| choose (n - 1, k), choose (n - 1, k - 1) |)
```

Similarly, here is a function to sum the leaves of a binary tree:

```
datatype tree = Lf of int | Br of tree * tree
fun trAdd t =
  case t of
    Lf i => i
  | Br (t1, t2) => add (| trAdd t1, trAdd t2 |)
```

As noted above, the implicitly-threaded parallel constructs are *hints* to the compiler about which computations are good candidates for parallel execution. As demonstrated by the previous examples, parallel tuples make it very easy to express parallel computations; indeed, they can often express more parallelism that can be effectively utilized. An important problem is to determine when parallel execution is likely to be profitable: the compiler and runtime must determine when the overhead of starting a parallel execution does not outweigh the benefits of parallel execution (else, sequential execution would be more efficient). By integrating analyses and transformations into the compiler and runtime system, we preserve a simple source language but provide sophisticated runtime behavior.

For example, the trAdd function concisely expresses the fact that one may sum the branches of a binary tree in parallel. However, it should be clear that summing *all* the branches of a binary tree in parallel would have poor performance: a balanced binary tree of depth N would induce the creation of $2^N - 2$ parallel sub-computations. Realizing each of these sub-computations as an independent thread would quickly result in more threads than physical processors, and many threads would be blocked waiting for the completion of sub-computations. Even reifying each of these sub-computations as a unit of work for a collection of work-stealing threads would induce an unacceptable overhead. In order to achieve high-performance executions, it is necessary to ensure that there is sufficient (sequential) computation to warrant the overhead of parallel execution. For example, we might wish to transform the treeAdd function as follows:

```
datatype tree = Tr of int * tree'
     and tree' = Lf' of int | Br' of tree * tree
fun Lf n = Tr (1, Lf' n)
fun Br (t1 as Tr (d1, _), t2 as Tr (d2, _)) =
  Tr (max(d1, d2) + 1, Br' (t1, t2))

fun trAdd (Tr (d,t')) =
   if (d < 16 orelse numIdleProcs () < 2)
      then tr'Add_seq t'
      else tr'Add_par t'
and trAdd_seq (Tr (_,t')) = tr'Add_seq t'
and tr'Add_seq t' =
  case t' of
     Lf' i => n
   | Br' (t1, t2) => add ( trAdd_seq t1, trAdd_seq t2 )
and tr'Add_par t' =
  case t' of
     Lf' i => n
   | Br' (t1, t2) => add (| trAdd t1, trAdd t2 |)
```

Under this transformation, the tree datatype maintains the depth of binary tree. We use the depth of the binary tree to ensure that any binary tree of depth less than 16 is summed as a sequential computation (trAdd_seq and trAdd'_seq). Similarly, we suppress parallel execution when there are insufficient computational resources available ($\texttt{numIdleProcs}$ () < 2). An important point is that we would like this transformation to be *automatically* generated by the compiler. The original $\texttt{trAdd}$ function is only two lines long and manifestly correct; the translated function above is significantly more complex. Making the analysis and transformation a duty of the compiler helps to ensure that the transformed program is semantically equivalent to the original program.

4.4   Parallel Bindings

Parallel arrays and tuples provide a fork-join pattern of computation, but in some cases more flexible scheduling is desirable. In particular, we may wish to execute some computations speculatively. Manticore provides a parallel binding form

> **pval** p = e

that spawns the evaluation of the expression e as a parallel thread. The sequential semantics of a parallel binding are similar to lazy evaluation: the binding is only evaluated (and only evaluated once) when one of the variables bound in the pattern p is demanded by the evaluation of some expression in the main thread of control. One important subtlety in the semantics of parallel bindings is that any exceptions raised by the evaluation of the binding must be postponed until one of the variables is touched, at which time the exception is raised at the point of the touched variable.

The distinguishing characteristic of the parallel-binding declaration form is that the spawned computation may be canceled before completion. When a (simple, syntactic) program analysis determines the program points at which a spawned computation is guaranteed never to be demanded, the compiler inserts a corresponding cancellation.

The following function computes the product of the leaves of a tree:

```
datatype tree = Lf of int | Br of tree * tree
fun trProd t=
  case t of
    Lf i => i
  | Br (t1, t2) =
      let
        pval p1 = trProd t1
        pval p2 = trProd t2
      in
        if p1 = 0
          then 0
          else p1 * p2
      end
```

This implementation short-circuits when the product of the left subtree of a $\texttt{Br}$ variant evaluates to zero. Note that if the result of the left product is zero, we do not need the result of the right product. Therefore its subcomputation and any descendants may be canceled. The short-circuiting behavior is not explicit in the function; rather, it is implicit in the semantics of the parallel-binding declaration form that when control reaches a point where the result of an evaluation is known to be unneeded, the resources devoted to that evaluation are freed and the computation is abandoned.

The analysis to determine when a future is subject to cancellation is not as straightforward as it might seem. The following example includes two parallel bindings linked by a common computation:

```
let
  pval x = f 0
  pval y = (| g 1, x |)
in
  if b then x else h y
end
```

In the conditional expression here, while the computation of y can be canceled in the **then** branch, the computation of x cannot be canceled in either branch. Our analysis must respect this dependency and similar subtle dependencies.

We will give more examples of the use of parallel bindings in Section 4.7. However, as a very simple example, we note that the behavior of parallel tuples may be encoded using parallel bindings; in particular, we encode (| e1, ..., en |) as

```
let
  pval x1 = e1
    ...
  pval xn = en
in
  (x1, ..., xn)
end
```

4.5 Parallel Cases

The parallel-case expression form is a nondeterministic counterpart to Standard ML's sequential-case expression form. In a parallel-case expression, the discriminants are evaluated in parallel and the match rules may include wildcard patterns that match even if their corresponding discriminants have not yet been fully evaluated. Thus, a parallel case expression nondeterministically takes any match rule that matches after sufficient discriminants have been evaluated. The parallel-case expression form leverages the familiar pattern-matching idiom and is flexible enough to express a variety of non-deterministic parallel mechanisms.

Unlike the other implicitly-threaded mechanisms, the parallel-case expression form is nondeterministic. We can still give a sequential semantics, but it requires including a source of non-determinism (*e.g.*, McCarthy's **amb** [28]), in the sequential language.

In many respects, the parallel-case expression form is syntactically similar to the sequential-case expression form:

```
pcase e1 & ... & en of
    pp11 & ... & pp1n => e'1
  | ...
  | ppm1 & ... & ppmn => e'm
  | otherwise => e
```

The metavariable pp denotes a *parallel pattern*, which is either

- a nondeterministic wildcard **?**,
- a handle pattern **handle** p, or
- a pattern p,

where p in the latter two cases signifies a conventional SML pattern. Further-more, **pcase** expressions include an optional **otherwise** branch (which must be the last branch) which has a special meaning as discussed below.

A *nondeterministic wildcard pattern* can match against a computation that is either finished or not. It is therefore different than the usual SML wildcard, which matches against a finished computation, albeit one whose result remains unnamed. Nondeterministic wildcards can be used to implement short-circuiting behavior. Consider the following parallel-case branch:

```
  | false & ? => 9
```

Once the constant pattern `false` has been matched with the result of the first discriminant's computation, the running program need not wait for the second discriminant's computation to finish; it can immediately return `9`.

A *handle pattern* catches an exception if one is raised in the computation of the corresponding discriminant. It may furthermore bind the raised exception to a pattern for use in subsequent computation.

We can transcribe the meaning of **otherwise** concisely, using SML/NJ-style or-patterns in our presentation for brevity. An **otherwise** branch can be thought of as a branch of the form:

```
  | (_ | handle _) & ... & (_ | handle _) => e
```

The fact that every position in this pattern is either a deterministic wildcard or a handle means it can only match when all computations are finished. It also has the special property that it takes lowest precedence when other branches also match the evaluated discriminants. In the absence of an explicit **otherwise** branch, a parallel-case expression is evaluated as though it were specified with the following branch:

```
  | otherwise => raise Match
```

To illustrate the use of parallel case expressions, we consider parallel choice. A parallel choice expression e1 |**?**| e2 nondeterministically returns either the result of e1 or e2. This is useful in a parallel context, because it gives the program the opportunity to return whichever of e1 or e2 evaluates first.

We might wish to write a function to obtain the value of some leaf of a given tree:

```
datatype tree = Lf of int | Br of tree * tree
fun trPick t =
  case t of
    Lf i => i
  | Br (t1, t2) = (trPick t1) |?| (trPick t2)
```

This function evaluates `trPick(t1)` and `trPick(t2)` in parallel. Whichever evaluates to a value first, loosely speaking, determines the value of the choice expression as a whole. Hence, the function is likely, but not required, to return the value of the shallowest leaf in the tree. Furthermore, the evaluation of the discarded component of the choice expression—that is, the one whose result is not returned—is canceled, as its result is known not to be demanded. If the computation is running, this cancellation will free up computational resources for use elsewhere. If the computation is completed, this cancellation will be a harmless idempotent operation.

The parallel choice operator is a derived form in Manticore, as it can be expressed as a **pcase** in a straightforward manner. The expression e1 |?| e2 is desugared to:

```
pcase e1 & e2 of
    x & ? => x
  | ? & x => x
```

Parallel case gives us yet another means to write the `trProd` function:

```
datatype tree = Lf of int | Br of tree * tree
fun trProd t =
  case t of
    Lf i => i
  | Br (t1, t2) =>
      (pcase trProd t1 & trProd t2 of
          0 & ? => 0
        | ? & 0 => 0
        | p1 & p2 => p1 * p2)
```

This function will short-circuit when either the first or second branch is matched, implicitly canceling the computation of the other sub-tree. Because it is nondeterministic as to which of the matching branches is taken, a programmer should ensure that all branches that match the same discriminants yield acceptable results. For example, if `trProd(t1)` evaluates to 0 and `trProd(t2)` evaluates to 1, then either the first branch or the third branch may be taken, but both will yield the result 0.

As a third example, consider a function to find a leaf value in a tree that satisfies a given predicate. The function should return an `int option` to account for the possibility that no leaf value in the tree match the predicate. We might mistakenly write the following code:

```
fun trFind (p, t) =
  case t of
     Lf i => if p i then SOME i else NONE
   | Br (t1, t2) => (trFind (p, t1)) |?| (trFind (p, t2))
```

In the case where the predicate p is not satisfied by any leaf values in the tree, this implementation will always return NONE, as it should. However, if the predicate is satisfied at some leaf, the function will nondeterministically return either SOME n, for a satisfying n, or NONE. In other words, this implementation will never return a false positive, but it will, nondeterministically, return a false negative. The reason for this is that as soon as one of the operands of the parallel choice operator evaluates to NONE, the evaluation of the other operand might be canceled, even if it were to eventually yield SOME n.

A correct version of trFind may be written as follows:

```
fun trFind (p, t) =
  case t of
     Lf i => if p i then SOME i else NONE
   | Br (t1, t2) =>
       (pcase trFind (p, t1) & trFind (p, t2) of
            SOME i & ? => SOME i
          | ? & SOME i => SOME i
          | NONE & NONE => NONE)
```

This version of trFind has the desired behavior. When either trFind(p, t1) or trFind(p, t2) evaluates to SOME n, the function returns that value and implicitly cancels the other evaluation. The essential computational pattern here is a parallel abort mechanism, a common device in parallel programming.

A parallel case can also be used to encode a short-circuiting parallel boolean conjunction expression. We first consider some possible alternatives. We can attempt to express parallel conjunction in terms of parallel choice using the following strategy. We mark each expression with its originating position in the conjunction; after making a parallel choice between the two marked expressions, we can determine which result to return. Thus, we can write an expression that always assumes the correct value, although it may generate redundant computation:

```
datatype z = L | R
val r = case (e1, L) |?| (e2, R) of
             (false, L) => false
           | (false, R) => false
           | (true, L)  => e2
           | (true, R)  => e1
```

This expression exhibits the desired short-circuiting behavior in the first two cases, but in the latter cases it must restart the other computation, having canceled it during the evaluation of the parallel choice expression. So, while this expression always returns the right answer, in non-short-circuiting cases its performance is no better than sequential, and probably worse.

We encounter related problems when we attempt to write a parallel conjunction in terms of **pval**, where asymmetries are inescapable.

```
val r =
  let
    pval b1 = e1
    pval b2 = e2
  in
    if (not b1)
      then false
      else e2
  end
```

This short-circuits when e1 is false, but not when e2 is false. We cannot write a parallel conjunction in terms of **pval** such that either subcomputation causes a short-circuit when false.

The **pcase** mechanism offers the best encoding of parallel conjunction:

```
val r =
  pcase e1 & e2 of
     false & ? => false
   | ? & false => false
   | true & true => true
```

Only when both evaluations complete and are true does the expression as a whole evaluate to true. If one constituent of a parallel conjunction evaluates to false, the other can be safely canceled. As soon as one expression evaluates to false, the other is canceled, and false is returned. As a convenience, Manticore provides |**andalso**| as a derived form for this expression pattern.

In addition to |**andalso**|, we provide a variety of other similar derived parallel forms whose usage we expect to be common. Examples include |**orelse**| and |*| (parallel multiplication, short-circuiting with 0). Because Manticore has a strict evaluation semantics for the sequential core language, such operations cannot be expressed as simple functions: to obtain the desired parallelism, the subcomputations must be unevaluated expressions. Thus, it may be desirable to provide a macro facility that enables a programmer to create her own novel syntactic forms in the manner of these operations.

4.6 Exceptions

The interaction of exceptions and parallel constructs must be considered in the implementation of the parallel constructs. Raises and exception handlers are first-class expressions, and, hence, they may appear at arbitrary points in a program, including in a parallel construct. For example, the following is a legal parallel-array expression:

```
[| 2+3, 5-7, raise A |]
```

Evaluating this parallel array expression should raise the exception A.

Note the following important detail. Since the compiler and runtime system are free to execute the subcomputations of a parallel array expression in any order, there is no guarantee that the first **raise** expression observed during the parallel execution corresponds to the first **raise** expression observed during a sequential execution. Thus, some compensation is required to ensure that the sequentially first exception in a given parallel array (or other implicitly-threaded parallel construct) is raised whenever multiple exceptions could be raised. Consider the following minimal example:

```
[| raise A, raise B |]
```

Although the exception B might be raised before A during a parallel execution, A must be the exception observed to be raised by the context of the parallel array expression in order to adhere to the sequential semantics. Realizing this behavior in this and other parallel constructs requires our implementation to include compensation code, with some runtime overhead.

In choosing to adopt a strict sequential core language, Manticore is committed to realizing a precise exceptions semantics in the implicitly-threaded parallel features of the language. This is in contrast to an imprecise exception semantics [34] that arise from a lazy sequential language. While a precise semantics requires a slightly more restrictive implementation of the implicitly-threaded parallel features than would be required with an imprecise semantics, we believe that support for exceptions and the precise semantics is crucial for systems programming. Furthermore, implementing the precise exception semantics is not particularly onerous.

It is possible to eliminate some or all of the compensation code with the help of program analyses. There already exist various well-known analyses for identifying exceptions that might be raised by a given computation [43,26]. If, in a parallel array expression, it is determined that no subcomputation may raise an exception, then we are able to omit the compensation code and its overhead. As another example, consider a parallel array expression where all subcomputations can raise only one and the same exception.

```
[| if x<0 then raise A else 0,
   if y>0 then raise A else 0 |]
```

The full complement of compensation code is unnecessary here, since any exception raised by any subcomputation must be the exception A.

Although exception handlers are first-class expressions, their behavior is orthogonal to that of the parallel constructs and mostly merit no special treatment in the implementation.

Note that when an exception is raised in a parallel context, the implementation should free any resources devoted to parallel computations whose results will never be demanded by virtue of the control-flow of raise. For example, in the parallel tuple

```
(| raise A, fact(100), fib(200) |)
```

the latter two computations should be abandoned as soon as possible.

4.7 Examples

We consider a few examples to illustrate the use and interaction of our language features in familiar contexts. We choose examples that stress the parallel binding and parallel case mechanisms of our design, since examples exhibiting the use of parallel arrays and comprehensions are covered well in the existing literature.

A Parallel Typechecking Interpreter. First we consider an extended example of writing a parallel typechecker and evaluator for a simple model programming language. The language in question, which we outline below, is a pure expression language with some basic features including boolean and arithmetic operators, conditionals, let bindings, and function definition and application. A program in this language can, as usual, be represented as an expression tree. Both typechecking and evaluation can be implemented as walks over expression trees, in parallel when possible. Furthermore, the typechecking and evaluation can be performed in parallel with one another. In our example, failure to type a program successfully implicitly cancels its simultaneous evaluation.

While this is not necessarily intended as a realistic example, one might wonder why parallel typechecking and evaluation is desirable in the first place. First, typechecking constitutes a single pass over the given program. If the program involves, say, recursive computation, then typechecking might finish well before evaluation. If it does, and if there is a type error, the presumably doomed evaluation will be spared the rest of its run. Furthermore, typechecking touches all parts of a program; evaluation might not.

Our language includes the following definition of types:

```
datatype ty = NatTy | BoolTy | ArrowTy of ty * ty
```

For the purposes of yielding more useful type errors, we assume each expression consists of a location (some representation of its position in the source program) and a term (its computational part). These are represented by the following datatype definition:

```
datatype term =
   NatTerm of int
 | AddTerm of exp * exp
 | BoolTerm of bool
 | IfTerm of exp * exp * exp
 | VarTerm of var
 | LetTerm of var * exp * exp
 | LamTerm of var * ty * exp
 | AppTerm of exp * exp
   . . .
withtype exp = loc * term
```

We assume that variables in the parse tree are uniquely identified.

For typechecking, we need a function that checks the equality of types. When we compare two arrow types, we can compare the domains of both types in parallel with comparison of the ranges. Furthermore, if either the domains or the ranges turn out to be not equal, we can cancel the other comparison. Here we encode this, in the ArrowTy case, as an explicit short-circuiting parallel computation:

```
fun tyEq (ty1, ty2) =
  case (ty1, ty2) of
    (BoolTy, BoolTy) => true
  | (NatTy, NatTy) => true
  | (ArrowTy (ty1a, ty1r), ArrowTy (ty2a, ty2r)) =>
      (pcase tyEq (ty1a, ty2a) & tyEq (ty1r, ty2r) of
          false & ? => false
        | ? & false => false
        | true & true => true)
  | _ => false
```

In practice, we could use the parallel-and operator |**andalso**| for the ArrowTy case

```
tyEq (ty1a, ty2a) |andalso| tyEq (ty1r, ty2r)
```

which would desugar into the expression explicitly written above.

We present a parallel typechecker as a function typeOfExp that consumes an environment (a map from variables to types) and an expression. It returns either a type, in the case that the expression is well-typed, or an error, in the case that the expression is ill-typed. We introduce a simple union type to capture the notion of a value or an error.

```
datatype 'a res = Ans of 'a | Err of loc
```

The signature of typeOfExp is

```
val typeOfExp : env * exp -> ty res
```

We consider a few representative cases of the `typeOfExp` function. To typecheck an `AddTerm` node, we can simultaneously check both subexpressions. If the first subexpression is not of type `NatTy`, we can record the error and implicitly cancel the checking of the second subexpression. The function behaves similarly if the first subexpression returns an error. Note the use of a sequential **case** inside a **pval** block to describe the desired behavior.

```
fun typeOfExp (G, e as (loc, term)) =
  case term of
     NatTerm _ => Ans NatTy
   | AddTerm (e1, e2) =
       let
         pval rty2 = typeOfExp (G, e2)
       in
         case typeOfExp (G, e1) of
            Ans NatTy =>
              (case rty2 of
                  Ans NatTy => Ans NatTy
                | Ans _ => Err (locOf e2)
                | Err loc => Err loc)
          | Ans _ => Err (locOf e1)
          | Err loc => Err loc
       end
```

The `IfTerm` case is similar to the `AddTerm` case. Its first component must have type `BoolTy`, and its second and third components must have the same type as one another.

```
   | BoolTerm _ => Ans BoolTy
   | IfTerm (e1, e2, e3) =
       let
         pval rty2 = typeOfExp (G, e2)
         pval rty3 = typeOfExp (G, e3)
       in
         case typeOfExp (G, e1) of
            Ans BoolTy =>
              (case (rty2, rty3) of
                  (Ans ty2, Ans ty3) =>
                    if tyEq (ty2, ty3)
                      then Ans ty2
                      else Err (locOf e)
                | (Err loc, _) => Err loc
                | (_, Err loc) => Err loc)
          | Ans _ => Err (locOf e1)
          | Err loc => Err loc
       end
```

In the `Apply` case, we require an arrow type for the first subexpression and the appropriate domain type for the second.

```
| ApplyTerm (e1, e2) =
    let
      pval rty2 = typeOfExp (G, e2)
    in
      case typeOfExp (G, e1) of
        Ans (ArrowTy (ty11, ty12)) =>
          (case rty2 of
             Ans ty2 =>
               if tyEq (ty2, ty11)
                 then Ans ty12
                 else Err (locOf e2)
            | Err loc => Err loc)
       | Ans _ => Err (locOf e1)
       | Err loc => Err loc
    end
```

Of course, when there are no independent subexpressions, no parallelism is available:

```
| VarTerm var =>
    (case envLookup (G, var) of
       NONE => Err (locOf e)
      | SOME ty => Ans ty)
| LamTerm (var, ty, e) =>
    (case typeOfExp (envExtend (G, (var, ty)), e) of
       Ans ty' => Ans (ArrowTy (ty, ty'))
      | Err loc => Err loc)
```

However, the representation of the environment (*e.g.*, as balanced binary tree) may enable parallelism in the envLookup and envExtend functions.

Throughout these examples, the programmer rather than the compiler is identifying opportunities for parallelism.

We have also written the typeOfExp function to report the earliest error when one exists. If we wished to report any error when multiple errors exist, then we could use a parallel case:

```
| ApplyTerm (e1, e2) =
    (pcase typeOfExp (G, e1) & typeOfExp (G, e2) of
       Ans ty1 & Ans ty2 =>
         (case ty1 of
            ArrowTy (ty11, ty12) =>
              if tyEq (ty11, ty2)
                then Ans ty12
                else Err (locOf e2)
           | _ => Err (locOf e1))
      | Err loc & ? => Err loc
      | ? & Err loc => Err loc)
```

For evaluation, we need a function to substitute a term for a variable in an expression. Substitution of closed terms for variables in a pure language is especially well-suited to a parallel implementation. Parallel instances of substitution are completely independent, so no subtle synchronization or cancellation behavior is ever required. Parallel substitution can be accomplished by means of our simplest parallel construct, the parallel tuple. We show a few cases here.

```
fun substExp (t, x, e as (p, t')) =
  (p, substTerm (t, x, t'))
and substTerm (t, x, t') =
  case t' of
     NumTerm n => NumTerm n
   | AddTerm (e1, e2) =>
       AddTerm (| substExp (t, x, e1),
                   substExp (t, x, e2) |)
   | BoolTerm b => BoolTerm b
   | IfTerm (e1, e2, e3)
       IfTerm (| substExp (t, x, e1),
                  substExp (t, x, e2),
                  substExp (t, x, e3) |)
  (* ... *)
```

Like the parallel typechecking function, the parallel evaluation function simultaneously evaluates subexpressions. Since we are not interested in identifying the first runtime error (when one exists), we use a parallel case:

```
exception EvalError
fun evalExp (p, t) =
  case t of
     NumTerm n => NumTerm n
   | AddTerm (e1, e2) =>
       (pcase evalExp e1 & evalExp e2 of
            NumTerm n1 & NumTerm n2 => NumTerm (n1 + n2)
          | otherwise => raise EvalError)
```

The IfTerm case is notable in its use of speculative evaluation of both branches. As soon as the test completes, the abandoned branch is implicitly canceled.

```
   | IfTerm (e1, e2, e3) =>
       let
         pval v2 = evalExp e2
         pval v3 = evalExp e3
       in
         case evalExp e1 of
            BoolTerm true => v2
          | BoolTerm false => v3
          | _ => raise EvalError
       end
```

We conclude the example by wrapping typechecking and evaluation together into a function that runs them in parallel. For this language, type checker, and evaluator, it is the case that a well-typed program cannot raise EvalError. If the typechecker discovers an error, the evaluation is implicitly cancelled. Note that even if the evaluation function raises an EvalError exception before the typechecking function returns an error, then the execution of the typechecking function continues until it returns an error (at which point, the first match rule applies). If the typechecking function returns any type at all, we simply discard it and return the value returned by the evaluator.

```
fun typedEval e : term res =
  pcase typeOfExp (emptyEnv, e) & evalExp e of
      Err loc & ? => Err loc
    | Ans _ & v => Ans v
```

Parallel Game Search. We now consider the problem of searching a game tree in parallel. This has been shown to be a successful technique by the Cilk group for games such as Pousse [2] and chess [12].

For simplicity, we consider the game of tic-tac-toe. Every tic-tac-toe board is associated with a score: 1 if X holds a winning position, ~1 if O holds a winning position, and 0 otherwise. We use the following polymorphic rose tree to store a tic-tac-toe game tree.

```
datatype 'a rose_tree =
    RoseTree of 'a * 'a rose_tree parray
```

Each node contains a board and the associated score, and every path from the root of the tree to a leaf encodes a complete game.

A player is either of the nullary constructors X or O; a board is a parallel array of nine player options, where NONE represents an empty square.

```
datatype player = X | O
type board = player option parray
```

Extracting the available positions from a given board is written as a parallel comprehension as follows:

```
fun availPositions (b: board) : int parray =
    [| i | s in b, i in [| 0 to 8 |] where isNone s |]
```

Generating the next group of boards given a current board and a player to move is also a parallel comprehension:

```
fun succBoards (b: board, p: player) : board parray =
    [| mapP (fn j => if i = j then SOME p else b!j)
            [| 0 to 8 |]
      | i in availPositions b |]
```

With these auxiliaries in hand we can write a function to build the full game tree using the standard minimax algorithm, where each player assumes the opponent will play the best available move at the given point in the game.

```
fun maxP a = reduceP (fn (x, y) => max (x, y)) ~1 a
fun minP a = reduceP (fn (x, y) => min (x, y)) 1 a
fun minimax (b: board, p: player) : board rose_tree =
  if gameOver b
    then RoseTree ((b, boardScore b), [| |])
    else let
            val ss = succBoards (b, p)
            val ch =
              [| minimax (b, flipPlayer p) | b in ss |]
            val chScores = [| treeScore t | t in ch |]
         in
           case p of
              X => Rose ((b, maxP chScores), ch)
            | O => Rose ((b, minP chScores), ch)
         end
```

Note that at every node in the tree, all subtrees can be computed independently of one another, as they have no interrelationships. Admittedly, one would not write a real tic-tac-toe player this way, as it omits numerous obvious and well-known improvements. Nevertheless, as written, it exhibits a high degree of parallelism and performs well relative both to a sequential version of itself in Manticore and to similar programs in other languages.

Using alpha-beta pruning yields a somewhat more realistic example. We implement it here as a pair of mutually recursive functions, maxT and minT:

```
fun maxT (b, alpha, beta) =
  if gameOver board
    then RoseTree ((b, boardScore b), [| |])
    else let
            val ss = succBoards (b, p)
            val t0 = minT (ss!0, alpha, beta)
            val alpha' = max (alpha, treeScore t0)
            fun loop i =
              if i = lengthP ss
                then [| |]
                else let
                        pval ts = loop (i + 1)
                        val ti = minT (ss!i, alpha', beta)
                     in
                       if (treeScore ti) >= beta
                         then [| ti |] (* prune *)
                         else concatP ([| ti |], ts)
                     end
            val ch = concatP ([| t0 |], loop 1)
            val chScores = [| treeScore t | t in ch |]
         in
           Rose ((b, maxP chScores), ch)
         end
  and minT (b, alpha, beta) = (* symmetric *)
```

Alpha-beta pruning is an inherently sequential algorithm, so we must adjust it slightly. This program prunes subtrees at a particular level of the search tree if they are at least as disadvantageous to the current player as an already-computed subtree. (The sequential algorithm, by contrast, considers every subtree computed thus far.) We compute one subtree sequentially as a starting point, then use its value as the pruning cutoff for the rest of the sibling subtrees. Those siblings are computed in parallel by repeatedly spawning computations in an inner loop by means of **pval**. Pruning occurs when the implicit cancellation of the **pval** mechanism cancels the evaluation of the right siblings of a particular subtree.

4.8   Conclusion

This section has discussed the implicit-parallelism mechanisms of Manticore. Although many of these mechanisms appear simple, that is a significant contribution to their appeal — they provide light-weight syntactic hints of available parallelism, relieving the programmer from the burden of orchestrating the computation. Furthermore, since **val** declaration bindings and **case** expressions are essential idioms in a functional programmer's repertoire, providing implicitly-threaded forms allows parallelism to be expressed in a familiar style.

5   Conclusion

These notes have described Manticore, a language (and implementation) for heterogeneous parallelism, supporting parallelism at multiple levels. By combining explicit concurrency and implicit parallelism into a common linguistic and execution framework, we hope to better support applications that might run on commodity processors of the near future, such as multimedia processing, computer games, small-scale simulations, *etc.* As a statically-typed, strict, functional language, Manticore (like other functional languages) emphasizes a value-oriented and mutation-free programming model, which avoids entanglements between separate threads of execution.

We have made steady progress on a prototype implementation of the Manticore language. A significant portion of the implementation is completed, and we have been able to run examples of moderate size (*e.g.* a parallel ray tracer). Some of the more novel features (*e.g.*, the **pcase** expression form) have only preliminary implementations, without significant optimization.

Acknowledgments. Portions of this work performed while Matthew Fluet was affiliated with the Toyota Technological Institute at Chicago.

Supported in part by National Science Foundation Grants 0811389 and 1010568 (transferred from 0811419). The views and conclusions contained herein are those of the authors and should not be interpreted as necessarily representing the official policies or endorsements, either expressed or implied, of these organizations or the U.S. Government.

References

1. Armstrong, J., Virding, R., Wikström, C., Williams, M.: Concurrent programming in ERLANG, 2nd edn. Prentice Hall International (UK) Ltd., Hertfordshire (1996)
2. Barton, R., Adkins, D., Prokop, H., Frigo, M., Joerg, C., Renard, M., Dailey, D., Leiserson, C.: Cilk Pousse(1998), http://people.csail.mit.edu/pousse/ (viewed on March 20, at 2:45 PM)
3. Blelloch, G.E.: Programming parallel algorithms. Communications of the ACM 39(3), 85–97 (1996)
4. Blelloch, G.E., Chatterjee, S., Hardwick, J.C., Sipelstein, J., Zagha, M.: Implementation of a portable nested data-parallel language. Journal of Parallel and Distributed Computing 21(1), 4–14 (1994)
5. Blelloch, G.E., Greiner, J.: A provable time and space efficient implementation of NESL. In: Proceedings of the 1996 ACM SIGPLAN International Conference on Functional Programming, pp. 213–225. ACM, New York (1996)
6. Blumofe, R.D., Leiserson, C.E.: Scheduling multithreaded computations by work stealing. Journal of the ACM 46(5), 720–748 (1999)
7. Carlisle, M., Hendren, L.J., Rogers, A., Reppy, J.: Supporting SPMD execution for dynamic data structures. ACM Transactions on Programming Languages and Systems 17(2), 233–263 (1995)
8. Chakravarty, M.M.T., Keller, G.: More types for nested data parallel programming. In: Proceedings of the Fifth ACM SIGPLAN International Conference on Functional Programming, pp. 94–105. ACM, New York (2000)
9. Chakravarty, M.M.T., Keller, G., Leshchinskiy, R., Pfannenstiel, W.: Nepal – Nested Data Parallelism in Haskell. In: Sakellariou, R., Keane, J.A., Gurd, J.R., Freeman, L. (eds.) Euro-Par 2001. LNCS, vol. 2150, pp. 524–534. Springer, Heidelberg (2001)
10. Chakravarty, M.M.T., Leshchinskiy, R., Peyton Jones, S., Keller, G.: Partial Vectorisation of Haskell Programs. In: Proceedings of the ACM SIGPLAN Workshop on Declarative Aspects of Multicore Programming, ACM, New York (2008)
11. Chakravarty, M.M.T., Leshchinskiy, R., Peyton Jones, S., Keller, G., Marlow, S.: Data Parallel Haskell: A status report. In: Proceedings of the ACM SIGPLAN Workshop on Declarative Aspects of Multicore Programming, pp. 10–18. ACM, New York (2007)
12. Dailey, D., Leiserson, C.E.: Using Cilk to write multiprocessor chess programs. The Journal of the International Computer Chess Association (2002)
13. Dean, J., Ghemawat, S.: MapReduce: Simplified data processing on large clusters. In: Proceedings of the Sixth Symposium on Operating Systems Design and Implementation, pp. 137–150 (December 2004)
14. Demaine, E.D.: Higher-order concurrency in Java. In: Proceedings of the Parallel Programming and Java Conference (WoTUG20)., pp. 34–47 (April 1997), http://theory.csail.mit.edu/~edemaine/papers/WoTUG20/
15. Flatt, M., Findler, R.B.: Kill-safe synchronization abstractions. In: Proceedings of the SIGPLAN Conference on Programming Language Design and Implementation (PLDI 2004), pp. 47–58 (June 2004)
16. Fluet, M., Ford, N., Rainey, M., Reppy, J., Shaw, A., Xiao, Y.: Status Report: The Manticore Project. In: Proceedings of the 2007 ACM SIGPLAN Workshop on ML, pp. 15–24. ACM, New York (2007)
17. Fluet, M., Rainey, M., Reppy, J., Shaw, A., Xiao, Y.: Manticore: A heterogeneous parallel language. In: Proceedings of the ACM SIGPLAN Workshop on Declarative Aspects of Multicore Programming, pp. 37–44. ACM, New York (2007)

18. Gansner, E.R., Reppy, J.H.: A Multi-threaded Higher-order User Interface Toolkit, Software Trends, vol. 1, pp. 61–80. John Wiley & Sons, Chichester (1993)
19. Gansner, E.R., Reppy, J.H. (eds.): The Standard ML Basis Library. Cambridge University Press, Cambridge (2004)
20. Gaudiot, J.L., DeBoni, T., Feo, J., Bohm, W., Najjar, W., Miller, P.: The Sisal model of functional programming and its implementation. In: Proceedings of the 2nd AIZU International Symposium on Parallel Algorithms / Architecture Synthesis (pAs 1997), pp. 112–123. IEEE Computer Society Press, Los Alamitos (1997)
21. Hammond, K.: Parallel SML: a Functional Language and its Implementation in Dactl. The MIT Press, Cambridge (1991)
22. Hauser, C., Jacobi, C., Theimer, M., Welch, B., Weiser, M.: Using threads in interactive systems: A case study. In: Proceedings of the 14th ACM Symposium on Operating System Principles, pp. 94–105 (December 1993)
23. Hofstee, H.P.: Cell broadband engine architecture from 20,000 feet (August 2005), http://www-128.ibm.com/developerworks/power/library/pa-cbea.html
24. Jones, M.P., Hudak, P.: Implicit and explicit parallel programming in Haskell. Tech. Rep. Research Report YALEU/DCS/RR-982, Yale University (August 1993)
25. Leroy, X.: The Objective Caml System (release 3.00) (April 2000), http://caml.inria.fr
26. Leroy, X., Pessaux, F.: Type-based analysis of uncaught exceptions. ACM Transactions on Programming Languages and Systems 22(2), 340–377 (2000)
27. Leshchinskiy, R., Chakravarty, M.M.T., Keller, G.: Higher order flattening. In: Alexandrov, V.N., van Albada, G.D., Sloot, P.M.A., Dongarra, J. (eds.) ICCS 2006. LNCS, vol. 3992, pp. 920–928. Springer, Heidelberg (2006)
28. McCarthy, J.: A Basis for a Mathematical Theory of Computation. In: Braffort, P., Hirschberg, D. (eds.) Computer Programming and Formal Systems, pp. 33–70. North-Holland, Amsterdam (1963), citeseer.ist.psu.edu/mccarthy63basis.html
29. MLton: Concurrent ML, http://mlton.org/ConcurrentML
30. Mohr, E., Kranz, D.A., Halstead Jr., R.H.: Lazy task creation: a technique for increasing the granularity of parallel programs. In: Conference record of the 1990 ACM Conference on Lisp and Functional Programming, pp. 185–197. ACM, New York (1990)
31. Nikhil, R.S.: ID Language Reference Manual. Laboratory for Computer Science. MIT, Cambridge (1991)
32. Nikhil, R.S.: Arvind: Implicit Parallel Programming in pH. Morgan Kaufmann Publishers, San Francisco (2001)
33. Olukotun, K., Hammond, L.: The future of microprocessors. ACM Queue 3(7) (September 2005), http://www.acmqueue.org
34. Peyton Jones, S., Reid, A., Henderson, F., Hoare, T., Marlow, S.: A semantics for imprecise exceptions. In: Proceedings of the SIGPLAN Conference on Programming Language Design and Implementation (PLDI 1999), pp. 25–36. ACM, New York (1999)
35. Reeves, W.T.: Particle systems — a technique for modeling a class of fuzzy objects. ACM Transactions on Graphics 2(2), 91–108 (1983)
36. Reppy, J., Russo, C., Xiao, Y.: Parallel Concurrent ML. In: Proceedings of the 14th ACM SIGPLAN International Conference on Functional Programming, pp. 257–268. ACM, New York (2009)

37. Reppy, J., Xiao, Y.: Toward a parallel implementation of Concurrent ML. In: Proceedings of the ACM SIGPLAN Workshop on Declarative Aspects of Multicore Programming. ACM, New York (2008)
38. Reppy, J.H.: CML: A higher-order concurrent language. In: Proceedings of the SIGPLAN Conference on Programming Language Design and Implementation (PLDI 1991), pp. 293–305. ACM, New York (1991)
39. Reppy, J.H.: Concurrent Programming in ML. Cambridge University Press, Cambridge (1999)
40. Russell, G.: Events in Haskell, and how to implement them. In: Proceedings of the Sixth ACM SIGPLAN International Conference on Functional Programming, pp. 157–168 (September 2001)
41. Shavit, N., Touitou, D.: Software transactional memory. In: Proceedings of the Fourteenth Annual ACM Symposium on Principles of Distributed Computing, pp. 204–213. ACM, New York (1995)
42. Shaw, A.: Data Parallelism in Manticore. Master's thesis, University of Chicago (July 2007), http://manticore.cs.uchicago.edu
43. Yi, K.: An abstract interpretation for estimating uncaught exceptions in Standard ML programs. Sci. Comput. Program. 31(1), 147–173 (1998)
44. Young, C., Szymanski, Y.N,L., Reppy, T., Pike, J., Narlikar, R., Mullender, G., Grosse, S.E.: Protium, an infrastructure for partitioned applications. In: Proceedings of the Twelfth IEEE Workshop on Hot Topics in Operating Systems (HotOS-XII), pp. 41–46 (January 2001)
45. Ziarek, L., Schatz, P., Jagannathan, S.: Stabilizers: a modular checkpointing abstraction for concurrent functional programs. In: Proceedings of the 11th ACM SIGPLAN International Conference on Functional Programming, pp. 136–147. ACM, New York (2006)

Non-monadic Models of Mutable References

Péter Diviánszky

Eötvös Loránd University, Fac. of Informatics, Programming Lang. and Compilers
Dep., Budapest, Hungary
divip@aszt.inf.elte.hu

Abstract. Pointers are known as mutable references in pure functional programming languages. In Haskell, IO-references and ST-references are the well-known monadic models of references. This paper propose a model of mutable references based on unique heaps. This model put less restriction on the evaluation order of basic reference operations. Moreover it has simpler, more tractable semantics and it supports features like shared references between heaps and virtual union of heaps.

The proposed model needs uniqueness typing. This need could be seen as a drawback but it can also be seen as a motivation for the spread of uniqueness typing in functional languages.

1 Introduction

Mutable references are well known in functional programming languages; they are called pointers in imperative languages. From now on, we will call mutable references just references.

Pointers and references are sources of several programming errors. One goal of this paper to give a safer model of references. In the pure functional language Haskell[15], references already have the following two safety properties:

- Referential transparency holds even for references.
- The are no references similar to null-pointers, so errors about null-pointers do not appear.

Haskell has monadic reference models which means that the functions on references produce computations rather than values (this is explained in Sect. 2). In the pure functional language Clean[17] there is a possibility for non-monadic models of references. These models use unique heaps which are explained in Sect. 3. Heap values represent part of the computer memory.

The difference between monadic and unique-state models is already discussed. In [20], Philip Wadler says that there is a tradeoff between monads and the unique world model (he compares the IO-monad with a unique-world IO model used in Clean): "[Unique worlds] require a sophisticated type system, and forces the code to be cluttered by passing around the current state. ... Although mentioning the state explicitly is something of a pain when there is just one state, it may become a boon if one fragments the state into separate components

Z. Horváth, R. Plasmeijer, and V. Zsók (Eds.): CEFP 2009, LNCS 6299, pp. 146–182, 2010.

representing portions of the world that do not interact. ... Further practical experience is needed to determine where the balance lies."

This paper shows how to split one component of the world, the heap. Moreover, we will also fragment the heap into several independent pieces. The evaluation order between operations on two distinct heaps is not fixed, which is an advantage over monadic models of references where the evaluation order of composed computations is fixed.

Once we have independent heap values, it is possible to explore more exciting features like shared references between heaps and virtual union of heaps (discussed in Sect. 3.8 and Sect. 3.9). These operations help to write safer pointer algorithms (examples can be found in Sect. 4).

1.1 Overview

In Sect. 2 the monadic models of IO-references and ST-references are introduced.

The proposed non-monadic model is described in Sect. 3.

It is not easy to design a new model of references because lots of different features can be supported by the model. The goal is to have a reference model with as many features as possible without sacrificing the simplicity of the semantics of the model, so I decided to include all but one the examined features.

The implementation is complicated, so we will start with a simple model, and add features one by one until we have reached the model with all the wanted features.

The examined features are the following:

feature name	introduced in	included in the proposed model
heap seeds	Sect. 3.3	No
homogeneous heaps	Sect. 3.5	Yes
separate seeds	Sect. 3.6	Yes
deletable references	Sect. 3.7	Yes
shared references	Sect. 3.8	Yes
union of heaps	Sect. 3.9	Optional

These are independent features, but the existence of all possible combinations of these features is not justified in this paper.

For each model a fast implementation and a pure implementation exist with the same interface. The pure implementations are much simpler and they help to understand the semantics of the models. Sect. 3.4 describes the background of the pure implementations of the examined models.

In Sect. 3.2 a common interface is defined which fits for each model to be examined.

Section 4 shows the expressive power of the proposed model by applications.

2   Monadic Models of References

In Haskell two types of references are defined in the base package[4]: IO-references in the `Data.IORef` module and ST-references in the `Data.STRef` module. Moreover, several unified monadic models exist, see 2.3.

IO-references and ST-references are monadic in the sense that their operations are *computations*. A computation has a side-effect and a return value. The return value of a computation cannot be used directly, which prevents the spread of side-effects in the program. Computations are values which can be composed into more complex computations. The structure of computations can be mathematically described as a monad, but the mathematical background is not needed to understand this section.

2.1 IO-References

The interface of IO-references is the following:

```
newIORef   ::        a      → IO (IORef a)
readIORef  :: IORef a       → IO a
writeIORef :: IORef a → a → IO ()
```

`IORef` σ is the type of IO-references where σ is the type of the referred value. `IO` σ is the type of IO-computations, which are computations with arbitrary side effects; σ is the type of the return value of the computation. `newIORef` maps a value to a computation which creates a reference to the value and returns the reference. `readIORef` maps a reference to a computation which reads the reference and returns the read value. `writeIORef` maps a reference and a value to a computation which writes the reference with the value and returns a unit[1] value. The exact semantics of IO-references are given in [10] and [19].

There is a syntactic sugar called do-notation[2], with which one can compose computations into more complex computations. The following function exchanges the referred values of two given references:

```
swap :: IORef a → IORef a → IO ()
swap x y = do
  a ← readIORef x
  b ← readIORef y
  writeIORef x b
  writeIORef y a
```

Let us see a simple application of `swap`:

```
main = do
  x ← newIORef 13
  y ← newIORef 14

  a ← readIORef x
  print a          -- prints 13
  swap x y
  a ← readIORef x
  print a          -- prints 14
```

---

[1] A unit value is returned in computations which are invoked only for its side effects.

[2] Do-notation can be read intuitively; the semantics of do-notation is given in [14].

Referential transparency says that same expressions should yield the same values. Referential transparency holds here because the `readIORef x` expressions denote the same computation of reading the variable x, and the two `print a` expressions are different because the variable a is defined twice[3].

2.2 ST-References

ST-references are introduced in [11]. The type of ST-references can separate different reference classes and encapsulation of references is also possible. The interface of ST-references is the following:

```
newSTRef   ::            a      → ST t (STRef t a)
readSTRef  :: STRef t a        → ST t a
writeSTRef :: STRef t a → a → ST t ()

runST      :: (∀t.ST t a) → a
```

STRef τ σ is the type of ST-references. σ is the type of the referred value and τ is always a type variable[4]. We call τ the *tag* of the reference.[5] The only purpose of the tag is to separate different reference classes.

ST τ σ is the type of an ST-computation. σ is the type of the return value of the computation and τ is a type variable which we call the *tag* of the ST-computation. An ST-computation tagged with τ can perform very limited side effects: it can only manipulate references tagged with τ.[6]

The `newSTRef`, `readSTRef` and `writeSTRef` functions perform the same task as the corresponding functions of IO-references.

`runST` is explained in 2.2.

Reference Classes. One can separate classes of ST-references via their tags. For example, the following functions swaps the referred values of two references with the same tag:

```
swap' :: STRef t a → STRef t a → ST t ()
swap' x y = do
  a ← readSTRef x
  b ← readSTRef y
  writeSTRef x b
  writeSTRef y a
```

The type of `swap` is the most general type which can be given because the typing rules of the do-notation unifies the tags between the combined computations.

---

[3] The second definition of a shadows the first variable a.

[4] This type variable could be instantiated, i.e. it could be replaced by a more specific type in applications, but the interface of ST-references provides meaningful operations only in case of not instantiated variables.

[5] It is originally called state variable, but we put the emphasis on classes of references rather than on computations with inner states.

[6] It can also manipulate other data structures like ST-arrays but we are interested in references in this paper.

Functional Encapsulation. There is a possibility to encapsulate references into values.

As an example we will see the encapsulation of references used in the Fibonacci number computation. First let us see the function which maps an integer to an ST-computation which computes the corresponding Fibonacci number:

```
fib :: Int → ST t Integer
fib n = do
  x ← newSTRef 0
  y ← newSTRef 1

  replicateM_ n $ do
    a ← readSTRef x
    b ← readSTRef y
    writeSTRef x b
    writeSTRef y (a + b)

  readSTRef x
```

The computation creates two ST-references, x and y and replicates a computation which updates x and y applying well-known computation steps. Finally it returns the value referred by x.

The type of the computation is ST t Integer. Note that the final Integer value does not depend on the tag t. In this case the return value can be safely extracted with the runST function:

```
pureFib :: Int → Integer
pureFib n = runST (fib n)
```

runST is a function in the interface of ST-references[7]:

```
runST :: (∀t.ST t a) → a
```

The short explanation of the type of runST is that the type variable a cannot be instantiated by a type which contains t because a appears at least once outside of the scope of t.

2.3 Monad-Independent Interfaces

One can define monad-independent interfaces for references with type classes. Such interfaces are already defined in the stateref package[5], in the Data.Ref.Universal module in the ArrayRef package[3], and in the Control.Monad.Adaptive.Ref module in the Adaptive package[2].

The interface defined in Data.Ref.Universal is the most succinct, it consists of one type class[8]:

---

[7] In fact, runST is defined in another module, Control.Monad.ST.

[8] Another type class is defined for unboxed references which is not discussed here.

```
class Monad m ⇒ Ref m r    where
  newRef    ::    a →      m (r a)
  readRef  :: r a →        m a
  writeRef :: r a → a → m ()
```

The corresponding instances:

```
instance Ref IO IORef    where
  newRef    = newIORef
  readRef  = readIORef
  writeRef = writeIORef

instance Ref (ST s) (STRef s)    where
  newRef    = newSTRef
  readRef  = readSTRef
  writeRef = writeSTRef
```

The interface defined in `Control.Monad.Adaptive.Ref` is similar to the interface defined in `Data.Ref.Universal`.

The interface defined in the stateref package has a more refined structure. Separate type classes are defined for reference creation, read and write:

```
class NewRef r m a    | r → a    where
  newReference    :: a → m r

class ReadRef r m a   | r → a    where
  readReference  :: r → m a

class WriteRef r m a | r → a    where
  writeReference :: r → a → m ()
```

These type classes have three type parameters: `r` is the type of the references, `m` is the type of the monad in which the actual computation occur, and `a` is the type of the referred values. `a` is determined by `r`, this is expressed by the functional dependency[9] $r \rightarrow a$ after the vertical bars.

Lots of instances are defined for these type classes in the stateref package. Three of them are:

```
instance ReadRef (IORef a)   IO    a
instance ReadRef (TMVar a)   IO    (Maybe a)
instance ReadRef (STRef s a) (ST s) a
```

The second instance could not be defined in the simpler interface defined in `Data.Ref.Universal` because the type of the referred value is not equal to the type parameter of the reference type constructor.

3   References Based on Unique Heaps

After the introduction of the well-known monadic models of references, we will explore non-monadic models of references. This section is the main contribution of the paper together with the examples described in the next section.

As stated in the overview in Sect. 1.1, we will start with a simple model, and add features one by one until we reach a sufficiently complex model. Sect. 3.1 is a short introduction to uniqueness typing. Sect. 3.2 defines a common interface for the examined models. The following subsections introduce the mentioned features with the exception of Sect. 3.4 which gives the background of the pure implementations of the examined models.

3.1   Uniqueness Typing

In the following models of references, heap values cannot be used arbitrarily by the programmer. The restrictions on heap values can be expressed in a so-called *uniqueness type system*.

The uniqueness type system developed in Nijmegen [6] is a special extension of the Milner/Hindley/Mycroft type inferencing/checking system.

The use of uniqueness typing in Haskell raise several questions. I try to answer these questions in the following subsections.

Introduction to Uniqueness Typing. The first question we need to consider what the programmer should know about uniqueness typing.

Uniqueness typing put more restrictions on functional programs via type attributes. Uniqueness typing can be seen as an extra phase after Hindley-Milner typing, so every program which is typeable in the uniqueness type system is also typeable if we omit the uniqueness type attributes.

This means that reading code which is typeable with uniqueness type attributes is as simple as reading it without uniqueness attributes while writing code typeable with uniqueness type attributes one has to obey more rules.

The uniqueness type system described in [6] has polymorphic type attributes, but in this paper we use only the monomorphic star attribute. Values with type $*\sigma$ are *unique*. Unique values should be used in a single-threaded way, with at most a single reference to it.

For example, suppose that the function `f` has type $*\mathtt{Heap} \to (\mathtt{Int}, *\mathtt{Heap})$. Suppose that we have an application `f h`. Then `h` should have type $*\mathtt{Heap}$ and the `h` value may not be referenced in other application. Suppose that we have a binding $(\mathtt{i}, \mathtt{h}') = \mathtt{f\ h}$. Then `h'` has type $*\mathtt{Heap}$ so it should be referenced at most once in an application which needs a unique value.

The benefit of uniqueness typing is that if a value has a unique type (like the heaps in this paper), a function applied to it can update the value in-place in the object code. In-place updates improve the efficiency of functional languages while maintaining referential transparency.

Practical Aspects. Uniqueness typing is not a supported extension to the Haskell language. The main obstacles for such an extension are the little motivation to use it, and the complex interaction between uniqueness typing and other type system extensions. The simplified uniqueness typing described in [7] recently brings this extension closer.

A more viable option is to use Clean with its uniqueness type system.[9] I did not have this option in this paper because I use the type families type system extension which is not supported by the Clean compiler. However, type families are used only in the common interface, so in a simplified setting (without multiple models, in case of a concrete application) type families are not needed.

Here I chose a third option. The uniqueness properties of the source code in this section and in the examples section was tested in *runtime*.[10] Testing cannot replace type checking but in this case it claimed to have the following property: Until a program does not halt with a uniqueness runtime error, every destructive update is as safe as in the type checked case.

Discussion. Using uniqueness typing has its drawbacks and advantages which is discussed already in the introduction in Sect. 1. Here I put another remark.

The drawbacks are not only the extra complexity in typing but also the fact that uniqueness typing invalidates some natural program transformation rules. From this point of view, a functional program with unique values has a lower abstraction level.

On the other side, every program which is typeable with uniqueness type attributes can also be typed without it, so the program with unique values is purely functional but it obeys some extra rules which allows the compiler to produce more efficient code from it. From this point of view, a functional program with unique values is a normal high-level functional program with some extra information.

3.2   The Common Interface

First a common interface is defined which fits for each model of references to be examined.

The common interface consists of four basic type classes introduced here: HeapRef, NewRef, Split and NewSeed. An additional type class will be defined in Sect. 3.9 and several auxiliary functions will be added in Sect. 3.7.

The type variables in the type classes have the following meaning:

type variable	denoted objects
h	heaps
r	references
s	seeds (explained in this section)
v	referred values
i	type-level integers (explained in Sect. 3.8)

Let us see the four basic type classes.

[9] The next version of the Clean compiler might allow mixed Clean and Haskell sources too.

[10] The runtime testing of uniqueness attributes was done by assigning a unique identifier to each unique value. For this purpose I had to reimplement the type class instances defined in Sect. 3.2. I omit further details here.

Reference Read and Write Functions. The `HeapRef` type class contains the reference read and write functions:

> **class** `HeapRef h r`   **where**
>
> **type** `Value h r`
>
> `readRef` :: $r \rightarrow *h \rightarrow (\text{Value } h\ r, *h)$
>
> `writeRef` :: $r \rightarrow \text{Value } h\ r \rightarrow *h \rightarrow *h$

The `HeapRef` class is parametrized by the type of heaps and the type of references, because these two types is not determined by each-other in general. However, the type of referred values is always determined by `h` and `r` together, but cannot be expressed with them in general, so we will use an associated type synonym[18] for it: `Value h r`. A functional dependency could also be used instead of the associated type synonym as in the stateref package shown in Sect. 2.3.

Stars in types are uniqueness type attributes: heaps should be used in a single-threaded way, see Sect. 3.1.

`readRef` returns the referred value of a given reference in a given heap; it also returns the given heap unchanged. The heap to be read cannot be used for other purposes, that is why a new, unique and unchanged heap is returned by `readRef`. `writeRef` replaces the referred value of a given reference in a given heap.

One can define `modifyRef` in terms of `readRef` and `writeRef`:

> `modifyRef` :: $\text{HeapRef } h\ r \Rightarrow r \rightarrow (\text{Value } h\ r \rightarrow \text{Value } h\ r) \rightarrow *h \rightarrow *h$
>
> `modifyRef r f h` $=$ `writeRef r (f v) h`$'$ **where**
>
> $(v, h') =$ `readRef r h`

`modifyRef` gets a reference, a value-modifying function and a heap and modifies the referred value of the given reference with the function in the heap.

Reference Creation. The `NewRef` type class contains the reference creation function:

> **class** `NewRef s r`   **where**
>
> **type** `InitValue s r`
>
> `newRef` :: $\text{InitValue } s\ r \rightarrow *s \rightarrow (r, *s)$

Reference creation is separated from the reference read and write operations in a distinct type class because in some models heaps cannot provide new references.

`InitValue   s   r` is an associated type synonym similar to `Value   h   r`. `InitValue s r` and `Value h r` are equal in some of the models but not in all.

The unique state for reference creation will be called seed. In the heap-seeds model defined in Sect. 3.3, heaps are seeds also.

`newRef` returns a fresh reference which is not already in domain of any heap. `newRef` also extends every heap with the new reference and the given referred value (this will not cause problems as we will see).

Unique State Splitting. The Split type class contains the function split_2 which splits a unique state:

    class Split s   **where**

        $\text{split}_2 :: *s \rightarrow (*s, *s)$

Note that after the split the original state cannot be used any more because the uniqueness type system prevents its usage.

    The idea behind unique state splitting is that in some models seeds are splittable (but not in all of them). Splittable seeds are handy in recursive functions which consume fresh references.

Seed Creation. The NewSeed type class provides a function for seed creation:

    class NewSeed s h   **where**

        newSeed :: $*h \rightarrow (*s, *h)$

With newSeed one can create new seeds from a given heap. The idea between NewSeed is that in some models it is possible to create seeds from heaps.

3.3   Heap Seeds

First we define a model of references similar to ST-references.[11] In this model one have two data types, Ref_{hs} v t for references (the v and t type parameters are explained later) and Heap_{hs} t for heaps. One can read, write and create references with heaps, so we will have the following two instances:

    instance HeapRef (Heap_{hs} t) (Ref_{hs} v t)
    instance NewRef (Heap_{hs} t) (Ref_{hs} v t)

The name of the model is heap seeds because heaps are seeds (i.e. sources of new references) in this model. We will use "heap seeds" as a name of feature too: each model in which heaps are seeds supports the "heap seeds" feature. Our first model supports the "heap seeds" feature and no other feature introduced later, so it is a simple model in this sense.

    First we give the fast implementation of the model. Fast means here (and also later in this paper) that the creation of a new reference, and writing and reading a reference are constant-time operations.

    The definitions of the data types are simple enough:

    newtype Ref_{hs} v t = Ref_{hs} (IORef v)

A reference is modeled with an IO-reference. v is the type of the referred value. The tag t is a phantom type variable[12] which helps to relate references to particular heaps.

---

[11] It is also possible to define a heap-based model of references similar to IO-references, but we omit that step because that model is too restrictive for out purposes.

[12] A phantom type variable is a type variable which appears only on the left hand side of a data type definition. Phantom type variables are used only in the static type checking of expressions.

```
data Heap_hs t = Heap_hs
```

Heaps are implemented with nothing at all, because the actual referred values are stored in the references (in the fast implementation).

Let us see the `HeapRef` instance definition:

```
instance HeapRef (Heap_hs t) (Ref_hs v t)    where
    type Value (Heap_hs t) (Ref_hs v t) = v
    readRef (Ref_hs r) Heap_hs = unsafePerformIO $ do
      v ← readIORef r
      return (v, Heap_hs)
    writeRef (Ref_hs r) v Heap_hs = unsafePerformIO $ do
      writeIORef r v
      return Heap_hs
```

The `Value` associated type synonym equals to the first parameter of the `Ref_hs` type constructor. In this model the type of references determines the type of the referred values but it is not the case in other models.

`readRef` and `writeRef` reads and writes the underlying IO-references. Both operations use `unsafePerformIO` which turns an IO-computation into its return value. We need `unsafePerformIO` here because we are not in an IO-monad but we would like to cause some side effect.

For every use of `unsafePerformIO` a proof should be given that its actual use is safe. A claim about it can be found in 3.4. A vague explanation is that the heap is used in a single-threaded way in all operation, so we have threaded heap objects at runtime. Suppose that the `t` tag is unique for heap objects, i.e. if two heaps have the same tag then one heap was created from the other with a sequence of `readRef`, `writeRef` or `newRef` operations. References tagged with `t` store the values of the heap object tagged with `t` at every moment at runtime. So we have to destructive update the reference value when we write a reference. The `unsafePerformIO` in reference read can be explained also in a similar way.

The `NewRef` instance definition is the following:

```
instance NewRef (Heap_hs t) (Ref_hs v t)    where
    type InitValue (Heap_hs t) (Ref_hs v t) = v
    newRef v Heap_hs = unsafePerformIO $ do
      r ← newIORef v
      return (Ref_hs r, Heap_hs)
```

The definition of `InitValue` is equal to the definition of `Value` in this model. `newRef` creates a new IO-reference with the help of `unsafePerformIO`.

The only function which is needed to turn this model usable is a function which creates a new unique heap:

```
newHeap_hs :: (∀t.*Heap_hs t → a) → a
newHeap_hs f = f Heap_hs
```

newHeap_{hs} maps a function to its return value. The parameter function gets a heap for free from newHeap_{hs}. Note that a cannot be instantiated with a type which contains t because a is outside of the scope of t. This makes possible the encapsulation of references as explained in Sect. 2.2 .

Running Example (v1). Will use doubly linked list implementations as a running example to show the differences between the models. Let us see the running example for heap seeds.

We need two data structure, one will point to the ends of the list and the other will be the list node.

```
data DList₁ a
    = Empty₁
    | ∀t.NonEmpty₁
        {first₁  :: Refₕₛ (DListNode₁ t a) t
        , last₁   :: Refₕₛ (DListNode₁ t a) t
        , nodes₁  :: Heapₕₛ t
        }
```

DList_1 is the main data structure for doubly linked lists. In case of non-empty lists it contains a reference to first and last nodes in the lists and a heap. The tag is encapsulated into the list; t is an *existentially quantified type variable*[13] here.

```
data DListNode₁ t a
    = DListNode₁
        {previous₁ :: Maybe (Refₕₛ (DListNode₁ t a) t)
        , next₁     :: Maybe (Refₕₛ (DListNode₁ t a) t)
        , value₁    :: a
        }
```

DListNode_1 is the data type of nodes. Each node contains two references which points to the previous and next nodes, respectively, and a value.

```
(◁) :: a → DList₁ a → DList₁ a
x ◁ Empty₁ = singleton₁ x
x ◁ (NonEmpty₁ r₁ r₂ n)
    = NonEmpty₁ r₁′ r₂ (modifyRef r₁ f n′)    where
      (r₁′, n′) = newRef v n
      v = DListNode₁
            {previous₁ = Nothing
            , next₁     = Just r₁
            , value₁    = x
            }
      f x = x {previous₁ = Just r₁′}
```

(◁) inserts an elem into the beginning of the list. In case of non-empty lists it performs the following operations: It creates a new reference, builds a new node, rewrites the $previous_1$ field of first reference with the new node, and replaces the first reference.

$$singleton_1 :: \forall a.a \rightarrow DList_1\ a$$
$$singleton_1\ x = newHeap_{hs}\ f \quad \textbf{where}$$

$$f :: Heap_{hs}\ t \rightarrow DList_1\ a$$
$$f\ h = NonEmpty_1$$
$$\{first_1 = r$$
$$, last_1\ \ = r$$
$$, nodes_1 = h'$$
$$\}\ \textbf{where}$$

$$(r,h') = newRef\ (DListNode_1\ Nothing\ Nothing\ x)\ h$$

$singleton_1$ creates a singleton list. It can use the $newHeap_{hs}$ function because the tag is encapsulated in the list and cannot escape.

3.4   Pure Implementation

The exact semantics of references can be given by a pure implementation. The pure implementation is quite simple, which is an advantage compared to the monadic models of references.

Heaps can be modeled with functions with finite domain so it is natural to use finite maps in the pure implementation.[13] For a short introduction to finite maps, here is a simplified interface of them:

```
empty :: Map k a
keys   :: Map k a → [k]

lookup :: Ord k ⇒ k →     Map k a → Maybe a
insert :: Ord k ⇒ k → a → Map k a → Map k a
delete :: Ord k ⇒ k →     Map k a → Map k a
```

Map $\kappa\ \sigma$ is the type of finite maps. κ is the type of map *keys* and σ is the map *values*. A finite map represents a function with a finite domain which maps keys to values. An ordering should be exists on keys, but for our purposes equality would be also enough. empty represents a function with an empty domain. keys returns the domain of the represented function. lookup applies the function represented by a given map on a given key. lookup returns a Maybe a value[14]; it returns Nothing if the key is not in the domain. insert returns a map which represents a function which is either extended with a given key and value or updated on the given key with the value. delete removes a given key from the function represented by the given map.

Let us see the pure implementation of references which support the "heap seeds" feature but nothing else.

---

[13] We could use association lists also but the interface of finite maps is closer to the interface of references.

[14] A value of type Maybe σ is either Nothing or Just v where v is a value of type σ.

newtype Ref'_{hs} v t $= \text{Ref}'_{hs}$ Integer

A reference has an identifying integer value which makes possible to distinguish two references with the same tag. The type of the referred value and the tag are phantom type variables. The referred value is not stored in the reference but in the heap.

data Heap'_{hs} t $= \text{Heap}'_{hs}$ Integer (`Map Integer Any`)

A heap is a finite map which represents the function which maps the identifiers of references to referred values. The additional `Integer` value is used to generate fresh keys for the map. An invariant property is that the keys of the map are always less than this value. Note that this value is not strictly needed (it could be defined as the maximum key of the map or 1 if the map is empty), but we would like to put emphasize on the fact that the heap is used as a seed also.

`Any` is a data type defined in the `GHC.Prim` module in the ghc-prim package. One can unsafely coerce any lifted type to it, and back. One could use dynamic types here too. The difference would be that with dynamics runtime type checking could be done at some cost. See the following documentation of the `readRef` member.

instance HeapRef $(\text{Heap}'_{hs}\ t)$ $(\text{Ref}'_{hs}\ v\ t)$ **where**

    type Value $(\text{Heap}'_{hs}\ t)$ $(\text{Ref}'_{hs}\ v\ t) = v$

    readRef $(\text{Ref}'_{hs}\ i)$ h@$(\text{Heap}'_{hs}\ \_\ m)$
      $=$ **case** lookup i m **of**
        Just x $\rightarrow$ (unsafeCoerce x, h)

    writeRef $(\text{Ref}'_{hs}\ i)$ v $(\text{Heap}'_{hs}\ s\ m)$
      $= \text{Heap}'_{hs}$ s (insert i (unsafeCoerce v) m)

The definition of `Value` is the same as in the fast implementation (it should be the same).

`readRef` looks up the referred value of a given reference in a given heap. Note that this function may not fail because every time a new reference is created a corresponding referred value is stored in the heap with the same tag. The type system guarantees that one can read a tagged reference in a heap with the same tag.

`writeRef` inserts the given reference and referred value into the map.

Unfortunately this implementation is not quite pure because it uses an unsafe type-casting function, `unsafeCoerce`. This is a shortcoming even if one can prove that the actual use of `unsafeCoerce` is safe. To cure this shortcoming, we will move on to other models of references.

instance NewRef $(\text{Heap}'_{hs}\ t)$ $(\text{Ref}'_{hs}\ v\ t)$ **where**

    type InitValue $(\text{Heap}'_{hs}\ t)$ $(\text{Ref}'_{hs}\ v\ t) = v$

    newRef v $(\text{Heap}'_{hs}\ s\ m)$
      $= (\text{Ref}'_{hs}\ s, \text{Heap}'_{hs}\ (s+1)\ (\text{insert s (unsafeCoerce v) m}))$

The definition of `InitValue` is the same as in the fast implementation (it should be the same).

`newRef` returns a fresh reference and extends the heap with the new reference and a given referred value.

$$\texttt{newHeap}'_{\texttt{hs}} \; :: \; (\forall \texttt{t}.*\texttt{Heap}'_{\texttt{hs}} \; \texttt{t} \to \texttt{a}) \to \texttt{a}$$
$$\texttt{newHeap}'_{\texttt{hs}} \; \texttt{f} = \texttt{f} \; (\texttt{Heap}'_{\texttt{hs}} \; 1 \; \texttt{empty})$$

New heaps are empty; the auxiliary value for creating fresh keys is initially 1.

The Correctness of the Fast Implementation. The following theorem formulates the correctness of the fast implementation:

Theorem. Let P be a program which uses the pure implementation. Let P' be a similar program which uses the fast implementation. If P' can be type checked by the uniqueness type system of Clean, then the observable behaviour of P and P' is the same.

As we said before fast implementation of references means that the creation of a new reference, and writing and reading a reference are constant-time operations.

The correct formulation of the theorem and the proof is future work.

3.5   Homogeneous Heaps

The primary cause that we could not give a completely pure implementation for the previous model is that the heaps were not homogeneous, i.e. a heap could store values with different types because the type of the values were determined by the type of the keys instead of the heaps.

This section we introduce homogeneous heaps, where the type of the stored values are determined by the type of the heaps. Whether this fact reduces the abstraction power of the model is a subject of further investigation. The applications shown in Sect. 4 suggest that the expression power is not reduced considerably.

The fast implementation of this model is similar to the fast implementation of the previous. Let us see the pure implementation of the model which supports "heap seeds" and "homogeneous heaps" but nothing else.

$$\textbf{data Heap}_{\texttt{hom}} \; \texttt{v} \; \texttt{t} = \texttt{Heap}_{\texttt{hom}} \; \texttt{Integer} \; (\texttt{Map Integer v})$$

In case of homogeneous heaps the type of the heap is parametrized by the type of the stored values.

$$\textbf{newtype Ref}_{\texttt{hom}} \; \texttt{t} = \texttt{Ref}_{\texttt{hom}} \; \texttt{Integer}$$

A reference is also just an integer. The type constructor is not parametrized by the referred value (it could be but it is not necessary).

instance HeapRef (Heap$_{hom}$ v t) (Ref$_{hom}$ t)   **where**
    type Value (Heap$_{hom}$ v t) (Ref$_{hom}$ t) = v
    readRef (Ref$_{hom}$ i) h@(Heap$_{hom}$ _ m) = **case** lookup i m **of**
      Just x → (x, h)
    writeRef (Ref$_{hom}$ i) v (Heap$_{hom}$ s m) = Heap$_{hom}$ s (insert i v m)

The referred value is now determined by the type of the heap. The definition of readRef and writeRef is similar to the definition in the previous model. No unsafeCoerce is needed this time.

The NewRef instance definition is similar to the definition in the simple tagged model, without unsafeCoerce.

The definition of newHeap$_{hom}$ is similar to the definition in the simple tagged model.

3.6 Separate Seeds

The previous models supported the "heap seeds" feature. Let us see the model which supports the "separate seeds" and "homogeneous heaps" but nothing else. Separate seeds means that the creation of references is possible without a heap as explained in Sect. 3.2.

The fast implementation of separate seeds is not complicated. Seeds are defined similarly to heaps:

    data Seed$_{sep}$ v t = Seed$_{sep}$

A seed is implemented with nothing at all; the actual values for new references will be stored in the references.

    instance NewRef (Seed$_{sep}$ v t) (Ref$_{sep}$ t)   **where**
      type InitValue (Seed$_{sep}$ v t) (Ref$_{sep}$ t) = v
      newRef v Seed$_{sep}$ = unsafePerformIO $ **do**
        r ← newIORef (unsafeCoerce v)
        return (Ref$_{sep}$ r, Seed$_{sep}$)

The creation of references is the same as defined in 3.3.

    instance Split (Seed$_{sep}$ v t)   **where**
      split$_2$ Seed$_{sep}$ = (Seed$_{sep}$, Seed$_{sep}$)

The split$_2$ do not have to do anything as seed values are trivial.

    newHeap$_{sep}$ :: (∀t.∗Heap$_{sep}$ v t → ∗Seed$_{sep}$ v t → a) → a
    newHeap$_{sep}$ f = f Heap$_{sep}$ Seed$_{sep}$

We have no heap seeds, so every time a heap is created a corresponding seed have to be created too.

Let us see the pure implementation of the model which supports the "separate seeds" and "homogeneous heaps" but nothing else.

data Ref'_{sep} t = Ref'_{sep} Any Integer

In case of separate seeds a pure reference should also contain the value which is given when the reference is created. It has type Any because the homogeneous reference type constructor is not parametrized by the type of the referred value. This renders the implementation less pure. We could cure this by adding the type of the referred value as a parameter to Ref'_{sep} but we will give an other solution in the next section.

newtype $\text{Heap}'_{\text{sep}}$ v t = $\text{Heap}'_{\text{sep}}$ (Map Integer v)

newtype $\text{Seed}'_{\text{sep}}$ v t = $\text{Seed}'_{\text{sep}}$ Integer

$\text{Heap}'_{\text{sep}}$ v t do not have to store an auxiliary Integer value for creating fresh keys; it is stored in $\text{Seed}'_{\text{sep}}$ v t.

instance HeapRef ($\text{Heap}'_{\text{sep}}$ v t) (Ref'_{sep} t)   **where**

   type Value ($\text{Heap}'_{\text{sep}}$ v t) (Ref'_{sep} t) = v

   readRef (Ref'_{sep} d i) h@($\text{Heap}'_{\text{sep}}$ m) = **case** lookup i m **of**
     Nothing → (unsafeCoerce d, h)
     Just v   → (v, h)

   writeRef (Ref'_{sep} d i) v ($\text{Heap}'_{\text{sep}}$ m) = $\text{Heap}'_{\text{sep}}$ (insert i v m)

The interesting point is the definition of readRef. If the lookup fails then that means that the reference was never written; the referred value is the value which was stored in the reference at its creation.

instance NewRef ($\text{Seed}'_{\text{sep}}$ v t) (Ref'_{sep} t)   **where**

   type InitValue ($\text{Seed}'_{\text{sep}}$ v t) (Ref'_{sep} t) = v

   newRef v ($\text{Seed}'_{\text{sep}}$ s) = (Ref'_{sep} (unsafeCoerce v) s, $\text{Seed}'_{\text{sep}}$ $(2*s)$)

newRef stores the initial value for the reference in the reference as it has no access to the heap. Note that the auxiliary Integer value is doubled; see the next definition.

instance Split ($\text{Seed}'_{\text{sep}}$ v t)   **where**

   split_2 ($\text{Seed}'_{\text{sep}}$ s) = ($\text{Seed}'_{\text{sep}}$ $(2*s)$, $\text{Seed}'_{\text{sep}}$ $(2*s+1)$)

A seed should yield infinitely many new Integer keys. The following invariant holds: $\text{Seed}'_{\text{sep}}$ i may yield keys whose binary form is prefixed by the binary form of i. This invariant holds for newRef and split_2 too. At the same time it is guaranteed that the two split seeds will yield different keys. Note that after the split the original seed cannot be used any more because the uniqueness type system prevents its usage.

$$\mathtt{newHeap'_{sep}} \ :: \ (\forall t.* \mathtt{Heap'_{sep}} \ v \ t \rightarrow *\mathtt{Seed'_{sep}} \ v \ t \rightarrow a) \rightarrow a$$
$$\mathtt{newHeap'_{sep}} \ f = f \ (\mathtt{Heap'_{sep}} \ \mathtt{empty}) \ (\mathtt{Seed'_{sep}} \ 1)$$

$\mathtt{newHeap'_{sep}}$ creates a new heap and a corresponding new seed with the same tag.

It is possible to define a model of homogeneous maps which supports both "heap seeds" and "separate seeds" but we are not interested in it.

3.7 Deletable References

Deletable references are references which can be deleted from the heap. From a point of view, deletable references are just normal references whose referred value's type is $\mathtt{Maybe}\ \sigma$ for some σ.

Let us see the pure implementation of the model which supports "homogeneous heaps", "separate seeds" and "deletable references".

> **data** $\mathtt{Seed_{del}}\ t = \mathtt{Seed_{del}}\ \mathtt{Integer}$

The main benefit of deletable references is that the seeds for deletable references should not parametrized by the referred type because the default $\mathtt{Nothing}$ value can be given for new references of any types. This will ease the implementation of the "shared references" feature.

> **newtype** $\mathtt{Heap_{del}}\ v\ t = \mathtt{Heap_{del}}\ (\mathtt{Map\ Integer\ v})$

> **newtype** $\mathtt{Ref_{del}}\ t = \mathtt{Ref_{del}}\ \mathtt{Integer}$

The definition of the heap and reference types did not change, but be aware that $\mathtt{Heap_{del}}\ v\ t$ corresponds to $\mathtt{Heap\ (Maybe\ v)\ t}$!

> **instance** $\mathtt{HeapRef}\ (\mathtt{Heap_{del}}\ v\ t)\ (\mathtt{Ref_{del}}\ t)$ **where**
>> **type** $\mathtt{Value}\ (\mathtt{Heap_{del}}\ v\ t)\ (\mathtt{Ref_{del}}\ t) = \mathtt{Maybe}\ v$
>> $\mathtt{readRef}\ (\mathtt{Ref_{del}}\ i)\ h@(\mathtt{Heap_{del}}\ m) = (\mathtt{lookup}\ i\ m, h)$
>> $\mathtt{writeRef}\ (\mathtt{Ref_{del}}\ i)\ \mathtt{Nothing}\ (\mathtt{Heap_{del}}\ m) = \mathtt{Heap_{del}}\ (\mathtt{delete}\ i\ m)$
>> $\mathtt{writeRef}\ (\mathtt{Ref_{del}}\ i)\ (\mathtt{Just}\ v)\ (\mathtt{Heap_{del}}\ m) = \mathtt{Heap_{del}}\ (\mathtt{insert}\ i\ v\ m)$

The $\mathtt{Value}$ definition is different because $\mathtt{Heap_{del}}$ v   t corresponds to $\mathtt{Heap\ (Maybe\ v)\ t}$, so the referred value is $\mathtt{Maybe}\ v$, not v.

The type system forces us to give $\mathtt{writeRef}$ a more sophisticated definition: if the new value is $\mathtt{Nothing}$, the reference is deleted from the heap. At the same time we do not have to make a case distinction on the $\mathtt{lookup}\ i\ m$ value in the definition of $\mathtt{readRef}$.

> **instance** $\mathtt{NewRef}\ (\mathtt{Seed_{del}}\ t)\ (\mathtt{Ref_{del}}\ t)$ **where**
>> **type** $\mathtt{InitValue}\ (\mathtt{Seed_{del}}\ t)\ (\mathtt{Ref_{del}}\ t) = ()$
>> $\mathtt{newRef}\ ()\ (\mathtt{Seed_{del}}\ s) = (\mathtt{Ref_{del}}\ s, \mathtt{Seed_{del}}\ (2 * s))$

InitValue cannot determine the type of the referred value because the type of seeds is not parametrized by it. The unit type seem to be a perfect choice here.

We can define specialized functions for deletable references. These functions could be added also to the general interface:

deleteRef :: (HeapRef h r, Value h r∼Maybe v) ⇒ r → h → h
deleteRef r h = writeRef r Nothing h

deleteRef deletes a deletable reference. Its type says that if the type of the referred value is Maybe v for some v (i.e. it is a deletable reference), then the reference can be indeed deleted.

insertRef :: (HeapRef h r, Value h r∼Maybe v) ⇒ r → v → h → h
insertRef r v h = writeRef r (Just v) h

insertRef writes a reference with a new value. insertRef wraps the given value in a Just constructor.

newDeletableRef :: (NewRef s r, InitValue s r∼()) ⇒ s → (r, s)
newDeletableRef s = newRef () s

newDeletableRef allow us to omit the mandatory unit argument in the creation of a deletable reference.

3.8 Shared References

In the previous models a reference could be stored in one heap at most. Models with the "shared references" feature allow references stored in more than one heap.

Type-Level Integers. Heaps will be tagged with type-level integers, so we need type-level integers.

Type-level integers are build with two type constructor, Zero and Succ:

data Zero

data Succ a

For convenience, we define the first four type level integers as type synonyms:

type I_0 = Zero
type I_1 = Succ I_0
type I_2 = Succ I_1
type I_3 = Succ I_2

We will need a function **num** which maps type-level integers to the corresponding Int values. Such a function can be defined with a type class member:

```
class I m   where
   num :: m → Int
```

The I type class should have an instance on all type-level integers so we define instances for Zero and Succ:

```
instance I Zero   where
   num _ = 0
instance I a ⇒ I (Succ a)   where
   num _ = 1 + num (⊥ :: a)
```

Note that we need the ScopedTypeVariables language extension for this Succ instance.

Fast Implementation. Let us see the fast implementation of the model which supports "homogeneous heaps", "separate seeds", "deletable references" and "shared references".

```
newtype Ref_sh t = Ref_sh (IOArray Int (Maybe Any))
```

Shared references are implemented with integer-indexed mutable arrays. In case of deletable references this array contains Maybe-values. The nth elem of the array will store the referred value corresponding to the nth map. The size of the array is determined by t.

```
data Heap_sh i v t = Heap_sh
data Seed_sh i t = Seed_sh
```

The type of heaps and heaps have and additional type variable i which is a type-level integer. v is the type of the values stored in the heap and t is the tag as usual.

```
heapIndex :: ∀i v t.I i ⇒ Heap_sh i v t → Int
heapIndex _ = num (⊥ :: i)
seedIndex :: ∀i t.I i ⇒ Seed_sh i t → Int
seedIndex _ = num (⊥ :: i)
```

heapIndex and seedIndex are two auxiliary functions which gives back the type-level integer index of heaps and seeds as Int values.

```
instance I i ⇒ HeapRef (Heap_sh i v t) (Ref_sh t)   where
   type Value (Heap_sh i v t) (Ref_sh t) = Maybe v
   readRef (Ref_sh r) h@Heap_sh = unsafePerformIO $ do
      v ← readArray r (heapIndex h)
      return (unsafeCoerce v, Heap_sh)
```

```
writeRef (Ref_sh r) v h@Heap_sh = unsafePerformIO $ do
  writeArray r (heapIndex h) (unsafeCoerce v)
  return Heap_sh
```

Value is defined as appropriate for deletable references. `readRef` and `writeRef` reads and writes the nth value of array of the reference where n is computed from the type-level integer index of the heap. Note that the calculation of n is done in compile-time if the type-level integer is known statically. This is the case in the example shown in 3.8.

```
instance I i ⇒ NewRef (Seed_sh i t) (Ref_sh t)    where

  type InitValue (Seed_sh i t) (Ref_sh t) = ()

  newRef () s@Seed_sh = unsafePerformIO $ do
    r ← newArray (0, seedIndex s) (unsafeCoerce Nothing)
    return (Ref_sh r, Seed_sh)
```

`InitValue` is defined as appropriate for deletable references. `newRef` creates a new array of n `Nothing` values where n is computed from the type-level integer index of the seed. Usually n is known statically.

```
instance Split (Seed_sh i t)    where

  split_2 Seed_sh = (Seed_sh, Seed_sh)
```

The definition of `split_2` is nothing special.

```
newHeaps_1 :: (∀t.*(∀v.Heap_sh I_0 v t) → *Seed_sh I_0 t → a) → a
newHeaps_1 f = f Heap_sh Seed_sh

newHeaps_2 :: (∀t. *(∀v.Heap_sh I_0 v t)
                → *(∀v.Heap_sh I_1 v t)
                → *Seed_sh I_2 t
                → a) → a
newHeaps_2 f = f Heap_sh Heap_sh Seed_sh
```

A family of definitions is needed for the creation of heaps and seeds for shared references.[15] Note the number of needed maps should be known in advance.

Pure Implementation. The pure implementation of homogeneous heaps with separate seeds and deletable shared references is quite easy.

```
newtype Heap'_sh i v t = Heap'_sh (Map Integer v)

newtype Seed'_sh i t = Seed'_sh Integer
```

The extra type-level integer is a phantom type in the definition of heaps and seeds.

The type-level integer has no role in the pure implementation because finite maps may share keys, so the definition of `HeapRef`, `NewRef` and `Split` instances are the same as for deletable references.

---

[15] It is possible to give only one definition instead of this family of definitions with the help of GADTs. The description of this method is future work.

Running Example (v2). Let us see the doubly linked list running example for shared references.

With shared references we can simplify the code of the doubly linked lists defined is Sect. 3.3.

The trick is that we use three heaps instead of a heap which contains $DListNode_1$ records:

```
data DList₂ a
     = Empty₂
     | ∀t.NonEmpty₂
          {first₂      :: Ref_sh  t
          , last₂      :: Ref_sh  t
          , previous₂ :: Heap_sh I₀ (Ref_sh t) t
          , next₂      :: Heap_sh I₁ (Ref_sh t) t
          , value₂     :: Heap_sh I₂ a        t
          , seed₂      :: Seed_sh I₂ t
          }
```

Note that the type-level integers are hard-coded for best performance. An extra $seed_2$ field is needed because the heaps used here do not store seeds. In the next version this field will be eliminated.

```
(◁₂) :: a → DList₂ a → DList₂ a
x ◁₂ Empty₂ = singleton₂ x
x ◁₂ (NonEmpty₂ r₁ r₂ p n v s)
   = NonEmpty₂
        {first₂     = r'₁
        , last₂     = r₂
        , previous₂ = insertRef r₁ r'₁ p
        , next₂     = insertRef r'₁ r₁ n
        , value₂    = insertRef r'₁ x v
        , seed₂     = s'
        }   where
             (r'₁, s') = newDeletableRef s
```

The definition of $(◁_2)$ is considerably clearer. One can see that inserting a new elem to the beginning of a doubly-linked lists needs three pointer operations.

```
singleton₂ :: ∀a.a → DList₂ a
singleton₂ x = newHeaps₃ f    where

  f :: (∀v.Heap_sh I₀ v t)
     → (∀v.Heap_sh I₁ v t)
     → (∀v.Heap_sh I₂ v t)
     → Seed_sh I₂ t
     → DList₂ a

  f p n v s = NonEmpty₂ r r p n (insertRef r x v) s'    where

     (r, s') = newDeletableRef s
```

Unfortunately in the code for $singleton_2$ one have to give the type of the inner function because its type is rank 2 polymorphic.

3.9   Union of Heaps

Doubly linked lists defined in 3.8 cannot be joined because if we open two $NonEmpty_2$ values the phantom type variables cannot be unified by the type system (which is all right).

It would be nice if we could join classes of references. For that purpose we define a new type constructor:

data $t_1 :|: t_2$

The data type $t_1 :|: t_2$ has no constructor. This type will be used for tagging and tags have no runtime values.

Tag Subtyping. If c is a type constructor then c $(t_1 :|: t_2)$ will denote a type which is a subtype of both c t_1 and c t_2.

There is no subtyping in Haskell; fortunately we need a restricted form of subtyping which is manageable. Three steps are needed.

The first step is to define a type class $Incl$ for inclusion functions:

```
class Incl c   where
    left :: c a → c (a :|: b)
    left = unsafeCoerce

    right :: c b → c (a :|: b)
    right = unsafeCoerce
```

The second step is to define instances of this type class. For every a data type with a tag type variable a new instance should be defined. Fortunately $Incl$ has default definitions so this task is easy enough:

```
instance Incl Ref_sh
instance Incl Ref_sep
instance Incl (Seed_sep v)
```

In the pure implementations the instances are somewhat trickier, but that is not need in real-world applications. For example the $Incl$ instance for Ref_{del} is the following:

```
instance Incl Ref_del   where
    left  (Ref_del i) = Ref_del (2 * i)
    right (Ref_del i) = Ref_del (2 * i + 1)
```

The third step is the most tiresome: we have to use the $left$, $right$, $fmap\ left$, $fmap\ right$, ... functions explicitly in the places where the subtyping is needed. An example will be given in Sect. 3.9.

We will need the generalization of the `Functor` type class too:

class $Functor_2$ (f :: $* \rightarrow * \rightarrow *$)   **where**
  $fmap_2$ :: $(a \rightarrow b) \rightarrow f\ a\ x \rightarrow f\ b\ x$

At one point we will have to use $fmap_2$ `left` on a value x with type $Heap_{sh}$ i v t. We cannot define such instance, however it is clear that $fmap_2$ `left` x $\equiv$ `unsafeCoerce` x.

One solution is to define a dummy $Functor_2$ instance on $Heap_{sh}$ i and give safe rewrite rules which eliminates the *runtime* invocation of $fmap_2$ `left`:

instance $Functor_2$ ($Heap_{sh}$ i)   **where**
  $fmap_2$ _ = `unsafeCoerce`


```
{-# RULES "fmap/left" forall x. fmap left x = unsafeCoerce x #-}
{-# RULES "fmap/right" forall x. fmap right x = unsafeCoerce x #-}
{-# RULES "fmap2/left" forall x. fmap2 left x = unsafeCoerce x #-}
{-# RULES "fmap2/right" forall x. fmap2 right x = unsafeCoerce x #-}
```

Rewrite rules are an extension to GHC. These rules apply program transformations during compilation.

The Union Type Class. We extend the general interface with a new type class:

class Union h   **where**
  union :: $h\ t_1 \rightarrow h\ t_2 \rightarrow h\ (t_1 :|: t_2)$

An instance of `Union` will be defined for heaps in models which support the "union" feature. In the fast implementations the `Union` instances are simple:

instance Union ($Heap_{sh}$ i v)   **where**
  union $Heap_{sh}$ $Heap_{sh}$ = $Heap_{sh}$

In the pure implementation the `Union` instance can be defined with the `Data.Map.union` function. This function returns the unions of two maps. We need disjoint union so first we translate the keys in the maps:

instance Union ($Heap'_{sh}$ i v)   **where**
  union ($Heap'_{sh}$ m_1) ($Heap'_{sh}$ m_2)
    = $Heap'_{sh}$ (Data.Map.union
        (mapKeys ($\lambda x \rightarrow 2 * x$) m_1)
        (mapKeys ($\lambda x \rightarrow 2 * x + 1$) m_2))

Running Example (v3). Let us see the doubly linked list running example for union of heaps.

In models with the "union" feature we can define the join operation for doubly linked lists.

```
data DList₃ a
      = Empty₃
      | ∀t.NonEmpty₃
          {first₃    :: Ref_sh t
          ,last₃     :: Ref_sh t
          ,previous₃ :: Heap_sh I₀ (Ref_sh t) t
          ,next₃     :: Heap_sh I₁ (Ref_sh t) t
          ,value₃    :: Heap_sh I₂ a t
          }
```

$\mathtt{DList_3}$ is similar to $\mathtt{DList_2}$ defined in Sect. 3.8. Note that we do not need the $\mathtt{seed_2}$ field any more, because we can always get fresh identifiers by joining a new class of identifiers.

```
(◁₃) :: a → DList₃ a → DList₃ a
a ◁₃ b = singleton₃ a ⋈ b
```

If we have join operation then inserting a new element to the beginning of the list is quite simple.

```
(⋈) :: DList₃ a → DList₃ a → DList₃ a
a                     ⋈ Empty₃ = a
Empty₃                ⋈ b      = b
NonEmpty₃ f l p n v ⋈ NonEmpty₃ f' l' p' n' v'

  = NonEmpty₃
      {first₃    = left f
      ,last₃     = right l'
      ,previous₃ = insertRef (right' p_u f') (left l) p_u
      ,next₃     = insertRef (left' n_u l) (right f') n_u
      ,value₃    = v 'union' v'
      }   where
              p_u = fmap₂ left p 'union' fmap₂ right p'
              n_u = fmap₂ left n 'union' fmap₂ right n'
              right' :: Incl d ⇒ c (t₁ :|: t₂) → d t₂ → d (t₁ :|: t₂)
              right' _ = right
              left' :: Incl d ⇒ c (t₁ :|: t₂) → d t₁ → d (t₁ :|: t₂)
              left' _ = left
```

The union of the $\mathtt{value_3}$ heaps is simple. The union of the $\mathtt{previous_3}$ and $\mathtt{next_3}$ heaps is more complicated: these heaps stores references, and their content should also lifted.

$\mathtt{right'}$ and $\mathtt{left'}$ help the type checking of associated type synonyms. $\mathtt{right'}$ and $\mathtt{left'}$ is not needed in case of a real-world library which contains only one model and need no associated type synonyms.

3.10   The Proposed Model

Let us see again the examined features:

feature name	introduced in	included
heap seeds	Sect. 3.3	No
homogeneous heaps	Sect. 3.5	Yes
separate seeds	Sect. 3.6	Yes
deletable references	Sect. 3.7	Yes
shared references	Sect. 3.8	Yes
union of heaps	Sect. 3.9	Optional

We have to decide which one is worth to be supported. Separate seeds are useful in case of shared references but separate seeds and heap seeds together overly complicates the pure implementation. So we chose all the features but exclude heap seeds. In this way the pure implementation of the model do not use unsafe operations.

The inclusion of the "union" feature is optional. One has to consider whether it worth the extra complexity in the fast implementation.

The implementation of the final model consists of the following definitions:

```
data Ref     t
data Heap i v t
data Seed i   t

instance HeapRef (Heap i v t) (Ref t)
instance NewRef  (Seed i t)   (Ref t)

instance Split   (Seed i t)

instance Union   (Heap i v)
```

$$\text{newHeaps}_1 :: (\forall t.* (\forall v.\text{Heap } I_0 \text{ v t}) \to *\text{Seed } I_0 \text{ t} \to a) \to a$$

$$\text{newHeaps}_2 :: (\forall t.\ * (\forall v.\text{Heap } I_0 \text{ v t})$$
$$\to * (\forall v.\text{Heap } I_1 \text{ v t})$$
$$\to *\text{Seed } I_2 \text{ t}$$
$$\to a) \to a$$

3.11   Extensions

The proposed model can be extended further with additional operations. Here we consider one small extension: reference equality check. Its type signature is the following:

$$\text{equalBy} :: \text{Ref t} \to \text{Ref t} \to *\text{Heap i a t} \to (\text{Bool}, *\text{Heap i a t})$$

The heap argument is needed because otherwise the following expression would have different meaning in the pure and the fast implementation:

$$\text{would\_be\_bad} = \text{equalBy (left r) (right r)}$$

This misuse is prevented by the additional parameter because a heap cannot be united with itself; the uniqueness type system rejects the expression

$$\texttt{rejected} = \texttt{equalBy} \, (\texttt{left r}) \, (\texttt{right r}) \, (\texttt{union h h})$$

It is easy to define `equalBy`. For example in the fast implementation of the proposed model it is defined as

$$\texttt{equalBy} \, (\texttt{Ref}_{\texttt{sh}} \, \texttt{a}) \, (\texttt{Ref}_{\texttt{sh}} \, \texttt{b}) \, \texttt{Heap}_{\texttt{sh}} = (\texttt{a} \equiv \texttt{b}, \texttt{Heap}_{\texttt{sh}})$$

The equality check in the definition is the built-in equality of mutable arrays.

4   Applications

The applications defined in this section use the proposed model defined in Sect. 3.10 with the extension defined in Sect. 3.11.

For the strongly connected components implementation the "deletable references" feature is essential; for the pointer reversal reversal implementation the "shared references" feature is essential; and all implementation is influenced by the "homogeneous heaps" feature. The "separate seeds" feature is important when one tries to construct the input graphs for these algorithms.

4.1   Strongly Connected Components

We define a strongly connected component calculation algorithm. The following type and function will be handy:

```
type Set i t = Heap i () t

memberRef :: I i ⇒ Ref t → *Set i t → (Bool, *Set i t)
memberRef x s = case readRef x s of
   (Nothing, s′) → (False, s′)
   (Just _,   s′) → (True,  s′)
```

Depth-First Walk. Consider the graph on Figure 1. The result of the depth-first walk started from node A is A, B, D, E, C, F, G, H.

We represent directed graphs as functions from nodes to the list of their children:

```
type Graph t = Ref t → [Ref t]
```

The `depthFirstWalk` function gets a graph, the set of already visited nodes (usually empty at the beginning) and the nodes to be visited (usually one node at the beginning), and produces the list of reachable nodes in a depth-first order:

```
depthFirstWalk :: I i ⇒ *Graph t → *Set i t → [Ref t] → [Ref t]
depthFirstWalk g _ [] = []
```

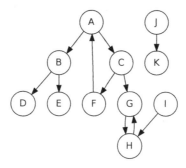

Fig. 1. Example Graph

```
depthFirstWalk g s (r : rs) = case r 'memberRef' s of
   (True,  s') →    depthFirstWalk g s' rs
   (False, s') → r : depthFirstWalk g (insertRef r () s') (g r ++ rs)
```

The implementation of **depthFirstWalk** makes a pattern match on list of nodes
to be visited. If it is not empty, it tests whether the first node is in the set of
already visited nodes. If it is not in the set, its result is a list. The head of list
is the node, and the tail of the is is the depth first walk of the same graph with
an extended set of visited nodes and an extended list of nodes to be visited (the
children of the node have to be visited).

Postorder Walk. Consider the graph on Figure 1. The result of the postorder
walk started from node A is D, E, B, F, H, G, C, A.

During the postorder walk we will use a task list. A task is an algebraic data
structure:

```
data Task a = Return a | Visit a
```

Return a is a task that the node **a** should be returned as the next node during
the walk. **Visit a** is a task that the node **a** should be visited (i.e. processed)
during the walk. The task list contains tasks which should be done in order: the
first task in the list should be done first.

The type of **postOrderWalk** is the same as the type of **depthFirstWalk**:

$$\text{postOrderWalk} :: I\ i \Rightarrow *\text{Graph } t \rightarrow *\text{Set } i\ t \rightarrow [\text{Ref } t] \rightarrow [\text{Ref } t]$$

```
postOrderWalk g s = collect s ∘ map Visit    where
   collect _ []             = []
   collect s (Return r : ts) = r : collect s ts
   collect s (Visit  r : ts) = case r 'memberRef' s of
      (True,  s') → collect s' ts
      (False, s') → collect (insertRef r () s')
                       (map Visit (g r) ++ Return r : ts)
```

The implementation first make a task list: all nodes should be visited in the given order. The local function `collect` is a recursive function.

It makes pattern matching on the task list. If it is not empty, and the first reference is a `Return` task then it returns it and goes on with the remained tasks. If the first reference is a `Visit` task then `collect` tests whether it is in the set of already visited nodes. If it is not in the set, it proceeds with an extended set and an extended task list.

The extended task list contains the children of the first reference (as `Visit` tasks) and the first reference as `Return` task, and the old tasks.

One can easily derive a variant of `postOrderWalk` which returns the visited nodes in reversed post-order and also returns the set of visited nodes:[16]

```
revPostOrderWalk
  :: I i ⇒ *Graph t → *Set i t → [Ref t] → (*Set i t, [Ref t])
```

The implementation of `revPostOrderWalk` is similar to the implementation of `postOrderWalk` but it uses a list which accumulates the nodes to be returned.

Mapped Walk. A "mapped" walk is a mapped depth-first walk, but the repeated nodes are removed from the result. In other words, `mapWalk` takes a list of nodes. It returns a list of lists with the same length as the input lists. The first list contains the nodes reachable from the first node. The second list contains the nodes reachable from the second node leaving nodes in the first list out, etc. A variant of this function will be used in the strongly connected component calculation.

Consider the graph on Figure 1. The result of the "mapped" walk started from nodes B, G, A is [E, D, B], [H, G], [F, C, A].

The type of `mapWalk` is similar to the type of `depthFirstWalk` but it returns list of lists of nodes:

```
mapWalk :: I i ⇒ *Graph t → *Set i t → [Ref t] → [[Ref t]]
mapWalk g _ []      = []
mapWalk g s (r : rs) = c : mapWalk g s' rs    where
  (s', c) = collect s [] [r]
  collect s a []      = (s, a)
  collect s a (r : rs) = case r 'memberRef' s of
    (True,  s') → collect s' a rs
    (False, s') → collect (insertRef r () s') (r : a) (g r ++ rs)
```

The `collect` local function is an accumulating variant of `depthFirstWalk`.

For the strongly connected component computation we need a variant of `mapWalk` which collects the nodes only which are *present* in the given set and returns the result in reversed order. Its type is the same as the type of `mapWalk`:

---

[16] Creation of reference maps is not simple so it is a good practice to return them after use.

$$\text{revMapWalk} :: \text{I i} \Rightarrow *\text{Graph t} \to *\text{Set i t} \to [\text{Ref t}] \to [[\text{Ref t}]]$$

The implementation of revMapWalk is similar to the implementation of mapWalk but it uses an accumulator, negates the result of the memberRef function and deletes the node from the set instead of insertion.

Strongly Connected Components. Consider the graph on Figure 1. Started from node A, the strongly connected components are {D}, {E}, {B}, {I, H, G}, {C, F, A}.[17]

The function gets a graph, the reverse of the first graph (the directed edges are reversed), an empty set and some initial nodes, and it returns the list of strongly connected components of reachable nodes in depth-first order:

$$\text{scc} :: \text{I i} \Rightarrow \text{Graph t} \to \text{Graph t} \to \text{Set i t} \to [\text{Ref t}] \to [[\text{Ref t}]]$$

```
scc g g' s
  = filter (¬ ∘ null)
  ∘ uncurry (revMapWalk g')
  ∘ revPostOrderWalk g s
```

The implementation is the composition of 3 phases: first it walks the graph in reversed post-order, then is maps a depth-first walk with the reversed graph on the node list and reverse the result, then it filters empty components out.

Note that the time consumption of the graph walks and the scc function defined here is proportional to the nodes in the graph provided that the number of the children and the parents of nodes in the graph is bounded.

4.2   Pointer Reversal Walk

```
replaceAndShiftOne :: Int → [a] → a → [a]
replaceAndShiftOne 0 [c] x = [x]
replaceAndShiftOne 0 (c : _ : cs) x = (x : c : cs)
replaceAndShiftOne n (c : cs) x = c : replaceAndShiftOne (n − 1) cs x
```

replaceAndShiftOne is a function which replaces a list's nth element and shift the old element one position to the right.

```
prWalk
  :: (I i, I j)
  ⇒ Heap i [Ref t] t    -- a graph
  → Heap j Int t        -- an empty map
  → Ref t               -- start node
  → [Ref t]             -- reachable nodes in depth first order
```

---

[17] If the nodes of the graphs are modules in a programming language, and the edges are dependencies between the modules, then this is the right compilation order if we want to compile the module A.

```
prWalk m₀ n t = follow m₀ n t t    where
   follow m n x t = case readRef t n of
      (Just _,  n') →    back m n' t x  -- already visited
      (Nothing, n') → t : case readRef t m of
         (Just (1 : u), m') → follow (insertRef t (x : u) m') (insertRef t 0 n') t 1
         (_,          m')  → back    m' (insertRef t 0 n') t x
   back m n x t = case equalBy x t m of
      (True,  m_) → []
      (False, m_) → let
            (Just ns, m') = readRef t m_
            (Just i, n')  = readRef t n
            m'' = insertRef t (replaceAndShiftOne i ns x) m'
            n'' = insertRef t (i + 1) n'
         in if (i + 1 ≡ length ns)
               then back   m'' n'' t (ns !! i)
               else follow m'' n'' t (ns !! (i + 1))
```

prWalk is the pointer reversal algorithm.

follow follows an edge, back goes back on an edge.

The index map contains already visited nodes. The index show how many children of the node was completely visited.

The graph is transformed in each step a little but at the end it will have its original shape.

4.3   Type Equations Solver

A type equations solving algorithm preceded by a disjoint set data structure implementation which is used in it.

Disjoint Sets type DSet i t = Heap i (Ref t) t

A disjoint set is heap with self-references.

```
follow' a m = case readRef a m of
   (Nothing, m') → (a, m')
   (Just b,  m') → follow' b m'
```

follow' follows the links until no link is found.

```
follow :: I i ⇒ Ref t → *DSet i t → (Ref t, *DSet i t)
follow a m = case readRef a m of
   (Nothing, m') → (a, m')
   (Just b,  m') → case readRef b m' of
      (Nothing, m'') → (b, m'')
      (Just c,  m'') → let
            (d, m''') = follow c m''
         in (d, insertRef a d m''')
```

follow is a faster version of follow'.

```
link :: I i ⇒ Ref t → Ref t → *DSet i t → *DSet i t
link a b m = case same a b m of
   (True,  m′) → m′
   (False, m′) → let (a′,m″) = follow a m′ in insertRef a′ b m″
```

link makes a link from the first reference to the second reference.

```
same :: I i ⇒ Ref t → Ref t → *DSet i t → (Bool, *DSet i t)
same a b m = equalBy a′ b′ m″   where

   (a′,m′) = follow a m
   (b′,m″) = follow b m′
```

same decides whether two reference are linked or not.

Type Equations Solver. This section shows an efficient type equations solver which uses type graphs.

```
type TypeGraph t = Ref t → TypePiece t
```

A type graph is a function from references to type pieces.[18]

```
data TypePiece t = Var | Con | App (Ref t) (Ref t)
```

A type piece is either a type variable, a type constructor, or a type application.

Note that type variables and type constructors do not need additional information because their positions identifies them in the type graph. Figure 2 shows the type graph of the type of the **head** function and Figure 3 shows the type graph of the type of the **map** function.

A type equation is a pair of references in the type graph:

```
type TEq t = (Ref t, Ref t)
```

The equation solving function need a type graph, type equations, and a fully separated disjoint set of the type graph nodes (which are the references of type pieces), and results a disjoint set which represents the unifications needed to solve the type equations[19]:

```
solveEquations
   :: I i ⇒ TypeGraph t → [TEq t] → DSet i t → DSet i t
```

The input type graph is the union of the type graphs made from the left and right hand sides of ordinary type equations. The input type equations are the pairs of root nodes of the type graphs made from the left and right hand sides of the ordinary type equations. For example, consider the ordinary type equations[20] (names beginning with lower letter are type variables):

---

[18] A reference map could also be used instead of a function. A function is used here because we do not alter the type graph, only read it.

[19] solveEqutions stops with an error message if there is no solution. One can easily modify this function such that is returns the unsolvable equations instead of raising an error message.

[20] These are the type equations of the single line program **f** x = (**head** x, **head** x).

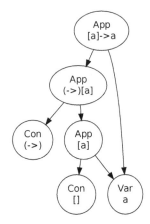

Fig. 2. Graph of the type of **head**

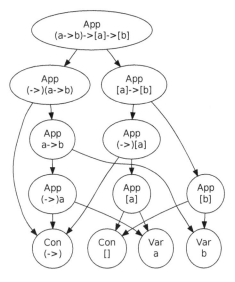

Fig. 3. Graph of the type of **map**

$$[a] \to a = x \to z$$
$$[b] \to b = x \to v$$
$$c \to d \to (c, d) = z \to v \to y$$
$$f = x \to y$$

The type graph is constructed from the pieces $[a] \to a$, $x \to z$, $[b] \to b$, $x \to v$, $c \to d \to (c, d)$, $z \to v \to y$, f and $x \to y$. There are four type equations, the first is (r_1, r_2) where r_1 is the root of $[a] \to a$ in the type graph and r_2 is the root of $x \to z$ in the type graph.

`solveEquations` is implemented as successive unification:

`solveEquations g es s = foldr (unify g) s es`

`unify` need a type graph, two nodes and a unification represented by a disjoint set, and it results a more general unification which also unifies the two subgraph of the type graph rooted in the given nodes:

`unify :: I i ⇒ TypeGraph t → (Ref t, Ref t) → DSet i t → DSet i t`

The code for `unify` is quite simple. If the nodes are equal according to the given unification, then there is nothing to do.

```
unify g (x, y) s = case same x y s of
   (True,  s′) → s′
   (False, s′) → let
      (x′, s″)  = follow x s′
      (y′, s‴) = follow y s″
   in case (g x′, g y′) of

      (App a b, App c d) → unify g (a, c) (unify g (b, d) (link x y s‴))
      (Var    , _)       → link x y s‴
      (_      , Var)     → link y x s‴
      (_      , _)       → error "The equations cannot be solved."
```

Note that the solution of the type equations may be cyclic types according to the algorithm given here, which can be seen as a feature.

The time consumption of `solveEquations` is linear; to be more precise it is proportional to the maximum of the number of type equations and the number of type application nodes in the type graph.

Here is a sketch of the proof: Let i the number of type equations and let n the number of `App` nodes in the type graph. The recursive case of `unify` happens n times in the worst case, because each time it happens, two `App` nodes are unified. Thus the total number of `unify` calls is at most $i + 2n$ because `unify` calls itself 2 times in the recursive case. Let t be the average time consumption of `unify` not counting the cost of the recursive calls. t is almost constant according to 4.3. So the time consumption of `solveEquations` is $t(i + 2n) < 3t \max\{i, n\}$ where t is an almost constant value.

5   Related Work

5.1   An Existing Model in Clean

References based on unique heaps appear in Clean compiler sources[1] and in the iTask system[16] but they are not documented. The interface is the following[21]:

---

[21] We use Haskell syntax in function types. The string `Ptr` is replaced by `HeapRef` in names.

```
newHeap          :: . Heap a
newRef           ::    a      → *Heap a → (Ref a, *Heap a)
readRef          :: Ref a     → *Heap a → (a,     *Heap a)
sreadRef_Clean   :: Ref a     →  Heap a →  a
writeRef         :: Ref a → a → *Heap a →          *Heap a
```

Ref σ is the type of references where σ is the type of the referred value. Heap σ is the type of heaps.

The dot attribute in the type of newHeap means that multiple use of newHeap is allowed and newHeap values can be seen as unique values. So new heaps can be created at any point of the program.

According our classification these are untagged homogeneous heaps.

Two Flavor of Reference Reads. A possible definition of swap in the Clean model is:

```
swap :: Ref a → Ref a → *Heap a → *Heap a
swap x y h₁ = writeRef y a (writeRef x b h₃)   where

   (a, h₂) = readRef x h₁
   (b, h₃) = readRef y h₂
```

If we can ensure that reading a reference in a heap is always done before writes on that heap, the sreadRef_Clean function can be used instead of readRef. For example, we can simplify the swap function:

```
swap′₂ :: Ref a → Ref a → *Heap a → *Heap a
swap′₂ x y h

   #! a = sreadRef_Clean x h
      b = sreadRef_Clean y h

   = writeRef y a (writeRef x b h)
```

#! is a special let expression, called let-before. Before evaluating the main expression of the let-before expression, the runtime system evaluates the bindings in the let-before expression. The uniqueness type system of Clean is smart enough to see that h is referenced only once at the point when is should be unique.

Problems. The introduced model in Clean has a serious problem: there is a interference between maps of the same type. Consider the following value:

```
x :: Char
x = sreadRef_Clean r h   where

   (r, _) = newRef 'a' newHeap
   (_, h) = newRef 'b' newHeap
```

x is either 'a' or 'b' depending on the evaluation order.

5.2   Other Related Works

The Disciplined Disciple Compiler (DDC)[12] is an explicitly lazy dialect of Haskell which supports destructive update and computational effects. It is related work because its effect system tracks what computational effects are being used in a program, without the need for state monads. But even if non-monadic references can be expressed in DDC, its effects system is more complicated than the basic form of uniqueness typing used in this paper.

Monadic regions[8] is technique for managing resources like memory areas, file handles and database connections. But it is a monadic framework.

6   Future Work

The correctness proof of the fast implementations is missing.

The models should be investigated in multithreading environment.

In theory the performance of the described models are comparable to the performance of pointer operations in imperative languages. In practice, however lots of details are missing, first of all measurements and benchmarks.

An interesting research area are the introduction of two non-destructive operations. The first is a non-destructive reference read operation, which does not return the heap:

```
sreadRef :: HeapRef h r ⇒ r → h → Value h r
sreadRef r h = fst (readRef r h)
```

The second is a non-destructive union operation which does not block the unified heaps. These operations are easy to define but it is not easy to extend the uniqueness type system so that it accepts these operations if they do not cause trouble.

7   Conclusion

The paper investigates non-monadic models of references based on unique heaps. The main advantage over monadic models is that the evaluation order between operations on two distinct heaps is not fixed, while the evaluation order of composed computations in monadic models is fixed. Another advantage is that the proposed model has a simple functional semantics (the semantics is close to the semantics of finite maps) so it is perfect for proving properties of pointer algorithms.

With independent heap values it is possible to model shared references between heaps and virtual union of heaps. These operations help to write safer pointer algorithms.

The main shortcoming that uniqueness typing is not yet supported in Haskell. Either one can consider references based on unique heaps as a motivating example to introduce a basic form of uniqueness typing in Haskell or one can use the Clean uniqueness type system. In the second case, one has to consider that this paper use several extensions to Haskell'98. The most important extensions are multi parameter type classes and rank n types which are also available in Clean. The type families extension is only needed if one needs a common interface of several models; this is not the case in practice. One need rewrite rules (a compiler pragma in GHC) for the virtual union of heaps.

References

1. The Clean compiler sources, `http://clean.cs.ru.nl/Download/download.html`
2. The Haskell Adaptive package, `http://hackage.haskell.org/package/Adaptive`
3. The Haskell ArrayRef package, `http://hackage.haskell.org/package/ArrayRef`
4. The Haskell base package, `http://hackage.haskell.org/package/base`
5. The Haskell stateref package, `http://hackage.haskell.org/package/stateref`
6. Barendsen, E., Smetsers, S.: Uniqueness typing for functional languages with graph rewriting semantics. Mathematical Structures in Computer Science 6(6), 579–612 (1996)
7. de Vries, E., Plasmeijer, R., Abrahamson, D.M.: Uniqueness typing simplified. In: Chitil, O., Horváth, Z., Zsók, V. (eds.) IFL 2007. LNCS, vol. 5083, pp. 201–218. Springer, Heidelberg (2008)
8. Fluet, M., Morrisett, G.: Monadic regions. SIGPLAN Not. 39(9), 103–114 (2004)
9. Jones, M.P.: Type classes with functional dependencies. In: Smolka, G. (ed.) ESOP 2000. LNCS, vol. 1782, pp. 230–244. Springer, Heidelberg (2000)
10. Jones, S.P.: Tackling the awkward squad: monadic input/output, concurrency, exceptions, and foreign-language calls in haskell
11. Launchbury, J., Jones, S.L.P.: Lazy functional state threads. SIGPLAN Not. 29(6), 24–35 (1994)
12. Lippmeier, B.: Type inference and optimisation for an impure world. PhD thesis, Australian National University (2009)
13. Läufer, K., Odersky, M.: Polymorphic type inference and abstract data types. ACM Transactions on Programming Languages and Systems 16 (1994)
14. Jones, S.P., et al.: The Haskell 98 language and libraries: The revised report. Journal of Functional Programming 13(1),0-255 (2003), `http://www.haskell.org/definition/`
15. Jones, S.P., Hughes, J., et al.: Report on the Programming Language Haskell 98, A Non-strict, Purely Functional Language (February 1999)
16. Plasmeijer, R., Achten, P., Koopman, P.: itasks: executable specifications of interactive work flow systems for the web. SIGPLAN Not. 42, 141–152 (2007)
17. Plasmeijer, R., van Eekelen, M.: Concurrent Clean Version 2.0 Language Report (2001)
18. Schrijvers, T., Jones, S.P., Chakravarty, M., Sulzmann, M.: Type checking with open type functions. In: ICFP 2008: Proceeding of the 13th ACM SIGPLAN international conference on Functional programming, , pp. 51–62. ACM, New York (2008)
19. Swierstra, W., Altenkirch, T.: Beauty in the beast: A functional semantics for the awkward squad. In:Haskell 2007: Proceedings of the ACM SIGPLAN workshop on Haskell workshop, pp. 25–36. ACM, New York (2007)
20. Wadler, P.: How to declare an imperative. ACM Comput. Surv. 29(3), 240–263 (1997)

Software Testing with QuickCheck

John Hughes

Chalmers University of Technology and Quviq AB

Abstract. This paper presents a tutorial, with extensive exercises, in the use of Quviq QuickCheck—a property-based testing tool for Erlang, which enables developers to formulate formal specifications of their code and to use them for testing. We cover the basic concepts of properties and test-data generators, properties for testing abstract data types, and a state-machine modelling approach to testing stateful systems. Finally we discuss applications of QuickCheck in industry.

1 Introduction

Testing is a major part of all real software development; its practical importance can hardly be overemphasized. Yet the *rigour* with which it is performed varies enormously, from the exacting standards demanded in the aerospace industry, to sloppy *ad hoc* tests and "letting customers find the bugs". Ideally, since testing is the main way we establish that software works, then it should be founded on a formal specification of what it *means* to "work"—yet this is very rarely the case. Indeed, it is rare that a formal specification even exists.

In this paper, we present a tutorial in the use of *QuickCheck*, a tool designed to address this problem. QuickCheck enables programmers to write and test formal *properties* of their code in a simple and practical way, making it easy and attractive both to formulate formal specifications, and to use them for testing. First developed in Haskell [4], QuickCheck has become the most-used testing tool in the Haskell community, and has been emulated in many other programming languages, including Scala (ScalaCheck), Microsoft's F# (FSCheck), and even Google's Go (quick.Check). A commercial version has been implemented in Erlang at Quviq AB, with many extensions.

This tutorial introduces the Erlang version, and is largely based on parts of Quviq's training course. There are three sections, each corresponding to a lecture of around 45 minutes, followed by extensive exercises. The first section introduces the fundamental QuickCheck concepts of *properties* and test data *generators*, using simple functions on lists as examples. The second section introduces the important idea of *symbolic test cases*—generated test cases which are essentially fragments of code, rather than test data—and applies it to test implementations of abstract data types using an approach that can be traced back to Hoare. Up to this point, all the code tested is purely functional—there are no side-effects involved, no hidden state. The third section shows how to apply similar ideas to test stateful code too, using Erlang's process registry as an example.

Z. Horváth, R. Plasmeijer, and V. Zsók (Eds.): CEFP 2009, LNCS 6299, pp. 183–223, 2010.

Finally, we report on some of the industrial applications of QuickCheck, which suggest that this approach to testing really can improve the quality of real software.

2   Properties and Generators

2.1   Testing and Test Automation

How do we know that software works? The answer, almost always, is that we test it. For example, consider the `delete` function in the Erlang `lists` module, which removes an element from a list. We might test it in the Erlang shell as follows:

```
4> lists:delete(2,[1,2,3]).
[1,3]
5> lists:delete(4,[1,2,3]).
[1,2,3]
```

See, it obviously works!

The biggest problem with testing is actually *not* that bugs may remain in well-tested code—although of course they may. The *biggest* problem is that reaching acceptable quality by testing is so inordinately expensive! Testing typically accounts for around half the cost of a software project—so finding ways to reduce its cost, without compromising the quality of the result, is very valuable indeed.

Running tests manually is the most expensive way to perform them. In practice, developers automate their tests in order to write them once, then run them many times. For example, the two tests above might be automated via the function definitions

```
delete_present_test() ->
    lists:delete(2,[1,2,3]) == [1,3].

delete_absent_test() ->
    lists:delete(4,[1,2,3]) == [1,2,3].
```

Many *unit testing* tools exist to find and run such tests automatically, of which EUnit [3] is the most popular for Erlang. Such tools make running the test suite very easy, which encourages developers to do so often. Running tests often, as software evolves, helps developers to catch mistakes that break something in the code as soon as the mistake is made. This practice is the foundation of *test-driven development*, which encourages developers to write their tests even before the code itself. Under test-driven development, the tests are used as a criterion for when the job is done—coding is considered complete when all the tests pass. This approach to development is claimed to improve quality and productivity (although the results of actual studies are somewhat mixed [12]).

Yet even automated testing is expensive. Thorough testing demands an enormous volume of test code: at Ericsson, 35% of all code written is test code. Even so, it can never be economic to write a test case for every possible scenario, with the result that there is always a risk that bugs remain undetected by the test suite. In practice, many test cases are added to the test suite to provoke an error already discovered by other means—such test cases do not help to *find* the error in the first place, but they do help developers to avoid making the same mistake twice.

2.2 Property-Based Testing

How can we reduce the cost of automated testing? Since the costly part is writing the test code in the first place, the key to doing so must be to *generalise the test functions*, so that each function covers not one test case, but many. In the case of the `lists:delete` function, let us generalise the element and the list, and write *one* test function that can test `delete` with *any* element and list:

```
...lists:delete(I,L)...
```

We run into a problem immediately: we can no longer predict the "expected" result, as we did in the two tests above, unless of course we reimplement the `delete` function in another way—which rather defeats the purpose. Instead, we must find some other way to determine whether the result of `delete` is correct. We can do so by identifying a *general property* of the result that should hold in all cases—such as, that I does not occur in the list after the deletion:

```
prop_delete0(I,L) ->
   not lists:member(I, lists:delete(I,L)).
```

This is not a complete test by any means—`lists:delete` might always return the empty list, for example, and still pass this test—but on the other hand, it is applicable in *any* test case. By identifying sufficiently many such properties, we can give a complete specification of the `delete` function, which can be used to test it with any inputs whatsoever.

Once we've identified a general property such as this, we would like to test it automatically in many different cases, *without* the effort of specifying each case manually. But since the property should now hold, whatever the inputs, then we can safely *generate* them instead of choosing them by hand. This is what QuickCheck [4, 5, 10] does—we rewrite the definition above as a *QuickCheck property*,

```
prop_delete1() ->
   ?FORALL({I,L},{int(),list(int())},
          not lists:member(I, lists:delete(I,L))).
```

and then test it using QuickCheck:

```
21> eqc:quickcheck(examples:prop_delete1()).
.........................................................................
.................................
OK, passed 100 tests
```

We can read the additional line of code *logically* as

$$\forall \{I,L\} \in \texttt{int()} \times \texttt{list(int())}....$$

making a universal statement of the truth of the property. QuickCheck instead interprets {int(),list(int())} as a *test data generator*, which produces pairs of an integer and a list of integers, and uses it to generate test cases which are bound to the pattern {I,L} in the rest of the test. Note that the first argument of ?FORALL is the *binding* occurrence of the variables I and L. Running quickcheck then performs (by default) 100 random tests of the property, and in this case, they all passed—each dot represents a successful test.

Of course, such a property is a partial *formal specification* of the delete function; using QuickCheck, we test code against a formal specification, rather than a set of test cases. We focus our effort on *formulating properties*, rather than on coming up with corner cases. We find this shift in perspective not only helps us test more effectively, but also improves our understanding of the code under test, and of the problem that it solves.

2.3   Failure Diagnosis and Shrinking

Having defined a QuickCheck property, we can test it in very many test cases— for example, as follows:

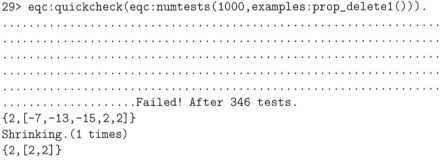

```
29> eqc:quickcheck(eqc:numtests(1000,examples:prop_delete1())).
.........................................................
.........................................................
.........................................................
.........................................................
.........................................................
....................Failed! After 346 tests.
{2,[-7,-13,-15,2,2]}
Shrinking.(1 times)
{2,[2,2]}
```

The numtests function sets the number of tests that should be performed to 1,000, and QuickCheck then begins testing—but after almost 350 tests, one of them fails! The next line of output

```
{2,[-7,-13,-15,2,2]}
```

is the failed test case itself; it is the data generated in the ?FORALL, and so is the value bound to the pattern {I,L}. So when I is 2, and L is [-7,-13,-15,2,2], then the property fails.

In this example, as in many cases, the randomly generated test case contains junk values that have nothing to do with the test failure itself. The next step is therefore to search for a *simpler*, but similar test case that also fails. We call this process "shrinking"—it is similar to Hildebrandt and Zeller's *delta-debugging* [8]—and its result in this case is the last line of output:

```
{2,[2,2]}
```

That is, the property fails when I is 2 and L is [2,2]. This is a minimal example, derived (in this case) by discarding irrelevant elements from the first failing case that was generated. We can think of shrinking as filtering away the "noise" from the test case, that random generation inevitably creates, leaving just the "signal" that is actually responsible for the test failure. Shrinking is tremendously important in making QuickCheck useful, since it automates the first stage of fault diagnosis—finding a minimal example that provokes failure. Without it, randomly generated failing cases would often be so large as to be almost useless.

When we see the result of shrinking, then the reason the property fails is almost obvious. In this case,

```
16> lists:delete(2,[2,2]).
[2]
```

we only delete the *first* occurrence of 2 from the list,

```
17> lists:member(2,[2]).
true
```

with the result that 2 is still a member of the list after deletion,

```
18> not true.
false
```

and the test fails.

Shrinking is performed via a search for smaller failing tests, using a customisable strategy (as we will see later). The number of shrinking steps reported is the number of smaller failing tests found during this search, which is of interest when optimising search strategies, but otherwise quite unimportant.

2.4   Conditional Properties

Now in fact, although the failed test does reveal a problem, it is not in the implementation of delete. Rather, the problem is sloppiness or a misconception on our part—the delete function does not delete *all* occurrences of the element from a list, but only *one* occurrence. From the documentation:

"Returns a copy of List1 where the first element matching Elem is deleted, if there is such an element."

So we must correct the *property*, not the definition of delete.

One way to correct the property is to note that it does indeed hold, *provided the list contains no duplicates*. So if we instead formulate a *conditional property*, then our tests should pass. We can define such a property as follows:

```
prop_delete2() ->
  ?FORALL({I,L},{int(),list(int())},
    ?IMPLIES(no_duplicates(L),
             not lists:member(I,lists:delete(I,L)))).

no_duplicates(L) -> lists:usort(L) == lists:sort(L).
```

where `no_duplicates(L)` returns `true` if L contains no duplicate elements, using the library function `lists:usort` which sorts a list and removes any duplicates in one go. The most interesting line here is

```
?IMPLIES(no_duplicates(L),...)
```

which we can read logically as `no_duplicates(L)` $\Longrightarrow$ ..., and which restricts test cases to those where the precondition holds.

With this new definition, testing the property succeeds:

```
39> eqc:quickcheck(examples:prop_delete2()).
.....................x........x...................x.x......xx....
.......x....x....xx....x..x............x.x.........x..
OK, passed 100 tests
```

The crosses ('x') in the output represent test cases which were generated, but were not run because the precondition was not satisfied; they are not counted among the 100 successful tests.

Note that, although each of these crosses represents a test case in which the generated list contains duplicates, it does not necessarily represent a test case that would cause the original property to fail. A list with duplicates is only a counterexample to the original property if the element we choose to delete (I) is the duplicated one—this is why counterexamples to the original property are far rarer than the crosses we see above.

Digression: on partial properties. We have just restricted our test cases to avoid lists with duplicated elements, and of course, one may wonder whether this is desirable. After all, `lists:delete` is intended to handle lists with duplicate elements also—so why should we exclude them from our tests?

The reason is quite simply that it enables us to formulate a simple property that clearly ought to hold. This property alone is not a complete specification of `lists:delete`—because it applies only to a part of the intended domain, and also because it checks only a part of the intended postcondition. (A version of `lists:delete` that always returns the empty list would satisfy this property, even though it is not correct). Thus this property is not *sufficient* for `lists:delete` to be correct, but it is *necessary*. In practice, we find that necessary conditions that are simple to formulate make good properties for testing—complemented, of course, with other tests covering the important missing cases.

We could also formulate a *necessary and sufficient* correctness property for `lists:delete`. Here is one way to do so:

```
prop_delete3() ->
  ?FORALL({I,L},{int(),list(int())},
    case lists:member(I,L) of
      false ->
        lists:delete(I,L) == L;
      true ->
```

```
    lists:any(
      fun(N) ->
        {Before,[_|After]} = lists:split(N,L),
        L == Before++[I]++After
        andalso
        lists:delete(I,L) == Before++After
        andalso
        not lists:member(I,Before)
      end,
      lists:seq(0,length(L)-1))
end).
```

That is, deleting an element from a list which does not contain it leaves the list unchanged, and deleting an element that does occur removes the first occurrence. This version of the property tests `delete` more thoroughly, but is also longer, more complex—and harder to understand.

In practice, there is a trade-off to be made between testing thoroughly and testing cheaply—complete necessary and sufficient correctness conditions may simply be too costly to formulate. Moreover, there is a risk that a programmer trying to compute a precise "expected value" for a test essentially replicates the code of the implementation—including any misconceptions in that code. For both these reasons, we find simple necessary correctness conditions, such as the simpler property of `delete` above, to be a cost-effective way of revealing bugs. For a detailed study of the effectiveness of such "partial oracles" in the setting of image compression algorithms, see Just and Schweiggert [11].

2.5   Custom Generators

Conditional properties can be very useful, but at the same time they incur a cost during testing—some test cases are generated, then discarded. If too many test cases are discarded, then testing will become very slow. Wouldn't it be better just to *generate* lists without duplicates in the first place?

QuickCheck provides an API for defining custom generators, and when test data satisfying complex invariants is needed, then writing a custom generator is the only reasonable approach. In this case, a good way to generate a random list without duplicates is first to generate a random list, and then remove duplicates from it. We can define a custom list generator which does so as follows:

```
ulist(Elem) ->
  ?LET(L,list(Elem),
     lists:usort(L)).
```

Here `Elem` is a *generator* for list elements, so `list(Elem)` is a generator for arbitrary lists of these elements. `?LET` *sequences* two generators: it binds L to the list generated by `list(Elem)`, then uses it in a second generator—in this case `lists:usort(L)`, which just returns L with the duplicates removed. Note that it would be wrong to write

```
ulist(Elem) ->
  L = list(Elem),
  lists:usort(L).
```

because `list(Elem)` returns a generator, not a list, and `lists:usort` would complain of an argument of the wrong type. Generators must be treated as an *abstract data type*, and sequenced using ?LET when multi-stage generation is needed[1].

Once a custom generator is defined, then we can use it like any other:

```
prop_delete4() ->
  ?FORALL({I,L},{int(),ulist(int())},
    not lists:member(I,lists:delete(I,L))).
```

When we test this property, then lists with duplicates are still generated by the `list(int())` generator, but rather than discarding them as ?IMPLIES does, the `ulist` generator converts them into a usable test case by removing the duplicates, and so no generated data need be discarded. In this example the gain is relatively small, because most generated lists lacked duplicates anyway, so discarding those that did was not so expensive—but in other examples ?IMPLIES may discard a large fraction of the generated test cases, and in that case replacing it by a custom test data generator can make testing very much more efficient.

2.6 Distribution of Test Cases

Returning to our original—buggy—property, note that the problem was quite hard to find: we had to run over 300 tests to do so. In retrospect, it's clear why: I is chosen from `int()`, while L is chosen from `list(int())`, and for the property to fail then I must occur in L not just once, but *twice*. The probability of finding a random integer twice in a randomly generated list is not very high! This is why many tests were needed to provoke the error.

However, it is dangerous to guess the probabilities of different kinds of test data; much better is to *measure* them. We can do so by instrumenting a QuickCheck property to collect statistics during testing. For example, we might instrument `prop_delete4` as follows, to measure how often I appears at all in L:

```
prop_delete5() ->
  ?FORALL({I,L},{int(),list(int())},
    collect(lists:member(I,L),
            not lists:member(I,lists:delete(I,L)))).
```

The effect of the line

```
collect(lists:member(I,L),...)
```

---

[1] Generators are a monad [13], and ?LET is its bind—for those familiar with those concepts.

is to collect the value of `lists:member(I,L)` in each test, and after testing is complete, to display the distribution of the values collected. In this case, testing the instrumented property yields

```
34> eqc:quickcheck(examples:prop_delete5()).
.............................................................
.....................................
OK, passed 100 tests
88% false
12% true
```

We can see from this that, most of the time, I doesn't even occur *once* in L, let alone twice!

Thus, almost ninety percent of the time, we are testing `lists:delete` in the case of an element that does not appear at all in the list. It is clear that this is not an efficient use of testing time. We can improve test efficiency by generating test cases more carefully, to increase the probability—or even to guarantee—that the element *will* occur in the list, at least once. One way to do so is to generate the list *first*, and then simply choose one of its elements to delete. We can express this by nesting ?FORALL,

```
prop_delete6() ->
  ?FORALL(L,list(int()),
    ?FORALL(I,elements(L),
      not lists:member(I,lists:delete(I,L)))).
```

where `elements(L)` generates a random element of the list L. In fact, this property has to be refined slightly further, since `elements([])` fails with an exception—what could it generate, after all? We add a precondition to avoid this case:

```
prop_delete7() ->
  ?FORALL(L,list(int()),
    ?IMPLIES(L /= [],
      ?FORALL(I,elements(L),
        not lists:member(I,lists:delete(I,L))))).
```

and now testing this revised property finds a counterexample quickly.

```
45> eqc:quickcheck(examples:prop_delete7()).
.xx.x.x.xx...x.x...x....x.......xx.....Failed! After 28 tests.
[-8,0,7,0]
0
Shrinking...(3 times)
[0,0]
0
```

In this small example, the poor distribution of tests data wasn't really important. We could find the fault quickly anyway, just by running a few hundred tests. In more complex situations, measuring the distribution of test data, and ensuring it is appropriate, is *essential* to find errors in a reasonable time.

(Why did we shrink three times, just to discard two elements from the list? Presumably because QuickCheck happened to try shrinking one of the numeric values before discarding the other element—the sequence of shrinking test cases could have been $[-8, 0, 7, 0] \rightarrow [0, 7, 0] \rightarrow [0, 0, 0] \rightarrow [0, 0]$ for example. There is no guarantee that QuickCheck will find the *shortest* shrinking path—only that the final result of shrinking can be shrunk no further.)

2.7   Properties That Fail

When a property fails, it is tempting just to correct it or delete it—after all, it was proven to be incorrect. Yet in some cases, it's worth retaining such properties, and recording the fact that they fail. We can do so by adding `fails` to the property definition:

```
prop_delete_misconception() ->
  fails(
    ?FORALL(L,list(int()),
      ?IMPLIES(L /= [],
        ?FORALL(I,elements(L),
          not lists:member(I,lists:delete(I,L)))))).
```

When such a property is tested, it is *expected* to fail:

```
49> eqc:quickcheck(examples:prop_delete_misconception()).
x...x.x....x..........OK, failed as expected. After 19 tests.
```

An error will be reported only if the property unexpectedly *passes*.

Failing properties serve two useful purposes.

- Firstly, they *document a misconception* that one might well harbour about the code. "You might think that XYZ holds, but oh no! Here is a counterexample." By documenting the misconception, we help to ensure that it will not be repeated.
- Secondly, they *test our test case generation*. If the distribution of test data that we generate is not good enough to falsify the property within the specified number of tests, then an error is reported.

2.8   Points to Remember

Using QuickCheck, we test code against a *formal specification*. Often, as in the example we presented, the errors that emerge are in the specification, not the code. Do not hold formal specifications in awe just because they are *called* specifications—they are as likely to be wrong as programs. Errors are revealed by *inconsistencies* between the properties and the code, which describe the same behaviour in two different ways. When an inconsistency is found, it is the developer's responsibility to decide whether the code or the specification is wrong, and make an appropriate correction. This results not only in high quality code, but in a *specification which has been tested against the code*, and is therefore much more likely to be correct than a formal specification which has simply been formulated.

The biggest danger in using QuickCheck is that we no longer *see* the test data—nor would we want to, there is far too much of it. As a result, we may be lulled into a false sense of security by a large number of passing tests, but fail to notice that the distribution is badly skewed. For example, if the list(int()) generator were always to generate the empty list, then all the tests in this section would pass—but that would mean very little. QuickCheck users cannot abdicate responsibility for the test data, just because they do not see it—but they exercise that responsibility at a higher level. Rather than focussing on individual test cases, we *collect statistics* on the test data, and satisfy ourselves that it is relevant and thorough. Traditional tools such as code coverage measures can be used to help evaluate the quality of our test data.

2.9   Exercises

1. **Getting Started.** The version of QuickCheck described in these notes is a commercial product, but you can download a free trial version from www.quviq.com. Follow the instructions to install QuickCheck and activate your trial licence.

   Once you have done so, you can start QuickCheck by starting an Erlang shell, and typing

   ```
   eqc:start().
   ```

   QuickCheck will download an activation from the licence server, and begin a session—you should see something like

   ```
   Starting eqc version 1.162 (compiled at {{2009,4,22},{16,10,31}})
   Licence reserved until {{2009,4,22},{19,1,51}}
   ```

   You can test whether QuickCheck is working by running

   ```
   eqc:quickcheck(true).
   ```

   which tests the property **true**—which should pass 100 tests, of course.

   QuickCheck is supplied with HTML documentation (generated by edoc); you should make a bookmark to it in your browser. The two modules needed for these exercises are eqc, which defines *properties* and the shell API, and eqc_gen which defines *generators*. Don't take more than a quick look at the documentation right now: it is more important to get on with some practical exercises.

   If you are using Emacs, then you should install the QuickCheck Emacs mode now: run

   ```
   eqc_emacs_mode:install().
   ```

   in an Erlang shell before starting Emacs.

In section 2.10 you will find the contents of a file `lecture1.erl`, containing the example properties presented above. You can either type in the file yourself, or download a copy from `http://www.chalmers.se/~rjmh/CEFP`. Open the file in an editor. If you are using Emacs, then you should find that a "QuickCheck" menu appears whenever you edit an Erlang file. Clicking on the menu, you should see sub-menus "Properties" and "Generators" that contain all the forms of property and generator that QuickCheck provides: if you're looking for something, this is a good way to find it. Choosing one of the functions from the menu prompts you for the parameters. The "full module header" entry under "Properties" can be used for quickly creating a new QuickCheck specification module. If you aren't using Emacs, then no such support is provided. You will need to manually insert

```
-include_lib("eqc/include/eqc.hrl").
```

at the head of each module that uses QuickCheck, to make the QuickCheck API available.

Compile the `lecture1` file, and use QuickCheck to test the two properties it contains.

```
c(lecture1).
eqc:quickcheck(lecture1:prop_delete()).
eqc:quickcheck(lecture1:prop_delete_misconception()).
```

2. **Simple numeric properties.** Add properties to the lecture1 file stating that the square of a real number is always positive, and that the square root of a real squares to the original real. You will need the generator for real numbers, which is called `real()`, and the square root function, which is called `math:sqrt`.

You may find this informal partial grammar of properties helpful:

```
<property> ::= ?FORALL(<pattern>,<generator>,<property>)
           |  ?IMPLIES(<boolean expression>,<property>),
           |  collect(<expression>,<property>)
           |  begin <erlang expressions>, <property> end
```

The last case was not presented above, and is just there to remind you that a `begin...end` block whose value is a property can also be used as a property. The Erlang expressions can also bind variables—for example, they might be

```
Y = math:sqrt(X)
```

3. **Properties of deletion.** The properties developed in the lecture are far from a complete characterization of deletion. To strengthen the specification, implement, test, and debug if necessary, these properties too:

   (a) Deleting an element that does *not* occur in a list leaves the list unchanged.

   (b) Deleting X from L1++[X]++L2 returns L1++L2.

   Together, these properties completely characterize deletion.

4. **Choice of test data.** So far, we have generated list elements using the primitive generator `int()`, which generates values between ±30, roughly. We could have specified the upper and lower bounds explicitly, using the generator `choose(-30,30)` instead. Use this generator to experiment with larger and smaller ranges of test data, and investigate the effect this variation has on the number of tests needed to falsify the property

```
prop_delete8() ->
   ?FORALL({I,L},{elem(),list(elem())},
            not lists:member(I, lists:delete(I,L)))
```

(where `elem()` is the element generator that you define). What general lesson can you draw about the choice of test data generator?

5. **Generating lists without duplicates.** We saw a simple way to generate lists without duplicate elements above: just generate a random list, then sort it with `usort`. One disadvantage of this method is that it only generates *sorted* lists, and so the properties we tested using it might only hold for sorted lists. Define your own generator for lists without duplicates that does not suffer from this limitation—rather, it should potentially be able to generate *any* list of elements without duplicates. You may find the function `eqc_gen:sample(G)` useful, which displays a selection of values generated by G; alternatively you can collect statistics about your generated values using a property of the form

```
prop_collect() ->
   ?FORALL(X,<my generator>,
            collect(<some property of X>,
                     true)).
```

Hint: one solution to this exercise uses the list difference operator `Xs--Ys`.

2.10   lecture1.erl

```
-module(lecture1).
-include_lib("eqc/include/eqc.hrl").

-compile(export_all).

prop_delete() ->
    ?FORALL({I,L},
             {int(),list(int())},
             ?IMPLIES(no_duplicates(L),
                       not lists:member(I,lists:delete(I,L)))).

no_duplicates(L) ->
    lists:usort(L) == lists:sort(L).
```

```
ulist(Elem) ->
    ?LET(L,list(Elem),
        lists:usort(L)).

prop_delete_misconception() ->
  fails(
    ?FORALL(L,list(int()),
      ?IMPLIES(L /= [],
        ?FORALL(I,elements(L),
          not lists:member(I,lists:delete(I,L)))))).
```

3   Symbolic Test Cases

3.1   An Abstract Data Type of Dictionaries

In this section we shall introduce a number of methods useful for testing data-structure libraries. As an example, we shall test the `dict` module from the Erlang standard libraries. This module implements a key-value store as an abstract data type, with a rich API containing such functions as

- `new()`—which returns a new, empty dictionary,
- `store(Key,Val,Dict)`—which returns a new dictionary extending `Dict` with the pair {Key,Val},
- `fetch(Key,Dict)`—which returns the value associated with `Key` in `Dict`.

It is important to note that these are *not* stateful operations: the Erlang dictionary implementation is *purely functional*. We will turn to testing stateful operations in section 4.

The representation of dictionaries is complex—in fact, they are hash tables—but our goal is not to understand it: we aim to test `dict` *without* needing to understand the internal representations. Thus we are engaged in **black box** testing, where we test the module's API, but need know nothing about the module internals. This is an appropriate kind of testing for the *user* of the `dict` module to apply.

We note in passing that the *developer* of the `dict` module would no doubt be interested in other properties, such as that invariants of the dictionary representation are preserved. This would be an example of "white box" testing, in which the module internals are also tested. Both kinds of testing are appropriate in some situations, and of course, QuickCheck can be used for either.

3.2   Generating Dictionaries

We begin by testing a very simple property indeed: the `dict` library provides a way to extract the list of keys from a dictionary; we shall check that each key is unique.

```
prop_unique_keys1() ->
  ?FORALL(D,dict(),
    no_duplicates(dict:fetch_keys(D))).
```

Now this property might or might not be true, depending on how the dict library is designed, but it is reasonable to test it in any case—by doing so, we will improve our understanding of the dict library. Thus at this point we are using QuickCheck as a program understanding tool, rather than a testing tool.

However, we cannot begin to test this property *until we can generate dictionaries*. Since we do not understand the structure of dictionaries, the only way we can do so is using the API that the dict library provides. To begin with, we shall use only the dict:new and dict:store operations to generate test data.

A first stab at a dictionary generator might be as follows:

```
dict() ->
  oneof([dict:new(),
        ?LET({K,V,D},{key(),value(),dict()},
            dict:store(K,V,D))]).
```

The oneof function is provided by QuickCheck: it combines a list of generators into a generator that chooses one of the generators randomly, and then uses it to generate its own result. In this case we either generate a new dictionary, or generate a dictionary in two stages (?LET), first by choosing a key, value, and (recursively) a dictionary, then by storing the key value pair in that dictionary D. Note that we can freely use values as generators (dict:new()), and use tuples (or lists for that matter) containing generators as generators themselves.

We can use oneof to generate more interesting data as keys and values also—for example,

```
key() -> oneof([int(),real(),atom()]).
value() -> key().
```

Here the atom() generator just chooses from a representative sample of atoms:

```
atom() -> elements([a,b,c,undefined]).
```

(where elements is another QuickCheck function that just generates one of the elements of a list). Here a, b, c and undefined are Erlang *atoms*—that is, symbolic constants—so remember that they are constants, not variables, when you see them shortly in generated test cases.

Now although the dict() generator above looks appealing, it does not actually work—and the reason is that Erlang is a strict programming language. The second choice in the list passed to oneof contains a recursive call of dict(), and this is an infinite recursion. Even though oneof only *uses* one element of its argument, the entire list, with all of its elements, must be evaluated since Erlang is strict. Thus, even when oneof chooses an empty dictionary, we still recursively construct another dictionary to store into—and the infinite loop is a fact.

We would often like to use *lazy evaluation* when building generators, so that only the part of the generator that is actually used is ever constructed. To make this possible, QuickCheck provides a generator construction ?LAZY(Gen), which is entirely equivalent to Gen, except that *constructing* the generator is always constant time. The price of constructing the argument is paid only if the generator is actually used. Thus we can avoid the infinite loop in the dict() generator as follows:

```
dict() ->
  ?LAZY(
    oneof([dict:new(),
           ?LET({K,V,D},{key(),value(),dict()},
                dict:store(K,V,D))])
      ).
```

Only one ?LAZY is needed to guarantee that recursive calls to dict() terminate at once.

Now we can test our simple property, and... surprise, surprise... it fails!

```
9> eqc:quickcheck(eqc:numtests(10000,examples2:prop_unique_keys1())).
..............................................................................
..............................................................................
..............................................................................
..............................................................................
..............................................................................
..............................................................................
...................................Failed! After 451 tests.
{dict,2,16,16,8,80,48,
    {[],[],[],[],[],[],[],[],[],[],[],[],[],[],[],[]},
    {{[[0.0|0.0],[0|0.0]],[],[],[],[],[],[],[],[],[],[],[],[],[],[]}}}
false
```

Thus this is an example of a dictionary which contains duplicate keys—but the failure report reveals a problem with our approach. Since we are engaged in *black box* testing, we do not understand the *representation* (as a hash table) of the problematic dictionary that QuickCheck has reported. We do not even know where the keys are in the structure that we see! Clearly, displaying the representation of failing test cases is not appropriate for black box testing—and in the next subsection, we will see how to avoid it.

3.3 Symbolic Test Cases

As we just saw, the *representation* of test data is often not useful for understanding a test failure. Instead, we would like to know *how the test data was constructed* using the API under test. We can indeed display this information instead—if we construct a *symbolic representation* of the test case, instead of its actual value.

QuickCheck supports a simple symbolic representation of function calls as Erlang terms: the term {call,*M*,*F*,*Args*} is used to represent the function call $M : F(...Args...)$. Symbolic representations can be interpreted using the function eval(X), which takes any term X *containing* symbolic function calls, and replaces each call by its value. Thus we can convert our dictionary generator to generate symbolic dictionaries instead, and add a call of eval to the property like this:

```
prop_unique_keys2() ->
  ?FORALL(D,dict(),
          no_duplicates(dict:fetch_keys(eval(D)))).
```

The symbolic dictionary generator can be defined as follows:

```
dict() ->
  ?LAZY(oneof([{call,dict,new,[]},
              {call,dict,store,[key(),value(),dict()]}])).
```

Note that we no longer need to use ?LET to generate the key, value, and recursive dictionary *before* constructing the call to dict:store...we can simply insert their generators directly into the symbolic call. These generators will still be converted to proper values *before* the call to dict:store is actually made, since this now happens later on in eval(D), rather than during the generation of the test data.

Now when we test the property, then the failing case is reported in an understandable form:

```
13> eqc:quickcheck(examples2:prop_unique_keys2()).
...Failed! After 4 tests.
{call,dict,store,
    [1,0.0,
     {call,dict,store,
         [0.0,undefined,
          {call,dict,store,
              [-1.0,c,
               {call,dict,store,
                   [0.0,1,
                    {call,dict,store,
                        [0,b,
                         {call,dict,store,
                             [1.0,1,
                              {call,dict,store,
                                  [a,-1.0,{call,dict,new,[]}]}]}]}]}]}]}]}
```

We can see exactly how the dictionary with non-unique keys was constructed using the dict API: it is the value of

```
dict:store(1,0.0,
  dict:store(0,0,undefined,
    dict:store(-1.0,c,
      dict:store(0.0,1,
        dict:store(0,b,
```

```
dict:store(1.0,1,
    dict:store(a,-1.0,
        dict:new())))))))
```

It must be admitted that this information is less useful than we might have hoped. It is hard to believe that such a complex construction is *necessary* to provoke the problem we have discovered. But wait... this is just the test case that QuickCheck first generated, which as we already learned contains a lot of random noise. Shouldn't it shrink to a simpler case? Indeed, it does—here is the result of shrinking in this case:

```
Shrinking.........(9 times)
{call,dict,store,
    [0,0.0,
     {call,dict,store,
         [0.0,a,
          {call,dict,store,
              [0.0,a,
               {call,dict,store,
                   [0.0,0,
                    {call,dict,store,
                        [0,a,
                         {call,dict,store,
                             [0.0,0,
                              {call,dict,store,
                                  [a,0.0,{call,dict,new,[]}]}]}]}]}]}]}]}
false
```

Unfortunately, this term is the same size as, and has the same structure as, the original. The only simplification is that some keys and values have been replaced by others—all the numbers are now zero, for example. Sadly, this is only of limited help in understanding the cause of the failure.

What we would like, of course, is to see QuickCheck simplify the test case be eliding unnecessary symbolic calls. Why doesn't this happen? The answer is that QuickCheck cannot know the *semantics* of the test data, and so cannot know which simplifications make sense. For example, *we* know that it makes sense to simplify {call,dict,store,[K,V,D]} to just D, because D is a simpler argument of the same type. But QuickCheck cannot know this—unless we tell it! In the next section we will see how to tailor QuickCheck's shrinking strategy so that it shrinks these examples well.

3.4   Shrinking Symbolic Tests

Shrinking is one of the most useful features of QuickCheck, and so in addition to built-in strategies, QuickCheck provides many ways to tailor the shrinking for particular kinds of test data. Shrinking is thus very much under the user's control, and can be used to replace test data by any data that the user considers "simpler"—even terms that are actually larger, if that is what the user wants. Shrinking is specified as a part of generators: a QuickCheck generator specifies a set of possible test data, a probability distribution over that set, and a shrinking strategy.

In particular, QuickCheck provides a construction

```
?LETSHRINK([X1,X2,...],
           [G1,G2,...],
           Result(X1,X2,...))
```

which is intended for use in recursive generators, such as the `dict()` generator above. `?LETSHRINK` generates a list of values using `[G1,G2,...]` (which are intended to be the recursive components of the result), binds them to the variables X1, X2,..., then returns a value generated by `Result`. Should the resulting test fail, then QuickCheck will try to simplify this result to each of the values X1, X2,... in turn—in addition to the other shrinking steps inherent in G1,G2,... and `Result`.

For example, to allow symbolic calls of `dict:store` to be elided, we could use `?LETSHRINK` as follows:

```
dict() ->
  ?LAZY(oneof([{call,dict,new,[]},
               ?LETSHRINK([D],[dict()],
                          {call,dict,store,[key(),value(),D]})]))).
```

Now symbolic calls `{call,dict,store,[K,V,D]}` can shrink to D.

With this revision to the `dict()` generator, failing test cases shrink much more effectively. For example,

```
20> eqc:quickcheck(examples2:prop_unique_keys2()).
...Failed! After 4 tests.
{call,dict,store,
      [-1.0,b,
       {call,dict,store,
             [-1,-1.0,
              {call,dict,store,
                    [c,c,
                     {call,dict,store,
                           [0,-1,
                            {call,dict,store,
                                  [1.0,b,{call,dict,new,[]}]}]}]}]}]}
Shrinking.....(5 times)
{call,dict,store,[-1.0,a,{call,dict,store,[-1,0.0,{call,dict,new,[]}]}]}
false
```

All but two calls of `store` shrink away, and we are left with a dictionary that just contains two keys— -1.0 and -1. Hmmm. Does this dictionary contain duplicate keys? That may depend very critically on the exact definition of "duplicate"...!

We will not diagnose this problem further, but just close by remarking that, just as in the last section, effective shrinking makes the *cause* of a test failure very easy to spot. Effective shrinking may require domain-specific shrinking strategies, which only the user can formulate, test, and debug—but QuickCheck provides customisation mechanisms to make such strategies easy to implement.

3.5 "Hoare Testing" of Abstract Data Types

We have now developed a good *generator* for dictionaries, but the property we are testing is still very weak—many incorrect implementations would satisfy this property. In this section, we shall see how to define stronger properties that characterize correct behaviour of the library. These properties are based on Hoare's 1972 article on proving the correctness of abstract data type implementations [9], and so we refer to this kind of testing as "Hoare testing".

The key idea is to relate the implementation to an *abstract model* of the data type, which is to taken to define correct behaviour. Hoare used set-theoretic models, but we need executable Erlang ones, and so we shall model dictionaries by lists of key-value pairs, or "property lists". With this simple representation, it is easy to see how each operation should behave; moreover we can use another Erlang library, the `proplists` library, to define the operations in the model.

Having chosen a model, the first step is to *relate the implementation to the model*. This is done by defining an *abstraction function* that uses the `dict` API to convert a dictionary representation into the corresponding abstract value. In this case, this is very easy, since the `dict` API already contains an operation to do precisely that:

```
model(Dict) -> dict:to_list(Dict).
```

Now, to test each operation, we need to define a corresponding operation in the model. For example, adding a key-value pair to a property list can be achieved by

```
model_store(K,V,L) -> [{K,V} | L].
```

Correctness of each operation can then be formulated as a commuting diagram:

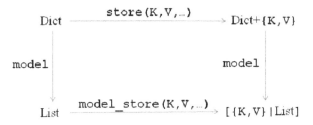

In other words, for any dictionary `Dict`, storing a key-value pair, and converting the result to its model, should give the same result as converting the original dictionary to its model, and adding the key-value pair using the model operation. If *every* operation in the API satisfies such a commuting diagram, then *any* program using the `dict` operations will behave in the same way as an abstract program using model operations instead. That is, if these properties hold, then `dict` is a correct implementation of the model.

Commuting diagrams such as these can easily be represented as QuickCheck properties. For example, the diagram above can be represented as:

```
prop_store() ->
  ?FORALL({K,V,D},
          {key(),value(),dict()},
    begin
      Dict = eval(D),
      model(dict:store(K,V,Dict)) == model_store(K,V,model(Dict))
    end).
```

A similar property can be written for each of the API operations; if all these properties pass an arbitrary number of tests, then we know that the implementation of dictionaries is correct. Thus, a complete test suite for the dict module should contain one such property for each API operation.

(The astute reader may worry that, with this approach, the two paths around the commuting diagram might result in *equivalent*, but *different* values, causing these properties to fail. For example, if we really intend to model a datatype by a mathematical set, but choose instead to use Erlang lists in our test code, then we might obtain two different lists representing the same set—two lists with the same elements, but in a different order. The solution is either to replace the equality test in the properties by an explicit test for equivalence, or to normalise the Erlang model so that equivalent values are always equal. In the case of lists representing sets, one can normalise by sorting the elements and removing duplicates: two such lists are equal if and only if they represent the same set.)

Yet the properties described, alone, are not enough to test the dict module thoroughly. It is also important that the dict() generator used in these properties can generate *any possible dictionary*—otherwise we are testing the correctness properties in only a subset of the relevant cases. The generator presented above may not do so, because it only constructs dictionaries using dict:new and dict:store. The real dict API provides a variety of other ways to construct dictionaries, such as append, update, filter and merge—and any one of these operations might break a dictionary invariant and construct a dictionary representation on which other operations fail. We therefore need to include *every* API operation that returns a dictionary in the dict() generator.

When we do so, then note that the property above does not only test the store operation, it actually tests store plus all of the operations used to construct the test data Dict—a much more thorough test.

We leave completion of the test suite as an exercise for the reader. For now, let us just test the property above—which reveals that it is not true!

```
29> eqc:quickcheck(examples2:prop_store()).
..Failed! After 3 tests.
{0,0.0,{call,dict,store,[0,0.0,{call,dict,new,[]}]}}
false
```

That is, when we insert the key-value pair {0,0.0} into a dictionary that already contains it, then the implementation and the model disagree. Assuming that a well-tested library module is probably correct, then there is a deficiency in our model—but it is far from clear what that might be. In the next section we will see how to debug failing properties of this sort.

3.6   Debugging Failing Properties

When a property fails, we often need more information than just the inputs to the test if we are to diagnose the failure easily. An easy way to generate this information is just to print additional values using io:format from within the property. Yet if we simply add such calls to our properties, then output is generated during *every* test QuickCheck runs—including the tests that pass, and the tests that QuickCheck runs while searching for a minimal failing example. The result is usually an enormous volume of information, almost all of which is irrelevant.

Ideally, we would like to add print-outs that are performed *only* in test cases that QuickCheck is reporting, namely the first failed test, and the final result of shrinking. QuickCheck provides another form of property to achieve this:

```
?WHENFAIL(Action,Property)
```

is equivalent to Property, but also performs Action when a failed test is re-ported to the user. Typically Action is a call to io:format that displays useful additional information.

For example, in the properties used in Hoare testing, then the property holds if two terms in the model are equal. We can replace the equality test by a call of the following function

```
equals(X,Y) ->
  ?WHENFAIL(io:format("~p /= ~p~n",[X,Y]),
            X==Y).
```

which is logically equivalent, but reports the two values that differ when a test fails[2]. With this modification, prop_store becomes

```
prop_store() ->
  ?FORALL({K,V,D},
          {key(),value(),dict()},
    begin
      Dict = eval(D),
      equals(model(dict:store(K,V,Dict),
             model_store(K,V,model(Dict)))
    end).
```

and retesting it generates the following output:

---

[2] Newer versions of QuickCheck include this function in the library, under the name equals.

```
31> eqc:quickcheck(eqc:numtests(10000,examples2:prop_store())).
Failed! After 1 tests.
{a,0,
 {call,dict,store,
       [a,undefined,
        {call,dict,store,
             [0,b,{call,dict,store,[undefined,0,{call,dict,new,[]}]}]}]}}
[{0,b},{a,0},{undefined,0}] /= [{a,0},{0,b},{a,undefined},{undefined,0}]
Shrinking...(3 times)
{a,0,{call,dict,store,[a,a,{call,dict,new,[]}]}}
[{a,0}] /= [{a,0},{a,a}]
false
```

The penultimate line displays the two abstract values that differ; we see immediately that the one on the right (produced by our `model_store` function) contains a duplicate key, which the real implementation avoided. Referring back to the definition of `model_store`,

```
model_store(K,V,L) -> [{K,V} | L].
```

we see at once that it does *not* model a dictionary which maintains only a *single* value per key—which is what `dict` is intended to do. So as we suspected, our model needs to be adjusted to match the real intent of the library.

In the exercises that follow, we will improve this specification of the `dict` library.

3.7   Exercises

In section 3.8 you will find the contents of a file `lecture2.erl`, which contains some of the definitions from this lecture—namely, a partial specification of the `dict` library. You can either type this file in, or download a copy from `http://www.chalmers.se/~rjmh/CEFP`. Compile the file, and run

```
eqc:module(lecture2).
```

which tests all the properties exported from the module. You will see that both properties fail.

1. **Property debugging.** The property `prop_dict()` expresses a correspondance between dictionaries constructed from a property list using the `from_list` function, and the original property list—but it fails. Generate several counter-examples using QuickCheck, examine them for common features, and form a hypothesis about why the property fails. Make a simple correction to the property so that it passes instead.

2. **Correcting the model.** The property `prop_store()` performs Hoare testing of the `store` operation, but it fails because the model is incorrect. Use QuickCheck to derive counterexamples to the property, then adjust the model (*i.e.* the functions `model` and `model_store`) until the property passes. Do *not* modify the property itself—there is no need to do so.

3. **Adding an operation.** So far, the only operations tested are `new` and `store`. Read the documentation of `dict:erase(Key,Dict)`, and define a model version `model_erase` and Hoare correctness property `prop_erase`. Use QuickCheck to check that your model is correct.

4. **Extending the generator.** To test `erase` properly, it should also be added to the `dict()` generator, since it provides yet another way to build dictionaries. Do so, and think specifically about how to shrink symbolic dictionaries once `erase` is introduced. In general, calling `erase` may make a dictionary smaller—does this mean that shrinking ought to *insert* calls of `erase`, rather than remove them?

5. **Controlling size in generators.** The purpose of this exercise is to add the `merge` function to the tested API—read the documentation of this function now. Testing `merge` demands that we construct a model and a Hoare property, but also that we add it to the `dict()` generator. This step is the trickiest, so it is the one we will focus on.

   To begin with, add a generator for calls of `merge` to the `dict()` generator, using the approach illustrated in the lecture. You will need to generate random 3-argument functions that return values, which you can do using the generator `function3(value())`. Compile your specification and test `prop_store()` again. You are likely to find that you run out of memory. The problem is that a symbolic call of `merge` contains *two* recursive dictionaries, with the result that generated terms can grow exponentially. In this situation, it is essential to limit the *size* of terms that `dict()` can generate. Add a natural number parameter `Size` to the `dict()` generator, and reduce it in the recursive calls, to ensure that generated terms cannot contain more than `Size+1` symbolic calls. (The smallest possible dictionary, {call,dict,new,[]}, contains one call, and must be generated when `Size` is zero). You can redefine an unparameterised dictionary generator via

   ```
   dict() -> ?SIZED(Size,dict(Size)).
   ```

   which gives control of the `Size` parameter to QuickCheck. Now check that your properties still pass using

   ```
   eqc:module(lecture2).
   ```

6. **Adding real numbers.** The `key()` generator provided in `lecture2.erl` generates only integers and atoms—real numbers, which caused problems in the lecture, have been omitted for simplicity. Add `real()` as a possible way to generate keys, and retest all the properties in your module using

   ```
   eqc:module({numtests,1000},lecture2).
   ```

   which returns a list of the properties that fail. You can inspect the counterexamples found using `eqc:counterexamples()`. Diagnose the failures, and correct your model so that the properties pass once again. *Hint:* read section 6.11 of the Erlang reference manual, on "Term Comparisons".

7. **Specifying merge.** Complete your specification of `merge`, by adding a
`model_merge` to the model, and a Hoare property `prop_merge()`. (This will
be easiest to do if you do *not* include real numbers in the test data).

This exercise can of course be continued much further. There are many more
operations in the `dict` module, waiting to be specified. There are other similar
modules—such as `orddict` and `gb_trees`—which provide related functionality
in a different way. These modules could be tested against the same (or a very
similar) model. Why not choose an abstract datatype implementation from the
Erlang libraries, and build a complete QuickCheck specification of your own?

3.8   lecture2.erl

```
-module(lecture2).
-include_lib("eqc/include/eqc.hrl").

-compile(export_all).

%% A generator for symbolic dictionaries

dict() ->
    ?LAZY(oneof(
      [{call,dict,new,[]},
       ?LETSHRINK([D],[dict()],
                  {call,dict,store,[key(),value(),D]})])).

%% Auxiliary generators

key() ->
    oneof([int(),atom()]).

value() ->
    key().

atom() ->
    elements([a,b,c,undefined]).

%% Dictionaries constructed using from_list behave
%% like property lists

prop_dict() ->
  ?FORALL(L,list({key(),value()}),
    ?IMPLIES(L/=[],
      ?FORALL(K,elements(proplists:get_keys(L)),
        equals(proplists:get_value(K,L) ,
               dict:fetch(K,dict:from_list(L)))))).

%% Hoare testing: the model
```

```
model(Dict) ->
    dict:to_list(Dict).
```

```
%% Hoare testing of store
```

```
model_store(K,V,L) ->
    [{K,V}|L].
```

```
prop_store() ->
    ?FORALL({K,V,D},
            {key(),value(),dict()},
            begin
              Dict = eval(D),
              equals(model(dict:store(K,V,Dict)),
                     model_store(K,V,model(Dict)))
            end).
```

```
%% Property auxiliary
```

```
equals(X,Y) ->
    ?WHENFAIL(io:format("~p /= ~p~n",[X,Y]),
             X==Y).
```

4   Testing Stateful Systems

4.1   The Process Registry

In many cases, real software manipulates internal state and offers a stateful API. A useful testing tool must be able to test stateful systems also, not just purely functional libraries. In this section we introduce QuickCheck's support for testing stateful software using abstract state machines.

The example we use for illustration is the Erlang *process registry*. This is a local name server that enables Erlang processes to find services running on the same node. Processes are named by atoms, and the central functions of the API are:

- register(Name,Pid)—which creates an association between an atom Name and a process identifier Pid,
- unregister(Name)—which removes any association for the given Name, and
- whereis(Name)—which returns the pid associated with Name, if any.

These functions are all in the erlang module containing built-in functions; detailed documentation can be found in the documentation of that module.

Interestingly, the process registry is really just another example of a key-value store—and we shall test it against a model in a similar way.

4.2   Testing Stateful Interfaces

Stateful APIs offer new challenges for testing (one good reason to prefer purely function APIs whenever possible!). The state is an implicit argument to and result from every API call, yet it is not directly accessible to the test code. We would like to model the state abstractly, just as we did in the previous section, and test in a similar way—but because the state is not directly observable, then we *cannot* define an abstraction function `model` which recovers the abstract state before and after a test. Although such a function should exist in principle, and the same diagram ought to commute as in the previous section, we cannot *implement* our tests in this manner. We must find an alternative.

However, although we cannot *observe* the abstract state directly, we can *compute* it using state transition functions that model the operations in the API under test. These functions correspond to `model_store`, `model_erase` and so on defined above, and are used in the same way to predict the model state after each operation—but whereas in the last section we could directly compare the predicted model state to the actual observed one, in this section we will only be able to use the *results* returned by the API operations. Our approach will thus be to test whether the real observed results of each API call are consistent with the *predicted* model state. If the predicted state and the actual state ever become inconsistent, then this inconsistency will eventually be observed via the result of some sequence of API calls—unless, of course, *no* sequence of calls can distinguish the two, in which case the difference is arguably of no importance.

The test cases we generate for stateful systems are *sequences* of API calls. We can gain a general idea of how such test cases are generated and used from the property used to test the registry:

```
prop_registry() ->
  ?FORALL(Cmds,commands(?MODULE),
    begin
      {H,S,Res} = run_commands(?MODULE,Cmds),
      cleanup(),
      ?WHENFAIL(
        io:format("History: ~p\nState: ~p\nRes: ~p\n", [H,S,Res]),
        Res == ok)
    end).
```

Referring to this definition, we see that:

- We *quantify* over a list of symbolic commands, `Cmds`, generated by the function `commands`, which is a part of QuickCheck. These correspond to the symbolic dictionaries of the previous section.
- We *execute* the list of commands using `run_commands`, another function provided by QuickCheck, which corresponds to `eval` in the previous section.
- The result of `run_commands` is a triple whose third component, `Res`, summarizes the outcome of the test. If this is the atom `ok`, then the test passed.
- The other components of the result contain debugging information; it is useful to display this when a test fails using `?WHENFAIL`.
- After each test, the registry must be restored to a known state in preparation for the next test; properties for testing stateful systems almost always need to contain clean-up code to do this.

- Both `commands` and `run_commands` take a *module name* as a parameter. This module provides callbacks that define the behaviour of the state machine model, and it is these callbacks that are the heart of the QuickCheck specification.

In the next sections we will explain the callbacks that make up a QuickCheck state machine specification. Definitions of these callbacks must be placed in, and exported from, the module whose name appears in the property above.

4.3 Generating Commands

The first callback we shall consider, called `command`, defines how the symbolic API calls that make up a test case should be generated. Since we intend to test `register`, `unregister` and `whereis`, then we might expect to define

```
command() ->
  oneof([{call,erlang,register,[name(),pid()]},
         {call,erlang,unregister,[name()]},
         {call,erlang,whereis,[name()]}
        ]).
```

where `name()` generates a random atom, and `pid()` generates a random process identifier. We generate names via

```
name() -> elements([a,b,c,d]).
```

choosing atoms from a small set so that a test case is likely to refer to the same name several times. But what about `pid()`? This should choose from a small pool of process identifiers—but process identifiers must be created dynamically. It is important to create *new* process identifiers each time a test case is run, since otherwise earlier tests may corrupt the test data (process identifiers) used in later ones, leading to test failures that are virtually impossible to diagnose.

It follows that process creation must be a part of the generated test cases. This is easy to achieve by defining a local function `spawn()` that just starts a process that does nothing, and including calls in test cases:

```
command() ->
  oneof([{call,erlang,register,[name(),pid()]},
         {call,erlang,unregister,[name()]},
         {call,erlang,whereis,[name()]},
         {call,?MODULE,spawn,[]}
        ]).
```

However, we still have to arrange for `pid()` to choose one the processes previously created by a `spawn()` in the same test case.

In order to do so, we maintain a *test case state* which collects all the process identifiers generated by `spawn()`, and we parameterise `pid()` (and `command()`) on this state so that previously spawned pids can be chosen:

```
command(S) ->
  oneof([{call,erlang,register,[name(),pid(S)]},
         {call,erlang,unregister,[name()]},
         {call,erlang,whereis,[name()]},
         {call,?MODULE,spawn,[]}
        ]).
```

The `command` callback is thus a one-argument function, not a zero-argument one as it appeared to be earlier. In fact, this kind of situation arises frequently: it is often the case that a resource allocated by one API call needs to be passed as a parameter to a later one, and so a mechanism for supporting this is an important part of a state machine testing framework.

We now need to maintain a test case state for two different reasons: firstly, as an abstract model of the state of the system under test, and secondly, so that we can generate call sequences that reuse the results of earlier calls later in the sequence. In principle we might track two separate states, but we have chosen instead to merge them into one. We are thus now in a position to choose a model state for testing the process registry: it is an Erlang record defined as follows:

```
-record(state,{pids=[],
               regs=[]
              }).
```

The first component is a list of the pids spawned in the current test, while the second is a property list modelling the state of the registry. With this definition, we can finally define

```
pid(S) -> elements(S#state.pids).
```

4.4 Modelling State Transitions

We have now defined how to generate the next command from a test case state, but we have yet to define how each command *changes* the state. We do this via a `next_state` callback, which maps the state before a call, and the symbolic call, into the resulting state afterwards. Since this state may depend on the actual result of the call, then this is also supplied as a parameter. For example, the clause for `spawn` adds the result of the call (the parameter V, a pid) to the list of pids in the test case state:

```
next_state(S,V,{call,_,spawn,_}) ->
  S#state{pids=[V|S#state.pids]};
```

The `next_state` function is used to simulate the test case state as a test case is generated, enabling the `command` generator in the previous section to refer to previously spawned pids.

Similarly, the state transitions for `register` and `unregister` make the expected changes to the modelled registry contents:

```
next_state(S,_V,{call,_,register,[Name,Pid]}) ->
  S#state{regs=[{Name,Pid}|S#state.regs]};
next_state(S,_V,{call,_,unregister,[Name]}) ->
  S#state{regs=proplists:delete(Name,S#state.regs)};
```

Finally, we include a catch-all clause specifying that other calls do not change the model state.

```
next_state(S,_V,{call,_,_,_}) ->
  S.
```

In this case the only other call is whereis, and sure enough, we do not expect it to change the registry state.

We also need to define the initial test case state, which is done by a third callback that can simply construct a state record with default field values:

```
initial_state() -> #state{}.
```

4.5   Conditional Generation

Glossing over a few details, we are now ready to run our first tests. When we do so, they fail immediately:

```
40> eqc:quickcheck(reg_eqc:prop_registry()).
Failed! Reason:
{'EXIT',{eqc,elements,[[]]}}
After 1 tests.
false
```

The error message indicates that the test failed because of an exception raised when elements([]) was called—to generate an element of the empty list! Of course, this is impossible, so elements should not be called in this way—we have a bug in our command generator. The problem is that in the initial test case state, S#state.pids is empty—and so if we try to generate a call of register, then we must choose a pid from the empty list, which raises the exception. The solution is to include register as an alternative in the list of possible commands *only* if S#state.pids is non-empty. We could do so using a case-expression, but we prefer a little trick which offers a very concise notation, so we revise our definition of command(S) again as follows:

```
command(S) ->
  oneof([{call,erlang,register,[name(),pid(S)]}
          || S#state.pids/=[]] ++
        [{call,?MODULE,unregister,[name()]},
         {call,erlang,whereis,[name()]},
         {call,?MODULE,spawn,[]}
        ]).
```

The first operand of ++ above is a *list comprehension with no generators*, a form one does not see very often, but which is just what we need here. Such a comprehension is evaluated as follows: [X||true] evaluates to [X], while [X||false] evaluates to []. Thus the effect is to include the call to register in the list from which oneof chooses precisely when the list of pids in the state is non-empty. In fact, the generator for register is not even evaluated if the condition is false—so such a list comprehension can be used as a kind of "if... then..." expression in Erlang, something many programmers more used to imperative languages miss sorely.

With this change, our command generator works, and we can start running tests for real.

4.6   Specifying Preconditions

Once again, when we try to test our property, then it fails immediately:

```
42> eqc:quickcheck(reg_eqc:prop_registry()).
Failed! After 1 tests.
[{set,{var,1},{call,reg_eqc,spawn,[]}},
 {set,{var,2},{call,erlang,whereis,[b]}},
 {set,{var,3},{call,erlang,unregister,[d]}},
 {set,{var,4},{call,reg_eqc,spawn,[]}},
 {set,{var,5},{call,reg_eqc,spawn,[]}},
 {set,{var,6},{call,erlang,register,[b,{var,5}]}},
 {set,{var,7},{call,erlang,whereis,[c]}},
 {set,{var,8},{call,erlang,whereis,[a]}},
 {set,{var,9},{call,erlang,whereis,[a]}},
 {set,{var,10},{call,erlang,register,[d,{var,1}]}},
 {set,{var,11},{call,erlang,unregister,[d]}},
 {set,{var,12},{call,erlang,register,[c,{var,1}]}}]
History: [{{state,[],[]},<0.2066.0>},{{state,[<0.2066.0>],[]},undefined}]
State: {state,[<0.2066.0>],[]}
Res: {exception,{'EXIT',{badarg,[{erlang,unregister,[d]},
                                  <...7 more lines...>]}}}
```

We can see from the output that test cases are more than just a list of symbolic commands: they are a list of *symbolic variable bindings*. Just as {call,M,F,Args} represents a function call symbolically, so {var,N} represents a variable... think of it as v_N. The test case above binds {var,1} to the result of spawn, {var,2} to the result of whereis, and so on. Variables can be reused in the arguments of later symbolic calls—for example, {var,1} is reused as an argument in the line binding {var,10}. One of the main differences between eval and run_commands is just that the latter manages these symbolic variable definitions, as well as performing symbolic calls.

Looking at the diagnostic output from the ?WHENFAIL, we see that the reason for the test failure was a badarg exception raised by unregister. However, the test case is too complex for us to understand the problem immediately. Luckily, it shrinks to a much simpler one—continuing the QuickCheck output, we see

```
Shrinking....(4 times)
[{set,{var,3},{call,erlang,unregister,[a]}}]
History: []
State: {state,[],[]}
Res: {exception,{'EXIT',{badarg,[{erlang,unregister,[a]},
                        <...7 more lines...>]}}}
false
```

This test does nothing other than call unregister(a). Now it is pretty clear
that the exception is raised because we are unregistering a name which has
not previously been registered—and indeed, the documentation confirms that
unregister is supposed to raise an exception in this case. We must revise our
model to reflect this.

One way to do so is to specify a *precondition* for unregister, stating that it
may only be called when the name to be unregistered is actually in the registry.
QuickCheck uses a fourth callback, precondition, to determine when API calls
may be made. We can define unregister's precondition as follows:

```
precondition(S,{call,_,unregister,[Name]}) ->
  unregister_ok(S,Name);
precondition(_S,{call,_,_,_}) ->
  true.

unregister_ok(S,Name) ->
  proplists:is_defined(Name,S#state.regs).
```

(where the second clause of the precondition callback was already present—
otherwise the tests would have failed with an undefined function). QuickCheck
ensures that all preconditions hold in every generated test case, so with this
addition then the problem we encountered can no longer occur.

4.7 Specifying Postconditions

The change we just made to the specification is an example of "positive
testing"—we restrict test cases to those in which we expect unregister to work.
Yet it is in a sense unsatisfactory. We know that unregister is *intended* to raise
an exception when called with a name that is not in the registry, but positive
tests will never test this case. We might therefore prefer *not* to specify a precondition for unregister, but instead allow arbitrary calls to be made, and check
that an exception is indeed raised whenever it ought to be. This kind of testing
is referred to as "negative testing", because we also test the (specified) error
behaviour of the system under test.

We can perform this kind of testing using QuickCheck by removing the precondition, and adding a *postcondition* for unregister instead. Postconditions
are defined via the fifth and final callback that makes up a QuickCheck state
machine model. This callback is passed the state before a call, the symbolic call,
and the actual result of the call, and is expected to return true or false. We
can add a postcondition for unregister as follows:

```
postcondition(S,{call,_,unregister,[Name]},Res) ->
  case Res of
    {'EXIT',_} -> not unregister_ok(S,Name);
    true ->        unregister_ok(S,Name)
  end;
postcondition(_S,{call,_,_,_},_Res) ->
  true.
```

where once again, the last clause was already present. Examining the code, we see that if the actual result Res is an exit value, then the postcondition holds only if the call was expected to fail, while if the actual result is true, then the postcondition holds only if the call was expected to succeed.

Note that we have made heavy use of unregister_ok, which defines when a call of unregister is expected to succeed. It is because such conditions are often moved between pre- and post-conditions that we defined a separate function to test it in the first place.

Our job is not quite complete. We have added a postcondition to *test* for an exception, but this will have no effect unless we arrange to *catch* the exception first—QuickCheck always considers an uncaught exception to be a test failure. We can catch the exception by defining a local version of unregister that does so,

```
unregister(Name) -> catch erlang:unregister(Name).
```

and replacing calls of erlang:unregister in test cases by calls of the local version:

```
command(S) ->
  oneof([...{call,?MODULE,unregister,[name()]},...]).
```

With these changes, we can now rerun our tests—and they will fail for a *different* reason!

```
44> eqc:quickcheck(reg_eqc:prop_registry()).
.Failed! After 2 tests.
<... 35 lines omitted ...>
Shrinking......(6 times)
[{set,{var,1},{call,reg_eqc,spawn,[]}},
 {set,{var,3},{call,erlang,register,[a,{var,1}]}},
 {set,{var,4},{call,erlang,register,[a,{var,1}]}}]
History: [{{state,[],[]},<0.2101.0>},{{state,[<0.2101.0>],[]},true}]
State: {state,[<0.2101.0>],[{a,<0.2101.0>}]}
Res: {exception,{'EXIT',{badarg,[{erlang,register,[a,<0.2101.0>]},
                           <... 7 lines omitted ...>]}}}
false
```

This time the failed test spawns a process, then tries to register it twice. We can see from the failure reason that one of the calls to register raised a badarg exception. The diagnostic information contains a history, in the form of the state before and result of each operation performed, and the final state after the last call—we can see that `spawn` returned the pid `<0.2101.0>`, the first call of `register` returned `true`, and that `{a,<0.2101.0>}` was in the model state after that call. It is not too big a stretch to guess that `register` is supposed to raise an exception when the name to be registered *is* already present in the registry, and so we now have enough information to refine our model further.

We will leave further model refinement to the exercises. For now, notice that the *same* property has revealed two *different* bugs—or rather, inconsistencies between the model and the real code. The ability to find different bugs using the same property is a major advantage of property-based testing over a fixed set of test cases, in which one test case can hardly ever reveal more than one bug.

4.8   Exercises

In section 4.9 you will find the contents of the file `reg_eqc.erl`, which provides an incomplete specification of the process registry. Type in this file, or download a copy from `http://www.chalmers.se/~rjmh/CEFP`. Note the line

```
-include_lib("eqc/include/eqc_statem.hrl").
```

at the top of the file, which is needed to make the QuickCheck state machine features available. Should you need to develop such a specification yourself, then a skeleton specification can be created by selecting "Complete eqc_statem spec" from the "State machine specs" menu in the QuickCheck Emacs mode.

1. **Adding a precondition.** Compile `reg_eqc.erl`, and use QuickCheck to test `prop_registry()`. You will find that the property fails, because `register` raises an exception. Define a function `register_ok(S,Name,Pid)` which returns `true` if `register(Name,Pid)` ought to succeed in state S, and use it to specify a precondition for `register` that enables this property to pass.
   Hint: the function `lists:keymember` may be useful.

2. **Adding a postcondition.** The previous exercise implements positive testing of `register`. Now we shall implement negative testing instead. First remove the precondition just added, and instead add a *postcondition* for `register` saying that an exception is raised precisely when `register_ok` is `false`. Revise your specification until `prop_registry()` passes.

3. **Testing whereis.** Add another postcondition to your specification, testing that `whereis` returns the correct result.

4. **Killing processes.** In this exercise, we shall investigate how the registry behaves when processes crash. Add the following definition to `reg_eqc.erl`:

```
stop(Pid) ->
  exit(Pid,kill),
  timer:sleep(1).
```

This function kills the process referred to by `Pid` (and then waits a millisecond for it to die completely). Add calls of `stop` to your generated test cases, and retest `prop_registry()`. Since the registry documentation does not mention dead processes, then we would expect `stop` to have no effect on test case behaviour. Since the default clauses in `next_state`, `precondition` and `postcondition` say that `stop` may be called at any time, and has no effect, then we would expect all tests to pass. If this is the case, then you are finished with this exercise.

If *not*, then your task is to revise the model so that the property passes again—*without* imposing restrictive preconditions on the operations, because the whole point of this exercise is to test what happens to the registry when relevant processes really do die.

Hint: the function `lists:keydelete` may be useful.

5. **Dealing with non-determinism.** This is an ambitious exercise, so don't worry if you find it puzzling or difficult.

Taking your passing specification from the previous exercise, remove the call to `timer:sleep(1)` from the definition of `stop`, and observe the effect on tests. Try to adjust your model so that tests pass again. You are likely to encounter evidence of non-deterministic behaviour, caused when the Erlang scheduler preempts your running test at an unpredictable point.

To make any further progress, you need to recover deterministic testing. This can be achieved by a combination of techniques:

   – Restrict your test cases to a maximum of 30 commands. This keeps them short enough to run to completion in one time slice.
   – Add `?SOMETIMES` to your property, to permit occasional failures (read the documentation, to be found in module `eqc`).

Once your tests run deterministically, then failed tests should shrink to a test case that makes diagnosis possible. Finish adjusting your model.

Finally, extend your command generator so as to add explicit calls of `timer:sleep(1)` to your test cases. Once again, you will need to adjust your model to make tests pass: having done so, you will have a good understanding of both the immediate, and the delayed effects of a process crash.

Having finished the exercises, why not select one of the Erlang library modules with a stateful interface, and construct a QuickCheck state machine specification of your own?

4.9   reg_eqc.erl

```erlang
-module(reg_eqc).

-include_lib("eqc/include/eqc.hrl").
-include_lib("eqc/include/eqc_statem.hrl").

-compile(export_all).

-record(state,{pids=[],      % pids spawned in this test
               regs=[]       % list of {Name,Pid} in the registry
              }).
```

```erlang
%% Initialize the state
initial_state() ->
    #state{}.

%% Command generator, S is the state
command(S) ->
    oneof([{call,erlang,register,[name(),pid(S)]}
           || S#state.pids/=[]] ++
          [{call,?MODULE,unregister,[name()]},
           {call,erlang,whereis,[name()]},
           {call,?MODULE,spawn,[]}
          ]).

-define(names,[a,b,c,d]).

name() ->
    elements(?names).

pid(S) ->
    elements(S#state.pids).

%% Next state transformation, S is the current state
next_state(S,V,{call,_,spawn,_}) ->
    S#state{pids=[V|S#state.pids]};
next_state(S,_V,{call,_,register,[Name,Pid]}) ->
    S#state{regs=[{Name,Pid}|S#state.regs]};
next_state(S,_V,{call,_,unregister,[Name]}) ->
    S#state{regs=proplists:delete(Name,S#state.regs)};
next_state(S,_V,{call,_,_,_}) ->
    S.

%% Precondition, checked before command is added to the
%% command sequence
precondition(_S,{call,_,_,_}) ->
    true.

%% Postcondition, checked after command has been evaluated
%% OBS: S is the state before next_state(S,_,<command>)
postcondition(S,{call,_,unregister,[Name]},Res) ->
    case Res of
        {'EXIT',_} ->
            not unregister_ok(S,Name);
        true ->
            unregister_ok(S,Name)
    end;
postcondition(_S,{call,_,_,_},_Res) ->
    true.

%% The conditions under which operations ought to succeed.
```

```
unregister_ok(S,Name) ->
    proplists:is_defined(Name,S#state.regs).

%% The main property.

prop_registry() ->
    ?FORALL(Cmds,commands(?MODULE),
      begin
        {H,S,Res} = run_commands(?MODULE,Cmds),
        cleanup(),
        ?WHENFAIL(
          io:format(
            "History: ~p\nState: ~p\nRes: ~p\n",
            [H,S,Res]),
          Res == ok)
      end).

cleanup() ->
    [catch erlang:unregister(Name) || Name <- ?names].

%% Exception-catching versions of the API under test

unregister(Name) ->
    catch erlang:unregister(Name).

%% Spawn a dummy process to use as test data.
%% Processes die after 5 seconds, long after the
%% test is over, to avoid filling the Erlang
%% heap with dummy processes.

spawn() ->
    spawn(timer,sleep,[5000]).
```

5   QuickCheck in Industry

In these notes, we show how to use QuickCheck to test parts of the Erlang standard libraries—relatively simple (and well-tested) code, in comparison to real industrial products. Yet the principles we have presented are equally applicable to testing real applications.

In a typical industrial scenario, QuickCheck might be used to test a system that communicates with the outside world using one of the standardized telecom or internet protocols. In this case, a QuickCheck state machine is used to generate test cases containing commands that send a protocol message to the system under test, then wait for and check the response. Typically the protocol messages are large and complex, and a significant amount of work goes into contructing suitable generators. This work can be partially automated—tools exist to convert both ABNF and ASN.1 grammars into QuickCheck generators—but manual intervention is needed to generate protocol messages that "make sense", as opposed to random rubbish. The state machine then models just enough of the internal state of the system to generate sensible message sequences, and validate the responses. When a test fails, then QuickCheck finds a minimal failing sequence as usual. We shall illustrate this with a couple of examples of real bugs found using QuickCheck.

For example, in one project (which cannot be identified for commercial reasons), QuickCheck was used to test a 3G radio base station for mobile telephony (RBS), by sending control messages using the NBAP[3] protocol and observing the responses. An RBS maintains a number of radio channels which are used to exchange information with the mobile phones in each cell. During a call, there is a dedicated radio channel between the handset and the base station, but even handsets which are not currently making a call need to communicate with the base station occasionally. A single signalling channel is used for this purpose, shared between all the handsets in a cell. Now, every channel needs to be set up, and parameters such as the power level assigned—this is done when another product, a Radio Network Controller, sends NBAP commands to the base station telling it how to set up each channel. Note that *even though there is only one signalling channel, it still needs to be set up and configured.* Thus there is a command in the NBAP protocol for this purpose. Although this command should only be sent once, since there can only be one such channel, it is of course possible to send it to the base station *more than once*—and it is easy to imagine situations in which this might really happen, for example when a Radio Network Controller has crashed and is coming back online. If the signalling channel has already been set up, than an RBS is supposed to *reject* subsequent attempts to set it up again. We found this to be true for the software we were testing—almost always. But QuickCheck found a combination of parameters in the first and second set-up messages which caused the RBS to *accept* the second set-up command—and to create *two* signalling channels at the same time. This violated a fundamental invariant of the base station software, leading within a few seconds to a hard failure, with the base station becoming unresponsive to all further commands. Interestingly, the first sign of trouble turned out to be Java exceptions in the base station log...which surprised us since we knew that the base station was implemented using C++! It transpired that Java had been used to build an operator GUI, which visualized the state of the base station, and this visualization was the first part of the software to crash when the signalling channel invariant was violated.

In another project, QuickCheck was used to test an Ericsson Media Proxy [1]. This is a kind of firewall for multimedia IP-telephony (that is, carried using the internet protocol); it is one component of a Session Border Gateway, that isolates an operator's network from the internet at large. The Media Proxy opens and closes "media pinholes" to allow the media streams making up a call to pass the firewall. It is controlled by the H.248 or Megaco protocol [7], which defines commands to add and remove callers from a call (or "terminations" from a "context", in Megaco-speak). A call is created when the first caller is added,

---

and deleted when the last caller is removed—and just as in the process registry tests, a call-ID is created by the first addition, and must be embedded in later messages to the Proxy concerning the same call.

The Megaco protocol supports any number of callers in a call, but the Media Proxy product is restricted to just two. Nevertheless, QuickCheck found the following command sequence that provoked a crash:

- First, two callers are added to a call (the normal situation).
- Now the call is "full", and no further caller can be added—but one caller can be *removed*.
- Now the call is not full: a third caller can be added, and then removed again.
- The call is still not full; a fourth caller can be added and removed. On this final removal, something inside the Proxy crashes!

This sequence of seven commands was minimal for provoking this crash.

This case is interesting for several reasons. Firstly, because it cannot reasonably be found using manually constructed test cases—no tester in their right minds would test this case! After all, if adding and removing a caller works once, and works twice, then "by induction" it *must* work three times—right? Yet it does not. More seriously, because it is expensive to construct test cases manually, then it is impractical to test *all* sequences of seven commands, and there is no *a priori* reason to suspect that this one is worth testing. Coverage measures would not help here—it is likely that all the code, all the paths, and all the state transitions were already covered by the first five commands, so coverage measures would not indicate that we should go on to test the last two also.

Secondly, this example illustrates the tremendous power of shrinking—this minimal test failure was extracted from a random failing sequence of over 160 commands. The problem was tricky enough to diagnose from this minimal example; from a sequence of 160 commands, diagnosis would have been impossible.

Thirdly, this case will probably never, ever arise in practice—but the failed case is just the *symptom* of a fault, not the cause. The cause turned out to be corruption of internal data-structures on removing a caller from a call—and this corruption occurred *every time* a caller was removed. It just so happened that, in the normal case, when the only thing following the removal of the first caller was the removal of the second, then the data corruption passed unobserved. The fourth to the seventh commands in the failing test are needed just in order to convert the corrupted data into a crash. Even if it was not causing a problem at the time, it was well worth while discovering and correcting this corruption. After all, in a year's time another developer might well modify the code, and would naturally assume that the data structures inside such a tried-and-tested product were correct—but they were not. The corrupt data would have been a trap lying in wait for future developers, if QuickCheck had not revealed it and enabled the problem to be fixed.

Interestingly, QuickCheck was able to reveal these corrupt data structures *even though we did not know of their existence!* Had we known about them, and added code to the specification to check their invariants after each call, then the fault would have been found more quickly, and with a shorter failing test—only the first three commands would have been needed to provoke a failure. But this more detailed specification was not *necessary* to reveal the fault. This is a general observation—we find that surprisingly simple properties often suffice to reveal deeply-hidden bugs. Once software *begins* to go wrong, then there is often some continuation which makes it go very wrong indeed—and so testing basic properties can often reveal subtle bugs, if we only run enough tests. For this reason it is often not worthwhile to formulate a *complete* formal specification of the system under test, which can be quite expensive—we can trade off specification effort against testing time instead.

Boberg reported an interesting study of two larger projects at Erlang Training and Consulting, one developed with and one without using QuickCheck [2]. An email gateway was developed using QuickCheck for system testing, and compared to an instant messaging gateway developed without using it. Boberg measured fault slip-through at each stage of testing—the percentage of faults which should have been found at an earlier stage—and found that 86% of the faults found during acceptance testing of the instant messaging gateway should have been found earlier, while the same was true of only 39% of the faults found during acceptance testing of the email gateway. This indicates that using QuickCheck for system testing improved the quality of the delivered system substantially, a conclusion which was also supported by a qualitative assessment of the developers' confidence in their code. Boberg's paper contains a wealth of other information also, including the somewhat surprising observation that the quality of *unit testing* of the email gateway appeared to *decline* as the study progressed! Boberg suggests that the developers spent less effort on unit testing (without QuickCheck), since they expected their errors to be found anyway during system testing (with QuickCheck).

6   Conclusions

In this tutorial we have shown how to write testable formal specifications in the form of QuickCheck properties, for both purely functional and stateful code. The appeal of the approach should be clear. However, proving that property-based testing is not only fun, but also a cost-effective way to find bugs in large-scale software, is still a challenge. The industrial experiences related above are encouraging, as is Boberg's study, which presents positive results in one context. An interesting small-scale experiment with students suggested that properties may be harder to write than unit tests, but once written are much more effective at revealing bugs [6]. But for definitive proof that this approach is cost-effective, we must await the results of larger scale industrial case studies, some of which will be completed in the not-too-distant future.

References

[1] Arts, T., Hughes, J., Johansson, J., Wiger, U.: Testing telecoms software with quviq quickcheck. In: Feeley, M., Trinder, P.W. (eds.) Erlang Workshop, pp. 2–10. ACM, New York (2006)

[2] Boberg, J.: Early fault detection with model-based testing. In: ERLANG 2008: Proceedings of the 7th ACM SIGPLAN workshop on ERLANG, pp. 9–20. ACM, New York (2008)

[3] Carlsson, R., Rémond, M.: Eunit: a lightweight unit testing framework for erlang. In: ERLANG 2006: Proceedings of the 2006 ACM SIGPLAN workshop on Erlang, pp. 1–1. ACM, New York (2006)

[4] Claessen, K., Hughes, J.: Quickcheck: a lightweight tool for random testing of haskell programs. In: ICFP 2000: Proceedings of the fifth ACM SIGPLAN international conference on Functional programming, pp. 268–279. ACM Press, New York (2000)

[5] Claessen, K., Hughes, J.: Specification based testing with QuickCheck. In: The Fun of Programming, Cornerstones of Computing, pp. 17–40. Palgrave (2003)

[6] Claessen, K., Hughes, J., Pałka, M., Smallbone, N., Svensson, H.: Ranking programs using black box testing. In: AST 2010: Proceedings of the 5th Workshop on Automation of Software Test, pp. 103–110. ACM, New York (2010)

[7] Greene, N., Ramalho, M., Rosen, B.: Rfc-2805, media gateway control protocol architecture and requirements. Technical report, Network Working Group (2000)

[8] Hildebrandt, R., Zeller, A.: Simplifying failure-inducing input. SIGSOFT Softw. Eng. Notes 25(5), 135–145 (2000)

[9] Hoare, C.A.R.: Proof of correctness of data representations. Acta Inf. 1, 271–281 (1972)

[10] Hughes, J.: Quickcheck testing for fun and profit. In: Hanus, M. (ed.) PADL 2007. LNCS, vol. 4354, pp. 1–32. Springer, Heidelberg (2006)

[11] Just, R., Schweiggert, F.: Automating software tests with partial oracles in integrated environments. In: AST 2010: Proceedings of the 5th Workshop on Automation of Software Test, pp. 91–94. ACM, New York (2010)

[12] Müller, M.M., Hagner, O.: Experiment about test-first programming. IEE Proceedings - Software 149(5), 131–136 (2002)

[13] Wadler, P.: Comprehending monads. In: LISP and Functional Programming, pp. 61–78 (1990)

An Effective Methodology for Defining Consistent Semantics of Complex Systems

Pieter Koopman, Rinus Plasmeijer, and Peter Achten

Nijmegen Institute for Computing and Information Sciences,
Radboud University Nijmegen, The Netherlands
{pieter,rinus,p.achten}@cs.ru.nl

Abstract. This paper has two contributions. First, it gives a semantics for the iTask workflow management system. Second, it describes an effective methodology to construct such a semantics.

Semantics is a formal description of the meaning of language constructs. Just like any other formal description there are umpteen ways of introducing flaws in such a description. Even trained people are not very effective in spotting issues in formal text. In this paper we show that it is very well possible to describe semantics of programming languages using a modern functional programming as carrier of the specification. This enables automatic sanity checks by the language compiler, simulation of the described semantics to validate the specification, and automatic testing of properties of the semantics.

We illustrate this technique with the well-known example of simple imperative language as well as the iTask workflow management system. In our experience this methodology works very well. The combination of sanity checks, simulation and automatic testing of properties really helped to construct a trustworthy semantics for the iTask system.

1 Introduction

The semantics of a system is a formal description of the meaning of that system. In these notes we define the semantics of programming language constructs like expressions, assignments, conditionals and loops. The definition of all language constructs and the way to combine them specifies the meaning of programs in that language. Although the formal semantics is usually a much simpler system than the system described, the semantics itself can be quite complicated as well. Since the semantics is a piece of formal language, the semantics itself is error prone just like any other large formal system (e.g. a computer program, or a mathematical proof). There are several kinds of potential problems with such a formal system: **1)** the system is incomplete, e.g. not all notions used are defined properly; **2)** the system is inconsistent, e.g. functions are used with the wrong number or type of arguments; **3)** the system does not possess the required properties, e.g. addition is not associative, commutative and distributive; **4)** the system does not prescribe the right semantics, e.g. the semantics of multiplication accidentally specifies addition. In these notes we show an effective way to tackle

Z. Horváth, R. Plasmeijer, and V. Zsók (Eds.): CEFP 2009, LNCS 6299, pp. 224–267, 2010.

these problems and illustrate our method by a well-known as well as a nontrivial example.

Problems 1) and 2) are avoided by using a high level functional programming language as carrier of the formal semantics. The burden of using such a language as formalism instead of ordinary mathematics appears to be very limited. The advantage is obvious; the compiler checks consistency and well-definedness of the semantics. Problem 4) can now be handled by simulating the specified semantics. In our experience such a validation is very effective. In these notes we show how problem 3) can be treated by stating desired properties of the semantics and test these properties automatically with the model-based test system G∀st. During the development of the semantics one does not want the burden of formal proofs of properties for intermediate versions of the semantics; a test system yields a solid approximation of correctness within seconds. In a next step one can use this semantics to test the real implementation of the specified system with G∀st.

The semantics is expressed in the functional programming language Clean instead of the more common Scott Brackets, denotational semantics [22], or horizontal bar style, structural operational semantics à la Plotkin [18]. The close correspondence between semantics and functional programs goes back at least to [15]. Expressing the operational semantics in a FPL is as concise as in Scott Brackets style. Using a functional programming language as carrier of the specification of the semantics has a number of advantages: **1)** the type system performs basic consistency checks on the semantics; **2)** the semantics is executable; **3)** using the iTask system it is easy to validate the semantics by interactive simulation; **4)** using the model-based test tool G∀st [8] it is possible to express properties about the semantics and equivalence of language constructs/tasks concisely, and to test these properties fully automatically. Although the semantics is executable, it is not a serious implementation of the described language itself. The semantics assigns a meaning to expressions represented by some data structure, a real implementation generally provides a parser and type checker to map textual representations to such a data structure. The iTask semantics is a model of the real system, it lacks for instance a frontend (user interface) as well as a backend (e.g. interface to a database).

Especially the ability to express properties of the specified semantics and to test them automatically appears to be extremely convenient in the development of the semantics and associated notions described in this paper. An alternative, more traditional, approach would be to define a semantics in a common mathematical style, state properties in logic, and formally prove these properties. Using a proof assistant like COQ [23] or SPARKLE [14] for this purpose requires a transformation of the semantics to the language of the proof assistant. In the past we have used this approach for the iData system [1]. In such a mathematically based approach it is much harder to experiment with different formulations of the semantics and to get the system consistent after a change. Proving a property of a new version of the semantics typical takes some days of human effort where testing the same property is done in seconds by a computer. When we have a final version of the semantics obtained in this way, we can decide to prove (some of) the tested properties in order to obtain absolute confidence in their correctness.

We will illustrate our approach with two case studies. The first one is the semantics of the very simple imperative language While to explain the concepts. This language, or a very similar language, can be found in many text books about semantics. We compare our formulation of semantics with standard ways to specify the semantics. The second case study is the iTask WFMS (WorkFlow Management System). A WFMS is a system that supports users and machines to execute tasks. The iTask systems consists of a language to describe the task to be executed, as well as the tools to administrate and guide the execution of these tasks via a web based user interface. The iTask example is a good test case since it is still under development and hence requires agile validation. It is a complex system, hence its properties are not cut and clear, and they require exploration.

In this paper we provide a basic rewrite semantics for iTasks as well as a number of useful contributions to reason about tasks, such as *needed events* and *equivalences* of tasks. As usual we omit many details in the semantics to express the meaning of the basic iTask combinators as clearly as possible.

Section 2 gives a short introduction to the various kind of semantics that exist and shows how this can be expressed concisely in a functional language. In section 3 we show how we model iTasks. We also define useful notions about subtasks, such as when they are enabled or needed. In section 4 we define the equivalence of tasks and how the equivalence of tasks can be determined in two different ways. Some important properties of the semantics of iTasks are given in section 5, we also show how these properties can be tested fully automatically. In the future we will use this semantics for model-based testing of the real iTask implementation, this will increase the confidence that the system obeys the semantics. Finally, we discuss related work in section 6 and there is a discussion and a conclusion in section 7.

2   Formal Semantics

The semantics [15] of a programming language defines the meaning of programs. In order to reason about the semantics we need a formal definition of the semantics, rather than an informal textual description. There is a considerable amount of research done in this field. As a result there are many different ways to describe the semantics of some programming language. The three main approaches are:

Operational semantics. This approach assigns a meaning to the syntactical constructs in a programming language. The meaning of each language construct is specified by the computations it induces when the construct is executed. This approach focusses on how the effect of each language construct is built in some kind of mathematical interpretation of the programming language.

Within the operational semantics we distinguish two approaches. The *structural operational semantics* (or *small-step* semantics) focusses on details of individual execution steps. The semantics is a mathematical interpreter of the programming language that hides details like storage allocation, but otherwise specifies the effect of each language construct in detail. The *natural semantics* (or *big step* semantics) hides even more details. There is no emphasis on specifying the meaning of individual execution steps, but one specifies the meaning of a language constructs in larger steps than in the structural operational semantics.

Denotational semantics. The focus in this approach is on the value that a language construct denotes, rather than how this value is obtained. For simple language constructs the denotational description resembles the operational semantics. For more complicated constructs like loops and recursive function applications one often uses a fixed point description. For instance, for a loop the denotational semantics specifies the state of the program after termination of the loop, while the operational semantics describes the state change by executing the loop once.

Axiomatic semantics. In this approach specific properties of executing language constructs are expressed as assertions. These properties specify the effect of language constructs, but there can be aspects of the execution that are ignored in an axiomatic semantics.

These approaches to specify the semantics have in common that they pattern match on the syntactic constructs of the language. A meaning is assigned to each of the alternatives in the syntax. For this reason we will represent the language by a data structure that has one constructor for each alternative in the syntax.

2.1 The Imperative Language While

In order to illustrate these approaches to specify the semantics and our own approach based on functional programming, we specify the semantics of a very simple imperative language called While in this section. Similar languages can be found in most textbooks about formal semantics. This language While and its semantics is taken from [15]. We start with the classical formal semantical description. Since this approach assigns a meaning to the syntactical constructs in a programming language, we need a specification of the syntax. For the language While we use the following meta-variables and catagories:

n ranges over integer numbers;
v ranges over variables;
a ranges over arithmetical expressions;
b ranges over Boolean expressions;
S ranges over statements.

These meta-variables can be primed or subscripted if we need more than one instance, e.g. v' and v_1 are also variables. We do not need to know the syntactical details of numbers and variables. Such details are usually omitted in the semantics. The syntax for the other constructs is:

$$a ::= v \mid n \mid a+a \mid a-a \mid a*a$$
$$b ::= \texttt{TRUE} \mid \texttt{FALSE} \mid a=a \mid a<a \mid \neg b \mid b \;\&\&\; b$$
$$S ::= x := a \mid \texttt{skip} \mid S1 \,;\, S2 \mid \texttt{if}\ b\ S1\ \texttt{else}\ S2 \mid \texttt{while}\ b\ S$$

The arithmetic expressions do not contain a division operator, /, since that would involve exceptions in the semantics. Division by zero is undefined, hence it cannot yield an ordinary number. It is perfectly possible to handle this in the semantical description of a language, but it makes things more complex as wanted in these notes.

2.2   The Semantics of Expressions in While

In order to specify the semantics we need an *environment*, also called *state*[1], that relates variables and their values. Usually this environment is modeled as a function from variables, modeled by the type Var, to their values, modeled by the type Int: State : Var $\rightarrow$ Int, i.e. a State is a function from variables to integers. Here we have to make our first semantic choice: do variables that did not occur on the left-hand side of an assignment have a value (and if they have a value, what is that value), or is the value of these variables undefined (and is the state a partial function Var $\hookrightarrow$ Int). For simplicity we assume that the state is a total function and that the value of all variables are initialized to 0.

In order to compare the classical mathematical way to define semantics with our functional programming based definitions, we repeat some of the classical definitions. In figure 1 we define the semantics of arithmetic expressions by a function from the expression and a state to an integer value. This definition is very similar to [15], the only difference is the resulting type of expressions. In the version of the Nielsons the result is a natural number, N, while our version produces its representation in computers, Int. Problems that are caused by a finite representation are ignored for the moment. It is perfectly possible to tackle these issues, but that complicates the definition.

In this function we use the Scott brackets $[\![$ $]\!]$ to denote a match on syntax using the syntactical categories defined above. This function specifies that the semantics of a number denotation n is the value of that denotation generated by $\mathcal{N}[\![n]\!]$. For brevity we ignored the syntactic details of numbers n, hence we also omit the definition of their semantics $\mathcal{N}$. The value of a variable v is obtained by looking it up in the state s. For operators we determine the values of the operands recursively and apply the mathematical operator corresponding to the operator indicated in the syntax. Note that the operators $+$, $-$ and $*$ occurring on the left in these equations are just syntax, while their counterparts on the right are the corresponding operations on values.

The function $\mathcal{A}$ is a mathematical entity that assigns a value to syntax. In [15] the Nielsons already indicate that there is a direct mapping from this mathematical function to a function in a functional programming language. In a modern functional programming language like Clean this can be further improved for instance by user defined infix operators and constructors. The advantages of using a functional language instead of a mathematics are **1)** the compiler of the

---

[1] While we follow the approach of the Nielson's we will call the relation between variables and their values state, just as they do. In our own work we call this function environment.

$$\mathcal{A} :: A \rightarrow \text{State} \rightarrow \text{Int}$$
$$\mathcal{A}[\![\,n\,]\!]\, s = \mathcal{N}[\![\,n\,]\!]$$
$$\mathcal{A}[\![\,v\,]\!]\, s = s\, v$$
$$\mathcal{A}[\![\,a_1 + a_2\,]\!]\, s = \mathcal{A}[\![\,a_1\,]\!]\, s + \mathcal{A}[\![\,a_2\,]\!]\, s$$
$$\mathcal{A}[\![\,a_1 - a_2\,]\!]\, s = \mathcal{A}[\![\,a_1\,]\!]\, s - \mathcal{A}[\![\,a_2\,]\!]\, s$$
$$\mathcal{A}[\![\,a_1 * a_2\,]\!]\, s = \mathcal{A}[\![\,a_1\,]\!]\, s \times \mathcal{A}[\![\,a_2\,]\!]\, s$$

Fig. 1. Classical definition of the semantics of arithmetic expressions

functional language can be used for static sanity checks of the specification (e.g. that all identifiers are defined and the specification is correctly typed); **2)** the specification can be executed. The execution of the semantics can for instance be used to validate the definition by interactive simulation, or to test properties of the semantics automatically. Possible drawbacks of using a functional language instead of mathematics are **1)** there are constructs in mathematics that cannot be expressed directly in a functional programming language; **2)** in general it is easier to add ad-hoc notation and new constructs to mathematics than in a functional language; **3)** in mathematics it is very well possible to reason about undefinedness and nontermination, if we are not careful this might cause run-time errors on nonterminating computations in a functional language. In this section we show that a modern functional language is very suited to express the semantics in a concise way.

As a first example we restate the semantics of arithmetic expressions in Clean instead of the mathematical formulation above. In order to mimic the syntactic match we model the arithmetic expressions by the datatype AExpr. This data type directly mimics the syntax of allowed expressions given above. In this datatype we append a dot to the names of infix operators (like +) that are defined with a different purpose in Clean. The priority of the operators is chosen such that expressions like Var "x" +. Int 2 *. Var "y" have the usual binding of operators (here Var "x" +. (Int 2 *. Var "y")). This detail is left unspecified or implicit above. If we do not want to specify those details we can simply label the infix constructors as **infix**.

```
:: AExpr
   = Int Int
   | Var Var
   | (+.) infixl 6 AExpr AExpr
   | (-.) infixl 6 AExpr AExpr
   | (*.) infixl 7 AExpr AExpr
:: Var :== String
```

If desired we can even reuse the the ordinary Clean infix symbols in right-hand sides of definitions by defining appropriate instances of the infix symbols.

```
instance - AExpr where (-) a b = a -. b
```

The environment used in the semantics is a function from variables, Var, to integers, Int.

```
:: Env := Var → Int
```

```
emptyEnv :: Env
emptyEnv = λx → 0
```

The equivalent of the mathematical semantic function $\mathcal{A}$ from figure 1 is the function A given in figure 2. Note that these functions have exactly the same length and structure. In the function A we are not bound to the naming conventions of $\mathcal{A}$. Hence we can use x and y instead of a_1 and a_2. The various elements of the language are determined by the type they obtain from the context in which they are used instead of the naming conventions.

```
A :: AExpr Env → Int                              1
A (Int i)  env = i                                2
A (Var v)  env = env v                            3
A (x +. y) env = A x env + A y env                4
A (x -. y) env = A x env - A y env                5
A (x *. y) env = A x env * A y env                6
```

Fig. 2. Semantics of arithmetic expressions in Clean

In exactly the same way we define a data type for Boolean expressions and the associated semantics in figure 3. This data type directly follows the syntax for B given above. Just like above we added priorities to the infix operators in order to assign the usual binding to Boolean expressions without parentheses.

```
:: BExpr                                          1
   = TRUE                                         2
   | FALSE                                        3
   | (=.) infix 4 AExpr AExpr                     4
   | (<.) infix 4 AExpr AExpr                     5
   | ¬. BExpr                                     6
   | (&&.) infixr 3 BExpr BExpr                   7
                                                  8
B :: BExpr Env → Bool                             9
B TRUE       env = True                           10
B FALSE      env = False                          11
B (x =. y)  env = A x env = A y env               12
B (x <. y)  env = A x env < A y env               13
B (¬. exp)  env = not (B exp env)                 14
B (x &&. y) env = B x env && B y env              15
```

Fig. 3. Boolean expressions and their semantics

According to these definitions the semantics of integers and Booleans in While inherits the semantics of Int and Bool in Clean. If this is not desired we can define tailor made data types and operations to describe the desired semantics.

2.3   Denotational Semantics

The goal of denotational semantics is to show the effect of executing a program. In the traditional formulation this is done by a function $\mathcal{DS} :: S \rightarrow$ State $\hookrightarrow$ State using a syntactic pattern match on statements. The state of a program is just its environment. The effect of an assignment is a change in the state or environment:

$$\mathcal{DS}\,[\![\,v := a\,]\!]\,s \;=\; s\,[\,v \mapsto \mathcal{A}\,[\![\,a\,]\!]\,s\,]$$

This reads that the same environment is returned that is received as argument, but the binding of variable v is mapped to the value of the arithmetic expression a. Note that v and a are meta variables, they represent all concrete variable and expressions that can occur in the language While.

The updated state function $s\,[\,x \mapsto i]$ associates the same value to every argument as s except the argument x is mapped to i:

$$(s\,[\,x \mapsto i]) \; x = i$$
$$(s\,[\,x \mapsto i]) \; y = s \; y, \; \text{if } x \neq y$$

In Clean we define the operator $\mapsto$ (written in plain text as |->) to achieve this effect, e.g. ("x" $\mapsto$ 1) emptyEnv.

```
(↦) infix :: Var Int → Env → Env
(↦) v i = λenv x.if (x=v) i (env x)
```

We use the functional language approach where the statements are represented by a data structure and an associated interpretation function as specified in figure 4. Again this is a direct transcription of the usual mathematical formulation of the denotational semantics using Scott brackets.

```
:: Stmt                                                              1
   = (:=.) infix 2 Var AExpr                                        2
   | (:.) infixl 1 Stmt Stmt                                        3
   | Skip                                                            4
   | IF BExpr Stmt Stmt                                             5
   | While BExpr Stmt                                               6
                                                                    7
ds :: Stmt Env → Env                                                8
ds (v :=. a)   env = (v ↦ A a env) env                             9
ds Skip        env = env                                            10
ds (s1 :. s2) env = ds s2 (ds s1 env)                              11
ds (IF c t e) env = if (B c env) (ds t env) (ds e env)             12
ds (While c stmt) env                                               13
   = fix (λf env2 . if (B c env2) (f (ds stmt env2)) env2) env     14
                                                                    15
fix :: (a → a) → a                                                  16
fix f = f (fix f)                                                   17
```

Fig. 4. Statements and their denotational semantics

The denotational semantics focusses on the meaning of programs and not on their detailed execution. For this reason the while-statement is not evaluated step by step in the semantics. The semantics simply states that the state produced by the semantics of the while statement (if any) is the fixed point of the given function. Of course there are statements (like `While TRUE Skip`) that have no fixed point. Technically the semantics is a partial function that assigns a meaning, state transformation, to correct terminating statements.

Example. As an example we show how the famous Euclid algorithm to compute greatest common divisors in the language While can be expressed as a data structure of type `Stmt`. This algorithm expects the arguments in the variables a and b and leaves the result in the variable b. Since the language While has no functions nor print statement this is about the best we can do.

```
gcdStmt
=  IF (va =. zero)
       (c :=. vb)
       (While (¬. (vb =. zero))
           (IF (vb <. va)
                 (a :=. va -. vb)
                 (b :=. vb -. va)
           ) :.
         c :=. va
       )
   where
       a = "a"; va = Var a
       b = "b"; vb = Var b
       c = "c"; vc = Var c
```

We can use the executability of the semantics to compute for instance the greatest common divisor of 294 and 546 by storing these values at the labels a (represented as `"a"`) and b (represented as `"b"`) in an (empty) environment (`emptyEnv`). The denotational semantics (`ds`) of the `gcdStmt` and this environment yields an environment that contains the result at `"c"`. Hence applying the environment to `"c"` yields the value given by the denotational semantics of this While program. This can be computed by the following one-liner in Clean:

```
Start = ds gcdStmt (("a" ↦ 294) (("b" ↦ 546) emptyEnv)) "c"
```

As expected this produces the value 42, which is the correct result.

2.4 Natural Semantics

The natural semantics is a big step semantics that focuses on the effect of the individual language constructs. Since this is a big step semantics it constructs the final state in one go by applying the semantic function recursively to intermediate results, just like the denotational semantics. For the while-statement it will evaluate the body once if the condition holds and continue with the semantics of the same loop in the new state. For all other statements the formulation

```
ns :: Stmt Env → Env                                                    1
ns (v :=. e)     env = (v ↦ A e env) env                                2
ns (s1 :. s2)    env = ns s2 (ns s1 env)                                3
ns Skip          env = env                                              4
ns (IF c t e) env |   B c env  = ns t env                               5
ns (IF c t e) env | ¬(B c env) = ns e env                               6
ns (While c s) env |   B c env  = ns (While c s) (ns s env)             7
ns (While c s) env | ¬(B c env) = env                                   8
```

Fig. 5. The natural semantics of statements

of the semantics in figure 5 is identical to the denotational semantics given in figure 4.

This natural semantics (ns) can be executed in exactly the same way as the denotational semantics (ds). As required this produces the same result for the gcdStmt shown above. Below we discuss how the equivalency of those semantics can be investigated more thoroughly.

In the traditional representation of the operational semantics, the semantics is often specified by a transition system. This system has two kind of configurations: a tuple $< S, s >$ connecting a statement S and a state s, or a final state s. Transitions are given in the form of axioms. If the premisses above the line and the condition to the right of the line holds, the conclusion below the line holds. For instance the natural semantics for the while-statement if the condition of the statement holds is expressed as:

$$[\text{while}_{\text{TRUE}}] \quad \frac{< S, s >\rightarrow s_1, \; < \text{while } b \; S, s_1 >\rightarrow s_2}{< \text{while } b \; S, s >\rightarrow s_2} \; \text{if } \mathcal{B}[\![b]\!] \, s$$

The part within the square brackets on the left is the name of this axiom. The phrase if $\mathcal{B}[\![b]\!] \, s$ is the condition. If this condition does not hold, the rest of the axiom cannot be applied.

The advantage of this approach is that it is not necessary to give an order in the reduction rules, nor to be complete (as in an axiomatic semantics). However, in order to obtain a deterministic semantics we have to prove that the result of semantics is independent of the order of applying these axioms, or we have to show that there is only one order. In figure 5 we use one function to represent all axioms. It is easy to see that the alternatives of the function ns all cover different cases, and hence these alternatives can be written in any order.

If necessary the natural semantics of While in Clean can be formulated in closer correspondence to the axiom by writing:

```
ns (While b s) env | B b env = env2
where env1 = ns s env; env2 = ns (While b s) env1
```

We prefer the equivalent formulation in figure 5 since it is shorter and shows the difference and similarity with the denotational semantics clearer.

2.5   Structural Operational Semantics

The structural operational semantics is a small-step semantics. It specifies the result of individual reduction steps. Hence the semantics does not always yield the final state, it can also yield an intermediate configuration consisting of a statement and the associated environment:

```
:: Config = Final Env | Inter Stmt Env
```

The structural operational semantics of our example language While is given in figure 6.

```
sosStep :: Stmt Env → Config                                              1
sosStep (v :=. e)  s = Final ((v ↦ A e s) s)                              2
sosStep Skip       s = Final s                                            3
sosStep (s1 :. s2) s                                                      4
  = case sosStep s1 s of                                                  5
      Final s'    = Inter s2 s'                                           6
      Inter s1' s' = Inter (s1' :. s2) s'                                 7
sosStep (IF c t e) s |   B c s  = Inter t s                              8
sosStep (IF c t e) s | ¬(B c s) = Inter e s                              9
sosStep (While c body) s = Inter (IF c (body :. While c body) Skip) s   10
```

Fig. 6. The structural operational semantics of statements

By applying this function repeatedly until we reach a `Final` configuration we obtain a trace of the reduction. For non terminating programs this trace will be an infinite list of configurations[2].

```
sosTrace :: Config → [Config]
sosTrace c=:(Final _)   = [c]
sosTrace c=:(Inter ss s) = [c: sosTrace (sosStep ss s)]
```

Using this trace we can construct a function `sos` with the same type as the other functions specifying the semantics. This function yields the state in the final state that can be found in the last configuration of the trace.

```
sos :: Stmt Env → Env
sos s env = env1 where (Final env1) = last (sosTrace (Inter s env))
```

There is much more to be said about semantics. For instance the language While can be extended by language constructs like pure functions and procedures. In a similar style we can also define the semantics of functional programming languages. Due to space limitations we will not elaborate on this here.

---

[2] The pattern c=:(Final s) for function arguments allows us to use the entire argument as c in the right-hand side, as well as to do a pattern match on a constructor and to use sub-arguments (like s) in the right-hand side.

2.6   Sanity Checks

Since our semantics is just a set of types and functions in a functional programming language, we can use the language implementation (here Clean) for elementary sanity checks of the specified semantics. In our examples the Clean compiler checks that all identifiers used are defined and used in a proper type context. Also the compiler checks the type correctness of each and every subexpression. Moreover the compiler can produce a warning if the semantics is a partial function, e.g. since no semantics is given for one of the language constructs. For a semantics defined in mathematics one has to rely on humans. If the semantics is formalized in some proof tool, this tool will provide similar support.

Although this sounds simple, it appears to be very useful. The draft version of these notes contained for a very long time the rule

$$\mathcal{DS} \llbracket v := a \rrbracket \, s \; = \; s \, [\, x \mapsto \mathcal{A} \llbracket a \rrbracket \, s \,]$$

Neither the authors nor the readers discovered that there was a wrong meta variable used in this definition[3] for a very long time. This mistake was found with a lot of luck. If we would have made the corresponding error in the semantics expressed in Clean(line 9 of figure 4), the Clean compiler would have indicated a problem immediately. We do not claim that the compiler of the host language will find all issues, but in our experience it really helps to get the semantics correctly.

2.7   Simulating the Semantics

Having the statements available as a data type and semantics available as functions in Clean we can use the fact that the semantics is executable. For instance we can make an editor for statements using iTasks. At the push of a button the iTask system can show the trace of the reduction of such a program using the structural operational semantics defined by sos, or the value of all used variables in the environment that is yielded by execution of the semantics. Since this is a straightforward application of iTasks that has its power in interactive simulation, we do not elaborate on this here.

2.8   Testing Properties of the Semantics

Another possibility is to test properties of the semantics using our model based test system G∀st. We now give a quick overview of model-based testing with logical properties as models, see [8] for details. Next we will show some applications of model-based testing for the semantics of While.

Model-Based Testing of Logical Properties. The main difference between model-based testing with logical properties and an ordinary automated test tool

---

[3] Another option is that the readers discovered it, but didn't tell it to the authors. Given the other feedback, this is highly unlikely.

like JUnit[4] is that the model-based test tool generates the test case while in JUnit they are always specified by the programmer. Both kind of test tools execute the tests automatically and give a verdict.

We will illustrate this with a few simple examples. First we introduce the enumeration type `Color` and the recursive algebraic data type `Tree`.

```
:: Color = Red | Yellow | Blue
:: Tree a = Leaf | Node (Tree a) a (Tree a)
```

The function `mirror` recursively flips the left and right subtree of nodes in the tree.

```
mirror :: (Tree a) → Tree a
mirror Leaf         = Leaf
mirror (Node l a r) = Node (mirror r) a (mirror l)
```

A desirable property of this `mirror` function is that applying it twice to a tree t yields the original tree. In logic this is:

$$\forall t \in \text{Tree } \tau \,.\, \text{mirror (mirror } t) \,=\, t$$

In a JUnit setting the user chooses some typical values for the tree t and checks the property for these values. For example `equal (mirror (mirror Leaf)) Leaf` and `equal (mirror (mirror (Node Leaf Red (Node Leaf Blue Leaf)))) (Node Leaf Red (Node Leaf Blue Leaf))`.

In the model-based test tool G∀st we only indicate the type of arguments that need to be generated, otherwise it is a direct translation of the logical property:

```
propMirror1 :: (Tree Color) → Bool
propMirror1 t = mirror (mirror t) == t
```

Any function yielding a Boolean, or special test value of type `Property`, can be interpreted as property where the arguments are interpreted as universal quantified variables. G∀st test this property by generating a large number of elements of type `Tree Color` and evaluates the function `propMirror1` for these test cases. We have to indicate the type in order to allow G∀st to generate the test cases.

The list of test cases is generated by the generic function `ggen`. In most situations we can just derive the generation from the generic algorithm:

derive ggen Color, Tree

For any data type this generic generation algorithm [6] produces a list of all instances of that type. If the instances of the type have more than one subtype, these instances are generated in a breadth first way. To make the testers happy

---

[4] JUnit is a well known test tool for the Java programming language. It executes a number of predefined tests (basically expression yielding a Boolean value). If such a test yields **True** it is regarded a success, otherwise it indicates an issue. JUnit generates a report giving the number of successes and issues. For the test yielding **False** JUnit prints the arguments of the test function. Originally JUnit was associated with Java, meanwhile it is ported to most mainstream languages.

there is some pseudo random perturbation of the order of elements compared to pure breadth first traversal. As a consequences elements can appear somewhat earlier or later in the list of test values. For instance the first 10 elements generated of type `Tree Color` are:

```
[Leaf
,Node Leaf Blue Leaf
,Node (Node Leaf Red Leaf) Blue Leaf
,Node Leaf Yellow Leaf
,Node (Node (Node Leaf Red Leaf) Red Leaf) Blue Leaf
,Node (Node Leaf Red Leaf) Yellow Leaf
,Node Leaf Blue (Node (Node Leaf Red Leaf) Red Leaf)
,Node (Node Leaf Yellow Leaf) Blue Leaf
,Node (Node (Node Leaf Red Leaf) Red Leaf) Yellow Leaf
,Node (Node Leaf Red Leaf) Blue (Node (Node Leaf Red Leaf) Red Leaf)
]
```

Executing `Start` = `test propMirror1` yields Pass[5], no counterexamples are found in the executed tests.

As a second property we might formulate that the function `mirror` should change its argument tree:

```
propMirror2 :: (Tree Color) → Bool
propMirror2 t = mirror t =!= t
```

The test system immediately finds a large number of counterexamples like `Leaf`, `Node Leaf Red Leaf` and so on. If we think a little harder we would realize that this property holds for nonsymmetric trees. An appropriate way to improve the property is by adding a precondition; only if the tree is not symmetric mirroring should change it:

```
propMirror3 :: (Tree Color) → Property
propMirror3 t = not (symmetric t) ==> mirror t =!= t

symmetric Leaf        = True
symmetric (Node l _ r) = l === r && symmetric l && symmetric r
```

Another direction to tackle the problems with the second property is by generating only asymmetric trees. The generic generation algorithm cannot do this all by itself. A possible solution is replacing the generic generation algorithm by a specific instance that transforms lists to list like trees (all left subtrees are empty):

```
ggen{|Tree|} f n r = map listToTree (ggen{|*→*|} f n r)

listToTree :: ([t] → Tree t)
listToTree = foldr (Node Leaf) Leaf
```

---

[5] Only in exceptional cases G∀st is able to *prove* properties by exhaustive testing. For such tests we either have to give a finite test suite by hand, or the only universal quantified variables are of nonrecursive algebraic data types or finite primitive types (like `Bool` and `Char`).

Now G∀st uses this generator of list-like trees in any property tested. If we want specific test cases only for one test, we should use the operator `For` (see below). Executing the test shows that this does not remove the problems with `propMirror2`, if there are less than two `Node`s in the tree, it is still symmetric.

Some other possibilities of the test system are introduced below, see [8] for a more elaborate and complete treatment.

Model-Based Testing of the Semantics of While. Now we turn to model-based testing properties of the semantics of While. Consider the factorial function in While:

```
facStmt :: Stmt
facStmt
  = y :=. one :.
    While (one <. vx)
    (
        y :=. vy *. vx :.
        x :=. vx -. one
    )
where
    x = "x"; vx = Var x
    y = "y"; vy = Var y
```

```
instance one AExpr where one = Int 1
```

Given any semantics `sem`, the semantics of the factorial function used with an environment that assigns 4 to the variable `"x"`, should produce an environment that associates 24 to the variable `"y"`. In logic this is:

$$\forall \, sem \in (\text{Stmt} \to \text{Env} \to \text{Env}) \, . \, sem \; facStmt \; (x \; \mapsto \; 4 \, (\lambda \, x \, . \, 0)) \, y \; = \; 24$$

In G∀st this property reads:

```
propFac :: (Stmt Env → Env) → Bool
propFac sem = sem facStmt (("x" ↦ 4) emptyEnv) "y" == 24
```

We can test this property for our three versions of the semantics (`ds`, `ns`, and `sos`) by executing:

```
Start = test (propFac For [ds, ns, sos])
```

Executing this program yields `Proof`. The Proof by exhaustive testing produced by the test system gives us confidence in the consistency and hence the correctness of the various semantics.

Of course one can think of many incorrect semantics that produce an incorrect environment in the example above. That is exactly the reason why we explicitly enumerate the semantics that needs to be used in testing this property, rather that let the test system generate a semantics.

Generating Terminating Statements. More general, the semantics of any statement should be equal for the natural semantics (**ns**) and the denotational semantics (ds). In order to guarantee that the test terminates we only want to consider statements that are known to terminate. We ensure this by generating only while-statements that correspond to for-loops with a limited number of iterations.

We cannot directly use the generic algorithm [6] to generate statements to be used in the tests: instances of the type Stmt. Since the generic generation algorithm has no notion of statements nor of their semantics, it will simply generate valid instances of this type without taking care of the desired properties. In general there are two ways to solve this kind of generation issues. First we can specify the generation completely by hand instead of using the generic algorithm. In this situation we need to derive ggen{|Stmt|} such that it yields (an infinite) list of terminating statements. In general this can be quite tricky. An easier and more elegant alternative is to define an additional data type that represents only terminating statements Gstmt and the associated transformation conv to statements. Once we start doing this we also introduce types to control the generation of numbers, variables and so on. The only interesting point is that we replace general while-loops that might cause nontermination with for-loops with a decreasing counter and a small counter value.

```
:: Gstmt
   = Assign Gvar GAExpr
   | Comp Gstmt Gstmt
   | Gskip
   | GIF GBExpr Gstmt Gstmt
   | GFor (Maybe GBExpr) Gvar GNat Gstmt

:: GNat = GNat Int
:: Gvar = Gvar String

:: GAExpr
   = GInt Int
   | GVar Gvar
   | GPlus GAExpr GAExpr
   | GMinus GAExpr GAExpr
   | GTimes GAExpr GAExpr
```

Instances of the generic generation function ggen for the natural numbers and variables are defined by hand: positive numbers and single letter variables.

```
ggen{|GNat|} n r = map GNat  [0..]
ggen{|Gvar|} n r = map (Gvar o toString)  ['a'..'z']
```

For all other and more complex types, we use the generic algorithm incorporated in G∀st. Since those types have many combinators and (double) recursion it would be rather cumbersome to define generation for those types manually.

derive ggen Gstmt, GAExpr, Maybe

For convenience we introduce a class conv to do the transformation from the generation types to the types used in the semantics.

```
class conv a b :: a → b
```

The transformation of expressions is a very simple one to one mapping:

```
instance conv GAExpr AExpr
where
    conv (GInt i)          = Int i
    conv (GVar (Gvar v))= Var v
    conv (GPlus x y)       = conv x +. conv y
    conv (GMinus x y)      = conv x -. conv y
    conv (GTimes x y)      = conv x *. conv y
```

The transformation of most statements is equally simple. Only in the transformation of for-loops to while-loops we need to do some work: we introduce a semi-fresh counter, initialize it with the given integer value and enter a while loop. The condition is the combination of the given boolean value (if the maybe type provides it) and the boolean expression that checks if the value of the counter is still positive. Since the introduced variable is only fresh in the body of the loop, introducing this variable can alter the semantics of the existing statement in Gstmt form. Since our only purpose is to generate valid and terminating statements, this is no problem whatsoever.

```
instance conv Gstmt Stmt
where
    conv (Assign (Gvar v) e)    = v :=. conv e
    conv (Comp x y)             = conv x :. conv y
    conv Gskip                  = Skip
    conv (GIF c t e)            = IF (conv c) (conv t) (conv e)
    conv (GFor b (Gvar v) (GNat n) s)
    =   counter :=. (Int n) :.
        While cond
            (body :.
             counter :=. Var counter -. one
            )
    where
        counter = fresh v (allvars body)
        cond    = case b of
                    Nothing = c0
                    Just b  = c0 &&. conv b
        body    = conv s
        c0      = Int 0 <. Var counter
```

The function allvars that yields all variables that occur on the left-hand side of an assignment in a program in the language While is defined as

```
allvars :: Stmt → [Var]
allvars (x :=. e)    = [x]
allvars (s :. t)     = allvars s + allvars t
allvars Skip         = []
allvars (IF c t e)   = allvars t + allvars e
allvars (While c b)  = allvars b

instance + [x] | Eq x where (+) x y = removeDup (x++y)
```

Having the generic generation of the new data types and the conversion of these data types to the data types used for statements in the semantics, we can define the generation of statements as a simple combination of these items.

```
ggen{|Stmt|}  n r = map conv stmts
where stmts :: [Gstmt]
      stmts = ggen{|*|} n r
```

Since Gstmt only contains quickly terminating statements, the statements of type Stmt generated in this way will also terminate.

The first 10 elements of the list of statements generated are:

```
[ a :=. a
, a0 :=. 0 :.
  While (0 <. a0 &&. -2147483648 <. a+.1+.0)
    (Skip :.
      a   :=. 0 :.
      a0 :=. a0 -. 1
    )
, b :=. a
, a :=. (0 *. (1 -. 0)) +. 2147483647
, Skip
, a :=. -2147483648 :.
  a :=. -2147483648 :.
  a :=. -1 :.
  a :=. -1
, IF TRUE
    (a :=. -1 -. a)
    (a :=. 2147483647)
, IF FALSE
    (a :=. -1 -. a)
    (a :=. 2147483647)
, c :=. a
, Skip :.
  a :=. 1
]
```

This generation of terminating statements is used in each and every property below that quantifies over statements.

Comparing Environments. The semantic functions yield the final environment which is a function. In general it is very hard to compare functions. Here it is sufficient to check that the environment produces the same value for all variables that occur in the statement. For this purpose we use the function allvars defined above. The function eqEnv that determines the equivalence of environments is straightforward.

```
eqEnv :: Env Env [Var] → Bool
eqEnv f g vars = and [f v = g v \\ v←vars]
```

Testing Semantic Properties of While Part 2. After these preparations, the property of testing equivalences between natural semantics and denotational semantics becomes:

```
prop1 :: Stmt → Bool
prop1 stmt = eqEnv (ns stmt emptyEnv) (ds stmt emptyEnv) (allvars stmt)
```

Similar properties can be stated for other combinations of the various versions of the semantics. Executing these tests yield Pass, which further increases the confidence in our definitions.

Our next property says that for all semantics and statements stmt, the semantics of that statement is equal to the semantics of Skip :. stmt.

```
propSkip :: (Stmt Env → Env) Stmt → Bool
propSkip sem stmt
 = eqEnv (sem stmt emptyEnv) (sem (Skip :. stmt) emptyEnv) (allvars stmt)
```

Another property used in the test is that the semantics for all terminating while-statements While b s is equivalent to the semantics of IF b (s :. While b s) Skip. This property needs some tweaking to generate terminating while statements corresponding to for loops.

```
propWhile :: (Stmt Env → Env) (Maybe GBExpr) Gvar GNat Gstmt → Bool
propWhile sem b v n s
 = eqEnv (sem stmt emptyEnv)
         (sem (decl :. IF cond loop Skip) emptyEnv)
         (allvars stmt)
where (stmt =: (decl :. loop =: (While cond body))) = conv (GFor b v n s)
```

Of course we do not require that this property holds for each and every semantics one can imagine. It is sufficient if this property holds for the three semantics introduced above. We achieve this by executing test (propWhile For [ds,ns,sos]) instead of test propWhile. Also this property passes the tests.

In the same spirit we can test whether for all of our three versions of the semantics the binding direction of the semi colon is irrelevant. In mathematics this reads $\forall s, t, u \in Stmt . sem ((s ; t) ; u) env = sem (s ; (t ; u)) env$. As a property in G∀st this reads:

```
propSemiColon :: (Stmt Env → Env) Stmt Stmt Stmt → Property
propSemiColon sem s t u
 = name ";"
    λsem .
   (eqEnv (sem (s :. (t :. u)) e)
          (sem ((s :. t) :. u) e)
          (allvars (s :. t :. u))
   )
where e = emptyEnv
```

Obviously we have chosen to test this with an empty environment. If desired we can of course extend the property, and hence the test to various environments. Fortunately also this properties passes the tests.

In our final example we extend the first test we used for Euler's algorithm to all our semantics and all integer arguments. we compute the desired result by the function gcd provided by Clean's standard libraries.

```
propGCD :: (Stmt Env → Env) (Int,Int) → Property
propGCD sem (a,b)
    = sem gcdStmt (("a" ↦ a) (("b" ↦ b) emptyEnv)) "c" = gcd a b
```

We can test this property for our three versions of the semantics and all arguments between 0 and 100 by executing:

```
Start = test ((λsem.propGCD sem For [(a,b) \\ a←[0..100], b←[0..100]])
                          For [ds,ns,sos])
```

If we allow sufficient test instances, G∀st is able to prove this property by exhaustive testing the property for the given values after executing 30603 test cases.

These examples illustrates how one can formulate properties about the semantics in G∀st and test these properties fully automatically. This leaves us with the problem how to find properties to be tested. We handle this question in the next paragraph.

Developing Properties to be Tested. There is always human intelligence necessary to define properties of a semantics that can be tested in order to gain confidence in the quality of specification. Nevertheless, it is not all black magic. A few simple guidelines provide helpful hints to construct properties.

1. First there are the general properties that are known to hold in the semantics of the language at hand. Examples of such properties are propSkip and propWhile above. It is straight forward to transform the known mathematical properties to G∀st and to execute the associated tests. This is an easy check after the basic sanity checks provided by the Clean compiler.
2. We can often easily indicate properties of a semantics or structures used in such a semantics.

    For instance for the environment used here: the empty environment should yield the value 0 for all variables, and after storing a result for some variable, looking up the value of that variable should produce the stored value.

```
pEnv1 :: Var → Bool
pEnv1 v = emptyEnv v = 0

pEnv2 :: Var Res → Bool
pEnv2 v i = (v ↦ i) emptyEnv v = i
```

In the same spirit, but slightly more advanced, storing a value with a different name in an environment does not change the value of the original variable in the environment.

```
pEnv3 :: Var Res Var Res → Property
pEnv3 v i w j = w ≠ v ==> (w ↦ j) ((v ↦ i) emptyEnv) v = i
```

The property `pEnv3` produces a `Property` instead of a Boolean as result since we used the logical combinator `=⇒`. This operator mimics implication, $\Rightarrow$, from logic and is used here as additional constraint on the values used in the tests.

3. Finally, the issues[6] found during the development of the semantics are a valuable source of testable properties. If there was ever an issue with the semantics of a specific construct and value, we can state the property that it should produce the correct value. It is even better if we can generalize such a property for all values and introduce a universal quantified variable. We will encounter some examples in the iTask semantics given below.

This completes our introduction to semantics and testing properties of such a semantics. In the next section we apply these techniques to give a semantics for iTask workflow management system.

3   A Semantics for iTasks

The iTask system supports workers executing the specified tasks by a web-based interface. Typical elementary user tasks in this system are filling in forms and pressing buttons to make choices. The elementary tasks are implemented on top of the iData system [16]. Based on an input the iTask system determines the new task that has to be done and updates the interface in the browser. Arbitrary complex tasks are created by combining (elementary) tasks. The real power of data dependent tasks is provided by the monadic bind operator that contains a *function* to generate the next task based on the value produced by the previous task.

The iTask implementation executes the tasks, but has to cope with many other things at the same time: e.g. i/o to files and database, generation of the multi-user web interface, client/server evaluation of tasks, and exception handling. The iTask system uses generic programming to derive interfaces to files, databases and web-browsers for data types. The combination of these things makes the implementation of iTasks much too complicated to grasp the semantics. To overcome these problems we develop a high level operational semantics for iTasks in this paper. The semantics in this paper is an extended version of our earlier work published in [9]. This semantics is used to explain the behavior of the iTask system, and to reason about the desired behavior of the system. In the future we will use this semantics as model to test the real iTask implementation with our model-based test tool G∀st. A prerequisite for model-based testing is an accurate model of the desired behavior. Making a model with the desired properties is not easy. Such a model is developed, validated, and its properties are tested in this paper.

---

[6] Issue is the notion used in model based testing to indicate any failing test. This includes all sources of failure. A failing test indicates not always an error in the tested software. Failing test can also be caused by, for instance, erroneous properties or invalid test data.

In the original iTask system a task is a state transformer of the strict and unique Task State TSt. The required uniqueness of the task state (to guarantee single threaded use of the state in a pure functional language) is in Clean indicated by the type annotation *. The type parameter a indicates the type of the result. This result is returned by the task when it is completely finished.

```
:: Task a :== *TSt → *(a,*TSt)    // an iTask is a state transition of type TSt
```

Hence, a Task of type a is a function that takes a unique task state TSt as argument and produces a unique tuple with a value of type a and a new unique task state. In these notes we consider only one basic task: the edit task.

```
editTask :: String a → Task a | iData a
```

The function editTask takes a string and a value of type a as arguments and produces a (Task a) under the context restriction that the type a is in the type class iData. The class iData is used to create a web based editor for values of this type. Here we assume that the desired instances are defined.

The editTask function creates a GUI to modify a value of the given type, and adds a button with the given name to finish the task. A user can change the value as often as she wants. The task is not finished until the button is pressed. There are predefined editors for all basic data types. For other data types an editor can be derived using Clean's generic programming mechanism, or a tailor-made editor can be defined for that type.

In these notes we focus on the following basic iTask combinators to compose tasks.

```
return            :: a                        → Task a      | iData a
(>>=)  infixl 1 :: (Task a) (a→Task b)       → Task b      | iData b
(-||-) infixr 3 :: (Task a) (Task a)         → Task a      | iData a
(-&&-) infixr 4 :: (Task a) (Task b)         → Task (a,b)  | iData a & iData b
```

The combinators return and >>= are the usual monadic *return* and *bind*. The return combinator transforms a value to a task yielding that value immediately. The bind combinator is used to indicate a sequence of tasks. The expression t >>= u indicates that first task t must be done completely. When this is done, its result is given to u in order to create a new task that is executed subsequently.

The expression t -||- u indicates that both iTasks can be executed in *any* order and *interleaved*, the combined task is completed *as soon as* any subtask is done. The result is the result of the task that completes first, the other task is removed from the system. The expression t -&&- u states that both iTasks must be done in any order (interleaved), the combined task is completed when *both* tasks are done. The result is a tuple containing the results of both tasks.

All these combinators are higher order functions manipulating the complex task state TSt. This higher order function based approach is excellent for constructing such a library in a flexible and type safe way. However, if we want to construct a program with which we can reason about iTasks, higher order functions are rather inconvenient. In a functional programming language like Haskell or Clean it is not possible to inspect which function is given as argument to a higher order function. The only thing we can do with such a function given as

argument is applying it to arguments. In a programming context this is exactly
what one wants to do with such a function. In order to specify the semantics
of the various iTask combinators however, we need to know which operator we
are currently dealing with. This implies that we need to replace the higher order
functions by a *representation* that can be handled instead. We replace the higher
order functions and the task state TSt by the algebraic data type ITask. We use
infix the constructor .||. for the or-combinator, -||-, and the combinator .&&.
for and-combinator, -&&-, from the original iTask library.

```
:: ITask
   = EditTask      ID       String  BVal         // an editor
   | .||. infixr 3 ITask    ITask                // OR-combinator
   | .&&. infixr 4 ITask    ITask                // AND-combinator
   | Bind          ID       ITask   (Val→ITask)  // sequencing-combinator
   | Return        Val                           // return the value

:: Val  = Pair Val Val  | BVal BVal
:: BVal = String String | Int Int   | VOID
```

Instances of this type ITask are called *task trees*. Without loss of generality we
assume here that all editors return a value of a basic type (BVal). In the real
iTask system, editors can be used with every (user defined) data type. Using only
these basic values in the semantics makes it easier to construct a simulator that
preserves types (see section 7). Since the right-hand side of the sequencing operator Bind is a normal function, this model has here the same rich expressibility
as the real iTask system.

In order to write ITasks conveniently we introduce two abbreviations. For the
monadic Bind operator we define an infix version. This operator takes a task and
a function producing a new task as arguments and adds a default id to the Bind
constructor.

```
(⇒) infixl 1 :: ITask (Val→ITask) → ITask
(⇒) t f = Bind id1 t f
```

For convenience we introduce also the notion of a button task. It executes the
given iTask after the button with the given label is pressed. A button task is
composed of a VOID editor and a Bind operator ignoring the result of this editor.

```
ButtonTask i s t = EditTask i s VOID ⇒ λ_ → t
```

No implementation of the iTask system will show an editor for the type VOID,
the only value of this type cannot be changed. As a consequence the GUI of
the ButtonTask will be only the button with the label s. This is exactly what is
required.

3.1   Task Identification

The task to be executed is composed of elementary subtasks. These subtasks
can be changed by events in the generated web-interface, like entering a value
in a text-box or pushing a button. In order to link these events to the correct

subtask we need an identification mechanism for subtasks. We use an automatic system for the identification of subtasks. Neither the worker (the user executing a task), nor the workflow developer has to worry about these identifications. The fact that the iTask system is a multi-user system implies that there are multiple views on the workflow. Each worker can generate events, input for the workflow, independently of the other workers. The update of the task tree can generate new subtasks as well as remove subtasks of other workers. This implies that the ids of subtasks must be persistent. Hence, the numbering system has to be more advanced than just a numbering of the nodes. The semantics in these notes ignore the multi-user aspect of the semantics, but the numbering system is able to handle this (just as the real iTask system).

Tasks are identified by a list of integers. These task identifications are used similar to the sections in a book. On top level the tasks are assigned integer numbers starting at 0. In contrast to sections, the least significant numbers are on the head of the list rather than on the tail. The data type used to represent these task identifiers, ID, is just a list of integers.

```
:: ID = ID [Int]
```

```
next :: ID → ID
next (ID [a:x]) = ID [a+1:x]
```

Whenever a task is replaced by its successor the id is incremented with the function next. For every id, i, we have that next i ≠ i. In this way we distinguish inputs for a specific task from inputs to its successor. The function splitID generates a list of task identifiers for subtasks of a task with the given id. This function adds two numbers to the identifier, one number uniquely identifies the subtask and one number serves as version for this subtask. This version number is increased each time when the task accepts an edit event. This implies that applying an event repeatedly to a task has at most once an effect. If we would use the same number for both purposes, one application of the function next would incorrectly transform the identification of the current subtask to that of the next subtask.

```
splitID :: ID → [ID]
splitID (ID i) = [ID [0,j:i] \\ j ← [0..]]
```

These identifiers of subtasks are used to relate inputs to the subtasks they belong to. The function nmbr is used to assign fresh and unique identifiers to a task tree.

```
nmbr :: ID ITask → ITask
nmbr i (EditTask _ s v) = EditTask i s v
nmbr i (t .||. u)       = nmbr j t .||. nmbr k u where [j,k:_] = splitID i
nmbr i (t .&&. u)       = nmbr j t .&&. nmbr k u where [j,k:_] = splitID i
nmbr i (Bind _ t f)     = Bind k (nmbr j t) f    where [j,k:_] = splitID i
nmbr i t=:(Return _)    = t
```

By convention we start numbering with id1 = ID [0] in these notes.

3.2   Events

The inputs for a task are called *events*. This implies that the values of input devices are not considered as values that change in time, as in FRP (Functional Reactive Programming). Instead changing the value of an input device generates an event that is passed as an argument to the event handling function. This function generates a new state and a new user interface.

An event is either altering the current value of an editor task or pressing the button of such an editor. At every stage of running an iTask application, several editor tasks can be available. Hence many inputs are possible. Each event contains the `id` of the task to which it belongs as well as additional information about the event, the `EventKind`.

```
:: Event      = Event ID EventKind | Refresh
:: EventKind  = EE BVal | BE
```

The event kind `EE` (*E*ditor *E*vent) indicates a new basic value for an editor. A *B*utton *E*vent `BE` signals pressing the button in an editor indicating that the user finished editing.

Apart from these events there is a `Refresh` event. In the actual system it is generated by each refresh of the user-interface. In the real iTask system this event has two effects: 1) the task tree is *normalized*; and 2) an interface corresponding to the normalized task is generated. In the semantics we only care about the normalization effect. Normalization of a task tree has an effect on all subtasks that can be rewritten without user events. For instance, the task `editTask "ok" 1 -||- return 5` is normalized to `return 5`. Similarly the task `return 7 >>= editTask "ok"` is replaced by `editTask "ok" 7`. We elaborate on normalization in the next section.

3.3   Rewriting Tasks Given an Event

In this section we define a rewrite semantics for iTasks by defining how a task tree changes if we apply an event to the task tree. Rewriting is defined by an operator `@.`, pronounced as *apply*. We define a class for `@.` in order to be able to overload it, for instance with the application of a list of events to a task.

```
class (@.) infixl 9 a b :: a b → a
```

Given a task tree and an event, we can compute the new task tree representing the task after handling the current input. This is handled by the main instance of the operator `@.` for `ITask` and `Event` listed in figure 7. It is assumed that the task is properly numbered and normalized, and that the edit events have the same type as stored currently in the editor.

This semantics shows that the `id`s play a dominant role in the rewriting of task trees. An event only has an effect on a task with the same `id`. Edit tasks can react on edit events (line 3) as well as button events (line 4). Line 14 shows why the `Bind` operator has an id. Events are never addressed to this operator, but the id is used to normalize (and hence number) the new subtask that is dynamically generated by `f v` if the left-hand side task is finished. All other constructs pass

```
instance @. ITask Event                                              1
where                                                               2
  (@.) (EditTask i n v) (Event j (EE w)) | i==j = EditTask (next i) n w 3
  (@.) (EditTask i n v) (Event j BE)     | i==j = Return (BVal v)    4
  (@.) (t .||. u) e  = case t @. e of                               5
                        t=:(Return _) = t                           6
                        t = case u @. e of                          7
                              u=:(Return _)  = u                     8
                              u             = t .||. u               9
  (@.) (t .&&. u) e  = case (t @. e, u @. e) of                     10
                        (Return v, Return w) = Return (Pair v w)    11
                        (t, u)               = t .&&. u             12
  (@.) (Bind i t f) e = case t @. e of                             13
                        Return v = normalize i (f v)               14
                        t        = Bind i t f                      15
  (@.) t e = t                                                     16
```

Fig. 7. The basic semantics of iTasks

the events to their subtasks and check if the root of the task tree can be rewritten after the reduction of the subtasks. The recursive call with @. e on line 13 can only have an effect when the task was not yet normalized, in all other situations applying the event has no effect.

An event is enabled if there is a task in the task tree that is rewritten when the event is applied. For an edit task the enabled events are the edit and button event with the corresponding id. Also the edit tasks that are composed with the combinators .||. and .&&. and on the left-hand side of the Bind operator in an enabled subtask are enabled. All events that belong to the right-hand side of a bins operator are not enabeled. All events that are not enabled are ignored (line 16).

A properly numbered task tree remains correctly numbered after reduction. Editors that receive a new value get a new unique number by applying the function next to the task identification number. The numbering scheme used guarantees that this number cannot occur in any other subtask. If the left hand task of the bind-operator is rewritten to a normal form, a new task tree is generated by f v. The application of normalize (next i) to this tree guarantees that this tree is normalized and properly numbered within the surrounding tree.

The handling of events for a task tree is somewhat similar to the reduction in combinator systems or in the λ-calculus. An essential difference of such a reduction system with the task trees considered here is that all needed information is available inside a λ-expression. The evaluation of task trees needs the event as additional information.

Event sequences are handled by the following instance of the apply operator:

instance @. t [e] | @. t e **where** (@.) t es = foldl (@.) t es

Normalization. A task t is *normalized* (or *well formed*) iff t @. Refresh = t. The idea is that all reductions in the task tree that can be done without a new input should have been done. In addition we require that each task tree considered is properly numbered (using the algorithm nmbr in section 3.1). In the definition of the operator @. we assume that the task tree given as argument is already normalized. Each task can be normalized and properly numbered by applying the function normalize1 to that task.

```
normalize :: ID ITask → ITask
normalize i t = nmbr i (t @. Refresh)


normalize1 :: ITask → ITask
normalize1 t = normalize id1 t
```

Enabled Subtasks. All editor tasks that are currently part of the task tree are *enabled*, which implies that they can be rewritten if the right events are supplied. The subtasks that are generated by the function on the right-hand side of a Bind construct are **not** enabled, even if we can predict exactly what subtasks will be generated. The subtasks in the right-hand side of a bind do not exists until the Bind operator is rewritten. Until this rewrite takes place there is just a function that will produce the new task. Sometime this is rather confusing for human reader since the subtasks in the function seem to be present. Textually these subtasks are there, but operationally they are there only after the evaluation of the function. For instance, in task t5 defined below the subtask ButtonTask id2 "c" .. is not enabled until EditTask id1 "b" (Int 5) is finished.

Events accepted by the enabled subtasks are called *enabled events*, this is the set of events that have an effect on the task when it is applied to such an event. Consider the following tasks:

```
t1 = EditTask id1 "b" (Int 1) .&&. EditTask id2 "c" (Int 2)
t2 = EditTask id1 "b" (Int 1) .||. EditTask id2 "c" (Int 2)
t3 = ButtonTask id1 "b" (EditTask id2 "c" (Int 3))
t4 = ButtonTask id1 "b" t4
t5 = EditTask id1 "b" (Int 5) ⇛ λv.ButtonTask id2 "c" (Return (Pair v v))
t6 = EditTask id1 "b" (Int 6) ⇛ λv.t6
t7 v p = EditTask id1 "ok" v ⇛ λr=:(BVal w).if (p w) (Return r) (t7 w p)
```

In t1 and t2 all integer and button events with identifier id1 and id2 are enabled. In t3 and t4 only the event Event id1 BE is enabled. In t5, t6 and t7 all integer and button events with identifier id1 are enabled. All other events can only be processed after the button event for the task with id1 on the left-hand side of the bind operator.

Task t4 rewrites to itself after a button event. In t6 the same effect is reached by a bind operator. The automatic numbering system guarantees that the tasks obtain another id after applying the enabled button events. Task t7 is parameterized with a basic value and a predicate on such a value, and terminates only when the worker enters a value satisfying the predicate. This simple example shows that the bind operator is more powerful than just sequencing fixed tasks. In fact any function of type Val→ITask can be used there.

Normal Form. A task is in *normal form* if it has the form `Return v` for some value `v`. A task in normal form is not changed by applying any event. The function `isNF :: ITask → Bool` checks if a task is in normal form. In general a task tree does not have a unique normal form. The normal form obtained depends on the events applied to that task. For task `t2` above the normal form of `t2 @. Event id1 BE` is `Return (BVal (Int 1))` while `t2 @. Event id2 BE` is `Return` `(BVal (Int 2))`. However, for any given scenario that produces a normal form the obtained normal form is unique. The recursive tasks `t4` and `t6` do not have a normal form at all.

Needed Events. An event is *needed* in task `t` if the subtask to which the event belongs is enabled and the top node of the task tree `t` cannot be rewritten without that event.

In task `t1` above the events `Event id1 BE` and `Event id2 BE` are needed. Task `t2` has no needed event. This task can evaluate to a normal form by applying either `Event id1 BE` or `Event id2 BE`. As soon as one of these events is applied, the other task disappears. In `t3` only `Event id1 BE` is needed, the event `Event id2 BE` is not enabled. Similarly, in `t4`, `t5` and `t6` (only) the event `Event id1 BE` is needed.

For an edit-task the button-event is needed. Any number of edit-events can be applied to an edit-task, but they are not needed. For the task `t1 .&&. t2` the needed events are the sum of the needed events of `t1` and the needed events of `t2`. For a monadic bind the only needed events are the needed events of the left hand task. The needed events of a task `t` are obtained by `collectNeeded`. To ensure that needed events are collected in a normalized task we apply `normalize1` before scanning the task tree. In the actual iTask system the task is normalized by the initial refresh event and needs no new normalization ever after. In the task `t1 .||. t2` none of the events is needed, the task is finished as soon as the task `t1` or the task `t2` is finished. Normalization is only included here to ensure that the task is normalized in every application of this function.

```
collectNeeded :: ITask → [Event]
collectNeeded t = col (normalize1 t)
where
  col (EditTask id n v) = [Event id BE]
  col (t1 .&&. t2)      = col t1 ++ col t2
  col (Bind id t f)     = col t              // no events from f
  col _                 = []                 // Return and the OR-combinator
```

In exactly the same spirit `collectButtons` collects all enabled button events in a task tree, and `collect` yields all enabled button events plus the enabled edit events containing the current value of the editors. The function `collectEdit` yields all enabled edit events in the given task tree with the current value of the editors in the tree. All edit events with the same id and another value of the same type will also be accepted when we apply them to the task tree. The list of events is needed for the simulation of the task discussed in section 7.

An event is *accepted* if it causes a rewrite in the task tree, i.e. the corresponding subtask is enabled. A sequence of events is accepted if each of the events causes a rewrite when the events are applied in the given order. This implies that an accepted sequence of events can contain events that are not needed, or even not enabled in the original tree. In task t2 the button event with id1 and id2 are accepted, also the editor event Event id1 (EE (Int 42)) is accepted. All these events are enabled, but neither of them is needed. The task t5 accepts the sequence [Event id1 BE, Event id2 BE]. The second event is not enabled in t5, but applying Event id1 BE to t5 enables it.

Value. The *value* of a task is the value returned by the task if we repeatedly press the left most button in the task until it returns a value. This implies that the value of task t1 is Pair (Int 1) (Int 2), the value of t2 is Int 1 since buttons are pressed from left to right. The value of t3 is Int 3 and the value of t5 is Pair (Int 5) (Int 5). The value of t4 and t6 is undefined. Since a task cannot produce a value before all needed events are supplied, we can apply all needed events in one go (there is no need to do this from left to right).

For terminating tasks the value can be computed by inspection of the task tree, there is no need to do the actual rewrite steps as defined by the ¢. operator. For nonterminating tasks the value is undefined, because these tasks never return a value. The class val determines the value by inspection of the data structure.

```
class val a :: a → Val
```

```
instance val BVal where val v = BVal v
instance val Val  where val v = v
instance val ITask
where
    val (EditTask i n e)    = val e
    val (Return v)          = val v
    val (t .||. u)          = val t    // priority for the left subtask
    val (t .&&. u)          = Pair (val t) (val u)
    val (Bind i t f)        = val (f (val t))
```

The value produced is always equal to the value returned by the task if the user presses all needed buttons and the leftmost button if there is no needed button. The property pVal in section 5 states this and testing does not reveal any problems with this property.

The value of a task can change after applying an edit event. For instance the value of task EditTask id1 "ok" (BVal (Int 2)) is BVal (Int 2). After applying Event id1 (BVal (Int 7)) to this task the value is changed to BVal (Int 7).

Type. Although all values that can be returned by a task are represented by the type Val, we occasionally want to distinguish several families of values within this type. This type is not the data type Val used in the representation of tasks, but the type that the corresponding tasks in the real iTask system would have. We assign the type *Int* to all values of the form Int i. All values of the form String s have type *String*. If value v has type *v* and value w has type *w* then the value Pair v w has type *Pair v w*. The types allowed are:

$$Type = Int \mid String \mid VOID \mid Pair\ Type\ Type$$

To prevent the introduction of yet another data type, we represent the types yielded by tasks in these notes as instance of `Val`. The type *Int* is represented by `Int` 0 and the type *String* is represented as `String ""`. We define a class `type` to determine types of tasks.

```
:: Type := Val
class type a :: a → Type
```

Instances of this class for `Val` and `ITask` are identical to the instances of `val` defined in section 3.3. Only the instance for `BVal` is slightly different:

```
instance type BVal
where
    type (Int i)    = BVal (Int 0)
    type (String s) = BVal (String "")
    type VOID       = BVal VOID
```

This reuse of the type `Val` to represent the type of instances of this type appears to be very handy in the generation of values needed to test properties of iTasks.

In the next section we use to semantics and notions introduces in this section to define equivalence of tasks.

4   Equivalence of Tasks

Given the semantics of iTasks we can define equivalence of tasks. Informally we want to consider two tasks equivalent if they have the same semantics. Since we can apply infinitely many update events to each task that contains an editor we cannot determine equivalence by applying all possible input sequences. Moreover, tasks containing a bind operator also contain a function and the equivalence of functions is in general undecidable. iTasks are obviously Turing complete and hence equivalence is also for this reason known to be undecidable. It is even possible to use more general notions of equivalence, like tasks are equivalent if they can be used to do the same job. Hence, developing a useful notion of equivalence for tasks is nontrivial.

In these notes we develop a rather strict notion of equivalence of tasks: tasks t and u are equivalent if they have an equal value after all possible sequences of events and at each intermediate state the same events are enabled. Since the identifications of events are invisible for the workers using the iTask system, we allow that the lists of events applied to t and u differ in the event identifications. The strings that label the buttons in t and u do not occur in the events, hence it is allowed that these labels are different for equivalent tasks.

This notion of equivalence is based on observational equivalence for workers. At any moment during the execution of a task the worker should have the same options for entering input (generating events), and both tasks should yield the same normal form for any sequence of inputs that produces a normal form in one of the tasks.

First we introduce the notion of *simulation*. Informally a task u can simulate a task t if a worker can do everything with u that can be done with t. It is very well possible that a worker can do more with u than with t. The notation $t \preccurlyeq u$ denotes that u can simulate t. Technically we require that: **1**) for each sequence of accepted events of t there is a corresponding sequence of events accepted by u; **2**) the values of the tasks after applying these events is equal; and **3**) after applying the events, all enabled events of t have a matching event in u. Two events are equivalent, $e_1 \cong e_2$, if they differ at most in their identification.

$$t \preccurlyeq u \equiv \forall i \in \text{accept}(t).\exists j \in \text{accept}(u).i \cong j \wedge val(t @. i) = val(u @. j)$$
$$\wedge collect(t @. i) \subseteq collect(u @. j)$$

The notion $t \preccurlyeq u$ is not symmetrical, it is very well possible that u can do much more than t. As an example we have that for all tasks t and u that are not in normal form $t \preccurlyeq t.||. u$, and $t \preccurlyeq u.||.t$. If one of the tasks is in normal form it has shape `Return v`, after normalization the task tree $u.||.t$ will have the value `Return v` too. Any task can simulate itself $t \preccurlyeq t$, and an edit task of any basic value `v` can simulate a button task that returns that value: `ButtonTask id1` `"b"` `(Return (BVal v))` $\preccurlyeq$ `EditTask id2 "ok" v`. In general we have $t.||.t \npreccurlyeq t$: for instance if t is an edit task, in $t.||.t$ we can put a new value in one of the editors and produce the original result by pressing the `ok` button in the other editor, the task t cannot simulate this. The third requirement in the definition above is included to ensure that $t.||.t \npreccurlyeq t$ also holds for tasks with only one button `ButtonTask id1 "b1" (BVal (Int 36))`.

Two tasks t and u are considered to be *equivalent* iff t simulates u and u simulates t.

$$t \cong u \equiv t \preccurlyeq u \wedge u \preccurlyeq t$$

This notion of equivalence is weaker then the usual definition of bisimulation [21] since we do not require equality of events, but just equivalency. Two editors containing a different value are not equivalent. There exist infinitely many event sequences such that these editors produce the same value. But for the input sequence consisting only of the button event, they produce a different value.

Since each task can simulate itself $(t \preccurlyeq t)$, any task is equivalent to itself: $t \cong t$. If t and u are tasks that are not in normal form we have $t.||.u \cong u.||.t$. Consider the following tasks:

```
u1  = ButtonTask id1 "b1" (Return (BVal (Int 1)))
u2  = EditTask id2 "b2" (Int 1)
u3  = EditTask id2 "b3" (Int 2)
u4  = EditTask id2 "b4" (String "Hi")
u5  = u1 .||. u2
u6  = u2 .||. u1
u7  = u2 .&&. u4
u8  = u4 .&&. u2
u9  = u2 ⇒ λv.Return (BVal (Int 1))
u10 = u2 ⇒ λx.u4 ⇒ λy.Return (Pair x y)
```

The trivial relations between these tasks are $u_i \preccurlyeq u_i$ and $u_i \cong u_i$ for all u_i. The nontrivial relations between these tasks are: `u1` $\preccurlyeq$ `u2`, `u1` $\preccurlyeq$ `u5`, `u1` $\preccurlyeq$ `u6`, `u1` $\preccurlyeq$

u9, u2 $\preceq$ u5, u2 $\preceq$ u6, u5 $\preceq$ u6, u6 $\preceq$ u5, u10 $\preceq$ u7, u10 $\preceq$ u8, and u2 $\cong$ u9, u5 $\cong$ u6. Note that u7 $\not\cong$ u8 since the tasks yield another value, a result of type Pair Int String can never be equal to a result of type Pair String Int. When we swap the elements in the resulting pair of either u7 or u8 these tasks are equivalent: for example u7 $\Rrightarrow$ λ(Pair a b) $\rightarrow$ Return (Pair b a) $\cong$ u8.

Due to the presence of functions in the task expressions it is in general undecidable if one task simulates another or if they are equivalent. This implies that an testing approach needs to approximate this equivalence relation in some, preferably safe, way. However, in many situations we can decide these relations between tasks by inspection of the task trees that determine the behavior of the tasks. The next sections show how equivalence can be approximated and used in test of the semantics of iTasks.

4.1   Determining the Equivalence of Task Trees

The equivalence of tasks requires an equal result for all possible sequences of accepted events. Even for a simple integer edit task there are infinitely many sequences of events. This implies that checking equivalence of tasks by applying all possible sequences of events is in general impossible.

In this section we introduce two algorithms to approximate the equivalence of tasks. The first algorithm, section 4.2, is rather straightforward and uses only the enabled events of a task tree and the application of some of these events to approximate equivalence. The second algorithm, section 4.3 is somewhat more advanced and uses the structure of the task trees to determine equivalence whenever possible.

We will use a four valued logic as for the result:

```
:: Result = Proof | Pass | CE | Undef
```

The result Proof corresponds to True and indicates that the relation is known to hold. The result CE (for *CounterExample*) is equivalent to False, the relation does not hold. The result Pass indicates that functions are encountered during the scanning of the trees. For the tried values the properties holds. The property might hold for all other values, but it is also possible that there exist inputs to the tasks such that the property does not hold. The value Undef is used as result of an existential quantified property ($\exists\, w.P\; x$) where no proof is found in the given number of test cases; the value of this property is undefined [8]. This type Result is a subset of the possible test results handled by the test system G$\forall$st. For these results we define disjunction ('or', $\vee$), conjunction ('and', $\wedge$), and negation ('not', $\neg$) with the usual binding power and associativity. In addition we define the type conversion from Boolean to results and the weakening of a result which turns Proof in Pass and leaves the other values unchanged.

```
class (∨) infixr 2 a b :: a b → Result     // a OR b
class (∧) infixr 3 a b :: a b → Result     // a AND b

instance ¬ Result                           // negation
```

```
toResult :: Bool → Result              // type conversion
toResult b = if b Proof CE

pass :: Result → Result                // weakens result to at most Pass
pass r = r ∧ Pass
```

For ∨ and ∧ we define instances for all combinations of Bool and Result as a straightforward extension of the corresponding operation on Booleans.

4.2 Determining Equivalence by Applying Events

In order to compare ITasks we first ensure that they are normalized and supply an integer argument to indicate the maximum number of reduction steps. The value of this argument N is usually not very critical. In our tests 100 and 1000 steps usually gives identical (and correct) results. The function equivalent first checks if the tasks are returning currently the same value. If both tasks need inputs we first check 1) if the tasks have the same type, 2) if the tasks currently offer the same number of buttons to the worker, 3) if the tasks have the same number of needed buttons, and 4) if the tasks offer equivalent editors. Whenever either of these conditions does not hold the tasks t and u cannot be equivalent. When these conditions hold we check equivalence recursively after applying events. If there are needed events we apply them all in one go, without these events the tasks cannot produce a normal form. If the tasks have no needed events we apply all combinations of button events and check if one of these combinations makes the tasks equivalent. We need to apply all combinations of events since all button events are equivalent. All needed events can be applied in one go since they are needed in order to reach a normal form and the order of applying needed events is always irrelevant. If there are edit tasks enabled, length et>0, in the task the result is at most Pass. This is achieved by applying the functions pass or id.

```
equivOper :: ITask ITask → Result
equivOper t u = equivalent N (normalize1 t) (normalize1 u)

equivalent :: Int ITask ITask → Result
equivalent n (Return v) (Return w) = v == w
equivalent n (Return v) _          = CE
equivalent n _          (Return w) = CE
equivalent n t u
  | n≤0
    = Pass
    = if (length et>0) pass id
      (type t == type u ∧ lbt == lbu  ∧ lnt == lnu ∧ sort et == sort eu
       ∧ if (lnt>0)
           (equivalent (n-lnt) (t @. nt) (u @. nu))
           (exists N [equivalent n (t @. i) (u @. j)\\(i,j)←diag2 bt bu]))
where
      bt = collectButtons t; nt = collectNeeded t
      bu = collectButtons u; nu = collectNeeded u
      et = collectEdit t;    eu = collectEdit u
      lnt = length nt; lnu = length nu; lbt = length bt; lbu = length bu
```

The function `exists` checks if one of the first N values are `Pass` or `Proof`.

```
exists :: Int [Result] → Result
exists n []    = CE
exists 0 l     = Undef
exists n [a:x] = a ∨ exists (n-1) x
```

The edit events are sorted before we compare them in order to get rid of possible different ids. We only compare the values of edit events in the comparison of events. Button events are considered to be smaller than edit events.

In this approach we do not apply any edit events. It is easy to design examples of tasks where the current approximation yields `Pass`, but applying some edit events reveals that the tasks are actually not equivalent (e.g. `t = EditTask id1` `(BVal (Int 5))` and `t ⇒ Return (BVal (Int 5)))`. We obtain a better approximation of the equivalence relation by including some edit events in the function `equivalent`. Due to space limitations and to keep the presentation as simple as possible we have not done this here.

4.3 Determining Equivalence of Tasks by Comparing Task Trees

Since the shape of the task tree determines the behavior of the task corresponding to that task tree, it is tempting to try to determine properties like $t \preccurlyeq u$ and $t \cong u$ by comparing the shapes of the trees for u and t. For most constructs in the trees this works very well. For instance it is much easier to look at the structure of the tasks `EditTask id1 "ok" (BVal (Int 5))` and `EditTask id2 "done"` `(BVal (Int 5))` to see that they are equivalent, than approximating equivalence of these tasks by applying events to these tasks and comparing the returned values. In this section we use the comparison of task trees to determine equivalence of tasks. The function `eqStruct` implements this algorithm.

There are a number of constructions that allow different task trees for equivalent tasks. These constructs require special attention in the structural comparison of task trees:

1. The tasks `ButtonTask id1 "b" (Return v) .&&. Return w` and `ButtonTask id1` `"b" (Return (Pair v w))` are equivalent for all basic values `v` and `w`. This kind of equivalent tasks with a different task tree can only occur if one of the branches of `.&&.` is in normal form and the other is not. On lines 9, 16 and 17 of the function `eqStruct` there are special cases handling this. The problem is handled by switching to a comparison by applying events, very similar to the `equivalent` algorithm in the previous section. The function `equ` takes care of applying events and further comparison.
2. The choice operator `.||.` should be commutative, `(t.||.u ≃ u.||.t)`, and associative `((t.||.u).||.v ≃ t.||.(u.||.v))`. In order to guarantee this, `eqStruct` collects all adjacent or-tasks in a list and checks if there is a unique mapping between the elements of those list such that the corresponding subtasks are equivalent (using `eqStruct` recursively). The implementation of the auxiliary functions is straightforward.

3. The `Bind` construct contains real functions, hence there are many ways to construct equivalent tasks with a different structure. For instance, we have that any task `t` is equivalent to the task `t` ⇒ `Return`, or slightly more advanced: `s.&&.t` is equivalent `(t .&&. s)` ⇒ λ`(Pair x y)`→`Return (Pair y x)` for all tasks `s` and `t`.

   The function `eqStruct` checks if the left-hand sides and the obtained right-hand sides of two bind operators are equivalent. If they are not equivalent the tasks are checked for equivalence by applying inputs, see line 13-15.

The `eqStruct` algorithm expects normalized task trees. The operator ≃ takes care of this normalisation.

class (≃) **infix** 4 a :: a a → Result   // *is arg1 equivalent to arg2?*

instance ≃ ITask **where** (≃) t u = eqStruc N (normalize1 t) (normalize1 u)

If the structures are not equal, but the task might be event equal we switch to applying inputs using the function `equ`. This function is very similar to the function `equivalent` in the previous section. The main difference is that the function `equ` always switches to `eqStruct` instead of using a recursive call. If a structural comparison is not possible after applying an event, the function `eqStruct` will switch to `equ` again.

```
eqStruc :: Int ITask ITask → Result                                          1
eqStruc 0 t u = Pass                                                         2
eqStruc n (Return v)        (Return w)       = v ≃ w                         3
eqStruc n (Return v)        _                = CE                            4
eqStruc n _                 (Return w)       = CE                            5
eqStruc n (EditTask _ _ e) (EditTask _ _ f) = e≃f                           6
eqStruc n s=:(a .&&. b)     t=:(x .&&. y)                                    7
 = eqStruc (n-1) a x ∧ eqStruc (n-1) b y ∨                                   8
   ((inNF a || inNF b || inNF x || inNF y) ∧ equ n s t)                      9
eqStruc n s=:(a .||. b)     t=:(x .||. y)                                   10
 = eqORn n (collectOR s) (collectOR t)                                      11
eqStruc n s=:(Bind i a f) t=:(Bind j b g)                                   12
 = eqStruc (n-1) a b ∧ eqStruc (n-2) (f (val a)) (g (val b)) ∨ equ n s t    13
eqStruc n s=:(Bind _ _ _) t                   = equ n s t                   14
eqStruc n s                t=:(Bind _ _ _) = equ n s t                      15
eqStruc n s=:(a .&&. b)    t                = (inNF a||inNF b) ∧ equ n s t   16
eqStruc n s                t=:(x .&&. y)    = (inNF x||inNF y) ∧ equ n s t   17
eqStruc n s                t                = CE                            18
```

This uses instances of ≃ for basic values (`BVal`) and values (`Val`). For these instances no approximations are needed. Line 10 and 11 implements the commutativity of the operator `.||.`: `collectOR` produces a list of all subtasks glued together with this operator, and `eqORn` determines if these lists of subtasks are equivalent in some permutations.

```
eqORn :: Int [ITask] [ITask] → Result
eqORn n xs ys
    = coversUnique (eqStruc n) xs ys ∧ coversUnique (eqStruc n) ys xs
```

The definitions are a direct generalization of the ordinary equality $=$.

The function coversUnique checks if there is an unique mapping between elements of the given lists using the comparison operator. As a simple example coversUnique (ab.toResult (a$=$b)) [1,1,2] [1,2,1] will produce OK, but comparing the list [1,1,2] and [1,2,2] as well as any list different length will produce CE.

```
coversUnique :: (a a→Result) [a] [a] → Result
coversUnique f xs ys = eq xs ys []
where
    eq [] ys zs = Proof
    eq [x:xs] [] zs = CE
    eq [x:xs] [y:ys] zs
        | f x y ≠ CE
            = eq xs (zs++ys) [] ∨ eq [x:xs] ys [y:zs]
            = eq [x:xs] ys [y:zs]
```

If the elements of the list can be sorted it is much easier to sort the lists of values and compare the elements one by one. The given algorithm works also if the lists cannot be sorted. We needed this to compare tasks, we have no less-then operator for tasks.

As indicated above the function equ takes care of applying events and further comparison of task trees. This function first checks if there are approximation steps to be done ($n{\leq}0$). If no steps can be done the result is Pass. Otherwise we check compare the current value of the task trees, the number of button events, the number of needed events, and the edit events. If there are needed events we apply them to the tasks. Otherwise we try if any pairs of button events for the tasks is structurally equivalent.

```
equ :: Int ITask ITask → Result
equ n t u
  | n≤0
    = Pass
    =     val t = val u ∧ lbt = lbu ∧ lnt = lnu
      ∧ sort (collectEdit t) = sort (collectEdit u)
      ∧ if (lnt>0)
            (eqStruc (n-lnt) (t @. nt) (u @. nu))
          (if (lbt>0)
            (exists N [ eqStruc (n-1) (t @. i) (u @. j)
                      \\ (i,j) ← diag2 bt bu
                      ]
          )
          (case (t,u) of
              (Return x,Return y) = x≃y
              _ = CE)
          )
where
    bt = collectButtons t; nt = collectNeeded t
    bu = collectButtons u; nu = collectNeeded u
    et = collectEdit t;    eu = collectEdit u
```

```
lnt = length nt;        lnu = length nu
lbt = length bt;        lbu = length bu
```

A similar approach can be used to approximate the simulation relation $\preccurlyeq$.

Property pEquiv in the next section states that both notions of equivalence yield equivalent results, even if we include edit events. Executing the associated tests indicate no problems with this property. This test result increases the confidence in the correct implementation of the operator $\simeq$. Since $\simeq$ uses the structure of the tasks whenever possible, it is more efficient than equivOper that applies events until the tasks are in normal form. The efficiency gain is completely determined by the size and contents of the task tree, but can be significant. It is easy to construct examples with an efficiency gain of one order of magnitude or more.

5   Testing Properties of iTasks

Above we mentioned a number of properties of iTasks and their equivalency like $\forall\ s,t \in \mathsf{iTask}.(\mathsf{s.||.t}) \simeq (\mathsf{t.||.s})$. Although we designed the system such that these properties should hold, it is good to verify that the properties do hold indeed. Especially during the development of the semantic description many versions have been created in order to find a concise formulation of the semantics and an effective check for equivalence.

The above property can be stated in G∀st as:

```
pOr :: GITask GITask → Property
pOr x y = normalize1 (t.||.u) ≃ normalize1 (u.||.t)
where t = toITask x; u = toITaskT (type t) y
```

Since some ITask constructs contain a function, we use an additional data type, GITask, to generate the desired instances. We follow exactly the approach as outlined in [7]. The type GITask contains cases corresponding to the constructors in ITask, for button tasks, for tasks of the form t $\Rightarrow$ Return, and for some simple recursive terminating tasks. For pOr we need to make sure the tasks t and u have the same type since we combine them with an or-operator. The conversion by toITask from the additional type GITasks used for the generation to ITasks takes care of that.

After executing 23 tests G∀st produces the first counterexample that shows that this property does not hold for t = Return (BVal (Int 0)) and u = Return (Pair (BVal (Int 0)) (BVal (Int 0))). Using the semantics from figure 7 it is clear that G∀st is right, our property is too general. A correct property imposes the condition that t and u are not in normal form:

```
pOr2 x y = notNF [t,u] ==> normalize1 (t.||.u) ≃ normalize1 (u.||.t)
where t = toITask x; u = toITaskT (type t) y
```

In the same way we can show that t.||.t $\not\simeq$ t for tasks that are not in normal form (p2) and test the associativity of the .||. operator (p3).

```
p2 :: GITask GITask → Property
p2 x y = notNF [s,t] ==> (s.||.t)≇t
where s = toITask x; t = toITaskT (type s) y
```

```
p3 :: GITask GITask GITask → Property
p3 x y z = (s .||. (t .||. u))≃((s .||. t) .||. u)
where s = toITask x; t = toITaskT (type s) y; u = toITaskT (type s) z
```

In total we have defined over 70 properties to test the consistency of the definitions given in these notes. We list some representative properties here. The first property states that needed events can be applied in any order. Since there are no type restrictions on the type t we can quantify over ITasks directly.

```
pNeeded :: ITask → Property
pNeeded t = (λj. t @. i ≃ t @. j) For perms i where i = collectNeeded t
```

In this test the fragment For perms i indicates an additional quantification over all j in perms i. The function perms :: [x] → [[x]] generates all permutations of the given list. In logic this property would have been written as $\forall t \in$ ITask, $\forall j \in$ perms (collectNeeded t). t @. (collectNeeded t) $\simeq t$ @. j.

The next property states that both approximations of equivalence discussed in the previous section produce equivalent results.

```
pEquiv :: ITask ITask → Property
pEquiv t u = (equivOper t u) ≃ (t≃u)
```

The type of a task should be preserved under reduction. In the property pType also events that are not well typed will be tested. Since we assume that all events are well typed (the edit events have the same type as the edit task they belong to), it is better to use pType2 where the events are derived from the task t.

```
pType :: ITask → Property
pType t = (λi.type t = type (t @. i)) For collect t
```

```
pType2 :: ITask → Property
pType2 t = pType t For collect t
```

The phrase For collect t indicates that for testing these properties the events are collected from the task tree rather than generated systematically by G∀st. However the tasks to be used in the test are generated systematically by G∀st.

The property pVal states that the value of a task obtained by the optimized function val is equal to the value of the task obtained by applying events obtained by collectVal until it returns a value. The function collectVal returns all needed events and the leftmost events if these are no needed events.

```
pVal :: ITask → Property
pVal t = val t = nf t
where
    nf (Return v) = v
    nf t = nf (t @. collectVal t)
```

When two tasks are equivalent it is not required that their buttons are exactly equivalent, some differences in layout and hence button labeling are allowed.

However, there should be an unique coverage of the buttons of those tasks. This is tested by property p50.

```
p50 :: ITask ITask→ Property
p50 s t = (s ≃ t) ==> (coversUnique (≃) (collect s) (collect t))
```

In general it is not enough to check that tasks are currently structural equivalent, this equivalence should be preserved after processing events. Details of this equivalence are beyond the scope of this paper. For our iTasksemantics we defined a notion of equivalent that covers this requirement. Many properties and hence use these notion of equivalence.

The definitions presented in these notes pass all stated properties. On a normal laptop (Intel core2 Duo (using only one of the cores), 1.8 GHz) it takes about 7 seconds to check all defined properties with 1000 test cases for each property. This is orders of magnitude faster and more reliable then human inspection, which is on its turn much faster than a formal proof (even if it is supported by a state-of-the-art tool). Most of these properties are very general properties, like the properties shown here. Some properties however check specific test cases that are known to be tricky, or revealed problems in the past. If there are problems with one of the properties, they are usually spotted within the first 50 test cases generated. It appears to be extremely hard to introduce flaws in the system that are not revealed by executing these tests. For instance omitting one of the special cases in the function eqStruct is spotted quickly. Hence testing the consistency of the system in this way is an effective and efficient way to improve the confidence in its consistency.

For iTasks it might be tempting to state properties in temporal logic. Currently temporal logic is not yet supported by G∀st, it is restricted to a slightly extended version of first order logic. G∀st does support also specifications by extended state machines and has a notion of behavioral equivalence of state machines. These state based specifications can be used to test state based properties of iTaskseffectively. However, this way of testing is outside the scope of this paper.

6   Related Work

This is certainly not the first paper on tool support for semantics, neither will it be the last one. There are several classes of related work.

The first class of papers aims to derive efficient implementations from the semantical description. Lakin and Pitts [10] propose a meta language for structural operational semantics. Their treated meta language is able to animate the described language, the long term goal is to execute it efficiently. They spend much effort in the implementation of a variable binding mechanism that is aware of α–equivalence, known as the *Barendregt variable convention* [3]. To that extend they implement *nominal unification* [24] to judge equivalence of environments (binding of variables to values). Cheney's scrap your nameplate [4] provides similar binding tools using generic programming techniques. We provide a more basic notion of binding without silent α–equivalence, nor do we aim to provide an efficient implementation. For the semantics given in this paper such an advanced notion of equivalence of environments is not needed. For specifying the semantics of, for instance, the λ-calculus, such a notion of equivalence would be a valuable addition. If necessary, such a notion of equivalence can be used instead of the simple environments used here.

A second class of related papers is about support for mechanical proofs of properties of the given semantics. These papers recognize that it is next to impossible to get a large semantical specification without an automatic sanity checking. To conquer this problem Sewell et al. [20] define the metalanguage Ott, specifications in this language are checked and can be compiled to LaTeX as well as code for proof assistants. Although proofs using a proof assistant are extremely valuable for semantical specifications and encouraging progress has been made with proof assistants in recent years, constructing such proofs still requires usually much human guidance [2]. If any detail of the semantics is changed the proofs need to be redone typically with new human guidance. For this reason proofs are typically delayed until the semantics is assumed to be correct, or omitted. Our test based approach gives quickly a fairly good approximation of the correctness of the properties stated. This appears to be very useful during the development of the semantics. We plan to investigate the combination of testing and proving properties as future research.

We neither aim to animate the semantics efficiently, nor do we directly target proof support. The possibilities for simulating the semantics using the iTask system as described in this paper are purely intended as an interactive way to create task and perform reductions. Efficiency is not an issue at all, the only purpose is the human validation of the observed reduction behavior.

Beauty, clearness and correctness of the semantics is our business. Our experience is that fast feedback from a test system is more valuable during the development of the semantics than support for proofs. Once the semantics is stable, off–line proofs do provide more confidence than tests. In our experience it is very hard to construct faithful properties for a semantics that does not hold and where the test system does not produce a counterexample quickly. In other words: if one of the stated properties does not hold, the test system G∀st is usually able to find a counterexample quickly. And if we have sufficient properties stated, issues in the semantics usually are indicated by counterexamples for one or more of the properties. Of course it would be nice to have a set of properties that completely fixes the desired semantics, but ad-hoc sets of properties appear to be effective as well.

Compared with these two classes of tools our approach has the advantage that no special purpose language needs to be designed, implemented and mastered. An existing and well-known language is reused for a new goal. We reuse all existing features of the language as well as all existing tooling (IDE, compiler, test-tool, ..), only a small number of tailor made features have to be provided to obtain a powerful embedded modeling language for semantics. A potential pitfall is that the semantics of the embedding functional language is silently inherited in the given semantics. The semantics of high level functional languages is usually not complete and rigourously defined. For Clean the basic semantics is given as a term graph rewrite system [17], de Mol [13] gives a precise definition of large parts of Clean. Since the semantics definitions directly corresponds to their counterparts in a mathematical formulation of the semantics the meaning of semantic formulation is never an issue. Moreover, only very basic rewrite semantics of the embedding language is used. All places where the semantics of the functional embedding language might be a little unclear are easily avoided.

The ability to test properties of the described semantics is an important contribution of our work.

In [5] Danvy describes various semantics in ML for simple systems and their transformation.

A third class of related papers is about semantics of workflow systems. The semantics of many other workflow systems is based on Petri-nets, e.g. [19], actor-oriented directed graphs (including some simple higher order constructs) [12], or abstract state machines (ASM) [11]. Neither of these alternatives is capable to express the flexibility covered by the dynamic generation of tasks of the monadic bind operation of the iTask system.

7   Discussion

In this paper we give a rewrite semantics for iTasks. Such a semantics is necessary to reason about iTasks and their properties, it is also well suited to explain their behavior. In addition we defined useful notions about iTasks and stated properties related to them. The most important notion is the *equivalence* of tasks.

Usually the semantics of workflow systems is based on Petri nets, abstract state machines, or actor-oriented directed graphs. Since the iTask system allows arbitrary functions to generate the continuation in a sequence of tasks (the monadic bind operator), such an approach is not flexible enough. To cope with the rich possibilities of iTasks our semantics incorporates also a function to determine the continuation of the task after a Bind operator.

We use the functional programming language Clean as carrier for the semantical definitions. The tasks are represented by a data structure. The effect of supplying an input to such a task is given by an operator modifying the task tree. Since we have the tasks available as data structure, we can easily extract information from the task, like the events needed or accepted by the task. A typical case of the operator @. (apply) that specifies the semantics is:

```
(@.) (EditTask i n e) (Event j BE) | i==j = Return (BVal e)
```

In the more traditional Scott Brackets style this alternative is written as:

$$\mathcal{A} \, [\![\, EditTask \; i \; n \; e \,]\!] \; (Event \; j \; BE) = Return \; (BVal \; e), \text{ if } i = j$$

Our representation has the same level of abstraction and has as advantages that it can be checked by the type system and executed (and hence simulated and tested).

Having the task as a data structure it is easy to create an editor and simulator for tasks using the iTask library. Editing and simulating tasks is helpful to validate the semantics. Although simulating iTasks provides a way to interpret the given task, the executable semantics is not intended as an interpreter for iTasks. In an interpreter we would have focused on a nice interface and efficiency, the semantics focusses on clearness and simplicity.

Compared with the real iTask system there are a number of important simplifications in our ITask representation. 1) Instead of arbitrary types, the ITasks can only yield elements of type Val. The type system of the host language is not able to prevent type errors within the ITasks. For instance it is possible to combine a task that yields an integer, BVal (Int i), with a task yielding a string, BVal (String s), using an .||. operator. In the ordinary iTasks the type system does not allow to combine (which indeed is semantically not desirable) tasks of type Task Int with Task String using a -||- operator. Probably GADTs would have helped us to enforce this condition in our semantical representation. 2) The application of a task to an event does not yield an HTML-page that can be used as GUI for the iTask system. In fact there is no notion at all of HTML output in the ITask system. 3) There is no way to access files or databases in the ITask system. 4) There is no notion of workers and assigning subtasks to them. 5) There is no difference between client site and server site evaluation of tasks. 6) There is only one workflow process which is implicit. In the real iTask system additional processes can be created dynamically. 7) The exception handling from the real iTask system is missing in this semantics.

Adding these aspects would make the semantics more complicated. We have deliberately chosen to define a concise system that is as clear as possible.

Using the model-based test system it is possible to test the stated properties fully automatically. We maintain a collection of over 70 properties for the iTask semantics and test them with one push of a button. Within seconds we do known if the current version of the system obeys all properties stated. This is extremely useful during the development and changes of the system. Although the defined notions of equivalence are in general undecidable, the given approximation works very well in practice. Issues in the semantics or properties are found very quickly (usually within the first 100 test cases). We attempted to insert deliberately small errors in the semantics that are not detected by the automatic tests, but we failed miserably. Many of these incorrect versions look very plausible for humans, without the test system one might believe that this version of the semantics is actually correct. This does give us confidence in the power of automatic testing of semantical properties. Nevertheless, a successful test is in general not a proof. Proving properties remains necessary to obtain maximum certainty about the properties. Using automatic testing as a first indication of correctness will reduce the proving effort significantly, there is a strongly reduced change that we try to prove incorrect versions of the semantics.

In the near future we want to test with G∀st if the real iTask system obeys the semantics given in this paper. In addition we want to extend the semantics in order to cover some of the important notions omitted in the current semantics, for instance task execution in a multi-user workflow system. When we are convinced about the quality and suitability of the extended system we plan to prove some of the tested properties. Although proving properties gives more confidence in the correctness, it is much more work then testing. Testing with a large number of properties has shown to be an extremely powerful way to reveal inconsistencies in the system.

References

1. Achten, P., van Eekelen, M., de Mol, M., Plasmeijer, R.: An Arrow based semantics for interactive applications. In: Morazán, M. (ed.) Proceedings of the 8th Symposium on Trends in Functional Programming, TFP 2007, New York, NY, USA, April 2-4 (2007)
2. Aydemir, B.E., Bohannon, A., Fairbairn, M., Foster, J.N., Pierce, B.C., Sewell, P., Vytiniotis, D., Washburn, G., Weirich, S., Zdancewic, S.: Mechanized metatheory for the masses: The poplmark challenge. In: Hurd, J., Melham, T. (eds.) TPHOLs 2005. LNCS, vol. 3603, pp. 50–65. Springer, Heidelberg (2005)
3. Barendregt, H.: The lambda calculus, its syntax and semantics (revised edition). Studies in Logic, vol. 103. North-Holland, Amsterdam (1984)
4. Cheney, J.: Scrap your nameplate (functional pearl). SIGPLAN Not. 40(9), 180–191 (2005)
5. Danvy, O.: From reduction-based to reduction-free normalization. In: Koopman, P., Plasmeijer, R., Swierstra, D. (eds.) AFP 2008. LNCS, vol. 5832, pp. 66–164. Springer, Heidelberg (2009)
6. Koopman, P., Plasmeijer, R.: Generic generation of elements of types. In: Proceedings of the 6th Symposium on Trends in Functional Programming, TFP 2005, Tallin, Estonia, Septmeber 23-24, pp. 163–178. Intellect Books, Bristol (2005) ISBN 978-1-84150-176-5
7. Koopman, P., Plasmeijer, R.: Automatic testing of higher order functions. In: Kobayashi, N. (ed.) APLAS 2006. LNCS, vol. 4279, pp. 148–164. Springer, Heidelberg (2006)
8. Koopman, P., Plasmeijer, R.: Fully automatic testing with functions as specifications. In: Horváth, Z. (ed.) CEFP 2005. LNCS, vol. 4164, pp. 35–61. Springer, Heidelberg (2006)
9. Koopman, P., Plasmeijer, R., Achten, P.: An executable and testable semantics for iTasks. In: Scholz, S.-B. (ed.) Revised Selected Papers of the 20th International Symposium on the Implementation and Application of Functional Languages, IFL 2008, pp. 53–64. University of Hertfordshire, UK (2008)
10. Lakin, M.R., Pitts, A.M.: A metalanguage for structural operational semantics. In: Morazán, M. (ed.) Trends in Functional Programming, vol. 8, pp. 19–35. Intellect (2008)
11. Lee, S.-Y., Lee, Y.-H., Kim, J.-G., Lee, D.C.: Workflow system modeling in the mobile healthcare B2B using semantic information. In: Gervasi, O., Gavrilova, M.L., Kumar, V., Laganá, A., Lee, H.P., Mun, Y., Taniar, D., Tan, C.J.K. (eds.) ICCSA 2005, Part II. LNCS, vol. 3481, pp. 762–770. Springer, Heidelberg (2005)
12. Ludäscher, B., Altintas, I., Berkley, C., Higgins, D., Jaeger, E., Jones, M., Lee, E., Tao, J., Zhao, Y.: Scientific workflow management and the Kepler system. Concurrency and Computation: Practice & Experience 18, 2006 (2005)

13. de Mol, M.: Reasoning About Functional Programs - Sparkle: a proof assistant for Clean. PhD thesis, Institute for Computing and Information Sciences, Radboud University Nijmegen,(2009) ISBN 978-90-9023885-2

14. de Mol, M., van Eekelen, M., Plasmeijer, R.: The mathematical foundation of the proof assistant Sparkle. Technical Report ICIS-R07025, Institute for Computing and Information Sciences, Radboud University Nijmegen, (November 2007)

15. Nielson, H., Nielson, F.: Semantics with applications: a formal introduction. John Wiley & Sons, Chichester (1992)

16. Plasmeijer, R., Achten, P.: iData for the world wide web - Programming interconnected web forms. In: Hagiya, M., Wadler, P. (eds.) FLOPS 2006. LNCS, vol. 3945, pp. 242–258. Springer, Heidelberg (2006)

17. Plasmeijer, R., van Eekelen, M.: Functional programming and parallel graph rewriting. Addison-Wesley Publishing Company, Reading (1993) ISBN 0-201-41663-8

18. Plotkin, G.D.: The origins of structural operational semantics. Journal of Logic and Algebraic Programming 60-61, 3–15 (2004)

19. Russell, N., ter Hofstede, A., van der Aalst, W.: newYAWL: specifying a workflow reference language using coloured Petri nets. In: Proceedings of the 8th 2007 (2007)

20. Sewell, P., Nardelli, F.Z., Owens, S., Peskine, G., Ridge, T., Sarkar, S., Strniša, R.: Ott: effective tool support for the working semanticist. SIGPLAN Not. 42(9), 1–12 (2007)

21. Stirling, C.: The joys of bisimulation. In: Brim, L., Gruska, J., Zlatuška, J. (eds.) MFCS 1998. LNCS, vol. 1450, pp. 142–151. Springer, Heidelberg (1998)

22. Stoy, J.E.: Denotational Semantics: The Scott-Strachey Approach to Programming Language Theory. MIT Press, Cambridge (1977)

23. Team, T.C.D.: The Coq proof assistant reference manual, (version 7.0) (1998), http://pauillac.inria.fr/coq/doc/main.html

24. Urban, C., Pitts, A.M., Gabbay, M.J.: Nominal unification. Theoretical Computer Science 323, 473–497 (2004)

Types for Units-of-Measure: Theory and Practice

Andrew Kennedy

Microsoft Research, Cambridge, UK
akenn@microsoft.com

1 Introduction

Units-of-measure are to science what types are to programming. In science and engineering, dimensional and unit consistency provides a first check on the correctness of an equation or formula, just as in programming the validation of a program by the type-checker eliminates one possible reason for failure.

Units-of-measure errors can have catastrophic consequences, the most famous of which was the loss in September 1999 of NASA's Mars Climate Orbiter probe, caused by a confusion between newtons (the SI unit of force) and lbf (pound-force, a unit of force sometimes used in the US). The report into the disaster made many recommendations [15]. Notably absent, though, was any suggestion that programming languages might assist in the prevention of such errors, either through static analysis tools, or through type-checking.

Over the years, many people have suggested ways of extending programming languages with support for static checking of units-of-measure. It's even possible to abuse the rich type systems of existing languages such as C++ and Haskell to achieve it, but at some cost in usability [19,6]. More recently, Sun's design for its Fortress programming language has included type system support for dimensions and units [2].

In this short course, we'll look at the design supported by the F# programming language, the internals of its type system, and the theoretical basis for units safety. The tutorial splits into three parts:

- Section 2 is a programmer's guide to units-of-measure in F#, intended to be accessible to any programmer with some background in functional programming.
- Section 3 presents details of the type system and inference algorithm.
- Section 4 considers the semantics of units, including a link with classical dimensional analysis.

The tutorial concludes with a brief discussion in Section 5. Each section contains a number of exercises; solutions to some of these can be found in an appendix.

2 An Introduction to Units-of-Measure in F#

We begin by taking a gentle tour through the units-of-measure feature of F#. For this you will need the F# command-line compiler (`fsc`) and interactive

Z. Horváth, R. Plasmeijer, and V. Zsók (Eds.): CEFP 2009, LNCS 6299, pp. 268–305, 2010.

```
/// For n>=0, compute the factorial of n
let rec fact n = if n=0 then 1 else n*fact(n-1)

let f5 = fact(5)
```
```
val fact : int -> int

For n>=0, compute the factorial of n

Full name: Program.fact
```

Fig. 1. Editing F# code in Visual Studio

environment (`fsi`), and optionally (available on Windows only), the Visual Studio integrated development environment. Throughout the tutorial we will present code snippets, like this,

```
let rec fact n = if n=0 then 1 else n * fact(n-1)
```

and also fragments of dialogue from `fsi`, like this:

```
> let rec fact n = if n=0 then 1 else n * fact(n-1);;

val fact : int -> int
```

If you are reading this tutorial online using a program such as Adobe Reader, you can copy-and-paste examples directly into `fsi`.

If you have Visual Studio you might instead prefer to try out code in its editor, as shown in Figure 1. The tooltips feature of VS is especially useful: if you hover the mouse cursor over an identifier, its type will be displayed in a box, along with information gathered from the "///" comment preceding its definition.

The F# programming language shares a subset with Caml; this subset will be familiar to Standard ML programmers, and unsurprising for Haskell programmers too. For the most part, we stay within this subset, extended with units-of-measure of course, even though some examples can be made slicker by using the object-oriented and other advanced features of F#. (One significant departure from Caml is the use of F#'s indentation based layout, similar to Haskell's 'offside rule'.) Sticking to this subset also illustrates how units-of-measure types and inference could usefully be added to other functional languages. (Language designers, take note!)

2.1 Introducing Units

We must first declare some base units. As it's the 21st century, we shall employ the SI unit system (*Système International d'Unités* [1]) and declare units for mass, length and time:

```
[<Measure>] type kg // kilograms
[<Measure>] type m // metres
[<Measure>] type s // seconds
```

The [<Measure>] attribute in front of type indicates that we're not really introducing types in the usual sense, but rather *measure constructors*, namely kg, m and s.

Now let's declare a well-known constant[1] with its units, which we can do simply by tacking the units onto a floating-point literal, in between angle brackets:

```
let gravityOnEarth = 9.808<m/s^2> // an acceleration
```

Notice how conventional notation for units is used, with / for dividing, and ^ for powers. Juxtaposition just means product (or you can write * if you prefer), and negative powers can be used in place of division. We could express the units of acceleration slightly differently:

```
let gravityOnEarth = 9.808<m * s^-2>
```

Or we might even go against recommended practice and write it this way:

```
let gravityOnEarth = 9.808<m/s/s>
```

What is the type of gravityOnEarth? In F# Interactive, the compiler tells us:

```
> let gravityOnEarth = 9.808<m/s/s>;;

val gravityOnEarth : float<m/s ^ 2> = 9.808
```

The float type is *parameterized* on units-of-measure, here instantiated with m/s^2, just as list takes a type parameter, as in list<int>. (In F#, ordinary type parameters can be written prefix, as in int list, or postfix in angle brackets, as in list<int>. Units-of-measure parameters must be written in the latter style.)

Now we can do some physics! If an object is dropped off a building that is 40 metres tall, at what speed will it hit the ground?[2] A little bit of Newtonian dynamics answers this question with the formula $\sqrt{2gh}$, in which g is acceleration due to gravity and h is the height. Let's do the calcu* uation in F#

```
> let heightOfBuilding = 40.0<m>;;

val heightOfBuilding : float<m> = 40.0
> let speedOfImpact = sqrt (2.0*gravityOnEarth*heightOfBuilding);;

val speedOfImpact : float<m/s> = 28.01142624
```

Note the units, computed automatically! Units-of-measure are not just handy comments-on-constants: they are there in the types of values, and, moreover, F# knows the "rules of units". When values of floating-point type are multiplied, the units are multiplied too; when they are divided, the units are divided too,

---

[1] Constant at a particular point on the surface of the earth, at least!
[2] Assuming no atmosphere!

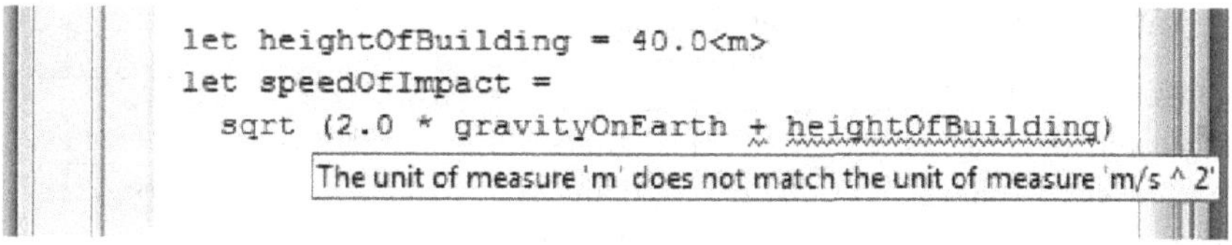

Fig. 2. A units error in Visual Studio

and when taking square roots, the same is done to the units. So by the rule for multiplication, the expression inside `sqrt` above must have units `m^2/s^2`, and therefore the units of `speedOfImpact` must be `m/s`.

What if we make a mistake?

```
> let speedOfImpact = sqrt (2.0*gravityOnEarth+heightOfBuilding);;

  let speedOfImpact = sqrt (2.0*gravityOnEarth+heightOfBuilding);;
  -----------------------------------------------^^^^^^^^^^^^^^^^

stdin(142,50): error FS0001: The unit of measure 'm' does not match
the unit of measure 'm/s ^ 2'
```

We've tried to add a height to an acceleration, and F# tells us exactly what we've done wrong. The units don't match up, and it tells us so! In Visual Studio, errors are shown interactively: a red squiggle will appear, and if you hover the mouse cursor over it, the error message will be shown, as in Figure 2.

Now let's do a little more physics. What force does the ground exert on me to maintain my stationary position?

```
> let myMass = 65.0<kg>;;

val myMass : float<kg> = 65.0

> let forceOnGround = myMass*gravityOnEarth;;

val forceOnGround : float<kg m / ^ 2> = 637.52
```

We've just applied Newton's Second Law of motion. Newton's eponymous unit, the newton, is the SI unit of force. Now instead of the cumbersome `kg m/s^2` we can introduce a derived unit and just write `N`, the standard symbol for newtons.

```
[<Measure>] type N = kg m/s^2
let forceOnGround:float<N> = myMass*gravityOnEarth
```

Derived units are just like type aliases: as far as F# is concerned, `N` and `kg m/s^2` mean exactly the same thing with respect to *checking* of types. Note, though, that when F# *displays* types, it won't automatically 'discover' derived units, as there are typically many ways of writing down equivalent units-of-measure.

2.2   Interlude: The F# PowerPack

The F# 'PowerPack' library declares all of the
SI base and derived units, under the namespace Microsoft.FSharp.Math.SI. It also defines
various physical constants in the namespace
Microsoft.FSharp.Math.PhysicalConstants. To
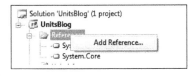
import this library, you will need to reference it from your project in Vi-
sual Studio, by right-clicking on *References* (see right) and then selecting the
FSharp.PowerPack component. Alternatively, you can use the #r directive in fsi,
as below:

```
> #r "FSharp.PowerPack";;

--> Referenced 'C:\Program Files\FSharp\bin\FSharp.PowerPack.dll'
```

Now let's use the units and constants from the PowerPack to implement Newton's law of universal gravitation:

$$F = G\frac{m_1 m_2}{r^2}$$

Here m_1 and m_2 are the masses of two bodies, r is the distance between them,
G is the gravitational constant and F is the force of attraction between the two
bodies. We can code this as follows:

```
> open Microsoft.FSharp.Math;;
> open SI;;
> let attract (m1:float<kg>) (m2:float<kg>) (r:float<m>) : float<N> =
-   PhysicalConstants.G * m1 * m2 / (r*r);;

val attract : float<kg> -> float<kg> -> float<m> -> float<N>
>
```

Figure 3 shows this function being defined in Visual Studio.

2.3   Unit Conversions

With SI units and standard physical constants built-in, this is no excuse for
physicists to go non-metric. But if you insist, you can define units from other
systems. Here is our earlier example, using feet instead of metres as the unit of
length.

```
[<Measure>] type ft
let gravityOnEarth = 32.2<ft/s^2>
let heightOfBuilding = 130.0<ft>
let speedOfImpact = sqrt (2.0 * gravityOnEarth * heightOfBuilding)
```

What if you need to convert between feet and metres? First, define a conversion
factor.

```
let feetPerMetre = 3.28084<ft/m>
```

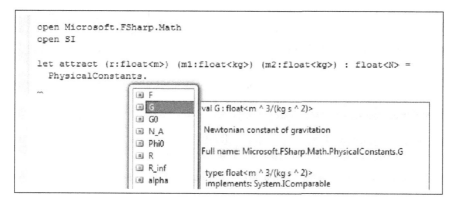

Fig. 3. Using the PowerPack in Visual Studio

Naturally enough, the units of `feetPerMetre` are feet per metre, or `ft/m` for short. Now we can convert distances...

```
let heightOfBuildingInMetres = heightOfBuilding / feetPerMetre
```

...and speeds...

```
let speedOfImpactInMPS = speedOfImpact / feetPerMetre
```

...and we can convert back the other way by multiplying instead of dividing:

```
let speedOfImpactInFPS = speedOfImpactInMPS * feetPerMetre
```

As far as F# is concerned, `ft` and `m` have nothing to do with each other. It's up to the programmer to define appropriate conversion factors. But the presence of units on the conversion factors makes mistakes much less likely. For example, what happens if we divide instead of multiply above? The type of the result suggests that something is awry, and will probably lead to a compile-time error later in the code:

```
> let speedOfImpactInFPS = speedOfImpactInMPS / feetPerMetre;;

val speedOfImpactInFPS : float<m ^ 2/(ft s)> = 8.500500698
```

It's a good idea to package up conversion factors with the unit-of-measure to which they relate. A convenient way to do this in F# is to make use of the ability to define static 'members' on types:

```
[<Measure>]
type ft =
  static member perMetre = 3.28084<ft/m>
```

Now we can just write `ft.perMetre`.

2.4 Interfacing Non-unit-aware Code

We've seen how to use syntax such as `2.0<s>` to introduce units-of-measure into the types of floating-point values. But what if a quantity is stored in a file, or entered by the user through a GUI, or in a web form? In that case it'll probably start out life as a `string`, to be parsed and converted into a `float`. How can we convert a vanilla `float` into, say, a `float<s>`? That's easy: just multiply by `1.0<s>`! Here's an example:

```
let rawString = reader.ReadLine()
let rawFloat = System.Double.Parse(rawString)
let timeInSeconds = rawFloat * 1.0<s>
```

If we want to convert back to a vanilla float, say, to pass to a non-units-aware function or method, we just divide by `1.0<s>`:

```
let timeSpan = System.TimeSpan.FromSeconds(timeInSeconds / 1.0<s>)
```

2.5   Dimensionless Quantities

But hold on – what's going on with that last example? The variable `timeInSeconds` has type `float<s>`, and we divided it by `1.0<s>` which has type `float<s>`. So the units cancel out, producing units which we write simply as the digit 1. Hence the type of `timeInSeconds / 1.0<s>` is `float<1>`. Such a quantity is called *dimensionless*. Conveniently, F# defines the ordinary `float` type to be an alias for `float<1>`, as if there is a definition

```
type float = float<1>
```

which makes use of overloading on the arity of the type constructor.

Traditionally, angles have been considered dimensionless, since they are defined as the ratio of arc length to radius. The built-in trigonometric functions `sin`, `cos`, and so on, accept dimensionless `floats`. There are, however, several *units* used to measure angles, such as *degrees*, or *revolutions*, in addition to the 'natural' unit *radians*. It's easy enough to define such units, and appropriate conversion factors, if stricter type-checking is required:

```
[<Measure>]
type deg =
  static member perRadian = 360.0<deg> / (2.0 * System.Math.PI)
[<Measure>]
type rev =
  static member perRadian = 1.0<rev> / (2.0 * System.Math.PI)

let l = sin (90.0<deg> / deg.perRadian)
```

2.6   Parametric Polymorphism

So far, we've seen how to write code that uses specific units-of-measure. But what about *generic* code that is independent of the units of the values? Let's start simple. What is the type of `fun x -> x*x`? Well, multiplication is overloaded, and F# defaults to integers:

```
> let sqr x = x*x;;
```

```
val sqr : int -> int
```

But if we annotate the argument, we can define squaring for all kinds of `floats`:

```
> let sqrLength (x:float<m>) = x*x;;
```

```
val sqrLength : float<m> -> float<m ^ 2>
> let sqrSpeed (x:float<m/s>) = x*x;;
```

```
val sqrSpeed : float<m/s> -> float<m ^ 2/s ^ 2>
```

This is very painful: we'd really like to write a single, *generic* squaring function, and then re-use it on values with differing units. And indeed, we can do just that:

```
> let sqr (x:float<_>) = x*x;;
```

```
val sqr : float<'u> -> float<'u ^ 2>
```

The underscore notation in `float<_>` tells the F# compiler to *infer* the unit-of-measure parameter, and as can be seen from the output, it infers a *generic* or *parametrically-polymorphic* type for squaring. The notation `'u` looks like a type variable, but is in fact a unit-of-measure variable that can be instantiated with any unit-of-measure expression. Let's use it on lengths and speeds:

```
> let d2 = sqr 3.0<m>;;
```

```
val d2 : float<m ^ 2> = 9.0
```

```
> let v2 = sqr 4.0<m/s>;;
```

```
val v2 : float<m ^ 2/s ^ 2> = 16.0
```

F# can fully infer polymorphic unit-of-measure types, with type annotations required only in situations where overloaded operators must be resolved. Moreover, as with ordinary ML-style type inference, it infers the most general, or *principal* type, of which all other possible types are instances. Here are some simple examples:

```
> let cube x = x*sqr x;;
```

```
val cube : float<'u> -> float<'u ^ 3>
```

```
> let pythagoras x y = sqrt (sqr x + sqr y);;
```

```
val pythagoras : float<'u> -> float<'u> -> float<'u>
```

```
> let average (x:float<_>) y = (x+y)/2.0;;
```

```
val average : float<'u> -> float<'u> -> float<'u>
```

Here's one that requires a bit of head-scratching to understand:

```
> let silly x y = sqr x + cube y;;

val silly : float<'u ^ 3> -> float<'u ^ 2> -> float<'u ^ 6>
```

We can now see that many of the built-in arithmetic operators and functions have a unit-polymorphic type as one possible overloading:

```
> let add (x:float<_>) y = x+y;;

val add : float<'u> -> float<'u> -> float<'u>

> let sub (x:float<_>) y = x-y;;

val sub : float<'u> -> float<'u> -> float<'u>

> let mul (x:float<_>) y = x*y;;

val mul : float<'u> -> float<'v> -> float<'u 'v>

> let div (x:float<_>) y = x/y;;

val div : float<'u> -> float<'v> -> float<'u/'v>

> fun (x : float<_>) -> sqrt x;;

val it : float<'u ^ 2> -> float<'u> = <fun:clo0>

> fun x -> sqrt x;;

val it : float -> float = <fun:clo0-1>
```

The last example here illustrates that without a type annotation, sqrt defaults to dimensionless float. This is in part to avoid units-of-measure confusing novice programmers, and in part to retain some compatibility with Caml.

Exercise 1. Without trying it out, what do you think is the most general type of the following function?

```
let sillier x y z = sqr x + cube y + sqr z * cube z
```

Now try it. Were you right?

2.7 Zero

Suppose we want to sum the elements of a list. In true functional style, we use one of the fold operators.

```
> let sum xs = List.fold (+) 0.0 xs;;

val sum : float list -> float
```

Oops – we don't have a nice polymorphic type! The reason is simple: unless units are specified, constants, including zero, are assumed to have no units, i.e. to be dimensionless. (This means that the subset of F# that coincides with Caml has the same static and dynamic behaviour as in Caml.) So instead, let's give `0.0` some units, but not tell F# what they are, by writing `0.0<_>`:

```
> let sum xs = List.fold (+) 0.0<_> xs;;

val sum : float<'u> list -> float<'u>
```

That's better!

Zero is the only numeric literal that is 'polymorphic' in its units, as is illustrated by the dialogue below.

```
> 0.0<_>;;
val it : float<'u> = 0.0
> 1.0<_>;;
val it : float = 1.0
```

Exercise 2. Can you think why this is so? (When we study the semantics of units, we will see the reason why it *must* be the case.) In fact, there are some other very special floating-point values that are polymorphic. Can you guess what they are?

2.8 Application Area: Statistics

Now let's do some statistics. First, we define the arithmetic mean μ of a list of n numbers $[a_1; \ldots; a_n]$, as given by the formula

$$\mu = \frac{1}{n} \sum_{i=1}^{n} a_i.$$

This is easy, using the `sum` function defined earlier:

```
> let mean xs = sum xs / float (List.length xs);;

val mean : float<'u> list -> float<'u>
```

Exercise 3. Write a unit-polymorphic function to compute the standard deviation σ of a list of n numbers $[a_1; \ldots; a_n]$, as given by the formula

$$\sigma^2 = \frac{1}{n} \sum_{i=1}^{n} (a_i - \mu)^2.$$

The *geometric mean* is given by

$$g = (a_1 \cdot a_2 \cdots a_n)^{\frac{1}{n}}$$

A straightforward implementation of this function does not get assigned a nice polymorphic type:

```
> let reciplen x = 1.0 / float (List.length x)

val reciplen : 'a list -> float

> let gmean (x:float<_> list) = List.reduce ( * ) x ** reciplen x;;

  let gmean (x:float<_> list) = List.reduce ( * ) x ** reciplen x;;
  --------------------^
```

```
stdin(15,21): warning FS0191: This code is less generic than
indicated by its annotations. A unit-of-measure specified using
 '_' has been determined to be '1', i.e. dimensionless. Consider
making the code generic, or removing the use of '_'.
```

```
val gmean : float list -> float
```

We have 'hinted' to the compiler that we want a parameterized `float` type, but it has inferred a dimensionless type, and so it helpfully emits a warning. But why did it not infer the type `float<'u> list -> float<'u>`? The answer lies in the type of the product *and* in the type of the exponentiation operator `**`. Consider first the expression `List.reduce ( * ) x`, which implements the product $a_1 \cdot a_2 \cdots a_n$. If x has type `float<'u> list` then we might expect it to have type `float<'u^n>`. But n is the length of the list, which is not known statically – we want a *dependent* type! Furthermore, the type of exponentiation is

```
val ( ** ) : float -> float -> float
```

in which both its arguments and result are dimensionless.

Exercise 4. With a little work, it is possible to write a function `gmean` that is assigned the polymorphic type that we expected. Hint: consider 'normalizing' the list before computing the product.

2.9 Application Area: Calculus

Now let's do some calculus. Higher-order functions abound here: for example, differentiation is a higher-order function $D : (\mathbb{R} \to \mathbb{R}) \to (\mathbb{R} \to \mathbb{R})$. To numerically differentiate a function f to obtain its approximate derivative f', we can use the formula

$$f'(x) \approx \frac{f(x+h) - f(x-h)}{2h},$$

where h represents a small change in x. Let's write this in F#:

```
> let diff (h:float<_>) (f:_ -> float<_>) = fun x -> (f(x+h)-f(x-h))
    / (2.0*h);;
-

val diff : float<'u> -> (float<'u> -> float<'v>) -> float<'u> ->
    float<'v/'u>
```

Notice how the type of `diff` precisely describes the effect of differentiation on the units of a function. For example, let's use it to compute the rate of change of the gravitational force between the earth and the author as the author moves away from the earth:

```
> let earthMass = 5.9736e24<kg>;;

val earthMass : float<kg> = 5.9736e+24

> diff 0.01<m> (attract myMass earthMass);;
val it : (float<m> -> float<kg/s ^ 2>) = <fun:it54-6>
```

The units `kg/s^2` appear a little strange, but we can confirm that they really are 'force per unit length':

```
> (diff 0.01<m> (attract myMass earthMass) : float<m> -> float<N/m>)
;;
val it : (float<m> -> float<N/m>) = <fun:it57-8>
```

We can likewise integrate a function, using one of the simplest methods: the trapezium rule [18, Section 4.1]. It is defined by the following formula, which gives an approximation to the area under the curve defined by f in the interval $a \leqslant x \leqslant b$ using $n + 1$ values of $f(x)$:

$$\int_a^b f(x)\, dx \approx \frac{h}{2}\left(f(a) + 2f(a+h) + \cdots + 2f(b-h) + f(b)\right), \quad h = \frac{b-a}{n}.$$

Here is an implementation in F#:

```
let integrate (a:float<_>) (b:float<_>) n (f:_ -> float<_>) =
  let h = (b-a) / (float n)
  let rec iter x i =
    if i=0 then 0.0<_>
    else f x + iter (x+h) (i-1)
  h * (f a / 2.0 + iter (a+h) (n-1) + f b / 2.0)
```

Exercise 5. Without typing it in, what do you think the unit-polymorphic type of `integrate` is?

Our final example is an implementation of the Newton-Raphson method for finding roots of equations, based on the iteration of

$$x_{n+1} = x_n - \frac{f(x_n)}{f'(x_n)}.$$

This method calculates a solution of $f(x) = 0$, making use of the derivative f'. The F# code is as follows:

```
let rec findRoot (f:float<_> -> float<_>) f' x xacc =
  let dx = f x / f' x
  let x' = x - dx
  if abs dx / x' < xacc
  then x'
  else findRoot f f' x' xacc
```

It accepts a function f, its derivative f', an initial guess x and a relative accuracy xacc. Its type is

```
val findRoot :
  (float<'u> -> float<'v>) ->
    (float<'u> -> float<'v/'u>) -> float<'u> -> float -> float<'u>
```

2.10 Unit-Parameterized Types

So far we have seen units applied to float, the built-in primitive type of double-precision floating-point numbers. The types float32 and decimal can be parameterized by units too:

```
[<Measure>] type USD
[<Measure>] type yr
let fatcatsalary = 1000000M<USD/yr> // decimal constants have suffix M
let A4paperWidth = 0.210f<m> // float32 constants have suffix f
```

It's natural to parameterize other numeric types on units, such as a a type for complex numbers, or a type for vectors in 3-space. Or a unit-parameterized numeric type might be required for a component of some other type, such as a scene model type for a ray-tracer, and so that type must be parameterized too. Such types are supported in F# simply by marking the parameters with the [<Measure>] attribute:

```
// Record types parameterized by units
type complex< [<Measure>] 'u> = { re:float<'u>; im:float<'u> }
type vector3< [<Measure>] 'u> = { x:float<'u>; y:float<'u>; z:float<'u> }
type sphere< [<Measure>] 'u> = { centre:vector3<'u>; radius:float<'u> }
// A discriminated union parameterized by units
type obj< [<Measure>] 'u> =
| Sphere of sphere<'u>
| Group of obj<'u> list
```

We can now instantiate such types with concrete units:

```
> let gravity = { x = 0.0<_>; y = 0.0<_>; z = -9.808<m/s^2> };;

val gravity : vector3<m/s ^ 2> = {x = 0.0;
                                  y = 0.0;
                                  z = -9.808;}
> let scene = Group [Sphere {centre={x=2.0<m>;y=3.0<m>;z=4.0<m>};
    radius = 1.5<m> }];;

val scene : obj<m> = Group [Sphere {centre = {x = 2.0;
                                              y = 3.0;
                                              z = 4.0;};
                                    radius = 1.5;}]
```

It's straightforward to write functions over such types, with appropriate unit-polymorphic types. For example, the dot product of two vectors can be defined as follows, with its type inferred automatically:

```
> let dot v w = v.x*w.x + v.y*w.y + v.z*w.z;;

val dot : vector3<'u> -> vector3<'v> -> float<'u 'v>
```

Here are functions to convert from and to the polar representation of complex numbers:

```
let fromPolar (m:float<_>) p = { re = m*cos p; im = m*sin p }
let magnitude c = sqrt (c.re*c.re + c.im*c.im)
let phase c = atan2 c.im c.re
```

It's desirable to define unit-polymorphic arithmetic operators for types such as `complex` and `vector3`. This is supported through the use of 'static members':

```
type complex< [<Measure>] 'u> = { re:float<'u>; im:float<'u>} with
  static member (+) (a:complex<'u>,b) = { re = a.re+b.re; im = a.im+a.im }
  static member (-) (a:complex<'u>,b) = { re = a.re-b.re; im = a.im-a.im }
  static member ( * ) (a:complex<'u>,b:complex<'v>) =
    { re = a.re * b.re - a.im * b.im; im = a.im * b.re + b.im * a.re }
```

We can now use complex numbers to do arithmetic on AC (alternating current) voltages:

```
> let voltage1 = fromPolar 2.0<V> 0.0;; // 2 volts

val voltage1 : complex<V> = {re = 2.0;
                             im = 0.0;}

> let voltage2 = fromPolar 3.0<V> (System.Math.PI/4.0);; // 3 volts
    at 45 degree phase

val voltage2 : complex<V> = {re = 2.121320344;
                             im = 2.121320344;}

> magnitude (voltage1 + voltage2);;
val it : float<V> = 4.635221826
> phase (voltage1 + voltage2);;
val it : float = 0.4753530566
```

2.11   Polymorphic Recursion

For our final example of unit-parameterized types we return to calculus. We saw that given a function of type `float<'u> -> float<'v>`, its derivative has type `float<'u> -> float<'v/'u>`. Naturally enough, its second-order derivative (the derivative of the derivative) has type `float<'u> -> float<'v/'u^2>`. What if we want to repeat this process, and create a list of successive derivatives? We can't just use the built-in `list` type, because it requires list elements to have identical types. We want a list in which the types of successive elements are *related* but not the same. We can define such a custom type as follows:

```
type derivs<[<Measure>] 'u, [<Measure>] 'v> =
| Nil
| Cons of (float<'u> -> float<'v>) * derivs<'u,'v/'u>
```

An expression `Cons(f,Cons(f',Cons(f'',...)))` of type `derivs<'u,'v>` represents a function `f` of type `float<'u> -> float<'v>`, its first-order derivative `f'` of type `float<'u> -> float<'v/'u>`, its second-order derivative `f''` having type `float<'u> -> float<'v/'u^2>`, and so on. The type makes use of *polymorphic recursion* in its definition, meaning that the recursive reference (`derivs`) is used at a type distinct from its definition. (This is also called a *nested* or *non-regular* datatype in the literature.)

In order to use such a type in a recursive function, the type of the function must be annotated fully with its type, as type inference for polymorphic recursion is in general undecidable. Here is a function that makes use of our earlier numerical differentiation function `diff` to compute a list of the first `n` derivatives of a function `f`.

```
let rec makeDerivs<[<Measure>] 'u, [<Measure>] 'v>
  (n:int)
  (h:float<'u>)
  (f:float<'u> -> float<'v>) : derivs<'u,'v> =
  if n=0 then Nil else Cons(f, makeDerivs (n-1) h (diff h f))
```

3   Polymorphic Type Inference for Units-of-Measure

Ever since Robin Milner's classic paper on polymorphic type inference [14], researchers have developed ever more sophisticated means of automatically inferring types for programs. Pottier's survey article presents a good overview of the state-of-the-art [17, §10]. The variety of parametric polymorphism described in Milner's original work has become known as "`let`-polymorphism", being equivalent in expressivity to the simple, monomorphic typing of a program after expanding all `let`-bindings. One fruitful direction for research has been to support 'first-class' polymorphism in the style of System F and beyond [12,11,23]. Others have extended inference to handle new type constructs such as Generalized Algebraic Data Types (GADTs) [20] or existentials. Another direction is to consider polymorphism over entities other than just types, for example records or effects. Units-of-measure are an instance of this last idea.

Before proceeding, we answer the question: how are units *different* from types? Even the original ML type system can be used to encode all sorts of invariants such as well-formed contexts [13] and well-formed lambda terms [4]. To encode units, we could define dummy type constructors `UOne`, `UProd` and `UInv`, together with base units, and then build derived units, e.g. `UProd<m,UInv<UProd<s,s>>>` encodes the units `m/s^2`. The crucial aspect of units-of-measure that is not captured by this encoding is *equations* that hold between syntactically distinct units. For example, the units `m s` are equivalent to `s m`; and `s s^-1` can be simplified to `1`. Any encoding of units in types must somehow encode this *equational theory* of units, typically requiring some syntax that *witnesses* the use of properties such as commutativity and associativity. It's better to build this theory in: moreover, it turns out that the equational theory associated with units has some very handy properties that support full type inference.

$$\frac{}{u =_U u}\ (\text{refl}) \qquad \frac{u =_U v}{v =_U u}\ (\text{sym}) \qquad \frac{u =_U v \quad v =_U w}{u =_U w}\ (\text{trans})$$

$$\frac{u =_U v}{u\hat{\ }\text{-}1 =_U v\hat{\ }\text{-}1}\ (\text{cong1}) \qquad \frac{u =_U v \quad u' =_U v'}{u * u' =_U v * v'}\ (\text{cong2}) \qquad \frac{}{u * 1 =_U u}\ (\text{id})$$

$$\frac{}{(u * v) * w =_U u * (v * w)}\ (\text{assoc}) \qquad \frac{}{u * v =_U v * u}\ (\text{comm}) \qquad \frac{}{u * u\hat{\ }\text{-}1 =_U 1}\ (\text{inv})$$

Fig. 4. Equational theory of units $=_U$

3.1 Grammar for Units

First let's pin down a formal grammar for unit expressions:

$$u, v, w ::= b \mid \alpha \mid 1 \mid u * v \mid u\hat{\ }\text{-}1$$

We use u, v and w for unit expressions. They're built from

- base units such as kg, ranged over by b, and drawn from a set UBase;
- unit variables, which we write as α, β, etc., and drawn from a set UVars;
- the 'unit' unit, written 1, representing dimensionless quantities without units;
- product of units, written $u * v$; and
- inverse of units, written $u\hat{\ }\text{-}1$.

Let $vars(u)$ be the unit variables occurring in unit expression u. For example, $vars(\alpha * \beta\hat{\ }\text{-}1) = \{\alpha, \beta\}$.

For the surface syntax, we de-sugar quotients and integer powers of units:

$$u/v = u * v\hat{\ }\text{-}1$$
$$u\hat{\ }n = \begin{cases} u * u\hat{\ }(n-1) & \text{if } n > 0, \\ 1 & \text{if } n = 0, \\ u\hat{\ }\text{-}1 * u\hat{\ }(n+1) & \text{if } n < 0. \end{cases}$$

For clarity, we will often write u^n for powers.

3.2 Equations for Units

Units of measure obey rules of associativity, commutativity, identity and inverses, and thus form an Abelian group. We can formalize this as an equivalence relation on unit expressions $=_U$, defined inductively by the rules of Figure 4. These rules just say that $=_U$ is the smallest congruence relation that is closed under the Abelian group axioms.

The relation $=_U$ is an example of an *equational theory*. Other common examples are AC (Associativity and Commutativity), AC1 (adding the identity axiom to AC), and ACI (adding an axiom for Idempotency to AC). These three theories are all *regular*, meaning that if a term t is equivalent to a term t' under the equational theory, then $vars(t) = vars(t')$. In contrast, our theory AG (Abelian groups) is *non-regular*, due to the axiom (inv) whose left and right sides do not have matching sets of variables.

Baader and Nipkow's book on term rewriting provides a good introduction to equational theories, and the problem of unification that we study later [3].

3.3 Deciding Equations

An obvious first question is: how can we *decide* whether two unit expressions u and v are equivalent, *i.e.* is the equation $u =_U v$ *valid*? It turns out that any unit expression is equivalent to a unique *normal form* with respect to $=_U$, as follows:

$$\alpha_1{}^{x_1} * \cdots * \alpha_m{}^{x_m} * b_1{}^{y_1} * \cdots * b_n{}^{y_n}$$

Here the x's and y's are non-zero integers, and the unit variables and base units are ordered alphabetically. (In fact the F# compiler does something similar when displaying units-of-measure, except that units with negative powers are separated from those with positive powers.)

One way of checking whether two unit-of-measure expressions are equivalent is to 'normalize' them by interpreting the rules of Figure 4 as oriented rewrite rules. In practice, one can go straight to the normal form of a unit expression u by calculating an exponent for each variable and base unit that occurs in u:

$$exp(u) \; : \; (\text{UBase} \cup \text{UVars}) \to \mathbb{Z}$$
$$exp(1)(w) = 0$$
$$exp(u * v)(w) = exp(u)(w) + exp(v)(w)$$
$$exp(u\text{\^{}-1})(w) = -exp(u)(w)$$
$$exp(\alpha)(w) = \begin{cases} 1, & \text{if } w = \alpha \\ 0, & \text{otherwise} \end{cases}$$
$$exp(b)(w) = \begin{cases} 1, & \text{if } w = b \\ 0, & \text{otherwise} \end{cases}$$

It's then easy to check equivalence of unit expressions u and v simply by checking that $exp(u)$ matches $exp(v)$ on all variables and base units in the expressions.

Exercise 6. Prove that $u =_U v$ if and only if $exp(u) = exp(v)$ (hard). Now prove the following corollary:

$$u =_U \alpha_1{}^{exp(u)(\alpha_1)} * \cdots * \alpha_m{}^{exp(u)(\alpha_m)} * b_1{}^{exp(u)(b_1)} * \cdots * b_n{}^{exp(u)(b_n)}$$

where $\alpha_1, \ldots, \alpha_m$ and $b_1, \ldots, b_n$ are respectively the unit variables and base units occurring in u.

3.4 Solving Equations

For languages such as Pascal and Java that support only type *checking*, it is relatively easy to add support for checking units-of-measure, using the procedure outlined in the previous section. But for F#, we go further, and support full type *inference*. To do this, we must not only *check* equations; we must *solve* them. Consider the following dialogue:

```
> let area = 20.0<m^2>;;

val area : float<m ^ 2> = 20.0

> let f (y:float<_>) = area + y*y;;

val f : float<m> -> float<m ^ 2>
```

In order to infer a type for f, the compiler will generate a fresh unit variable α for the units of y, and will then solve the equation

$$\alpha^2 =_U \mathrm{m}^2$$

in order to satisfy the requirements of the addition operation. Of course, this equation is easy to solve (just set $\alpha := \mathrm{m}$), but in general, the equation can have arbitrarily complex units on either side.

Moreover, there may be many ways to solve the equation. Consider the equation

$$\alpha * \beta =_U \mathrm{m}^2$$

for which $\{\alpha := \mathrm{m}, \beta := \mathrm{m}\}$, $\{\alpha := \mathrm{m}^2, \beta := 1\}$, and $\{\alpha := 1, \beta := \mathrm{m}^2\}$ are three distinct solutions. These solutions are all *ground*, meaning that they contain only base units and no variables. All three, though, are subsumed by the non-ground, 'parametric' solution $S = \{\alpha := \beta\hat{\ }{-1} * \mathrm{m}^2\}$, in the following sense: each can be presented as $\{\beta := u\} \circ S$ for some u. (To verify this, instantiate u to be m, 1 and m^2 respectively.) In fact, here S is the *most general* solution for this equation from which all others can be derived by instantiation.

Exercise 7. Present solutions in α and β to the equation

$$\alpha * \beta =_U \mathrm{kg} * \mathrm{s}$$

Can you express a *most general* solution? Can you express a most general solution without using the inverse operation?

The idea of solving equations by computing a syntactic substitution for its variables is known as *unification*, and will be familiar to anyone who has studied the type inference algorithms for ML, Haskell, or other similar languages. The well known *principal types* property for those languages relies on the following property of syntactic unification: if two types are unifiable, then there exists a *most general* unifier from which all other unifiers can be derived.

For units-of-measure we must solve equations with respect to the equational theory of Abelian groups. In general, for an equational theory $=_E$, an *E-unification problem* is the following: for given terms t and u, find a substitution S such that $S(t) =_E S(u)$.

If the terms are unifiable at all, there can be an infinite number of possible unifiers. We say that a unifier S_1 is *more general than* a unifier S_2 and write $S_1 \preceq_E S_2$ if $R \circ S_1 =_E S_2$ for some substitution R. (And we say that S_2 *is an instance of* S_1.) In contrast to syntactic unification, for equational unification there may not be a single most general unifier. For example, in the presence of nullary constants, unification problems in $AC1$ may have a finite set of unifiers of which all unifiers are instances, but which are not instances of each other. This was hinted at in Exercise 7: under $AC1$, in which the rule (inv) of Abelian groups is not available, there are in fact four incomparable unifiers, namely $\{\alpha := \mathsf{kg}, \beta := \mathsf{s}\}$, $\{\alpha := \mathsf{s}, \beta := \mathsf{kg}\}$, $\{\alpha := 1, \beta := \mathsf{kg} * \mathsf{s}\}$ and $\{\alpha := \mathsf{kg} * \mathsf{s}, \alpha := 1\}$.

3.5   A Unification Algorithm

We are fortunate that the theory of Abelian groups (AG) with nullary constants is *unitary*, the technical term for "possesses most general unifiers". Rather few equational theories have this property; one other is the theory of Boolean Rings. Moreover, AG-unification is decidable, and the algorithm is straightforward to implement.

Figure 5 presents the algorithm *Unify*, which takes a pair of unit expressions u and v and either returns a substitution S such that $S(u) =_U S(v)$, or returns fail indicating that no unifier exists. First observe that the equation

$$u =_U v$$

is equivalent (i.e. has the same set of solutions) to

$$u * v\text{^-1} =_U 1,$$

and so unification can be reduced to the problem of matching against 1.

The core algorithm *UnifyOne* is a variant of Gaussian elimination, and works by iteratively applying a solution-set-preserving substitution that reduces the size of the minimum exponent in the normal form until it reaches an equation containing at most one variable. Consider each subcase in turn:

$Unify(u, v) = UnifyOne(u * v\text{^-1})$

$UnifyOne(u) =$
  let $u =_U \alpha_1^{x_1} * \cdots * \alpha_m^{x_m} * b_1^{y_1} * \cdots * b_n^{y_n}$
    where $\alpha_1, \ldots, \alpha_m, b_1, \ldots, b_n$ distinct, $x_1, \ldots, x_m, y_1, \ldots, y_n$ positive, $|x_1| \leqslant |x_2|, \cdots, |x_m|$
  in
    if $m = 0$ and $n = 0$ then id
    if $m = 0$ and $n \neq 0$ then fail
    if $m = 1$ and $x_1 \mid y_i$ for all i then $\{\alpha_1 \mapsto b_1^{-y_1/x_1} * \cdots * b_m^{-y_n/x_1}\}$
    if $m = 1$ otherwise then fail
    else $S_2 \circ S_1$ where
      $S_1 = \{\alpha_1 \mapsto \alpha_1 * \alpha_2^{-\lfloor x_2/x_1 \rfloor} * \cdots * \alpha_m^{-\lfloor x_m/x_1 \rfloor} * b_1^{-\lfloor y_1/x_1 \rfloor} * \cdots * b_n^{-\lfloor y_n/x_1 \rfloor}\}$
      $S_2 = UnifyOne(S_1(u))$

Fig. 5. Unification algorithm for units-of-measure

- If there are no variables ($m = 0$) then either we have 1 ($n = 0$), and so we're done, or we have just base units ($n \neq 0$), and so there is no unifier.
- If there is exactly one variable ($m = 1$) then we check to see if its exponent divides all of the exponents of the base units. If not, then there is no unifier: an example would be the unification problem $\alpha^2 =_U \text{kg}^3$. If it does divide, then the unifier is immediate: an example would be the problem $\alpha^2 =_U \text{m}^2 * \text{s}^{-4}$ with unifier $\{\alpha := \text{m} * \text{s}^{-2}\}$.
- Otherwise, we recurse, after applying a substitution S_1, whose effect is to transform the unit expression to

$$\alpha_1^{x_1} * \alpha_2^{x_2 \bmod x_1} * \cdots * \alpha_m^{x_m \bmod x_1} * b_1^{y_1 \bmod x_1} * \cdots * b_n^{y_n \bmod x_1}.$$

Termination is ensured as the size of the smallest exponent, which was x_1, has been reduced, as each of the _ mod x_1 is smaller than x_1.

The following theorem characterizes the result of *Unify* as the most general unifier.

Theorem 1 (Soundness and completeness of *Unify*).
(Soundness) If Unify$(u, v) = S$ then $S(u) =_U S(v)$.
(Completeness) If $S(u) =_U S(v)$ then Unify$(u, v) \preceq_U S$.

Proof. See [7].

Exercise 8. Compute the most general unifier to the equation $\alpha^2 * \beta =_U \text{m}^6$.

3.6 Types

As we saw in Section 2.10, type constructors in F# can take both types and units-of-measure as parameters. The distinction is enforced by a trivial *kind* system, in which type parameters are one of two kinds, *type*, the default, and *measure*, as indicated by the attribute [<Measure>]. We won't formalize this kind system here, and simply use the same set of variables for both types and units, relying on the context to distinguish their kinds.

Suppose that the grammar of types is really simple, consisting just of type variables, floating-point types parameterized by units and functions:

$$\tau ::= \alpha \mid \text{float<}u\text{>} \mid \tau \text{ -> } \tau$$

This will be enough to illustrate the process of type inference.

The relation $=_U$ extends in an obvious way to types, the important point being that float<u> $=_U$ float<v> if and only if $u =_U v$. A simple unification algorithm for types with respect to $=_U$ makes use of our existing unification algorithm for units in the case for float. This is shown in Figure 6. The most general unifier property for units of measure extends to types.

Theorem 2 (Soundness and completeness of *UnifyTy*).
(Soundness) If UnifyTy$(\tau_1, \tau_2) = S$ then $S(\tau_1) =_U S(\tau_2)$.
(Completeness) If $S(\tau_1) =_U S(\tau_2)$ then UnifyTy$(\tau_1, \tau_2) \preceq_U S$.

Proof. See [7].

$$UnifyTy(\alpha, \alpha) = id$$

$$UnifyTy(\alpha, \tau) = UnifyTy(\tau, \alpha) = \begin{cases} \text{fail} & \text{if } \alpha \text{ in } \tau \\ \{\alpha := \tau\} & \text{otherwise.} \end{cases}$$

$$UnifyTy(\texttt{float<u>}, \texttt{float<v>}) = Unify(u, v)$$

$$UnifyTy(\tau_1 \texttt{ -> } \tau_2, \tau_3 \texttt{ -> } \tau_4) = S_2 \circ S_1$$
$$\text{where } S_1 = UnifyTy(\tau_1, \tau_3)$$
$$\text{and } S_2 = UnifyTy(S_1(\tau_2), S_1(\tau_4))$$

Fig. 6. Unification algorithm for types

3.7   Type Schemes

Polymorphic types as displayed in F# are in fact shorthand for type *schemes* of the form

$$\sigma ::= \forall \alpha_1, \ldots, \alpha_n.\tau$$

Top-level type schemes as presented to the programmer are always *closed*, meaning that all variables in the type τ are bound by the $\forall$ quantifier: the variables are *implicitly* quantified. Internally, the F# type system and inference algorithm make use of *open* schemes such as $\forall \alpha.\texttt{float<}\alpha\texttt{> -> float<}\beta\texttt{>}$ in which β occurs *free*. Nevertheless, for the purposes of these notes, we will study in detail only closed type schemes, and in Section 3.10 briefly discuss some interesting challenges that are presented by open type schemes.

Type schemes can be *instantiated* to types by replacing occurrences of unit variables by unit expressions. Formally, we write $\sigma \preceq \tau$ if $\sigma = \forall \alpha_1, \ldots, \alpha_n.\tau'$ instantiates to τ, that is $\tau = \{\alpha_1 := u_1, \ldots, \alpha_n := u_n\}\tau'$ for some unit expressions $u_1, \ldots, u_n$. We write $\sigma \preceq_U \tau$ if $\sigma \preceq_U \tau'$ and $\tau' =_U \tau$ for some τ': in other words, τ is an instance of σ with respect to the rules of units.

Exercise 9. Show that $\forall \alpha.\texttt{float<}\alpha \texttt{ * kg> -> float<}\alpha \texttt{ * kg>} \preceq_U \texttt{float<1> -> float<1>}$.

3.8   A Type System and Inference Algorithm

We are finally ready to present a small subset of the F# type system. As with all members of the ML family, parametric polymorphism is introduced through `let` bindings, as in the following sample:

```
> let pair =
-   let id = fun y -> y in (id 5, id true);;

val pair : int * bool = (5, true)
```

Here the type system will assign the `let`-bound identifer `id` a polymorphic type scheme $\forall \alpha.\alpha \texttt{ -> } \alpha$, which is instantiated to `int -> int` and `bool -> bool` at its uses. Contrast the following code, which is not typeable under the type system and is rejected by F#'s type checker:

Expressions: $\Gamma \vdash e : \tau$

$$(var)\frac{}{\Gamma, x{:}\sigma \vdash x : \tau}\ \sigma \preceq \tau \qquad (app)\frac{\Gamma \vdash e_1 : \tau_1 \text{ -> } \tau_2 \quad \Gamma \vdash e_2 : \tau_1}{\Gamma \vdash e_1\ e_2 : \tau_2}$$

$$(abs)\frac{\Gamma, x{:}\tau_1 \vdash e : \tau_2}{\Gamma \vdash (\textbf{fun } x \text{ -> } e) : \tau_1 \text{ -> } \tau_2} \qquad (eq)\frac{\Gamma \vdash e : \tau_1}{\Gamma \vdash e : \tau_2}\ \tau_1 =_U \tau_2$$

Top-level: $\Gamma \vdash t : \sigma$

$$(let)\frac{\Gamma \vdash t_1 : \sigma_1 \quad \Gamma, x{:}\sigma_1 \vdash t_2 : \sigma_2}{\Gamma \vdash \textbf{let } x = t_1 \textbf{ in } t_2 : \sigma_2} \qquad (gen)\frac{\Gamma \vdash e : \tau}{\Gamma \vdash e : \forall \overline{\alpha}.\tau}\ \overline{\alpha} = vars(\tau)$$

Fig. 7. Typing rules

```
> let pair =
-   let applyFun id = (id 5, id true) in applyFun (fun y -> y);;

    let applyFun id = (id 5, id true) in applyFun (fun y -> y)
    ---------------------------^^^^

stdin(4,28): error FS0001: This expression was expected to have type
    int
but here has type
    bool
```

In this example id is λ-bound, and so cannot be used polymorphically.

The full type system permits let expressions to appear *locally*, under λ-abstractions. For our presentation, to avoid the need for open type schemes in type inference we allow let constructs to appear only at top-level, specifying the following grammar for expressions and top-level expressions:

$$\begin{array}{lll} \text{(expressions)} & e ::= x \mid \textbf{fun } x \text{ -> } e \mid e\ e \\ \text{(top-level)} & t ::= e \mid \textbf{let } x = t \textbf{ in } t \end{array}$$

Here t represents *top*-level expressions consisting of a sequence of let bindings followed by an expression e to evaluate. Expressions consist of variables, λ-abstractions, and function application. Constants and primitive operations are assumed to be declared in some 'pervasive' environment.

Figure 7 presents a polymorphic type system for this language. Here the typing judgment $\Gamma \vdash e : \tau$ assigns a type τ to an expression e under the environment Γ that maps variables to type schemes. Top-level expressions are assigned type *schemes* using the judgment $\Gamma \vdash t : \sigma$.

In essence, it is a very modest extension to the usual ML type system, such as that presented in Pierce's book on types and programming languages [16]. Apart from the stratification of syntax into expressions and top-level expressions, the main addition is the rule (eq), that incorporates the equational theory $=_U$ into

$$Infer(\Gamma \cup \{x : \forall \overline{\alpha}.\tau\}, x) = (id, \{\overline{\alpha} := \overline{\beta}\}\tau) \quad \text{where } \overline{\beta} \text{ are fresh}$$

$$Infer(\Gamma, \text{fun } x \rightarrow e) = (S, S(\alpha) \rightarrow \tau)$$
$$\text{where } Infer(\Gamma \cup \{x : \alpha\}, e) = (S, \tau) \quad \text{for fresh } \alpha$$

$$Infer(\Gamma, e_1 \, e_2) = (S_3 \circ S_2 \circ S_1, S_3(\alpha))$$
$$\text{where } Infer(\Gamma, e_1) = (S_1, \tau_1)$$
$$Infer(S_1(\Gamma), e_2) = (S_2, \tau_2)$$
$$UnifyTy(S_2(\tau_1), \tau_2 \rightarrow \alpha) = S_3$$

$$InferTop(\Gamma, \text{let } x = t_1 \text{ in } t_2) = \sigma_2$$
$$\text{where } InferTop(\Gamma, t_1) = \sigma_1$$
$$InferTop(\Gamma \cup \{x : \sigma_1\}, t_2) = \sigma_2$$

$$InferTop(\Gamma, e) = \forall \overline{\alpha}.\tau$$
$$\text{where } Infer(\Gamma, e) = (S, \tau)$$
$$vars(\tau) = \overline{\alpha}$$

Fig. 8. Type inference algorithm

the type system. (Compare the subsumption rule from systems that support subtyping.)

Exercise 10. Suppose that

$$\Gamma = \{ \, \texttt{+} : \forall \alpha.\texttt{float<}\alpha\texttt{> -> float<}\alpha\texttt{> -> float<}\alpha\texttt{>},$$
$$\texttt{recip} : \forall \alpha.\texttt{float<}\alpha\texttt{> -> float<}\alpha\texttt{\^{}-1>}\}.$$

Present a typing derivation for

$$\Gamma \vdash \texttt{fun } x \texttt{ -> fun } y \texttt{ -> } x + \texttt{recip } y : \forall \alpha.\texttt{float<}\alpha\texttt{> ->float<}\alpha\texttt{\^{}-1> ->float<}\alpha\texttt{>}.$$

The usual inference algorithm for ML can be adapted very easily to this system, simply by replacing the use of syntactic unification by our equational unification algorithm *UnifyTy*. Figure 8 presents the algorithm.

Exercise 11. Dry-run the algorithm on the top-level expression from Exercise 10.

Theorem 3 (Soundness and completeness of *InferTop*). *Suppose Γ is closed. Then:*
(Soundness) If $InferTop(\Gamma, t) = \sigma$ then $\Gamma \vdash t : \sigma$.
(Completeness) If $\Gamma \vdash t : \sigma$ then $InferTop(\Gamma, t) \preceq_U \sigma$.

Proof. First prove that if $Infer(\Gamma, e) = (S, \tau)$, then $S(\Gamma) \vdash e : \tau$ (soundness for *Infer*), and that if $S(\Gamma) \vdash e : \tau$ then $Infer(\Gamma, e) = (S_0, \tau_0)$ such that $\tau =_U S'(\tau_0)$ and $S =_U S' \circ S_0$ for some S' (completeness for *Infer*). (This proof will make use of Theorem 2.) The result concerning *InferTop* then follows straightforwardly.

3.9   Type Scheme Equivalence

A type scheme represents an infinite family of types, and we define

$$Insts_U(\sigma) = \{\tau \mid \sigma \preceq_U \tau\}.$$

This provides a natural notion of type scheme equivalence, namely that two schemes are equivalent if they instantiate to the same set of types. We write

$$\sigma_1 \cong_U \sigma_2 \text{ iff } Insts_U(\sigma_1) = Insts_U(\sigma_2)$$

For vanilla ML types, type scheme equivalence is trivial: the only way that schemes can differ is in naming and redundancy of type variables. For example, writing $\cong$ for equivalence, we have

$$\forall\alpha\beta\gamma.\alpha \text{ -> } \beta \text{ -> } \alpha \cong \forall\alpha\beta.\beta \text{ -> } \alpha \text{ -> } \beta.$$

For units-of-measure, in addition to naming, we have the underlying equivalence $=_U$ on types, but it goes further than that. For example, consider the following three equivalent type schemes for the division operation:

$$\forall\alpha\beta.\text{float<}\alpha\text{> -> float<}\beta\text{> -> float<}\alpha * \beta\text{^-1>} \tag{1}$$
$$\forall\alpha\beta.\text{float<}\alpha * \beta\text{> -> float<}\alpha\text{> -> float<}\beta\text{>} \tag{2}$$
$$\forall\alpha\beta.\text{float<}\alpha\text{> -> float<}\beta\text{^-1> -> float<}\alpha * \beta\text{>} \tag{3}$$

The bodies of these type schemes differ even with respect to $=_U$, yet they instantiate under $\preceq_U$ to the same set of types.

We can characterize type scheme equivalence in terms of substitutions that map from one type scheme to the other and vice versa. Suppose $\sigma_1 = \forall\overline{\alpha}.\tau_1$ and $\sigma_2 = \forall\overline{\alpha}.\tau_2$. Then $\sigma_1 \cong_U \sigma_2$ if and only if $\sigma_1 \preceq_U \tau_2$ and $\sigma_2 \preceq_U \tau_1$. In other words, recalling the definition of $\preceq_U$ from Section 3.7, to show two type schemes equivalent we must merely find substitutions both ways.

Exercise 12. Demonstrate the equivalence of the types for reciprocal just presented. Hint: you can halve the number of substitutions required by mapping (1) to (2) to (3) and back to (1).

As far as the theory of units is concerned, the form of type schemes doesn't much matter. But for the programmer, it could be confusing to be presented with seemingly-different schemes that are in fact equivalent. Partly for this reason, F# presents type schemes to the programmer in a consistent way, putting them in a *normal form*.

This normal form has pleasant properties (e.g. it minimizes the number of quantified and 'free' variables) and corresponds to a well-known form (the Hermite Normal Form) from algebra. There is not space in these notes to present details; if you are interested, consult the author's thesis [7].

3.10   Open Type Schemes and Generalized Let

We now consider type schemes in which not every variable is bound by a quantifier. Consider the following three type schemes:

$$\forall\alpha.\texttt{float<}\alpha\texttt{> -> float<}\alpha\texttt{\^{}-1>}$$
$$\forall\alpha\beta.\texttt{float<}\alpha * \beta\texttt{> -> float<}\alpha\texttt{\^{}-1 * }\beta\texttt{\^{}-1>}$$
$$\forall\alpha.\texttt{float<}\alpha * \beta\texttt{\^{}-1> -> float<}\alpha\texttt{\^{}-1 * }\beta\texttt{>}$$

The first of these is clearly the type that one would expect of the reciprocal function `fun (x:float<_>) -> 1.0/x`. In fact, the other two schemes are equivalent, despite the presence of a 'redundant' bound variable β in the second scheme, and a redundant free variable β in the third scheme.

Now suppose that we generalize our type system to support polymorphic `let` underneath λ's. We can add the following standard rule:

$$\frac{\Gamma \vdash e_1 : \tau_1 \quad \Gamma, x{:}\forall\overline{\alpha}.\tau_1 \vdash e_2 : \tau_2}{\Gamma \vdash \texttt{let } x = e_1 \texttt{ in } e_2 : \tau_2} \quad \overline{\alpha} \text{ not free in } \Gamma$$

Then we can extend the type inference algorithm with the standard clause:

$$Infer(\Gamma, \texttt{let } x = e_1 \texttt{ in } e_2) = (S_2 \circ S_1, \tau_2)$$
$$\text{where } Infer(\Gamma, e_1) = (S_1, \tau_1)$$
$$vars(\tau_1) \setminus vars(S_1(\Gamma)) = \overline{\alpha}$$
$$Infer(S_1(\Gamma) \cup \{x : \forall\overline{\alpha}.\tau_1\}, e_2) = (S_2, \tau_2)$$

Unfortunately, although this algorithm is sound (it does not accept ill-typed expressions), it is not complete (it rejects typeable expressions). The problem lies with its use of $vars(\Gamma)$: as we saw from the open type scheme illustrated above, the notion of 'free' variable in a type scheme or environment is rather slippery: it's not respected by type scheme equivalence. It's not even enough to minimize 'free' variables by simplifying type schemes in the environment with respect to type scheme equivalence, as the following example demonstrates. Suppose

$$\Gamma_0 \equiv \{ \texttt{ div} : \forall\alpha\beta.\texttt{float<}\alpha * \beta\texttt{> -> float<}\alpha\texttt{> -> float<}\beta\texttt{>},$$
$$\texttt{mass} : \texttt{float<kg>},$$
$$\texttt{time} : \texttt{float<s>}\}$$

and we wish to type-check the following expression under Γ_0 (assuming that we've added pairs to the language):

$$e \equiv \texttt{fun } x \texttt{ -> let } d = \texttt{div } x \texttt{ in } (d \texttt{ mass}, d \texttt{ time})$$

Now there *is* a typing derivation of $\Gamma_0 \vdash e : \texttt{float<}\alpha\texttt{> -> float<}\alpha * \texttt{kg\^{}-1> -> float<}\alpha * \texttt{s\^{}-1>}$. The `let`-bound variable d is given a polymorphic type, which is used at two instances when applied to `mass` and `time`. Unfortunately, the inference algorithm will reject e. If you run the algorithm until the crucial point in the new rule for `let`, you will find that

$$\tau_1 \quad = \texttt{float<}\alpha\texttt{> -> float<}\beta\texttt{>}$$
$$S_1(\Gamma) = \Gamma_0 \cup \{x : \texttt{float<}\alpha * \beta\texttt{>}\}$$

for some fresh variables α and β. Hence there is no possible generalization of variables, as all of the variables present in the type τ_1 of x also occur in the environment.

Exercise 13. As is usual, our type system has a substitution property, namely, that if $\Gamma \vdash e : \tau$ then for any substitution S there is a derivation of $S(\Gamma) \vdash e : S(\tau)$. Furthermore, one can show that if $\Gamma_1 \cong_U \Gamma_2$ and $\Gamma_1 \vdash e : \tau$ then $\Gamma_2 \vdash e : \tau$. (Optional: prove these results.) Now use these two properties and find a substitution that can be applied to the judgment of

$$\Gamma_0 \cup \{x : \texttt{float<}\alpha * \beta\texttt{>}\} \vdash \texttt{div } x : \texttt{float<}\alpha\texttt{>} \texttt{ -> float<}\beta\texttt{>}$$

to 'reveal' a generalizable variable in the type of $\texttt{div } x$.

The above exercise suggests a means of fixing the inference algorithm: before applying the usual rule ("generalize over variables not free in the context"), apply a substitution that reveals the generalizable variables. There are a couple of ways that this can be done [7,8]. The end result is that full $\texttt{let}$-polymorphism for units-of-measure shares with ML the existence of principal type schemes and an inference algorithm.

4 Semantics of Units

In his original paper on polymorphic type inference, Milner defined a denotational semantics for a small ML-like language [14]. This semantics incorporated a value **wrong** to correspond to the detection of a failure at run-time, such as applying a non-functional value as the operator of an application. Milner proved that "well-typed programs don't go wrong", showing that if a program passes the type-checker, then no run-time failure occurs.

When working with a small-step operational semantics, as has become popular more recently, one instead proves *syntactic type soundness*, stating that

1. reduction *preserves* types: if $e : \tau$ and $e \rightarrow e'$ then $e' : \tau$; and
2. reduction makes *progress*: if e is not a final value then there exists an e' such that $e \rightarrow e'$.

Both the idea of **wrong** values and the notion that programs make 'reductions' until reaching a final value are convenient fictions that don't really correspond to the actual execution of real programs. (Machine instructions do not do β-reduction!) Nevertheless, for a language with, say, just integers and function values, it can be argued that the attempted 'application' of an integer really does constitute a run-time failure (which might be manifested as a memory violation), so syntactic type soundness is saying something about program safety.

4.1 Units Going Wrong

For units-of-measure, though, this argument makes no sense. What "goes wrong" if a program contains a unit error? If run-time values do not carry their units, as is the case with F# and other systems [19], then syntactic type soundness tells us precisely *nothing*. Of course, we could incorporate units into the semantics and ensure that operations with mismatched units evaluate to wrong (denotationally), or get stuck (in a small step operational semantics). But that's cheating: we have *instrumented* the semantics and thereby changed it to match some refinement of the type system, when in fact the behaviour of programs with and without unit annotations should be the same.

Instead, let's use *nature* as our guide – after all, we are talking about units of measure. Nature does not seg-fault or throw ClassCastException! In nature, physical laws are independent of the units used, i.e. they are invariant under changes to the unit system. This, then, is the real essence of unit correctness: the ability to *change the unit system* without affecting behaviour.

Consider the following 'correct' function and sample data that an airline might use as part of its check-in procedure:

```
let checkin(baggage:float<lb>, allowance:float<lb>) =
    if baggage > allowance then printf "Bags exceed limit"

checkin(88.0<lb>, 44.0<lb>)
```

Now suppose that we metricate the program by replacing lb with kg and converting all constants from pounds to kilograms.

```
let checkin(baggage:float<kg>, allowance:float<kg>) =
    if baggage > allowance then printf "Bags exceed limit"

checkin(40.0<kg>, 20.0<kg>)
```

The *behaviour remains the same*, namely, the passenger is turned away.

Now consider an 'incorrect' program that breaks the rules of units, confusing the weight limit with the length limit:

```
let checkin(baggage:float<lb>, allowance:float<cm>) =
    if baggage > allowance then printf "Bags exceed limit"

checkin(88.0<lb>, 55.0<cm>)
```

No run-time errors occur, and the passenger is turned away – but clearly the business logic used to arrive at this conclusion is faulty. Again, let's metricate:

```
let checkin(baggage:float<kg>, allowance:float<cm>) =
    if baggage > allowance then printf "Bags exceed limit"

checkin(40.0<kg>, 55.0<cm>)
```

This time, after metrication, the passenger can fly: the behaviour of the program changed when using a different system of units!

The fact that this program was *not* invariant under change-of-units revealed an underlying units error. This is the essence of unit correctness. Notice that in contrast to syntactic type soundness this is inherently a *relational* property: it does not say anything about the behaviour of a single program, but instead tells us about the relationship between one program and a transformed one.

4.2   Polymorphic Functions Going Wrong

Suppose we have a polymorphic function such as

```
val f : float<'u> -> float<'u^2>
```

How do we characterize 'going wrong' for such a function? We certainly know it when we see it: if we were told that f was implemented by

```
let f (x:float<'u>) = x*x*x
```

then we would rightly be suspicious of its type! But it's clearly not enough to consider just changes to the base units, as none are used here.

Furthermore, f might not even be implemented in F#. Suppose that f were implemented in assembly code, or by dedicated hardware. What *test* applied to f would refute its type? The answer is: it should be *invariant under scaling* in 'u, in the following sense: if its argument is scaled by some factor k (corresponding to the units 'u) then its result should scale by k^2 (corresponding to the units 'u^2). That is:

$$\forall k > 0, \mathtt{f}(k*x) = k^2*\mathtt{f}(x)$$

So if we fed f the value 2, and it responded with 8, and we then fed it 4, and it responded with 64, we would know that its type 'lied'.

4.3   Parametricity

We've now seen how the semantics of base units and of unit polymorphism can be explained in terms of invariance under scaling. This is reminiscent of the idea of *representation independence* in programs: that the behaviour of a program can be independent of the representation of its data types. For example, we can choose to represent booleans as a zero/non-zero distinction on integers, or we could use a string "F" for false and "T" for true. As long as the underlying representation can't be 'broken' by a client of the boolean type, then it should not be possible to observe the difference.

The similarity goes deep, in fact, as one popular characterization of representation independence, namely *relational parametricity*, can be applied very fruitfully to units-of-measure. We first define a map ψ from unit variables to positive 'scale factors', which we call a 'scaling environment'. This can be extended to full unit *expressions* in an obvious way:

$$\psi(\mathtt{1}) = 1$$
$$\psi(u * v) = \psi(u) \cdot \psi(v)$$
$$\psi(u\mathtt{\char`\^-1}) = 1/\psi(u)$$

So if $\psi = \{\alpha \mapsto 2, \beta \mapsto 3\}$ then $\psi(\alpha * \beta^2) = 18$.

We then define a binary relation $\sim_\tau^\psi$, indexed by types, and parameterized by ψ, whose interpretation is roughly "has the same behaviour when scaled using ψ".

$$x \sim_{\mathtt{float<u>}}^\psi y \quad \Leftrightarrow \quad y = \psi(u) * x$$
$$f \sim_{\tau_1 \to \tau_2}^\psi g \quad \Leftrightarrow \quad \forall xy, x \sim_{\tau_1}^\psi y \Rightarrow f(x) \sim_{\tau_2}^\psi g(y)$$

The interpretation of a type scheme $\forall\bar{\alpha}.\tau$ is then "related for all possible scalings for unit variables $\bar{\alpha}$". Formally:

$$x \sim_{\forall\bar{\alpha}.\tau} y \quad\Leftrightarrow\quad \forall\bar{k}, x \sim_\tau^{\{\bar{\alpha}\mapsto\bar{k}\}} y$$

It's then possible to prove a 'fundamental theorem' that states that an expression with closed type is related to itself at that type, i.e. if $e : \sigma$, then $e \sim_\sigma e$. From this simple idea flow many consequences.

4.4 Theorems for Free

For first-order types, we immediately get what Wadler describes as 'theorems for free' [24], namely theorems that hold simply due to the *type* of an expression, irrespective of the details of the code. For example, if f has type $\forall\alpha\beta.\texttt{float<}\alpha\texttt{>} \texttt{ -> float<}\beta\texttt{>} \texttt{ -> float<}\alpha * \beta\texttt{\^-1>}$ then we know that for any positive k_1 and k_2, we have

$$\texttt{f } (k_1 * x) \, (k_2 * y) = (k_1/k_2) * \texttt{f } x \, y$$

We can even prove such theorems for higher-order types, such as the type of diff from Section 2.9:

$$\texttt{diff } h \, f \, x \;=\; \frac{k_2}{k_1} * \texttt{diff} \left(\frac{h}{k_1}\right) \left(\lambda x.\frac{f(x * k_1)}{k_2}\right) \left(\frac{x}{k_1}\right).$$

4.5 Zero

We can now explain semantically why zero is polymorphic in its units (i.e. it has type $\forall\alpha.\texttt{float<}\alpha\texttt{>}$) whilst all other values are dimensionless (i.e. they have type $\texttt{float<1>}$). It's easy: zero is invariant under scaling (because $k * 0.0 = 0.0$ for any scale factor k) whilst other values are not.

4.6 Definability

Another well-known application of parametricity is to prove that certain functions cannot be defined with a particular type – and even, to show that there are *no* functions with a particular type, i.e. the type is uninhabited, or at least that there are no *interesting* functions with that type.

Exercise 14. In a statically-typed pure functional language with only total functions, what functions can you write with type $\forall\alpha.\alpha \texttt{ -> } \alpha \texttt{ -> } \alpha$? What happens if you add general recursion to the language?

Exercise 15. Do any functions have the type $\forall\alpha\beta.\alpha \texttt{ -> } \beta$? Can you explain?

For units-of-measure, it's possible to use parametricity to show similar definability results. For example, in a pure functional language with only total functions we can tell that the only function f with type type $\forall\alpha.\texttt{float<1> -> float<}\alpha\texttt{>}$ is the constant zero function, because by invariance under scaling we must have $f(x) = k * f(x)$ for any k.

Exercise 16. Can you think of any functions with the type $\forall \alpha \beta.$float$<\alpha * \beta>$ -> float$<\alpha>$*float$<\beta>$? Can you think of any *interesting* ones? Why not? Can you give a formal argument based on parametricity?

Most interestingly of all, if the relation $\sim_\tau^\psi$ is beefed up a bit, it's possible to show that in a language with only basic arithmetic (i.e. +, -, * and /), there are no interesting functions with type $\forall \alpha.$float$<\alpha^2>$ -> float$<\alpha>$. In other words, square root is not definable.

Exercise 17. Can you think why not? Hint: try using Newton's method from Section 2.9 to construct such a function.

4.7   Semantic Typing

For some program code, the type assigned by a type system for units-of-measure might be strictly weaker than the code's true 'semantic type'. A trivial example is fun x -> x + 1.0 - 1.0, which is assigned the type float<1> -> float<1> by F# (because 1.0 is dimensionless), but semantically has the more general type float<'u> -> float<'u>. But what do we mean by 'semantic type'? The answer is: a type that corresponds to the code's behaviour with respect to scaling. Formally, if an expression e satisfies $e \sim_\sigma e$ then e has semantic type σ.

We've already seen a more sophisticated example of this phenomenon, in Exercise 4. The naive definition of gmean is assigned a dimensionless type, even though it satisfies the following scaling property: for any $k > 0$,

$$\text{gmean (map (fun x -> } k\text{*x) } y) = k * \text{gmean } y$$

This scaling property corresponds to float<'u> list -> float<'u>, the most general semantic type of gmean.

4.8   Type Isomorphisms

Two types τ and τ' are said to be *isomorphic*, written $\tau \cong \tau'$, if there are functions $i : \tau \rightarrow \tau'$ and $j : \tau' \rightarrow \tau$ such that $j \circ i = \text{id}_\tau$ and $i \circ j = \text{id}_{\tau'}$ where id_τ and $\text{id}_{\tau'}$ are identity functions on τ and τ' respectively. We need to be a bit more precise about what we mean by *function* (should it be definable in the programming language?) and = (is this observational equivalence?). For simple isomorphisms, the distinction doesn't matter. For example, it's obvious that int*bool $\cong$ bool*int by the (definable) functions

```
let i (p:int*bool) = (snd p, fst p)
let j (q:bool*int) = (snd q, fst q)
```

Exercise 18. Show that the types int*bool -> unit*int and bool*int -> int are isomorphic.

More subtle isomorphisms make use of parametricity. For example:

$$\tau \cong \forall \alpha.(\alpha \rightarrow \tau) \rightarrow \tau$$
$$\forall \alpha.(\tau_1 \rightarrow \tau_2 \rightarrow \alpha) \rightarrow \alpha \cong \tau_1 * \tau_2$$

These latter isomorphisms are not definable in ML (or F#), because they require functions that take polymorphic arguments.

Exercise 19. For each isomorphism above, write down maps i and j that exhibit the isomorphisms, supposing that you had a language with 'first-class' polymorphism à la System F.

For units-of-measure, some rather surprising isomorphisms hold. Suppose for a moment that all values of `float` type are positive, and that operations on floats preserve this invariant (this rules out ordinary subtraction, for example). Then the following isomorphism between types

$$\forall \alpha.\texttt{float<}\alpha\texttt{>} \rightarrow \texttt{float<}\alpha\texttt{>} \cong \texttt{float<1>}$$

holds, *i.e.* the set of unary polymorphic functions that simply preserve their units is isomorphic to the set of dimensionless values! This isomorphism can be demonstrated by the maps $i : (\forall \alpha.\texttt{float<}\alpha\texttt{>} \rightarrow \texttt{float<}\alpha\texttt{>}) \rightarrow \texttt{float<1>}$ and $j : \texttt{float<1>} \rightarrow (\forall \alpha.\texttt{float<}\alpha\texttt{>} \rightarrow \texttt{float<}\alpha\texttt{>})$ below:

$$i(f) = f(1.0)$$
$$j(x) = \lambda y.y * x$$

We now prove that these maps compose to give the identity. First, $i \circ j = id$, by simple equational reasoning:

$$
\begin{array}{ll}
i \circ j & \\
= \lambda x.i(j(x)) & \text{(definition of composition)} \\
= \lambda x.i(\lambda y.y * x) & \text{(applying } j) \\
= \lambda x.1.0 * x & \text{(applying } i) \\
= \lambda x.x & \text{(arithmetic identity)}
\end{array}
$$

Now, $j \circ i = id$, by scaling invariance:

$$
\begin{array}{ll}
j \circ i & \\
= \lambda f.j(i(f)) & \text{(definition of composition)} \\
= \lambda f.j(f(1.0)) & \text{(applying } i) \\
= \lambda f.\lambda y.y * f(1.0) & \text{(applying } j) \\
= \lambda f.\lambda y.f y & \text{(instance of scaling invariance)} \\
= \lambda f.f & \text{(eta)}
\end{array}
$$

This is a semi-formal argument, which can be made completely rigorous [10].

For a less formal but perhaps more intuitive explanation, consider a concrete inhabitant of the type $\forall \alpha.\texttt{float<}\alpha\texttt{>} \rightarrow \texttt{float<}\alpha\texttt{>}$. What can it do with an argument x of type `float<`α`>`? It cannot add x to anything except for zero or x

itself, as there are no other values of type float<α> available. It *can* multiply or divide by a dimensionless value, as this results in a value with the appropriate type. But that's it: in fact, the function must be observably equivalent to one having the form $\lambda x.k * x$ for some k. In other words, a value k of type float<1> completely determines the function.

Exercise 20. Prove the following isomorphism:

$$\forall \alpha.\text{float<}\alpha\text{> -> float<}\alpha\text{> -> float<}\alpha\text{>} \cong \text{float<1> -> float<1>}$$

4.9 Dimensional Analysis

The invariance of physical laws under changes to the units not only provides a simple check on the correctness of formulae, it also makes it possible to *derive* laws simply through consideration of the units. This is called *dimensional analysis* [21] and its origins go back at least a century.

The idea is simple: when investigating some physical phenomenon, if the equations governing the phenomenon are not known but the parameters *are* known, one can use the dimensions of the parameters to narrow down the possible form the equations may take. (Dimensions are classes of units: for example, an acceleration has dimensions LT^{-2} where L and T stand for units of length and time respectively.)

For example, consider investigating the equation which determines the period of oscillation t of a simple pendulum. Possible parameters are the length of the pendulum l, the mass m, the initial angle from the vertical θ and the acceleration due to gravity g. After performing dimensional analysis it is possible to assert that the equation must be of the form $t = \sqrt{l/g}\,\phi(\theta)$ for some function ϕ of the angle θ. Let's see how this is done. We first write down the *dimensions* of the parameters:

parameter	name	dimensions
period of oscillation	t	T
length of pendulum	l	L
mass of pendulum	m	M
angle from vertical	θ	1
acceleration due to gravity g		LT^{-2}

We now suppose that there is some relationship between the parameters, described by a function f:

$$f(t, l, m, \theta, g) = 0$$

Now supposing that the parameters are measured in some particular system of units, under the assumption that physical laws are invariant under *changes* to the units we can assume that

$$f(Tt, Ll, Mm, \theta, LT^{-2}g) = 0$$

Now we can set the scale factors T, L and M arbitrarily. Let's set $T = 1/t$, and $L = 1/l$, and $M = 1/m$ (it's not always this easy!). We then obtain

$$f(1,1,1,\theta,\frac{gt^2}{l}) = 0$$

In other words, there are actually only two degrees of freedom in the system, described by θ and $\frac{gt^2}{l}$. Assuming that the above relationship is functional, and rearranging a little, we must have

$$t = \sqrt{l/g}\,\phi(\theta)$$

for some function ϕ.

By experiment or through application of Newtonian mechanics one can determine that for small angles $\phi(\theta) \approx 2\pi$, but dimensional analysis got us a long way! (Note in particular that the period of oscillation turned out to be independent of the mass m.)

In general, any dimensionally consistent equation over several variables can be reduced to an equation over a smaller number of dimensionless terms which are products of powers of the original variables. This is known as the Pi Theorem [5].

Theorem 4 (Pi Theorem). *Fix a set of m base dimensions $B_1, \ldots, B_m$ and let $x_1, \ldots, x_n$ be positive variables with the exponent of B_j in the dimension of x_i being given by the i, j'th element of an $m \times n$ matrix of integers A. Then any scale-invariant relation of the form*

$$f(x_1, \ldots, x_n) = 0$$

is equivalent to a relation

$$f'(\Pi_1, \ldots, \Pi_{n-r}) = 0$$

where r is the rank of the matrix A and $\Pi_1, \ldots, \Pi_{n-r}$ are dimensionless power-products of $x_1, \ldots, x_n$.

Proof. See Birkhoff [5].

In our pendulum example, we have three base dimensions M, L and T, and five variables t, l, m, θ and g. The matrix A is then

	t	l	m	θ	g
M	0	0	1	0	0
L	0	1	0	0	1
T	1	0	0	0	-2

We can now make a link with the type isomorphisms described in Section 4.8. There, we showed that certain polymorphic function types are isomorphic to dimensionless types over fewer parameters; compare the example of the pendulum in which we reduced a relation over several parameters to one over fewer parameters that are dimensionless power-products of the original parameters.

Assuming that `float` values are positive, we can prove the following result analogous to the Pi Theorem concerning type isomorphisms for first-order unit-polymorphic types.

Theorem 5 (Pi Theorem for programming). *Let τ be a closed type of the form*

$$\forall \alpha_1, \ldots, \alpha_m.float{<}u_1{>} \; \text{->} \cdots \text{->} \; float{<}u_n{>} \; \text{->} \; float{<}u_0{>}.$$

Let A be the $m \times n$ matrix of unit variable exponents in $u_1, \ldots, u_n$, and B the m-vector of unit variable exponents in u_0. If the equation $AX = B$ is solvable for integer variables in X, then

$$\tau \cong float{<}1{>} \; \text{->} \overset{n-r}{\cdots} \text{->} \; float{<}1{>} \to float{<}1{>}$$

where r is the rank of A.

Proof. See [9].

We can now apply this theorem to the pendulum example, recast in type-theoretic terms. Suppose that the square of the period of a pendulum is determined by a function

$$p : \forall M.\forall L.\forall T.float{<}M{>} \; \text{->} \; float{<}L{>}$$
$$\text{->} \; float{<}L * T^{-2}{>} \; \text{->} \; float{<}1{>} \; \text{->} \; float{<}T^2{>}$$

whose arguments represent the mass and length of the pendulum, the acceleration due to gravity and the angle of swing. Then for positive argument values `float<1> -> float<1>` is an isomorphic type.

5   Discussion

In this tutorial, we've studied types for units-of-measure from the viewpoint of three parties: the programmer (Section 2), the implementer (Section 3), and the theorist (Section 4).

There are two ways in which F#'s type system as described in Section 2 might be extended. The first is some kind of automated unit conversion, a feature that is often requested. For example, one might extend the base unit declaration syntax to incorpate a conversion factor:

```
[<Measure>] type ft = 0.3048<m>
```

This simple idea does inhabit a sizeable design space, though. Is `ft` a distinct unit-of-measure, or simply a convenient means of writing constants, such as `2.0<ft>`? If it's a separate unit-of-measure, how do conversions lift through the type structure? Can I pass a value of type `float<ft> -> float<m>` to a function expecting an argument of type `float<m> -> float<ft>`? How do multiple conversions get ordered, bearing in mind that in practice floating-point arithmetic doesn't satisfy even basic properties such as associativity of multiplication?

The second possible extension is a *kind* system richer than the current type-measure dichotomy. This crops up as soon as one tries to parameterize over both the underlying numeric type (e.g. to support `float` and `float32`) and units-of-measure. We might introduce a syntax for kinds less clunky than the current `[<Measure>]`, and write something like

```
type Matrix<'t : measure=>type, 'u : measure> = 't<'u> list list
```

Here a matrix type is parameterized by a unit-of-measure and an element type *constructor*, using the notation => for type-level functions. So the instantiated type `Matrix<float32,kg>` would expand to `float32<kg> list list`.

As we saw in Section 3, although the core of type inference for units-of-measure, namely unification, is straightforward, there are subtleties associated with supporting principal types in the presence of local `let`-polymorphism. Indeed, the current implementation of F# doesn't actually use the more sophisticated algorithm hinted at in Section 3.10. Recent work suggests that local `let`-polymorphism is rarely used in practice, and can always be worked around via explicit type annotations [22].

It might seem that the theoretical results of Section 4 have little relevance to practice. Far from it! Imagine a units-refactoring tool that uniformly changes code to use a different system of units. That this refactoring is semantics-preserving is guaranteed by our scaling invariance results, and any 'holes' in the type system (e.g. the ability to cast polymorphically from one unit to another) would break this. The idea of 'semantic type' is applicable to foreign-function interfaces. We might wish to provide an interface utilising units-of-measure for a numeric library implemented in a language (e.g. C++) that does not support units. The scaling invariance propositions associated with the interface type are exactly the proof obligations appropriate for safety. Finally, it's conceivable that type isomorphisms such as those studied in Section 4.8 might be used in an optimizing compiler to generate more efficient code, reducing the number of arguments to a function.

Acknowledgements

The author would like to thank Nick Benton, James Margetson, Simon Peyton Jones, Claudio Russo, Don Syme and Dimitrios Vytiniotis for numerous discussions on the topics covered in this tutorial, the anonymous reviewers of the published version of the lecture notes for their very helpful remarks, and the attendees at the CEFP'09 (Komarno, Slovakia) and "Types at Work" (Copenhagen, Denmark, 2009) summer schools for their keen interest.

References

1. The International System of Units (SI). Technical report, Bureau International des Poids et Mesures (2006)
2. Allen, E., Chase, D., Hallett, J., Lunchangco, V., Maessen, J.-W., Ryu, S., Steele Jr., G.L., Tobin-Hochstadt, S.: The Fortress Language Specification, Version 1.0 (2008)
3. Baader, F., Nipkow, T.: Term Rewriting and All That. Cambridge University Press, Cambridge (1988)
4. Bird, R.S., Paterson, R.: de brujn notation as a nested datatype. Journal of Functional Programming 9(1), 77–92 (1999)

5. Birkhoff, G.: Hydrodynamics: A Study in Logic, Fact and Similitude. Princeton University Press, Princeton (1960)
6. Buckwalter, B.: dimensional: statically checked physical dimensions for Haskell (2008)
7. Kennedy, A.J.: Programming Languages and Dimensions. PhD thesis, University of Cambridge (1995)
8. Kennedy, A.J.: Type inference and equational theories. Technical Report LIX/RR/96/09, École Polytechnique, Paris, France (1996)
9. Kennedy, A.J.: Relational parametricity and units of measure. In: POPL 1997: Proceedings of the 24th ACM SIGPLAN-SIGACT Symposium on Principles of Programming Languages, pp. 442–455. ACM Press, New York (1997)
10. Kennedy, A.J.: Formalizing an extensional semantics for units of measure. In: 3rd ACM SIGPLAN Workshop on Mechanizing Metatheory, WMM (2008)
11. Le Botlan, D., Rémy, D.: MLF: Raising ML to the power of System F. In: 8th ACM SIGPLAN International Conference on Functional Programming, ICFP (2003)
12. Leijen, D.: HMF: Simple type inference for first-class polymorphism. In: 13th ACM SIGPLAN International Conference on Functional Programming, ICFP (2008)
13. Lindley, S.: Many holes in Hindley-Milner. In: Proceedings of the 2008 Workshop on ML (2008)
14. Milner, R.: A theory of type polymorphism in programming. Journal of computer and system sciences 17, 348–375 (1978)
15. NASA. Mars Climate Orbiter Mishap Investigation Board: Phase I Report, (November 1999)
16. Pierce, B.C. (ed.): Types and Programming Languages. MIT Press, Cambridge (2002)
17. Pierce, B.C. (ed.): Advanced Topics in Types and Programming Languages. MIT Press, Cambridge (2005)
18. Press, W.H., Teukolsky, S.A., Vetterling, W.T., Flannery, B.P.: Numerical Recipes: The Art of Scientific Computing, 3rd edn. Cambridge University Press, Cambridge (2007)
19. Schabel, M.C., Watanabe, S.: Boost.Units (2008)
20. Schrijvers, T., Peyton Jones, S., Sulzmann, M., Vytiniotis, D.: Complete and decidable type inference for GADTs. In: International Conference on Functional Programming, ICFP (2009)
21. Szirtes, T.: Applied Dimensional Analysis and Modeling, 2nd edn. Butterworth-Heinemann, Butterworths (2007)
22. Vytiniotis, D., Peyton Jones, S., Schrijvers, T.: let should not be generalized. In: Proceedings of the ACM SIGPLAN Workshop on Types in Language Design and Implementation, TLDI (2010)
23. Vytiniotis, D., Weirich, S., Peyton Jones, S.: FPH: First-class polymorphism for Haskell. In: 13th ACM SIGPLAN International Conference on Functional Programming, ICFP (2008)
24. Wadler, P.: Theorems for free! In: Proceedings of the 4th International Symposium on Functional Programming Languages and Computer Architecture (1989)

Appendix: Solutions to Selected Exercises

Exercise 2. Non-zero literals cannot be polymorphic, else we would be able to "cheat" the type system and assign any old polymorphic type to an expression. For example, we would be able to write

```
let cube (x:float<'u>) = x*x*1.0<'u>
```

in order to "pretend" that squaring has the type `float<'u> -> float<'u^3>`!

There are three other special values that are polymorphic in their units: positive and negative infinity, and the special `NaN` (not a number) value. Like zero, these are all invariant under scaling.

```
> open Microsoft.FSharp.Math.Measure;;
> infinity;;
val it : float<'u> = infinity
> nan;;
val it : float<'u> = nan
```

Exercise 4. Suppose the list parameter has type `float<'u>`. Pick an element from the list (e.g. the head). Divide all elements of the list by this value, obtaining a list of type `float<1> list`. Pass this list to the original **gmean** function, then multiply the result by the original head, obtaining a result of type `float<'u>`.

```
> let gmean' (xs:float<_> list) =
-     let h = List.head xs in h * gmean (List.map (fun z -> z/h) xs);;

val gmean' : float<'u> list -> float<'u>
```

Exercise 7. A most general solution is $\{\beta := \alpha\text{^}-1 * \text{kg} * \text{s}\}$. There is no most general solution that does not use inverse.

Exercise 12. The substitution $\{\alpha := \alpha * \beta, \beta := \alpha\}$ takes us (1) to (2). The substitution $\{\alpha := \beta\text{^}-1, \beta := \alpha * \beta\}$ takes us from (2) to (3). The substitution $\{\beta := \beta\text{^}-1\}$ takes us from (3) to (1), thus proving that all three are equivalent.

Exercise 13. The substitution $\{\alpha := \alpha * \beta\text{^}-1\}$ can be applied, to obtain a derivation of

$$\Gamma_0 \cup \{x : \text{float}<\alpha>\} \vdash \text{div } x : \text{float}<\alpha * \beta\text{^}-1> \text{ -> float}<\beta>.$$

From this, the variable β can be generalized.

Exercise 14. There are two functions with type $\forall \alpha. \alpha \text{ -> } \alpha \text{ -> } \alpha$:

$$\lambda x.\lambda y.x \text{ and}$$
$$\lambda x.\lambda y.y$$

In a (call-by-value) language with general recursion, there is one additional function:

$$\lambda x.\lambda y.\Omega$$

where Ω is a divergent term.

Exercise 15. In a pure functional language with only total functions, no functions have type $\forall\alpha\beta.\alpha \rightarrow \beta$. Informally, given a parameter of type α, how can a function possibly produce a value of type β? More formally, a consequence of parametricity (representation independence) is that for a function f of type $\forall\alpha\beta.\alpha \rightarrow \beta$,

$$f(\psi(x)) = \phi(f(x))$$

for any changes of representation ψ and ϕ. Now take β to be `bool`, ϕ to be negation, and ψ to be the identity, and we get a contradiction.

Exercise 16. There is just one pure total function with type $\forall\alpha\beta.$`float<`α `* `β`> -> ` `float<`α`>*float<`β`>`:

$$f(x) = (0, 0)$$

Informally, it's clear that f can't 'take apart' its argument to obtain values of type `float<`α`>` or `float<`β`>`, and as the only unit-polymorphic value is zero (ignoring infinities and NaNs), it must therefore return a pair of zeroes. More formally, scaling invariance tells us that for any $k_1, k_2 > 0$, we have

$$f(x) = (y, z) \Rightarrow f(k_1 k_2 x) = (k_1 y, k_2 z)$$

Now first set $k_1 = 1$ and $k_2 = 2$, and then set $k_1 = 2$ and $k_2 = 1$, giving

$$f(x) = (y, z) \Rightarrow f(2x) = (y, 2z) = (2y, z)$$

and so $y = 2y$ and $z = 2z$. Hence $y = z = 0$.

Exercise 17. Let's try using Newton's method. For an input a we wish to find x such that $x^2 - a = 0$. Hence let $f(x) = x^2 - a$ and its derivative is $f'(x) = 2x$. So using the code from Section 2.9 we might write

```
let sqrt (a:float<'u^2>) : float<'u>
  = newton (fun x -> x*x - a) (fun x -> 2.0*x) ? 0.001
```

But what can we write for the initial estimate ? above? It has to be of type `float<'u>` but the only value of that type at our disposal is zero, which will not converge to the root.

Exercise 18. We can write F# functions to map between these types:

```
let i (f:int*bool -> unit*int) = fun x:bool*int -> snd (f (snd x, fst x))
let j (g:bool*int -> int) = fun y:int*bool -> ((), g(snd y, fst y))
```

Functional Programming with C++ Template Metaprograms

Zoltán Porkoláb

Eötvös Loránd University, Faculty of Informatics
Dept. of Programming Languages and Compilers
Pázmány Péter sétány 1/C H-1117 Budapest, Hungary
gsd@elte.hu

Abstract. Template metaprogramming is an emerging new direction of generative programming. With the clever definitions of templates we can force the C++ compiler to execute algorithms at compilation time. Among the application areas of template metaprograms are the expression templates, static interface checking, code optimization with adaption, language embedding and active libraries. However, as template metaprogramming was not an original design goal, the C++ language is not capable of elegant expression of metaprograms. The complicated syntax leads to the creation of code that is hard to write, understand and maintain. Although template metaprogramming has a strong relationship with functional programming, this is not reflected in the language syntax and existing libraries. In this paper we give a short and incomplete introduction to C++ templates and the basics of template metaprogramming. We will enlight the role of template metaprograms, and some important and widely used idioms. We give an overview of the possible application areas as well as debugging and profiling techniques. We suggest a pure functional style programming interface for C++ template metaprograms in the form of embedded Haskell code which is transformed to standard compliant C++ source.

1 Introduction

Templates are key elements of the C++ programming language [3,26]. They enable data structures and algorithms to be parameterized by types, thus capturing commonalities of abstractions at compilation time without performance penalties at runtime [29]. *Generic programming* [22,21,14] is a popular programming paradigm, which enables the developer to implement reusable codes easily. Reusable components – in most cases data structures and algorithms – are implemented in C++ with the heavy use of templates. The most notable example, the Standard Template Library [14] is now an unavoidable part of professional C++ programs.

In C++, in order to use a template with some specific type, an *instantiation* is required. This process can be initiated either implicitly by the compiler when a template with a new type argument is referred, or explicitly by the programmer.

Z. Horváth, R. Plasmeijer, and V. Zsók (Eds.): CEFP 2009, LNCS 6299, pp. 306–353, 2010.

During instantiation the template parameters are substituted with the concrete arguments, and the generated new code is compiled.

This instantiation mechanism enables us to write smart template codes that execute algorithms at compilation time. To demonstrate the power of C++ templates, in 1994 Erwin Unruh wrote a program [28] which displayed a list of prime numbers as part of the error messages emitted by the compiler during the compilation process. In fact, Unruh used C++ templates and the template instantiation rules to write a program that is "executed" as a side effect of compilation. It turned out that a cleverly designed C++ code is able to utilize the type-system of the language and force the compiler to execute a desired algorithm [31]. These compile-time programing is called C++ *Template Metaprograming* and has been proved to be a Turing-complete sublanguage of C++ [8].

In the last fifteen years lots of effort have been spent to improve the process of template metaprogramming. Essential compilation time algorithms have been identified, and used for basic metaprogram libraries. Data structures are implemented in various forms to hold compile time informations. Despite of the growing number of positive examples, developers are still wary of using template metaprogramming in strict, time-restricted software projects.

One of the reasons is the improper syntax of C++ to express template metaprograms. The syntax of a programming language is often a major factor when developing programs in a new paradigm. C++ has a strong heritage of imperative programming (namely from C and Algol68) influenced by object-orientation (Simula67). In the same time, template metaprogramming is much closer to functional programming. Furthermore, the syntax of the C++ templates is especially complicated. Therefore, metaprogram implementors are forced to use alien techniques and unnecessary complex syntax. As a result, C++ template metaprograms are hard to read, understand and often hopeless to maintain [1,2,5,8,10].

The relationship between C++ template metaprograms and functional programming is well-known: most properties of template metaprograms are closely related to the principles of the functional programming paradigm. The compiler evaluates constant and enumerated values, determines types, etc. Once a certain entity has been evaluated or computed, it will be immutable during the rest of the compilation process. There is no assignment in template metaprograms. This is the same as referential transparency in functional programming. The control structures of metaprograms are based on pattern matching, similarly to functional programming languages. We will discuss further similarities in the paper.

The author strongly believe that in an ideal situation the syntax of the programming language should support the appropriate programming paradigm. Therefore, a pure functional programming interface could produce a more effective programming environment for C++ template metaprograms.

In this paper we give an overview C++ templates and the basic concepts of template metaprogramming with the help of short, motivating examples. To improve development process and code maintenance, we suggest a pure functional style programming interface for C++ template metaprograms in the form of embedded Haskell code which is transformed to standard compliant C++ source. The lack of essential tools, such as debuggers and profiles supporting metaprogram development is a serious restriction in industrial projects. Therefore we suggest metaprogram debugging and profiling techniques.

The paper is organized as follows. In Section 2 we give a short informal introduction to C++ template mechanism. In Section 3 C++ template metaprogramming is presented and compared to runtime functional programming. We discuss the fundamental connections between functional programming and C++ template metaprogramming in Section 4. In Section 5 we examine the possibility of pure functional style programming interface for C++ template metaprograms. We explain possible debugging and profiling techniques in Section 6. Related work is presented in Section 7. We support our material with sample programs. Inside the text of the article mostly smaller – and sometimes incomplete – code snippets are shown. However, in Appendix A we present a full set of complete examples which the reader can examine, compile, and run. For the full, syntactically correct examples we will refer in the form of (*example NN*). The examples are also available at `http://aszt.inf.elte.hu/~gsd/cefp/`.

2   Informal Introduction to C++ Templates

Templates are an essential part of the C++ language, by enabling data structures and algorithms to be parameterized by types. This abstraction is frequently needed when using general algorithms such as finding an element in a data structure, or defining data types such as a *matrix* of elements of the same type. The mechanism behind a matrix containing integer or floating point numbers, or even strings is essentially the same, it is only the *type* of the contained objects that differs. With templates we can express this abstraction in one chunk of code, avoiding code duplication, thus the *generic* language construct aids code reuse and the introduction of higher abstraction levels. The abstraction over type parameters – often called *parametric polymorphism* – emphasizes that the variability is supported by compile-time template parameter(s).

In the following we give an informal introduction to templates in the C++ language. We will sometimes simplify the complex rules of templates for the sake of general understanding of the whole mechanism. To those who are interested in the detailed rules, a fundamental source is [29]. For language lawyers the best source is the C++ standard itself [3]. We will be less rigorous in C++ syntactical rules, often omitting headers like `<iostream>`, and namespace tags, like `std::`.

Let us start with a very simple problem: we have to compute the maximum of two parameters – a rather trivial task in most programming languages. However, without some kind of abstraction mechanism over the type of the parameters we soon end up in a nasty, unmanageable code duplication:

```
// a max function for "int" type
int max( int a, int b)
```

```
{
  if ( a > b )
    return a;
  else
    return b;
}

// a  max function for "double" type
double max( double a, double b)
{
  if ( a > b )
    return a;
  else
    return b;
}

// and a lot of other overloadings for other parameter types.
```

While overloading allows us in most modern programming languages to write the correct, type-safe functions, the result is a number of overloaded versions of the max() function. Should we modify the algorithm (in a more realistic case), we have to update all of their overloaded instances in a consistent way.

Moreover, we can write overloading functions only for the already defined types. If somebody creates a new type with a well-defined *less-then* operator to compare the objects, we have to write a new overloading version. We cannot implement and compile a max() function on type T *before* creating T, even if we know what that function will look like. Strongly typed programming languages allows writing programs on non-existing types only a very restricted manner[1].

It is tempting to try non-typesafe solutions. For a C/C++ programmer a precompiler macro seems to solve the problem:

```
#define MAX(a,b)    a > b ? a : b
```

As precompiler macro functions are *typeless*, this will work not only for the existing types, but on every future type too. Unfortunately, precompiler macros are not the answer for writing generic algorithms over types. Precompiler macros are replaced before the running of the C++ compiler, therefore we may encounter a huge number of side-effects and type-safety problems (*example 01*). Apart from that, the attempt to solve more complex problems with macros is hopeless.

To demonstrate this, let us implement a swap function, which changes the values of two parameters. Here is the trivial solution in C++ for parameters of type int:

---

[1] Polymorphic functions may be defined on base classes and work on derived classes defined later. In many cases, however, the runtime overhead of polymorphism are not acceptable.

```
void swap( int& x, int& y)
{
  int temp = x;
  x = y;
  y = temp;
}
```

This is simple. The **&** symbols in the parameter list denote that the parameter passing should happen by *reference*, therefore x and y inside the function body yield the original variables which we want to swap via the temporary variable temp. Variable **temp** should have the same type as the function parameters.

At this point we are in trouble. Since precompiler macros are replaced *before* the C++ compiler itself starts, we cannot use any type inference information from the C++ compiler. We are not able to identify the type of the parameters of the swap macro in an automated way[2]. What we need is an intelligent macro-like feature working together with the type system of the C++ language. This language element in C++ is called *template*.

Templates allow us to write both the **max** and **swap** in a generic way in one code snippet working over different types:

```
template <class T>
T max( T a, T b)
{
  if ( a > b )
    return a;
  else
    return b;
}
```

```
template <typename T>
void swap( T& x, T& y)
{
  T temp = x;
  x = y;
  y = temp;
}
```

The **typename** and the **class** keywords are interchangeable in the template definitions and declarations, but we should repeat them for all parameters. It is important to understand that templated **max** and **swap** are not functions in the traditional sense. They are not compiled and they will be not called during the execution of the program. Templates are rather skeletons, describing a manufacturing process of real functions instantiated by the compiler in an automated

---

[2] The new C++ standard, C++0x provides the **auto** keyword, which allows us to define a variable of the specific type corresponding to the actual initializer. This is a nice feature, but does not invalidate our message here on the lack of type inference regarding macros.

way during the compilation process. Therefore we call them: *function templates* rather than *template functions*.

The automated instantiation process is the most remarkable feature of the C++ templates. In the following example (*example 02*) we apply this process to the function template `max()`:

```
int i = 3, j = 4, k;
double x = 3.14, y = 4.14, z;
const int ci = 6;

k = max(i, j);     // -> max(int, int)
z = max(x, y);     // -> max(double, double)
k = max(i, ci);    // -> max(int, int)
```

The compilation of the above code snippet requires a number of distinct actions from the compiler. In the first step, the compiler has to decide whether a function template is applicable at the calling sites of `max()`. Then the parameter type(s) should be decided. Parameter types are normally decided based on the actual arguments: `i,j,x,y,ci`. This process is called *template parameter deduction*. In our example the first and third call of `max` leads to calling an instance of `max(int,int)`, while the second indicates to call `max(double,double)`. These concrete versions of templates are called *specializations*.

When a specialization is not available, the compiler generates it. Thus one `max` function with two `int` parameters and one with two `double` parameters are created and will be called. Let us recognize that the first and third call will refer to the same specialization. The concrete implementation process may be compiler dependent, and later we will see that we should be extremely careful with such situations.

Which specialization will be called in the following case?

```
z = max(i, x);     // syntax error
```

Under the parameter deduction process, from the type of the argument `i` the compiler deduces the template parameter type `T` to be `int`. However, the second argument `x` contradicts this, suggesting a `double` parameter. Therefore the parameter deduction process will fail and the compiler raises a syntax error.

How can we fix this problem? As you might expect, templates may be defined with two or more type parameters. Thus we can provide another templated `max()`, accepting two different type parameters (*example 03*):

```
template <typename T, typename S>
T max( T a, S b)
{
  if ( a > b )
    return a;
  else
    return b;
}
```

```
int     i = 3;
double  x = 3.14;

z = max(i, x);      // -> max(int, double)
std::cout << z << std::endl;
```

At first sight, everything seems to have been solved. The parameter deduction identifies parameter T as int and parameter S as double based on the types of actual arguments i and x. The instantiation process creates the max(int,double) specialization, and the right function will be called during runtime.

However, the result printed to the output will be 3 and not 3.14 as we may expect. This is a consequence of the template mechanism we discussed above. When parameters have been decided in the deduction process, also the return type has been determined. Yielded by T in the code of max, it will be int as well as the type of the first parameter. When the function is called in run-time, a>b evaluates as false, and 3.14 is to return. However, as the return type has been defined at compilation time as int, this 3.14 value will be converted to integer, and thus we get 3 assigned to z. It is clear that any attempt to change the role of parameters T and S could lead us to the same problem.

It is also irrelevant that the return value will be assigned to z – a variable of type **double**. Programming languages rarely provide overloading on return types, and never do parameter deduction on them.

Can we construct a better max(), a template which returns with the type of the *greater value*? Not in a strongly typed programming language like C++, unfortunately. In such languages, types are fully decided during compilation time: in run-time we cannot change them anymore. As templates are compile-time language features, once the template parameter deduction decides template parameters, these decisions are final. Whether the first or the second argument of the max(i,x) call is greater is a completely run-time property. Compilation time and run-time are fundamentally separated in strongly typed, compiled programming languages.

Even if we understand this phenomenon, it may be a bit embarassing. Looking at the actual code it seems natural for the programmer to define **double** as the return type of the max function called with an integer and a floating point argument. Programmers understand that **double** is "wider" then **int**. Why were we not able to tell this to the compiler?

The root of the problem is that when speaking about templates we have to consider not only two stages – compilation time and run-time – of the full process, but also the very first one: the *definition time* of the template function. When we had defined the templated max(T,S) with two different type parameters T and S, we had no idea about its usage environment. We had to decide whether the type T or S or some other type would be the appropriate return type. At that point, however, we had no information about whether the actual arguments in a call environment would be of type int, double or something else. We still had to make final decisions.

In the next stage, in compilation time, the compiler instantiates the code of `max(i,x)`, with actual `i` and `x` arguments. Now the compiler apprehends the environment of the call, recognizes the actual types of `i` and `x`, but cannot overrule the decisions made in template definition time.

Finally, in run-time the program works with the given set of types and rules, and is able only to decide, whether the value of `i` or `x` is the greater, but is unable to overrule the type and the conversion rules regarding the return value.

In the next table we summarized the main stages of programming with templates.

Table 1. Programming with templates

Stage	Template definition	Compilation time	Run-time
Role	Design of algorithms The templated code has been defined	Template instantiation Types used in program is being decided	Execution of algorithm Program evaluates expressions
Example	Return type of max(T,S) has been decided	Parameter deduction determines T and S	Greater argument value is chosen to return

The two fundamental problems we have: (1) the gap between template definition time and compilation/template instantiation time: this inhibits choosing the "better" return type out of `int` and `double`, and (2) the gap between compilation and the run-time: this inhibits choosing the type of the greater value to return. Dynamic and script languages sometimes can help in the second problem. Template metaprograms will give us the power to bridge the first gap in C++.

Before we proceed with template metaprograms, we have to learn some more technicalities on templates.

We may be tempted to improve our `max()` template with a third type parameter, which yields the return type:

```
template <class R, class T, class S>
R max( T a, S b)
{
  if ( a > b )
    return a;
  else
    return b;
}
```

Unfortunately, the parameter deduction will fail as there is no information about type `R`. There are a number of reasons why template parameters are not deduced based on return values, but to understand the potential problems consider the following example:

```
int     i = 3;
double  x = 3.14, z;

z = max(i, x);        // (1)
cout << max(i, x);    // (2)
```

Deduction (theoretically) may work in case (1), but there is no reasonable way to choose the correct return type in case (2). However, inventive C++ programmers found the way to smuggle the return type into ordinary arguments, to make it deducible (*example 04*):

```
template <class R, class T, class S>
R max( T a, S b, R)
{
  if ( a > b )
    return a;
  else
    return b;
}

double z = max(i, x, 0.0);
```

The extra argument works, but it is ugly and possibly misleading. The C++ standard committee recognized this requirement, and introduced a more readable notation (*example 05*):

```
template <class R, class T, class S>
R max( T a, S b)
{
  if ( a > b )
    return a;
  else
    return b;
}

double z = max<double>(i, x);
long   l = max<long, int, long>(i, x);
```

This syntax above is called *explicit specialization*. In the first case max() will be instantiated with template parameters: R=double given explicitly, and T=int, and S=double deduced from function arguments. In the second case, all the parameters are given explicitly: R=long, S=int, and T=long. Actual parameter x will be converted to long as well as the return value. The shortage of this solution is that we have to decide the actual type parameters manually.

We can further specialize templates by eliminating all the template parameters.

```
template <> const char *max( const char *s1, const char *s2)
{
  return  strcmp( s1, s2) < 0;
}


char *s1 = "Hello";
char *s2 = "world";


cout << max(s1, s3);
```

It is clear that the original algorithm of `max()` would not work properly when comparing the pointer values rather than the contents of the char arrays. We provided a *user specialization* for defining an exceptional behavior of the maximum algorithm for character arrays.

Different template definitions may exist with the same name: overloading of templates is possible. Hence we may define all previously discussed versions of max at the same time (*example 06*).

```
template <typename T> T max(T,T);
template <typename R, typename T, typename S> R max(T,S);
template <> const char *max( const char *s1, const char *s2);
```

When instantiating `max` template, the compiler will choose the *most specific* version of template definitions applicable for the actual call.

Up to this point we mainly discussed function templates. Class templates play a similarly important role when implementing abstract data structures like list, generalized array, matrix, etc. In the rest of this section we will discuss class templates in detail as they form the base of template metaprogramming.

The following code snippet defines a matrix class template. The typename of the matrix elements yielded by T is the parameter of the class. Apart from the usual set of constructor, copy constructor, destructor and assignment operator we have methods to retrieve size parameters with `rows`, and `cols` parameters, and accessing elements with the pair of `at` methods.

C++ uses value semantics, i.e. when copying a matrix we have to copy each stored element one by one. We implement the copy semantic with the help of the private `copy` method.

```
template <typename T>
class matrix
{
public:
  matrix(int i, int j);                      // constructor
  matrix(const matrix &other);               // copy constructor
  ~matrix();                                  // destructor
  matrix& operator=(const matrix &other); // assignment
```

```
int rows() const { return x; }     // returns x dimension
int cols() const { return y; }     // returns y dimension

T& at(int i, int j);       // element at position x,y
T  at(int i, int j) const; // element at position x,y for read

matrix& operator+=(const matrix &other); // A += B
private:
  int  x;
  int  y;
  T    *v;
  void copy(const matrix &other); // helper to copy elements
};
```

Note that each method of a class template is a function template itself. This seems natural for methods explicitly referring the template parameter, like the at method, but also holds for other member functions like rows() and cols(), which are also templated by T.

As object constructors' parameters do not hold relevant information on class template parameters, objects of class templates are instantiated explicitly specifying their type parameters. Here we define matrix objects with type parameter int, double, and matrix<double> respectively:

```
matrix<int>             im;
matrix<double>          dm;
matrix<matrix<double> > dmm;
```

A possible implementation of the matrix allocates x*y objects of type T dynamically. This is a fair solution unless T is (logically) very small. Allocating an x*y length array of type bool does not neccessary give what one expects. In some implementions bool type has a size of 4 bytes (for compatibility with int type). Even if sizeof(bool)==1, we can work out a better implementation by storing 8 boolean values on every single byte.

Naturally, this economical solution may require a totally different representation. Additional attributes, methods, different function bodies should be implemented in a *class specialization*.

```
template <>
class matrix<bool>
{
  // a totally different implementation
};
```

The specialization and the original template only share their *names*, otherwise they are considered separate classes. A specialization does not need to provide the same functionality, interface, or implementation as the original one. It is possible, but generally a bad practice to change the public interface between specializations.

We have to mention that not only typenames, but constant expressions of certain types (`bool`, `int`, etc..) are also allowed as template arguments:

```
template <typename T, int SIZE>
class array
{
  T  t[SIZE];
  //...
};
```

With a *partial specialization* we can bind one or more types of arguments:

```
template<class T, class U>
class A { ... };

template <class U>
class A<int,U> { ... };
```

This partial specialization will be selected by the compiler if `A` is instantiated with its first argument being `int`.

Templates can not always accept arbitrary type parameters. For example, abstract priority queues should contain types which are *comparable*, accumulator functions applies for *additive* types. These assumptions are restrictions against genericity. In some programming languages the constraints could be expressed explicitly by the language. Among others, Java's *wildcards* [27], the inheritance hierarchy in Eiffel, and the `with` keyword in Ada serves this purpose. If we break the constraints, we get clear and straightforward error messages from the compiler.

C++ has no language-level support to describe explicit requirements for certain template properties, i.e. C++ templates are not constrained [9]. When we pass a type without proper comparison methods to an abstract priority queue, we do not experience an immediate syntax error. In contrast, the instantiation process starts and it will fail only when the lacking method is explicitly referred, in most cases somewhere deeply in the chain of instantiations. The canonical example is the standard template library (STL), where algorithms require certain types of iterators. E.g. the `sort` algorithm requires parameters in form of *random access iterators*. When `sort` is called with parameters only satisfying the criteria of *forward iterators* we end up with a few pages of error messages and none of them will explicitly tell us the root of the problem.

Due to lack of compiler support, the problem had to be remedied on the library level. Complex language constructs have been created to inspect the characteristics of types. Existence of certain attributes or methods, usage of polymorphism, inheritance relationships, etc. can be determined at compilation time using template metaprograms [35]. Based on the inspections, in case of certain conditions,

the designer of the program may decide to abort compilation. This area of research is called *static interface checking* or *concept checking* [16,20].

The ANSI C++ committee started to work on a proposal to extend C++
with language-based concepts. With the help of *concepts* [19] programmers could
specify the requirements against template parameters of classes and functions
in a clear syntax, and could separate concept checking from the instantiation
process. Unfortunately, this enhancement requires enourmous amount of work
– especially reimplementing existing libraries by the enrichment of concepts. In
the summer of 2009 the C++ standardization committee excluded concepts from
the already late C++0X standard. Concepts are not forgotten but it is hard to
predict when they will be part of the official C++ standard. Until then, we
may utilize library based concepts implemented mostly by means of template
metaprograms [36,35].

3   C++ Template Metaprograms

In 1994 Erwin Unruh wrote and circulated at C++ standards committee meeting
a very interesting C++ program. The program did not even succesfully compile,
but when the compiler printed the error messages, parts of them were the prime
numbers appeared in increasing order.

```
// Erwin Unruh, untitled program,
// ANSI X3J16-94-0075/ISO WG21-462, 1994.

template <int i>
struct D
{
    D(void *);
    operator int();
};
template <int p, int i>
struct is_prime
{
    enum { prim = (p%i) && is_prime<(i>2?p:0), i>::prim };
};
template <int i>
struct Prime_print
{
    Prime_print<i-1>    a;
    enum { prim = is_prime<i,i-1>::prim };
    void f() { D<i> d = prim; }
};
struct is_prime<0,0> { enum { prim = 1 }; };
struct is_prime<0,1> { enum { prim = 1 }; };
struct Prime_print<2>
```

```
{
    enum { prim = 1 };
    void f() { D<2> d = prim; }
};
void foo()
{
    Prime_print<10> a;
}
// output:
// unruh.cpp 30: conversion from enum to D<2> requested in Pri..
// unruh.cpp 30: conversion from enum to D<3> requested in Pri..
// unruh.cpp 30: conversion from enum to D<5> requested in Pri..
// unruh.cpp 30: conversion from enum to D<7> requested in Pri..
// unruh.cpp 30: conversion from enum to D<11> requested in Pri..
// unruh.cpp 30: conversion from enum to D<13> requested in Pri..
// unruh.cpp 30: conversion from enum to D<17> requested in Pri..
// unruh.cpp 30: conversion from enum to D<19> requested in Pri..
```

Erwin Unruh's prime number computing template demonstrated that it is possible to use the C++ template system to write compile-time programs. Such programs are called template metaprograms. A metaprogram is a program that manipulates other programs; for example, compilers, partial evaluators, parser generators and so forth are metaprograms. Template metaprograms are special ones in the sense that they are self-contained: the program which manipulates the code is the C++ compiler itself.

The canonical template metaprogram for showing the basic behavior is the compile time evaluation of factorial numbers. Let us compare a run-time solution and the metaprogram version.

The run-time version is straightforward. Basically the similar code could be implemented in various programming languages ranging from FORTRAN to Pascal.

```
// runtime recursion
int Factorial(int N)
{
    if ( 1 == N )  return 1;
    return          N * Factorial(N-1);
};

int main()
{
    int r = Factorial(5);
    cout << r << endl;
    return 0;
}
```

There are other possibilities to implement the algorithm: specially we may use loop instead of recursion.

The template metaprogram solution takes two template definitions: one for the generic solution of Factorial, and another for the specialization of the parameter value 1 (*example 07*).

```cpp
// compile-time recursion
template <int N>
struct Factorial
{
  enum { value = N * Factorial<N-1>::value };
}

template<>
struct Factorial<1>
{
  enum { value = 1 };
};

int main()
{
  int r = Factorial<5>::value;
  cout << r << endl;
  return 0;
}
```

Let us analyze what happens here. The main() function is used to start the instantiation steps. When the assignment refers to Factorial<5>::value the compiler is forced to instantiate the Factorial template with argument 5. As we have a correspondent template definition, the compiler starts the instantiation and reaches the initialization of enumeration value inside Factorial. Here we refer to Factorial<4>::value. The instantiation of Factorial<5> is suspended and the compiler starts to instantiate Factorial<4>::value. This way we imitate recursion, which will descend down to the instantiation request of Factorial<1>. Here the compiler will find a full specialization template for Factorial with argument value 1, which is "more specialized" than the generic one. Therefore the full specialization is used to generate the requested class, and instantiation of Factorial<1> completes.

At this point we are coming back from the instantiation chain. In this process Factorial<1>::value is used to finalize Factorial<2>, etc... The suspended instantiations are completed in the reverse order. At the end, this results in generating five classes; four of them instantiated from the generic template definition and one from the template specialization.

As the compiler has Factorial<5>::value in hand, it simply replaces the right hand side of the assignment in main(). In run-time, we will execute only the output statement. Hence, we "executed" the factorial algorithm – a C++ template metaprogram – at compilation time.

Two important template rules have been tacitly used here: (1) Templates which are not referred must not be instantiated – C++ template mechanism is *lazy*. (2) Constant expressions – which can be evaluated at compilation time – must be evaluated at compilation time. Such constant expression appears on the left side of the enumeration initialization of `value` in class `Factorial`.

Lazyness is essential for writing template metaprograms. Let us consider the following example:

```
template <bool condition, class Then, class Else>
struct IF
{
  typedef Then RET;
};

template <class Then, class Else>
struct IF<false, Then, Else>
{
  typedef Else RET;
};

int main()
{
  IF< sizeof(int)<sizeof(long), long, int>::RET  i;
  cout << sizeof(i) << endl;
  return 0;
}
```

This seems a bit more cryptic than the factorial example. First let us draw up an inventory. We have a generic version of a template called `IF` and a *partial specialization* for it. It is partial, since only one, the leftmost argument has been specialized to the `false` boolean value. The first type parameter of the class `IF` is a (constant) value, the remaining arguments are type parameters.

When we instantiate the `IF` template, we provide a boolean expression as the first argument. In our example this is `sizeof(int)<sizeof(long)`. The expression is evaluated at compilation time. If this is `true`, then the generic template is instantiated, and hence the `typedef Then RET` is in effect. With the actual arguments this defines `RET` as `long`. However, when the expression is evaluated as false, we have a "better" specialization, and `typedef Else RET` means `RET` is defined as `int`. As a result, based on whether the size of `int` is smaller than the size of `long`, we define `i` as a variable of the widest type.

The construct is symmetric – it would be an equally working solution to define the generic function typedefing the `Else` branch, and writing a specialization for the `true` value as the first parameter.

The `IF` construct – the generic template and the specialization – works like a branching metaprogram. Having recursion and branching with pattern matching we have a complete programming language – executing programs at compilation time. In 1966 Bohm and Jacopini proved, that Turing machine implementation is equivalent to the existence of conditional and looping control structures in a programming language [4]. C++ template metaprograming forms a Turing complete programming language executed at compilation time [8].

Now we can revisit the max() function we discussed earlier (*example 09*):

```
template <class T, class S>
IF< sizeof(T)<sizeof(S), S, T>::RET max(T x, S y)
{
  if ( x > y )
    return x;
  else
    return y;
}
```

This version of max() is able to choose the "widest" of the argument types and define it as the return type. In the template definition we did not commit ourselves to any return type. Instead of choosing one of the argument types, we defined a small metaprogram which will be executed during compilation, i.e. template instantiation time. When the template is instantiated the actual types of T and S are known and the metaprogram is evaluated. Either T or S will be selected as typedef of IF<...>::RET, based on the metaprogram's algorithms.

When this template is instantiated with argument types int and double, the return value will be double. Similarly, when the arguments are short and long, the latter will be chosen as the return type.

Table 2. Programming with template metaprograms

Stage	Template definition	Compilation time	Run-time
Role	Design of algorithms The templated code has been defined	Template instantiation Parameter deduction Metaprograms are executed	Execution of algorithm Program evaluates expressions
Example	Return type of max(T,S) defined with metaprogram	Parameter deduction determines T and S. IF<T,S>::RET is selected	Greater argument value is chosen to return

It is important to understand two facts. First, we cheated a bit. The "widest" type – which has the greater sizeof value – is not always the best return type. Sometimes the size of a class is unrelated to the arithmetical representation – this is true especially for classes allocating extra space in the heap. But conceptually this is not a problem for us: anyway, we are in a Turing complete language, so we are able to define as complex algorithms as we wish.

Second, we were still not able to choose the type of the greater value, we have chosen the type which seemed better during compilation. It is still possible that `double` has been chosen as return type, but the `int` run-time value is greater. In such situation the return type value will be converted to `double`. In other words, we are not breaking the rules of strongly typed programming languages. Types are not selected in run-time. What we added to the earlier version of `max` is the possibility of selecting the return type not in template definition/design time, but latter, at compilation time, when the template is instantiated. We delegated an algorithm written in design time, executed at compilation time which – based on the actual types of the template arguments – was able to select the better return type. This has happened in an automated way with the execution of a small and simple template metaprogram.

4 Connection between Functional Programming and C++ Template Metaprograms

In our context the notion *template metaprogram* stands for the collection of templates, their instantiations, and specializations, whose purpose is to carry out operations at compilation time. Their expected behavior might be either emitting messages or generating special constructs for the runtime execution. Henceforth we will call a *runtime program* any kind of runnable code, including those which are the results of template metaprograms. Executing programs in either way means executing pre-defined actions on certain entities. It is useful to compare those actions and entities between runtime programs and metaprograms.

C++ template metaprogram actions are defined in the form of template definitions and they are "executed" when the compiler instantiates them. Templates can refer to other templates, therefore their instantiation can instruct the compiler to execute other instantiations. This way we get an instantiation chain very similar to a call stack of a runtime program. Recursive instantiations are not only possible, but occur regularly in template metaprograms to model loops.

In metaprograms we use `static const` and enumeration values to store quantitative information. Results of computations during the execution of a metaprogram are stored either in other constants or enumerations. Furthermore, the execution of a metaprogram may trigger the creation of new types by the compiler. These types may hold information that influences the further execution of the metaprogram [34].

However, there is a fundamental difference between usual runtime programs and C++ template metaprograms: once a certain entity (constant, enumeration value, type) has been evaluated or constructed, it will be immutable. There is no way to change its value or meaning. When we initialized a constant or enumeration we are not able to change its value. When a type has been constructed, it is not possible to redefine it. Therefore metaprogram assignment does not exist. In this sense metaprograms are similar to pure functional programming languages, where *referential transparency* is obtained. That is the reason why we use recursion and specialization to implement loops: we cannot change the value of any

Table 3. Comparison of functional programs and template metaprograms

	Runtime functional program	C++ template metaprogram
values	run-time data (constant, literal)	static const and enum class members
variables	variables	symbolic names (typenames, typedefs)
initialization	constants generators	static const initialisation enum definition
assignment	no	no
I/O helpers	monads	warnings, error messages no interactive input
branching	pattern matching function specialization	pattern matching template specialization
looping	recursive functions	recursive templates
subprogram	function	(template) class
data types	abstract data structures	typelists, boost::vector
types	type class (Haskell)	concepts

loop variable. Immutability – as in functional languages – has a positive effect too: unwanted side effects do not occur.

Based on these observations we can say that C++ template metaprogramming is part of the functional programming paradigm. In the following table we summarized the main similarities, tools, and language features.

Abrahams and Gurtovoy [1] defined the term template metafunction as a special template class: the arguments of the metafunction are the template parameters of the class, the value of the function is a nested type of the template called `type`.

Metafunctions – as we can expect in a functional programming language – are first class citizens in C++ template metaprogramming. In the following example we show a metaprogram `Accumulate` which summarizes the value of a function given as a parameter at points in the interval 0..N. The function will be a metaprogram itself, and it can be specified as an argument of `Accumulate`.

```
// Accumulate(n,f) := f(0) + f(1) + ... + f(n)
template <int n, template<int> class F>
struct Accumulate
{
  enum { RET = Accumulate<n-1,F>::RET + F<n>::RET };
};

template <template<int> class F>
struct Accumulate<0,F>
{
  enum { RET = F<0>::RET };
};
```

```
template <int n>
struct Square
{
  enum { RET = n*n };
};

int main()
{
  cout << Accumulate<3,Square>::RET << endl;
  return 0;
}
```

Previous examples show that there are sophisticated ways to build up, pass as parameter, and execute functions at compilation time. We have similar professional tools to express lists, vectors, etc. as compile-time data structures.

Complex data structures are also available for metaprograms. Recursive templates store information in various forms, most frequently as tree structures, or sequences. Tree structures are the favorite forms of implementation of expression templates [32]. The canonical examples for sequential data structures are typelist [2] and the elements of the boost::mpl library [37].

We define a typelist with the following recursive template:

```
class NullType {};
struct EmptyType {};          // could be instantiated

typedef Typelist< char, Typelist<signed char,
         Typelist<unsigned char, NullType> > > Charlist;
```

In the example we store the three character types in a typelist. We can use helper macro definitions to make the syntax more readable.

```
#define TYPELIST_1(x)         Typelist< x, NullType>
#define TYPELIST_2(x, y)      Typelist< x, TYPELIST_1(y)>
#define TYPELIST_3(x, y, z)   Typelist< x, TYPELIST_2(y,z)>
#define TYPELIST_4(x, y, z, w) Typelist< x, TYPELIST_3(y,z,w)>
// ...
typedef TYPELIST_3(char, signed char, unsigned char)  Charlist;
```

Essential helper functions – like Length, which computes the size of a list at compilation time – have been defined in Alexandrescu's Loki library[2] in pure functional programming style. Let us consider the typical template metaprogram components. We began with the declaration of the Length template. This is followed by the specific version of Length applicable for the empty list as a specialization for NullType. This template will be instantiated only at the end of a typelist. Finally, we define the generic case on template parameter Typelist<T,U> with further recursion on U.

```
template <class TList> struct Length;
template <>
struct Length<NullType>
{
    enum { value = 0 };
};
template <class T, class U>
struct Length <Typelist<T,U> >
{
    enum { value = 1 + Length<U>::value };
};
```

Length reads the size of the list. The `IndexOf` metafunction takes a type parameter and returns the position of that parameter in the list. If the actual argument
is not found in the list it returns the value -1.

```
template <class TList, class T> struct IndexOf;

template <class T>
struct IndexOf< NullType, T>
{
    enum { value = -1 };
};
template <class T, class Head, class Tail>
struct IndexOf< Typelist<Head, Tail>, T>
{
private:
    enum { temp = IndexOf<Tail, T>::value };
public:
    enum { value = (temp == -1) ? -1 : 1+temp };
};
```

Similar data structures and algorithms can be found in the `boost::mpl` metaprogramming library.

5   Functional Interface for Template Metaprograms

Writing programs today is largely supported by various automated tools, such
as code generators mapping UML notations to source code, model driven architectures, cross-compilers, RAD tools, etc. Coding, however, is still considerably
influenced by personal experiences, conventions, traditions, and customs. The
syntax and the semantics of the programming language is a major factor as it
seriously drives the programmer's attitude. It is possible, but it is not easy to
program in a style which is not directly supported by the actual programming
language. It is even worse if the required programming paradigm is not supported by the language. Similarly, as the spoken language has impact on human

perception, the programming language may drive the programmer's style. In an ideal situation the applied programming language supports the paradigm in which the task has to be solved.

C++ templates are designed to express genericity on data structures and algorithms – i.e. parametric polymorphism. Template metaprogramming has been discovered almost as a side effect. At that time template syntax has already been formulated, and it is far from expressive regarding template metaprograms.

Let's examine the following C++ template metaprogram which decides at compilation time whether its parameter is a prime number.

```cpp
#include <iostream>

namespace { int helper_begin(char*); }

template <int n>
struct Print { enum{ helper_begin_=sizeof(helper_begin(""))}; };

template <bool condition, class True, class False>
struct If : True {};

template <class True, class False>
struct If<false, True, False> : False {};

template <bool b>
struct Bool { static const bool value = b; };

template <class a, class b>
struct And : Bool<a::value && b::value> {};

template <int from, int to, int n>
struct IsPrimeImpl : If< from <= to,
                         And< Bool<n%from!=0>,
                              IsPrimeImpl<from+1,to,n>
                            >,
                         Bool<true>
                       > {};
template <int n>
struct IsPrime {
  static const bool value=IsPrimeImpl<2,n/2,n>::value;
};

struct Nop {};

template <int n>
struct PrintIfPrime : If< IsPrime<n>::value,
                          Print<n>,
```

```
                       Nop
                     > {};

template <class A, class B>
struct Sequence
{
  A a;
  B b;
};

template <int from, int to>
struct PrintPrimes : If< from <= to,
                         Sequence<PrintIfPrime<from>,
                         PrintPrimes<from+1,to>
                       >, Nop> {};
int main()
{
  std::cout << IsPrime<337>::value << std::endl;
}
```

As we have seen in Section 4, the behavior of C++ template metaprograms is very close to the functional programming paradigm. Although this relationship is well-known, current C++ template metaprogramming libraries do not support functional programming directly. Metaprogram implementors are forced to use alien techniques and extremely intricate syntax to implement their own concepts. This often leads to cryptic, unmanageable and fragile code as the sample above.

In this section we propose a functional programming interface for C++ template metaprograms. Using that idea metaprogram developers write embedded Haskell code to express compile time algorithms and data structures inside the C++ host language. These Haskell fragments are automatically translated to native C++ code, which then can be compiled by any standard-compliant C++ compiler. Haskell snippets can communicate with the surrounding C++ environment and – via the host language – each other.

With the help of a translator we can write the previous prime-decider program in the following way:

```
#include <lambda.h>

__BEGIN(Haskell)
  divides b a = (a 'mod' b == 0)
  hasDivider n from to = (from <= to) && ((divides from n) ||
                          (hasDivider n (from + 1) to));
  isPrime 1 = False;
  isPrime n = not (hasDivider n 2 (n 'div' 2));
```

```
  main = print (isPrime 1);
__END(Haskell)

#include <iostream>

int main()
{
  cout << lambda::Reduce< HaskellMain >::type::value << endl;
}
```

To implement this idea we use a step-wise transformation using intermediate languages. Intermediate languages not only make the implementation more stable but are also useful for executing everyday tasks like debugging. Our experimental transformator uses *Yhc.Core*, the York Haskell Compiler's core language [40] as the first intermediate language, and *Lambda*, our own language for expressing lambda expressions [23] as the second intermediate language. Therefore the transformation proceeds in three major steps. First, Haskell code is translated to *Yhc.Core* with the Yhc compiler. In the second step the Yhc.Core is adjusted to our *Lambda* language. In the last step, Lambda is used to generate standard compliant C++ source. Then users may compile the final result with any recent C++ compiler.

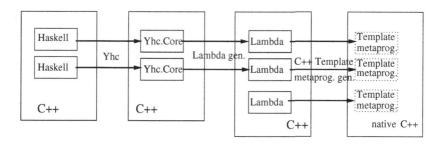

Fig. 1. Transformation schema of embedded Haskell to template metaprograms

There are other possible transformation schemas. Instead of Yhc, one can consider using the Glasgow Haskell Compiler [39] to utilize better parsing possibilities. Another experimental project uses *EClean*, a subset of the *Clean* functional language [6,12]. A Clean to Template Metaprogram translator has been written, and tested on various applications [24].

5.1   Generating Yhc.Core Code

Yhc.Core [13,40] is a core Haskell-like language in which all Haskell programs can be expressed. It uses a small number of structures making it easy to process further translating steps. Haskell programs can be transformed into Yhc.Core using the York Haskell Compiler using the `--showcore` argument. It generates a human readable code which is easy to use for further processing. The Core language can be treated as a subset of Haskell with restrictions:

- Case statements examine their outermost constructor
- Does not contain type classes
- Does not contain `where` statements
- Has only top level functions
- Has fully qualified names
- Constructors and primitives are fully applied

Currently lambda expressions are guaranteed not to appear in the output of the Haskell to Core transformation. The syntax of Yhc Core is found in [13].

5.2   Generating Lambda Expressions

We defined our Lambda language to express lambda expressions. Lambda is a full-featured language. Programmers may embed Lambda code into C++ [23] and generate C++ template metaprograms. However, in this case Lambda is used as an intermediate language.

We use the definition of non-typed enriched lambda expressions from [17]. We express the λ symbol with the \ character. Our solution supports naming lambda expressions.

The code generated by Yhc contains a list of function definitions. Each function definition is converted into a named lambda expression with a corresponding name. Functions taking arguments are converted into lambda abstractions: a new abstraction is introduced for each argument of the function. These lambda abstractions wrap each other in their order of appearance in the argument list. The lambda abstraction generated for the leftmost argument is the outermost. The innermost lambda abstraction encapsulates the body of the function.

Function applications are handled by our lambda expressions. The `let` expressions and the `case` expressions are transformed into lambda expressions supported by our syntax based on the transformation techniques described in [17].

5.3   Generating Template Metaprograms

In the next step lambda expressions are transformed into C++ template metaprograms which can be compiled by any standard C++ compiler. These metaprograms have the ability to access any other part of the C++ code. Therefore they provide interoperability between independent lambda expressions (and thus individual Haskell functions).

During the execution of the generated template metaprograms the C++ compiler builds the graph of the expression and reduces it lazily. Our compiler compiles named lambda expressions into C++ classes (metafunction classes [1]) implementing the lambda expression. The names of the classes are the names of the lambda expressions indicating that they have to be valid C++ identifiers.

Since these expressions are translated into C++ classes they can be at any part of the code where classes can be defined [3] indicating that Haskell code can be embedded at any part of the C++ code where classes can be defined.

Lazy and eager evaluation. Our compiler supports lazy evaluation of lambda expressions: every (sub)expression is evaluated only when its value is needed. It makes implementation of infinite data structures (such as infinite lists) possible. Eager evaluation is supported by the classes implementing the lambda expressions in C++ but are not supported directly in the lambda expressions themselves.

Currying. Currying is supported: when the number of elements applied to a function symbol is less than the number of elements required by the function symbol, then the result is a new function symbol. For example: we have an anonymous function requiring two elements to be applied to it: `\x.\y. + x y`. When only one element is applied to this function the result is a new function requiring one element to be applied to it. `(\x.\y. + x y) 5` is equivalent to `\y. + 5 y`.

Lambda abstractions. Lambda abstractions are implemented by metafunction classes whose embedded `apply` metafunction takes exactly one argument. The name of the argument is the name of the variable the lambda abstraction bounds. Let us consider the following lambda expression and its implementation:

```
// The lambda expression
__lambda I = \x. y;

// It's implementation
struct I {
  template <class x>
  struct apply {
    typedef y type;
  };
};
```

Variables. Variables are implemented by their names. A name symbol from the lambda expression becomes a name symbol in C++. Binding of the names in lambda abstractions is done by the C++ compiler. As we could see it in the previous example the lambda expression y becomes `typedef y type` in the C++ template metaprogram. The example has a lambda abstraction binding x. This lambda abstraction is represented by a template metafunction taking one argument called x. When this metafunction is instantiated the x symbol in its body (if there are any) are replaced by the class with which the metafunction is instantiated.

Eagerly evaluated applications. Eager application of a lambda expression to a lambda abstraction is implemented by the evaluation of the `apply` meta-function. The C++ compiler does β conversion during the instantiation because the name of the bounded variable is the name of the argument of the nested `apply` metafunction (and the variables are implemented by their names).

The `I` lambda expression defined in the previous code example can be evaluated either in an eager or a lazy way. To specify eager evaluation, the user should use the following C++ construct:

```
typedef I::apply<I>::type ApplicationOfIToItself;
```

Currying in built-in functions. Built-in functions (such as the arithmetical or logical operators) have more than one arguments. Their implementation has to support currying. They have to be implemented as lambda abstractions. For example applying an element to the `plus` operator has to evaluate to another lambda abstraction, applying another element to that has to evaluate to a constant (and the value of it has to be the sum of the arguments). It can be implemented easily using nested types and templates. Let us consider the implementation of the `plus` operator:

```
struct OperatorPlus {
  template <class a>
  struct apply {
    struct type {
      template <class b>
      struct apply {
        // ... implementation of addition,
        // possibly by boost::mpl
      };
    };
  };
}
```

We assume that every built-in function supports partial evaluation (to a lambda abstraction).

5.4   Lazy Application

Applications in lambda expressions (and in Haskell) are evaluated only when their value is needed, they cannot be translated into eager applications. We use the following template to implement lazy application:

```
template <class left, class right>
struct Application {};
```

Using this metafunction lazily evaluated template expressions can be built as binary trees of applications: the instances of the `Application` template represent the application nodes of the tree, the `left` and `right` arguments represent the sub-trees of the application nodes.

We define a metafunction implementing reduction of expressions to weak head normal form [7]. Standalone lambda abstractions, constants and built-in functions are in weak head normal form. Lazy applications are never in weak head normal form, since we assume that every built-in function supports partial evaluation. These considerations simplify the reduction algorithm:

```
while (the top level element is a lazy application)
  reduce the left side of the top level element to
    weak head normal form
  evaluate the top level application
```

We implemented this in a metafunction called `Reduce`:

```
template <class T> struct Reduce {typedef T type;};

template <class left, class right>
struct Reduce< Application<left, right> > {
  typedef
    typename Reduce<
      typename
      Reduce<left>::type::template
      apply<right>::type
    >::type  type;
};
```

The general case handles lambda expressions which are already in weak head normal form. There is a specialization of the template for reducing lazy applications in normal order reduction: it reduces the left sub-expression of the application to weak head normal form (`typename Reduce<left>::type`) after which the left side is in weak head normal form, so the next redex is this application:

```
typename Reduce<left>::type::template apply<right>::type
```

Finally the resulting expression is reduced as well.

5.5   Interoperability with Directly Implemented C++ Metafunctions

Lambda expressions are translated to their C++ equivalents. The generated code is valid C++ source with template definitions. Such templates can be written directly, without implementing their Lambda equivalents. Directly implemented Lambda expressions can be used in generated Lambda expressions as constants. For example:

```
struct DirectLambdaExpression {
  // implementation...
};
```

```
__lambda f = \n. DirectLambdaExpression 2 n;
```

It makes extension of the built-in operators possible and parts of the expressions can be implemented using other techniques.

Lambda expressions can be used by directly implemented C++ template metaprograms as well. After they are translated into template metaprograms there is no difference between a directly implemented lambda expression and a translated one. Lambda expressions can be used as built-in functions in other lambda expressions, for example:

```
__lambda add = \a.\b. + a b;
__lambda f = \n. * n (add 6 7);
```

Lambda expressions can be used in their own definition simplifying the creation of recursive expressions:

```
__lambda rec = \n. (< n 1) 13 (rec (- n 1));
```

Due to the visibility rules of C++ [3] lambda expressions are visible after their declaration. For example the following code cannot be compiled because b is defined after a:

```
__lambda a = \n. b n;
__lambda b = \n. + 1 n;
```

Our compiler supports forward declaration of lambda expressions by ensuring that every lambda expression translated to C++ is implemented as a struct. In the previous example b can be declared before a is defined:

```
struct b;
__lambda a = \n. b n;
__lambda b = \n. + 1 n;
```

Haskell functions are visible in the whole Haskell block. To support this our Yhc.Core to lambda expression transformation tool adds forward declaration of the named lambda expressions to the beginning of each lambda expression list generated from an embedded Haskell block. Note that this makes functions visible to each other within an embedded Haskell block. Visibility of functions defined in separate Haskell blocks depend on the C++ visibility rules [3] because Haskell functions are transformed into C++ classes.

5.6   Evaluation

Ideally, the syntax of a programming language should match the paradigm the program is written in. Template metaprogramming, a Turing-complete subset of the C++ language, is many times regarded as a pure functional language. Unfortunately, the current way of writing metaprograms is far from ideal, mainly due to the complicated template syntax and the different original design goals of C++.

In this section we described a method which makes metaprogram developers able to express their intentions directly in functional style using Haskell syntax. Haskell code snippets are embedded into the C++ program and are translated into native C++ code. The translation process uses a stepwise approach; and the last step generates C++ template metaprograms which can be compiled by any standard conformant C++ compiler.

We have shown that using embedded Haskell simplifies template metaprograms, makes them easier to write and maintain. The developer can focus on the functionality of the metaprogram, reusing a huge number of existing algorithms and data structures implemented as Haskell libraries making them available to the C++ metaprogramming community.

6   Debugging Template Metaprograms

Debuggers are software tools helping the debugging process. The main objective of a debugger is to help us understand the hidden sequence of events that led to the error. In most cases this means following the program's control flow, retrieving information on memory locations, and showing the execution context. Debuggers also offer advanced functionality to improve efficiency of the debugging process. These include stopping the execution at a certain *breakpoint*, continuing the execution step by step, step into, step out, or step over functions, etc. Still, debugging can be one of the most difficult and frustrating tasks for a programmer.

In this section we describe possible debugging strategies for C++ template metaprograms. First we discuss the ontology of template metaprogram errors [25], then we give an overview of possible implementation strategies for debugging template metaprograms.

6.1   Ontology of Template Metaprogram Errors

As we have seen in section 3, Unruh's first template metaprogram emitted error messages to print prime numbers. The program is erroneous in the traditional sense, as it would not compile and therefore is unable to run. Was this program correct or erroneous as a template metaprogram? As the goal of the program – printing prime numbers – has been achieved, we should consider Unruh's code a correct metaprogram. This example points out the difference of the notions *correct* and *erroneous* behavior between traditional runtime programs and template metaprograms.

Let us examine the `Factorial` metaprogram described in Section 3, and let us suppose that the template specialization `Factorial<1>` has a syntactic error: a semicolon is missing at the end of the class definition.

```
template <int N>
class Factorial
{
public:
  enum { value = N*Factorial<N-1>::value };
};
template<>
class Factorial<1>
{
public:
  enum { value = 1 };
} // ; missing
```

This is an *ill-formed* template metaprogram, with a *diagnostic message*. The metaprogram was not executed: no template instantiation happened. Another *ill-formed* template metaprogram with *diagnostic message* is shown in the next example. However, it starts to "run", i.e. the compiler starts to instantiate the Factorial classes, but the metaprogram *aborts* (at compilation time).

```
template <int N>
class Factorial
{
public:
  enum { value = N*Factorial<N-1>::value };
};
template<>
class Factorial<1>
{
// public: missing
  enum { value = 1 };
};
int main ()
{
  const int f = Fibonacci<4>::value;
  const int r = Factorial<5>::value;
}
```

As the full specialization for Factorial<1> is written in form of a class, the default visibility rule for a class is private. Thus enum { value=1 } is a private member, so we receive a compile-time error when the compiler tries to acquire the value of Factorial<1>::value, when Factorial<2> is being instantiated. The main difference from the earlier *ill-formed* example is that here instantiations are started. For example, the Fibonacci<4>::value is computed.

In our next example we remove the full specialization Factorial<1>:

```
template <int N>
struct Factorial
```

```
{
  enum { value = N*Factorial<N-1>::value };
};
// specialization for N==1 is missing
int main ()
{
  const int r = Factorial<5>::value;
}
```

As the `Factorial` template has no explicit specialization, the `Factorial<N-1>` expression will trigger the instantiations of `Factorial<1>` followed by the instantiation of `Factorial<0>`, `Factorial<-1>` etc. We have written a compile-time infinite recursion. This is an *ill-formed* template metaprogram with *no diagnostic message*, equivalent to infinite loops of run-time programs.

The C++ standard requires a maximum of 17 level of recursive template instantiations. Therefore portable metaprograms must not exceed this limit. However, different compilers have rather diverse behavior.

Compiler `g++ 3.4` halts the compilation process after the 17 levels of implicit instantiations is reached, as defined by the C++ standard. This limit can be modified by compiler flags. The `MSVC 6` compiler runs until its resources are exhausted (reached `Factorial<-1308>` in our test). `MSVC 7.1` halted the compilation reaching a certain recursion depth. The error message received was *fatal error C1202: recursive type or function dependency context too complex*.

However, some compilers, like `g++` can be parameterized to accept deeper instantiation levels. In this case the compiler continues the instantiation risking that the resources will be exhausted. In that unfortunate situation the compiler crashes.

6.2 Debugging Techniques

Tools used for debugging in run-time programming are not available in the well–known way when dealing with metaprograms. We have no command for printing to the screen (in fact we have practically no commands at all), and we have no framework to manage running code. On the other hand, we still have some options. Having a set of good debugging tools in the runtime world and a strong analogue between the runtime and compile-time realm, we can attempt to implement a template metaprogram debugging framework. In the following we explain the structure of *Templight*, a template metaprogram debugger framework [18].

A common property of debugging tools is that they analyze a specific execution of the program. In the case of debugging C++ template metaprograms our goal is to retrieve the chain of template instantiations with as much additional information (template parameters, etc.) as we can.

In the most favorable case the execution does not depend on the usage of the debugging tool. In such cases it does not matter whether we are using the tool on the running program itself or we analyze a previously generated trace of its runtime steps. Most compilers generate additional information for debuggers and profilers. Obviously, the simplest way for providing trace information on instantiations would be the implementation of another compiler feature. However, an immediate and more portable solution is to use external tools cooperating with standard C++ language elements. The appropriate compiler support could be an ideal long-term solution.

Without the modification of the compiler the only way of obtaining any information during compilation is generating informative warning messages that contain the details we are looking for [1]. Therefore the task is the *instrumentation* of the source, i.e. its transformation into a functionally equivalent modified form that triggers the compiler to emit talkative warning messages. The concept of such instrumentation is common in the field of debuggers, profilers and program slicers. Everytime the compiler starts to instantiate a template, defines an inner type etc. the inserted code fragments generate detailed information on the actual template-related event. Similar warnings should be emitted when we reach the end of the template. Embedded start and end markers unambigously identifies the chain of template instantiations – similar to the stack frames of runtime programs. We have to collect the desired information from the corresponding warning messages in the compilation output and form a trace file. A front-end tool may use this information to implement various debugging features and visualization of the instantiations.

The input of the process is a C++ source file and the output is a trace file, containing a list of events like *instantiation of template X began*, *instantiation of template X ended*, *typedef definition found* etc. The procedure begins with the execution of the preprocessor with exactly the same options as if we were to compile the program. As a result we acquire a single file, containing all #included template definitions and the original code fragment we are debugging. The preprocessor decorates its output with #line directives to mark where the different sections of the file come from. This information is essential for a precise jump to the original source file positions as we step through the compilation while debugging. To simplify the process we handle the mapping of the locations in the single processed file to the original source files in a separate thread. Simple filter scripts move the location information from #line directives into a separate mapping file and delete #line directives.

At this point we have a single preprocessed C++ source file, that we transform into a C++ token sequence. To make our framework as portable and self-containing as possible we apply the `boost::wave` C++ parser. Note that even though `boost::wave` supports preprocessing, we still use the original preprocessor tool of the compilation environment to eliminate the chance of bugs occurring due to different tools being used. Our aim is to insert warning-generating code fragments at the instrumentation points. As `wave` does no semantic analysis we can only recognize these places by searching for specific token patterns. We go through the token sequence and look for patterns like *template keyword + arbitrary tokens + class or struct keyword + arbitrary tokens + {* to identify template definitions. The end of a template class or function is only a } token that can appear in quite many contexts, so we should track all { and } tokens in order to correctly determine where the template contexts actually end. This pattern matching step is called annotating, its output is an XML file containing annotation entries in a hierarchical structure following the scope.

The instrumentation takes this annotation and the single source and inserts the warning-generating code fragments for each annotation at its corresponding location in the source. Therefore a source is produced that emits warnings at each annotation point during its compilation. The next step is the execution of the compiler to have these warning messages generated. The inserted code fragments are intentionally designed to generate warnings that contain enough information about the context and details of the actual event. Since the compiler may produce output independently of our instrumentation, it is important for debugger warnings to have a distinct format that differentiates them. This is the step where we ask the compiler for valuable information from its internals. Here the result is simply the build output as a text file. The warning translator takes the build output, looks for the warnings with the aforementioned special format and generates an event sequence with all the details. The result is an XML file that lists the events that occurred during the compilation in chronological order. The annotations and the events can be paired. Each event signals that the compiler went through the corresponding annotation point. We can say events are actual occurrences of the annotation points in the compilation process.

6.3 Profiling

Unfortunately, implementations of template metaprograms are typically far from optimal [1]. One reason is that compilers are optimized to generate efficient run-time code and not designed to maximize efficiency of the compilation process itself. Another reason is that programmers are not familiar with all the background costs of the metaprogram constructs. This may result in a very long compilation time and huge memory usage. With a profiling tool we should be able to identify these "noisy" code segments that hold up the compilation process. Since traditional profiler tools are unapplicable to metaprograms running at compilation time, the development of metaprogram-specific profiling tools is crucial. Unfortunately, today there are no C++ template metaprogram profiling tools available. In this subsection we describe methods for template metaprogram profiling, which could serve as foundations of an optimization process.

Measuring compilation units. The simplest method for measuring compile-time performance is measuring the full compilation of units. Compilation of full source files does not require code modification, therefore this is a non-intrusive method, and does not add overhead or significant distortion. Although filtering out all perturbations is not easy, most operating systems provide fair tools to measure the experienced real-time, user- and system times on a compilation session.

In most cases locating, loading, and parsing header files is a non-trivial effort. To filter out this effect we can run the precompiler in a separate session

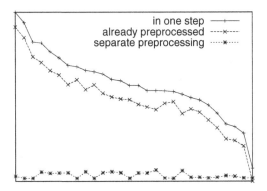

Fig. 2. Compilation time with separate precompilation

and measure only further compilation stages. Figure 2 shows that separating precompiler tasks changes the compilation times significantly.

Compiling full programs or compilation units can reveal significant behavioral patterns of programs or template constructs. Abrahams and Gurtovoy measured template metaprogram constructs in [1] with this method and could point to fundamental differences in strategy and tactics of different compilers. They have shown the effect of certain techniques, like memoization and have measured structural complexity of metaprograms.

However, measuring full compilation time has shortages. It is not always trivial to write wrapper programs around specific template constructs without seriously distorting measurement results. The full session of compilation includes activities we are not interested in: initializations, solving non-template metaprogram related tasks. Code generation, optimization steps produce significant overhead too. When we analyze the results we get the compilation times, but no implications on how this gross time splits among different code components. Measuring full compilation is great to prove concepts but hard to use for analysis.

Measuring with instrumenting. Most compilers generate additional information for profilers. An appropriate compiler support for measuring template metaprogram profiles would be the ideal solution. However, as this support is unavailable today, an immediate and portable method is to use external tools cooperating with standard C++ language elements.

Using the Templight tool – described in subsection 6.2 – is a natural choice instrumenting the source code providing profiling information. With the Templight framework we have to execute only one compilation that emits warnings for each instantiation, and a post processing pipelined tool memorizes the timestamps whenever a warning occurs. This way we have timestamps for each template-related event, and the processing time of a certain template instance can easily be computed by subtracting the timestamps stored at the corresponding template-begin and template-end events (warning messages).

A factor of distortion is the way we add timestamps to the emitted warning messages. Compilers do not decorate warnings with timestamp info. In the simplest solution an external program reads compiler output and records the actual time whenever it sees some of our special warning messages being produced by the instrumented fragments. In this case the delay between the warning is generated and timestamped can be sigificant. It is better to have the timestamp generated inside the compiler when constructing the warning message, as this delay can be eliminated. However, this requires the modification of the compiler.

Inheritance relationships require special attention when using Templight. As warnings emitted by the injected code appear at the begin and end of templated code, the end marker of the base class will be emitted *before* the begin marker of the derived class. This could be solved by the extra decoration of the (first) base class.

```
template <typename T>
class Derived : public ReportInherit<Derived<T>, Base<T> >::Base
{
  /* skipping this instrumentation point */
  // ..
  /* remaining instrumentation point */
};
```

Modification of the compiler. The most accurate way of evaluating compilation times is by acquiring timing information from the compiler itself. As our metaprogram is executed on a meta-level from the viewpoint of C++, a meta-level profiler is needed, i.e. one measuring the compiler's action times. The naïve approach – to use a profiler tool (like `gprof`) and measure the compiler's runtime – does not work, since we cannot identify which metaprogram elements of the subject code are under compilation at a certain moment. Even though we would be able to measure individual compiler method's running time in general, we could not disambiguate certain instantiations. In other words, we could acquire the sum of all instaniation times, but would not be able to measure each instantiation separately.

To gain the required detailed data on particular instantiations we have to modify the compiler for the purpose. We instrument the code with Templight, but generate warnings decorated with timestamps via the modified compiler. Figure 3 shows the compilation time after we instrumented the GNU `g++` compiler (version 3.4.3) The modification consists of generating timestamps when entering and exiting these functions and adding it to the emitted message. We used this approach to eliminate the distortion of generating the warning itself. Experiments showed that in many cases the time we spent in these functions is significant.

The measured code contains recursive template instantiation. The `raw` data shows the observed times, i.e. the time the compiler spent on instantiating up to 2500 instances of the measured class *plus* the time of the warning generation

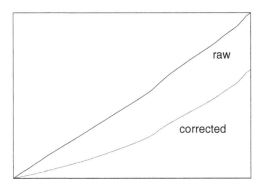

Fig. 3. Compilation time with the time spent for warnings (raw) and without it (corrected) in a test of increasing template depth

due to code instrumentation. The `corrected` data has been constructed by subtracting the time the compiler spent with warning generation from the observed time.

7   Related Work

7.1   FC++

FC++ is a C++ library providing runtime support for functional programming [15]. Using the tools the library provides functional programs can be written in C++ from which the expression graph is built and evaluated at runtime. They do not require any external tools (such as a translator), but use standard language features only. The library focuses on runtime execution.

7.2   Boost Metaprogramming Library

Boost has a template metaprogramming library called `boost::mpl` which implements several data types and algorithms following the logic of STL [11]. Our solution is designed to be compatible with it (the lambda expressions produced by our compiler are designed to be template metafunction classes taking one argument). `Boost::mpl` has lambda expression support: the library provides tools to create lambda abstractions easily: placeholders (_1, _2, etc.) are provided and arguments of metafunctions can be replaced by them. The result of evaluating a metafunction with a placeholder argument is not directly usable, a metafunction called `lambda` generates a metafunction class from them. Using these lambda abstractions, partial function applications can be implemented, but since `lambda` bounds every placeholder, lambda abstractions with other lambda abstractions as their value can't be defined. For example $\lambda x.\lambda y.+xy$ can't be expressed (and neither can be the Y fixpoint operator) [38].

7.3   Haskell Type Classes

Zalewski et al. defined a mapping from generic Haskell specifications to C++ with concepts [33]. Haskell multi-parameter type classes with functional dependencies have been translated to ConceptC++, an experimental implementation of the concept feature of C++0x. The translation process consists of three major parts: the division of Haskell class variables into ConceptC++ concept parameters and associated types, the corresponding division of superclasses in the context of a type class, and the flattening of Haskell AST to the concrete syntax of ConceptC++. The main motivation of the authors was to model software components in Haskell type classes, then transform them to C++ concepts. Thus the implementation in C++ is checked against the constraints defined originally in Haskell.

7.4   Debugging and Profiling

Template metaprogramming was first investigated in Veldhuizen's articles [31,30]. Static interface checking was introduced by McNamara [16] and Siek [20]. The compile-time assertion appeared in Alexandrescu's work [2]. Vandevoorde and Josuttis introduced the concept of a *tracer*, which is a specially designed class that emits runtime messages when its operations are called [29]. When this type is passed to a template as an argument, the messages show in what order and how often the operations of that argument class are called. The authors also defined the notion of an *archetype* for a class whose sole purpose is checking that the template does not set up undesired requirements on its parameters. In their book [1] Abrahams and Gurtovoy devoted a whole section to diagnostics, where the authors showed methods for generating textual output in the form of warning messages. They implemented the compile-time equivalent of the aforementioned runtime tracer (`mpl::print`, see [37]).

8   Conclusion

In this paper we gave a brief and incomplete introduction to C++ templates and template metaprogramming. We learned the fundamental methods of writing metaprograms, and discussed the connection of C++ metaprogramming and the functional programming paradigm. We proposed a pure functional interface in form of embedded Haskell code to improve metaprogram development. Techniques for supporting tools – debugger and profiler – have been presented.

Ideally, the syntax of a programming language should match the paradigm the program is written in. Template metaprogramming, a Turing-complete subset of the C++ language for implementing compile-time algorithms is many times regarded as a pure functional language. Unfortunately, the current way of writing metaprograms is far from ideal, mainly due to the complicated template syntax and the different original design goals of C++. Therefore template metaprograms are hard to read, understand and maintain.

The author's idea is to write template metaprograms in functional style with the help of a functional programming language. Haskell code fragments embedded into C++ host language can be compiled into template metaprograms. Thus we are able to write clear, maintainable metaprogram code, reusing a huge number of the existing codebase of the Haskell community.

Acknowledgements

The author would like to thank Zoltán Csörnyei and Péter Diviánszky for clarifying the details of the functional programming paradigm, and József Mihalicza for his indispensable work on debugging and profiling metaprograms. Norbert Pataki and Melinda Simon helped to develop various metaprogram examples. Ábel Sinkovics, Ádám Sipos, and Viktória Zsók made fundamental work on implementing translators from Haskell and Clean to C++ template metaprograms. Zalán Szűgyi and István Zólyomi inspired me and made important contributions on various topics of C++ template metaprogramming.

References

1. Abrahams, D., Gurtovoy, A.: C++ template metaprogramming, Concepts, Tools, and Techniques from Boost and Beyond. Addison-Wesley, Boston (2004)
2. Alexandrescu, A.: Modern C++ Design: Generic Programming and Design Patterns Applied. Addison-Wesley, Reading (2001)
3. ANSI/ISO C++ Committee. Programming Languages – C++. ISO/IEC 14882:1998(E). American National Standards Institute (1998)
4. Bohm, C., Jacopini, G.: Flow Diagrams, Turing Machines and Languages with Only Two Formation Rules. Communications of the ACM 9(5), 366–371 (1966)
5. Bravenboer, M., Vermaas, R., Vinju, J., Visser, E.: Generalized Type-Based Disambiguation of Meta Programs with Concrete Object Syntax. In: Glück, R., Lowry, M. (eds.) GPCE 2005. LNCS, vol. 3676, pp. 157–172. Springer, Heidelberg (2005)
6. Brus, T.H., van Eekelen, C.J.D., van Leer, M.O., Plasmeijer, M.J.: CLEAN: A language for functional graph rewriting. In: Kahn, G. (ed.) FPCA 1987. LNCS, vol. 274, pp. 364–384. Springer, Heidelberg (1987)
7. Csörnyei, Z., Dévai, G.: An introduction to the lambda-calculus. In: Horváth, Z., Plasmeijer, R., Soós, A., Zsók, V. (eds.) Central European Functional Programming School. LNCS, vol. 5161, pp. 87–111. Springer, Heidelberg (2008)
8. Czarnecki, K., Eisenecker, U.W.: Generative Programming: Methods, Tools and Applications. Addison-Wesley, Reading (2000)
9. Garcia, R., Järvi, J., Lumsdaine, A., Siek, J., Willcock, J.: A Comparative Study of Language Support for Generic Programming. In: Proceedings of the 18th ACM SIGPLAN OOPSLA, pp. 115–134 (2003)
10. Juhász, Z., Sipos, Á., Porkoláb, Z.: Implementation of a Finite State Machine with Active Libraries in C++. In: Lämmel, R., Visser, J., Saraiva, J. (eds.) Generative and Transformational Techniques in Software Engineering II. LNCS, vol. 5235, pp. 474–488. Springer, Heidelberg (2008)
11. Karlsson, B.: Beyond the C++ Standard Library, A Introduction to Boost. Addison-Wesley, Reading (2005)
12. Koopman, P., Plasmeijer, R., van Eeekelen, M., Smetsers, S.: Functional programming in Clean (2002)

13. Mitchell, N., Runciman, C.: A Supercompiler for Core Haskell. In: Chitil, O., Horváth, Z., Zsók, V. (eds.) IFL 2007. LNCS, vol. 5083, pp. 147–164. Springer, Heidelberg (2008)
14. Musser, D.R., Stepanov, A.A.: Algorithm-oriented Generic Libraries. Software-practice and experience 27(7), 623–642 (1994)
15. McNamara, B., Smaragdakis, Y.: Functional programming in C++. In: Proceedings of the Fifth ACM SIGPLAN International Conference on Functional Programming, pp. 118–129 (2000)
16. McNamara, B., Smaragdakis, Y.: Static interfaces in C++. In: First C++ Template Programming Workshop, Erfurt (October 2000)
17. Jones, S.L.P.: The Implementation of Functional Languages, pp. 4–45. Prentice-Hall, Englewood Cliffs (1987)
18. Porkoláb, Z., Mihalicza, J., Sipos, Á.: Debugging C++ template metaprograms. In: Jarzabek, S., Schmidt, D.C., Veldhuizen, T.L. (eds.) Proceedings Generative Programming and Component Engineering, 5th International Conference, GPCE 2006, Portland, Oregon, USA, October 22-26, pp. 255–264. ACM, New York (2006)
19. Gregor, D., Järvi, J., Siek, J.G., Reis, G.D., Stroustrup, B., Lumsdaine, A.: Concepts: Linguistic Support for Generic Programming in C++. In: Proceedings of the 2006 ACM SIGPLAN Conference on Object-Oriented Programming, Systems, Languages, and Applications, OOPSLA 2006 (October 2006)
20. Siek, J., Lumsdaine, A.: Concept checking: Binding parametric polymorphism in C++. In: First C++ Template Programming Workshop, Erfurt (October 2000)
21. Siek, J., Lumsdaine, A.: Essential Language Support for Generic Programming. In: Proceedings of the ACM SIGPLAN 2005 Conference on Programming Language Design and Implementation, New York, NY, USA, pp. 73–84 (2005)
22. Siek, J.: A Language for Generic Programming. PhD thesis, Indiana University (August 2005)
23. Sinkovics, Á., Porkoláb, Z.: Expressing C++ Template Metaprograms as Lambda expressions. In: Horváth, Z., Zsók, V., Achten, P., Koopman, P. (eds.) Tenth symposium on Trends in Functional Programming (TFP 2009), Komarno, Slovakia, June 2 - 4, pp. 97–111 (2009)
24. Sipos, Á., Porkoláb, Z., Zsók, V.: Meta<fun> – Towards a functional-style interface for C++ template metaprograms. In: Frentiu, et al. (eds.) Studia Universitatis Babes-Bolyai Informatica LIII,Cluj-Napoca, pp. 55–66 (Febraury 2008)
25. Sipos, Á.: Effective development of C++ Template Metaprograms. PhD thesis. Eötvös Loránd University, Budapest, Hungary (2009)
26. Stroustrup, B.: The C++ Programming Language Special Edition. Addison-Wesley, Reading (2000)
27. Torgersen, M., Hansen, C.P., Ernst, E., Ahe, P., Bracha, G., Gafter, N.: Adding Wildcards to the Java Programming Language. In: Proceedings of the 2004 ACM Symposium on Applied Computing (SAC) 2004, pp. 1289–1296 (2004)
28. Unruh, E.: Prime number computation. ANSI X3J16-94-0075/ISO WG21-462
29. Vandevoorde, D., Josuttis, N.M.: C++ Templates: The Complete Guide. Addison-Wesley, Reading (2003)
30. Veldhuizen, T.L., Gannon, D.: Active libraries: Rethinking the roles of compilers and libraries. In: Proceedings of the SIAM Workshop on Object Oriented Methods for Inter-operable Scientic and Engineering Computing (OO 1998), pp. 21–23. SIAM Press, Philadelphia (1998)
31. Veldhuizen, T.: Using C++ Template Metaprograms. C++ Report 7(4), 36–43 (1995)

32. Veldhuizen, T.: Expression Templates. C++ Report 7(5), 26–31 (1995)
33. Zalewski, M., Priesnitz, A.P., Ionescu, C., Botta, N., Schupp, S.: Multi-language library development: From Haskell type classes to C++ concepts. In: MPOOL 2007 Ecoop workshp (2007)
34. Zólyomi, I., Porkoláb, Z., Kozsik, T.: An extension to the subtype relationship in C++. In: Pfenning, F., Smaragdakis, Y. (eds.) GPCE 2003. LNCS, vol. 2830, pp. 209–227. Springer, Heidelberg (2003)
35. Zólyomi, I., Porkoláb, Z.: Towards a template introspection library. In: Karsai, G., Visser, E. (eds.) GPCE 2004. LNCS, vol. 3286, pp. 266–282. Springer, Heidelberg (2004)
36. Boost Concept checking,
    http://www.boost.org/libs/concept_check/concept_check.htm
37. Boost Metaprogramming library,
    http://www.boost.org/libs/mpl/doc/index.html
38. The boost lambda library,
    http://www.boost.org/doc/libs/1_40_0/doc/html/lambda.html
39. Glasgow Haskell Compiler,
    http://www.haskell.org/ghc/
40. York Haskell Compiler,
    http://community.haskell.org/~ndm/yhc/

A   Appendix: The Sample Programs

In this appendix we publish a selection of examples. All the examples could be independently compiled and run. We tested the examples with **g++** version 4.3 compiler, however most of them will work fine with other compilers. Notable exceptions are example 15 and 16 which generate warnings for debugging purposes. Here passing a string literal to a **char*** parameter emits the warning. In the case of older compilers or compiler versions the assingment unsigned int i = -1.0   will generate warning. All the examples could be downloaded from http://aszt.inf.elte.hu/~gsd/cefp/.

```
//-------------------------------------------------
// example 01
// side effects of C/C++ macros
//-------------------------------------------------
#include <iostream>
#define MAX(a,b)  a > b ? a : b

int main()
{
  int i = 3;
  double d = 3.14;

  std::cout << "MAX( i, d ) = "
            << (MAX( i, d))   << std::endl;
  std::cout << "MAX( i, d )*2 = "
            << (MAX( i, d)*2) << std::endl;
```

```
    std::cout << "MAX( ++i, d ) = "
              << (MAX( ++i, d)) << std::endl;
    return 0;
}


//--------------------------------------------------
// example 02
// simple template with on type argument
//--------------------------------------------------
#include <iostream>

template <typename T>
T max( T x, T y)
{
  if ( x > y )
    return x;
  else
    return y;
}
int main()
{
  int i = 3, j = 4;
  double d = 3.14, e = 2.71;

  std::cout << "max( i, j ) = "
            <<  max( i, j) << std::endl;
  std::cout << "max( d, e ) = "
            <<  max( d, e) << std::endl;
  // syntax error:
  std::cout << "max( i, d ) = "
            <<  max( i, d) << std::endl;
  return 0;
}


//--------------------------------------------------
// example 03
// template with two type arguments
//--------------------------------------------------
#include <iostream>

template <typename T, typename S>
T max( T x, S y)
{
  if ( x > y )
    return x;
```

```
  else
    return y;
}
int main()
{
  int i = 3;
  double d = 3.14;

  std::cout << "max( d, i ) = "
            <<  max( d, i) << std::endl;
  std::cout << "max( i, d ) = "
            <<  max( i, d) << std::endl;
  return 0;
}


//------------------------------------------------
// example 04
// template with three type arguments
//------------------------------------------------
#include <iostream>

template <typename R, typename T, typename S>
R max( T x, S y, R)
{
  if ( x > y )
    return x;
  else
    return y;
}
int main()
{
  int i = 3;
  double d = 3.14;

  std::cout << "max( d, i, 0.0 ) = "
            <<  max( d, i, 0.0) << std::endl;
  std::cout << "max( i, d, 0.0 ) = "
            <<  max( i, d, 0.0) << std::endl;
  return 0;
}


//------------------------------------------------
// example 05
// explicit specialization
//------------------------------------------------
```

```cpp
#include <iostream>

template <typename R, typename T, typename S>
R max( T x, S y)
{
  if ( x > y )
    return x;
  else
    return y;
}
int main()
{
  int i = 3;
  double d = 3.14;

  std::cout << "max<double>( d, i ) = "
            <<  max<double>( d, i) << std::endl;
  std::cout << "max<double>( i, d ) = "
            <<  max<double>( i, d) << std::endl;
  return 0;
}


//---------------------------------------------------
// example 06
// overloading of templates
//---------------------------------------------------
#include <iostream>

template <typename T>
T max( T x, T y)
{
  std::cout << "T max( T x, T y) = ";
  if ( x > y )
    return x;
  else
    return y;
}
template <typename R, typename T, typename S>
R max( T x, S y)
{
  std::cout << "R max( T x, S y) = ";
  if ( x > y )
    return x;
  else
    return y;
```

```
}
int main()
{
  int i = 3;
  double d = 3.14;

  std::cout << max( 2, i) << std::endl;
  std::cout << max<double>( i, d ) << std::endl;

  return 0;
}

//-------------------------------------------------
// example 07
// the factorial template metaprogram
//-------------------------------------------------
#include <iostream>

template <int N>
struct Fact
{
  enum { value = Fact<N-1>::value * N };
};
template <>
struct Fact<1>
{
  enum { value = 1 };
};
int main()
{
  std::cout << Fact<6>::value << std::endl;
  return 0;
}

//-------------------------------------------------
// example 08
// the fibonacchi template metaprogram
//-------------------------------------------------
#include <iostream>

template <int N>
struct Fib
{
  enum { value = Fib<N-1>::value + Fib<N-2>::value };
};
```

```cpp
template <>
struct Fib<0>
{
  enum { value = 0 };
};
template <>
struct Fib<1>
{
  enum { value = 1 };
};
int main()
{
  std::cout << Fib<6>::value << std::endl;
  return 0;
}


//--------------------------------------------------
// example 09
// if-then-else template metaprogram
//--------------------------------------------------
#include <iostream>

template <bool cond, typename Then, typename Else>
struct If
{
  typedef Then Ret;
};
template <typename Then, typename Else>
struct If<false, Then, Else>
{
  typedef Else Ret;
};
template <typename T, typename S>
If<sizeof(T)<sizeof(S), S, T>::Ret max( T x, S y)
{
  if ( x > y )
    return x;
  else
    return y;
}
int main()
{
  int i = 3;
  double d = 3.14;
```

```
  std::cout << "max( d, i ) = "
            <<   max( d, i) << std::endl;
  std::cout << "max( i, d ) = "
            <<   max( i, d) << std::endl;

  return 0;
}

//------------------------------------------------
// example 10
// debugging the factorial metaprogram
//------------------------------------------------
#include <iostream>

static inline int f(char *s){ return 1;}

template <int N>
struct Fact
{
  enum { begin = sizeof (f("")) };
  enum { value = Fact<N-1>::value * N };
  enum { end = sizeof (f("")) };
};
template <>
struct Fact<1>
{
  enum { begin = sizeof (f("")) };
  enum { value = 1 };
  enum { end = sizeof (f("")) };
};
int main()
{
  std::cout << Fact<6>::value << std::endl;
  return 0;
}

//------------------------------------------------
// example 11
// debugging the fibonacchi metaprogram
//------------------------------------------------
#include <iostream>

static inline int f(char *s){ return 1;}

template <int N>
```

```cpp
struct Fib
{
  enum { begin = sizeof (f("")) };
  enum { value = Fib<N-1>::value + Fib<N-2>::value };
  enum { end = sizeof (f("")) };
};
template <>
struct Fib<0>
{
  enum { value = 0 };
};
template <>
struct Fib<1>
{
  enum { value = 1 };
};
int main()
{
  std::cout << Fib<6>::value << std::endl;
  return 0;
}
```

Embedding a Proof System in Haskell*

Gergely Dévai

Eötvös Loránd University, Faculty of Informatics
Dept. of Programming Languages and Compilers
Pázmány Péter sétány 1/C H-1117 Budapest, Hungary
deva@elte.hu

Abstract. This article reports about a work-in-progress project that aims at embedding a proof system [4] in the *Haskell* programming language. The goal of the system is to create formally verified software using the *correctness by construction* principle. Using *Haskell* as the host language provides a powerful and flexible environment so that programming language tools can be used to build proofs.

The main contribution of this paper is the systematic analysis of different techniques for language embedding. We present design decisions by pointing out which techniques are applicable and which ones are inappropriate or inconvenient to use when embedding a proof system like the our one. We also point out the advantages of the embedding compared to a previous implementation of the same system.

1 Introduction

Correctness by construction [20] is a reasonable way of producing formally verified software. Writing the specification first and deriving a program from it helps in design decisions. We can also avoid making too much effort to prove a program that is actually wrong, while this can happen in case of posterior verification.

Deriving a program means that one replaces the original specification with a more detailed one using refinement rules. This refinement process results in a proof that can be validated automatically.

In systems like the B-method [5] there are refinement rules that introduce programming structures. This means that the refinement process results in a program which is a solution for the problem defined by the specification. In our system it is not necessary to derive a program by hand during the refinement process: It is possible to automatically generate program code from the axioms used to complete the proof. This way, the system is independent of the target programming language, it can be equipped with sets of axioms and code generator modules for different programming languages.

Our system was first implemented as a standalone specification and proof language. It supports the construction of imperative programs with a C++ backend. The proof checker itself was also implemented in C++. The expressive power of

---

* This work is supported by ELTE IKKK (KMOP-1.1.2-08).

Z. Horváth, R. Plasmeijer, and V. Zsók (Eds.): CEFP 2009, LNCS 6299, pp. 354–371, 2010.

this language was tested by implementing axioms about pointer operations [13] and containers in the C++ Standard Template Library [14].

We concluded that generalizing and parametrizing often used proof fragments made proof construction much more effective. We introduced a meta language [12] on top of the proof language to be able to define and reuse these generalized proof fragments that we call templates. Adding more features to this meta language made proof templates more flexible and powerful: We were able to use them as proof generators. However, the lack of λ-abstraction was a severe restriction.

These observations inspired the embedding of our system in a functional language. In case of deep embedding, one defines data types in the host language to represent constructs of the embedded language. To complete the embedding, a set of functions has to be defined to make the manipulation of the represented constructs convenient. This means that the host language becomes a meta language: It is possible to use all its power to generate programs of the embedded language. Haskell, as a pure, lazy functional language with an unobtrusive syntax is especially well-suited to be a host language.

The current status of the project is the following. We have embedded our proof-system in Haskell by implementing the necessary data structures, the frontend library and the proof verification algorithm. The next step is to port the axioms and proof templates created for the earlier C++ implementation into the new, Haskell-based one. The C++ code generator backend is also to be re-implemented in Haskell to complete the system.

In the next section we give an overview on the proof system that we have embedded in Haskell. In section 3 we discuss design decisions we had to make during the embedding process and point out the advantages and disadvantages of the different approaches. Section 4 presents the frontend of the language. It is a library that defines the "syntax" of the language and makes construction of expressions, formulas and proofs more convenient. In the last section we point out that using the functional programming paradigm and language embedding technologies can make the implementation simpler and more powerful at the same time. Finally we present related and future work.

2   Overview of the Proof System

This section informally presents the proof system we would like to embed in Haskell. It uses classical first order logic and a special type of temporal logic. It is suitable both for imperative and purely functional programs. The system was designed for program development using the correctness by construction paradigm.

2.1   Proof Structure

Specification statements of the system consist of progress and safety properties. Progress properties are built up of a *pre-* and a *postcondition*. In case of imperative programs, a progress property states that whenever the program reaches a state where the precondition holds, it has to reach eventually a state where the postcondition is true. Purely functional programs have no state, therefore pre- and postconditions in that case define the relation between the inputs and outputs of functions: For all possible input that makes the precondition true, the function's result has to satisfy the postcondition.

While the semantics of pre- and postconditions are different for imperative and functional programs, their refinement rules are identical. We use three refinement rules to split up a specification: sequence, selection and induction.

Sequence introduce an intermediate step in-between the precondition and postcondition. If we can prove that an imperative program makes the intermediate condition true starting from the precondition, and reaches the postcondition from the intermediate one, then we can conclude that it eventually reaches the postcondition from the precondition. In case of purely functional programs, the sequencing rule is even more simple: If we can prove the intermediate condition from the precondition and the postcondition from the intermediate one, we have proved the postcondition from the precondition. These sequencing rules can easily be generalized for more than one intermediate steps as well.

In case of *selection*, we split the precondition into several conditions, such that their disjunction follows from the precondition. If the imperative program reaches the postcondition from each of these conditions, it reaches the postcondition from the precondition as well. In case of purely functional programs, this rule splits the proof in several cases.

While proving a theorem in this system, we may use the statement of the theorem itself with different arguments in order to complete the proof. In order to ensure the well-foundness of the *induction* one has to prove that the new set of arguments is positive and strictly less than the original arguments of the theorem (according to a suitable ordering on the possible values and a zero element).

In case of imperative programs, progress properties can be extended by safety properties. A program satisfies such an extended property, if during the progress from the precondition to the postcondition, in case the safety property becomes true it remains true at least until the program reaches the postcondition. In order to prove a safety property attached to a progress property, the system checks all the temporal axioms used to complete the proof of the progress property if they maintain the safety property.

A property and its proof can be represented by a proof tree. The root of the tree is the property to prove. If the proof is a sequence or selection, the proof obligations we mentioned earlier will be the child nodes in the tree. These child nodes may also have children according to the corresponding proof. A leaf of the proof tree is either a inductive application of the theorem in the root, or an *axiom*.

2.2   Program Extraction

Axioms may describe mathematical properties of functions (eg. transitivity of equality) or properties of elementary constructs of the target programming language (eg. temporal properties of an assignment). In the second case, a representation of the programming construct is encapsulated in the axiom. This representation can be arbitrary data structure, its form is up to the programmer who implements the axiomatization of the given target programming language.

A theorem to prove is in fact a specification of the program to develop. Using the constructs described in the previous subsection, one creates a proof for the theorem in a top-down manner. Proofs can be completed by using some of the available axioms.

The proof checker algorithm provided by the system validates this proof. Its result is either a set of error messages, or a list of program fragments collected from the axioms used in the proof. This algorithm terminates for all proofs and is sound (i.e. it only accepts valid proofs). This proof checking algorithm is implemented by the `validate` function mentioned in section 3.4.

The list of program fragments collected by the proof checker can be transformed to program text according to the syntax of the target programming language. This transformation is completely independent of the proof system itself, it has to be provided by the library supporting the given target language. This design makes the proof system highly extensible.

Correctness by construction means, that the generated program fulfils the specification provided at the beginning of the development process. The soundness of the program has two conditions: both the implementation of the proof system and the axioms about the target programming language have to be sound.

3 Design Decisions

Creating an embedded language consists of the following tasks:

- *representing* the constructs of the embedded language using the features of the host language,
- creating *frontend*, that is, a library that provides an easy way for users to express embedded language programs,
- writing *backend*, that is, a compiler, interpreter or some other program that implements the semantics of the embedded language.

The current section of this paper discusses the first task, the *representation* of the language constructs. Section 4 presents briefly the *frontend* library. The *backend* is mainly out of scope of this paper, but the proof checking rules and basics of program extraction are informally presented in section 2 (see [11] for formal discussion).

If we want to embed a proof system like the one described in section 2, we need a host language that makes symbolic manipulation of expressions and formulas easy. This suggests declarative languages. We used Haskell, because it is an advanced functional programming language with a sophisticated type system. In addition, Haskell has a minimalistic syntax that makes it especially suitable for being a host language.

We had to make several design decisions while embedding the proof system in Haskell. In this section we summarize the most important ones by presenting solutions we applied together with other techniques that have turned out to be not or hardly applicable for our problems.

3.1 Shallow or Deep Embedding

Shallow embedding means that entities of the embedded language and the host language coincide. In our case this means that functions in the specification statements would be Haskell functions. A logical formula then could be a Haskell function of return type *Bool*. This would be an option only if Haskell supported symbolic manipulation of functions, which is not the case. It is not possible to infer a == c from a == b && b == c if these are Haskell expressions of type *Bool*. The inference function would have type

```
infer :: Bool -> Bool -> Bool
```

and it would not be possible to observe the structure of the expressions passed to this function.

Deep embedding encodes the constructs of the embedded language using data types. A naive representation of expressions and formulas could be implemented using the following data structures.

```
data Expression
  = Symbol String
  | Appl Expression Expression
  | Lambda String Expression

data Formula
  = Literal Expression
  | And Formula Formula
  | Or Formula Formula
  | Not Formula
  | Forall String Formula
  | Exists String Formula
```

The previous formula a == b && b == c could then be encoded as follows[1].

```
And
  (Literal $ Appl (Appl (Symbol "==") (Symbol "a")) (Symbol "b"))
  (Literal $ Appl (Appl (Symbol "==") (Symbol "b")) (Symbol "c"))
```

In case of deep embedding, an inference function would get Formulas as parameters and could perform pattern matching on them:

```
infer :: Formula -> Formula -> Bool
```

3.2 Typed Expressions

Types and static type checking is crucial for our proof system. Partly because writing sound axioms or meaningful specification is quite difficult using expressions without types, partly because the system mainly targets statically typed programming languages.

---

[1] The $ operator in Haskell stands for function application and it has low precedence. It can be used to spare parentheses: One writes `f $ g $ h x` instead of `f (g (h x))`.

One possibility to introduce typed expressions is to extend the data types shown above with type parameters. In order to do this we need an extra data type that represents the possible types.

```
data Type
  = Simple String
  | Arrow Type Type
```

This `Type` type could then be used to extend the `Expression` data type:

```
data Expression
  = Symbol String Type
  | Appl Expression Expression
  | Lambda String Expression
```

This approach unfortunately allows ill-typed expressions like the following one.

```
Appl (Symbol "f" $ Arrow (Simple "Int") (Simple "Char"))
     (Symbol "x" $ Simple "Bool")
```

This means that we need a type-checking function that computes the types of compound expressions and finds type errors. Writing such a function is a straightforward but tiresome task.

Fortunately, we can use the type checking algorithm of the Haskell compiler to perform this work for us. There is an extension to the Haskell language supported by the Glasgow Haskell Compiler tools, called generalized algebraic data types (GADTs)[16]. In case of GADTs, the type parameters are flexible in the constructors' types, making it possible to implement typing rules for our expressions.

```
data Expression t where
  Symbol :: String -> Expression a
  Appl   :: Expression (a -> b) -> Expression a -> Expression b
  Lambda :: String -> Expression b -> Expression (a -> b)
```

This way we can reuse Haskell types for our expressions and can use the Haskell compiler to catch type errors. Here is our previous ill-typed expression encoded using the new representation.

```
Appl (Symbol "f" :: Expression (Int -> Char))
     (Symbol "e" :: Expression Bool)
```

The Haskell compiler reports in this case the following error.

```
Couldn't match expected type 'Int' against inferred type 'Bool'
...
```

Note, that the Haskell compiler cannot always infer all types. Sometimes the user has to explicitly declare the types of certain expressions; however, this burden is outweighed by the safety that static type checking provides.

3.3   Parameters

Embedding of parametric entities. Let us observe how to implement beta-reduction for expressions defined in the previous section. In order to perform the reduction

```
Appl (Lambda ''x'' $ Symbol ''x'') (Symbol ''a'')     ⟶     Symbol ''a''
```

we have to find all occurrences of Symbol ''x'' inside the λ-expression and replace them with the right-hand side of the application. Furthermore, such a reduction function has to take care of variable scopes and name capture too.

Again, this work can be saved by making use of the Haskell machinery. The idea is to use a Haskell function inside the lambda expression. We change the declaration of the Lambda constructor to the following one.

```
Lambda :: (Expression a -> Expression b) -> Expression (a -> b)
```

This way, the expression seen above is encoded as follows.

```
Appl (Lambda $ \x -> x) (Symbol a)
```

Implementation of reduction[2] becomes quite straightforward: We have to apply the function inside the λ-expression on the second argument of the application.

```
reduce :: Expression a -> Expression a
reduce (Symbol s) = Symbol s
reduce (Appl (Lambda f) e) = reduce $ f e
reduce (Appl f e) = Appl (reduce f) (reduce e)
reduce (Lambda f) = Lambda $ \x -> reduce $ f x
```

The same technique can be applied in several cases while embedding our proof system. For example, the parameters of universal and existential quantifiers can also be Haskell functions from expressions to formulas. It is possible to make use of this technique to add parameters to theorems too.

The next code snippet shows the altered representation of formulas. As expressions have a type parameter which formulas does not, we need a GADT again.

```
data Formula where
    Literal :: (Expression Bool) -> Formula
    Forall  :: (Expression a -> Formula) -> Formula
    Exists  :: (Expression a -> Formula) -> Formula
    ...
```

Note, how simple it is to express that an expression inside a literal has to have boolean type. Also note, that the type variable a in the types of Forall and

---

[2] Note, that the goal of the reduce function is just to simplify expressions to help the validation of proofs. It is not an interpreter that could be used to evaluate expressions.

Exists are unbound. According to the rules of Haskell, there is an implicit universal quantifier on these type variables.

However, there is a possible problem with this approach. The parameter of the **Forall** constructor may be a function that performs pattern matching on its parameter and results in different formulas depending on it, like in the following example.

```
Forall $ \expr -> case expr of
    Symbol "x"  -> Literal $ Symbol "a"
    otherwise   -> Literal $ Symbol "b"
```

It is not clear which logical formula is encoded by this example. The solution is to forbid the user to observe the internal structure of expressions. This can be achieved by hiding the constructors and any other function that deconstructs formulas and expressions. The frontend of the language should export functions only to construct them.

Unique parameters. We have implemented the simple inference function `infer :: Formula -> Formula -> Bool`, that tries to infer a formula from another one. Such a function can be sound, but, of course, cannot be complete. It returns **True** if it succeeds to prove the inference and **False** otherwise, but in the latter case it is still possible that the second formula is a consequence of the first one. The algorithm is described in detail in [10]. It first converts formulas to a generalized conjunctive normal form. The inference is first done between conjunctive chains, then between disjunctive chains and finally between formulas which are either literals or quantified formulas. This inference algorithm performs well, if the proof requires axioms of propositional logic only, but its capabilities are limited when working with quantified formulas.

To conclude `Forall $ \x -> p x` $\Rightarrow$ `Forall $ \y -> q y`, the algorithm tries to prove `p t` $\Rightarrow$ `q t`, where `t` is a parameter not contained in `p` and `q`. We extend the data type **Expression** with a new constructor[3]:

```
Parameter :: Id -> Expression a
```

This constructor is not visible in the frontend of the language, it can only be used by the proof checking algorithm. The argument of a **Parameter** has to be a unique identifier. There are basically two solutions for generating such a fresh identifier: an elementary one and one using monads.

In the first solution, it is handy to use integers as **Id**s. We can generate a fresh identifier by first applying `p` and `q` to a dummy, parameter-free expression, and then traversing the resulting formulas to find the maximal integer used as an identifier of a **Parameter** in any of them. Adding one to this maximum gives a suitable identifier for the fresh parameter we need.

The same solution can be applied when plugging fresh parameters into a parametric proof in order to validate it. However, traversing huge proofs each time when a fresh identifier is needed can be inefficient.

---

[3] If we used the **Symbol** constructor for parameters, the generated identifiers could clash with the user-defined ones.

In the other solution Id is the Unique data type from the standard Haskell Data.Unique module. The module exports the function newUnique :: IO Unique, that generates a fresh identifier within the *IO monad* each time we call it. This way the generation of a fresh parameter is possible in constant time, but the inference algorithm (and consequently the entire proof checking) is monadic. Here is an example code fragment from the inference algorithm.

```
infer :: Formula -> Formula -> IO Bool
infer (Forall e1) (Forall e2) = do
    id <- newUnique
    infer (e1 $ Parameter id) (e2 $ Parameter id)
```

In order to infer one universally quantified formula from another one, this program first generates a new, unique identifier (id), plugs a parameter with this identifier into the quantified expressions and calls the inference function recursively on the results.

3.4 Proof Representation

Data structures. Proofs presented in section 2 can be represented using Haskell data structures in several ways. A series of experiments led us to the relatively compact representation that we describe in this section.

The most important data structure is Statement, consisting of a precondition, a postcondition and safety properties.

```
data Statement
    = Statement
    { pre       :: Formula
    , post      :: Formula
    , safeties  :: [Formula]
    }
```

Precondition and postcondition together form a *progress property*, while each element of the safeties list defines a *safety property* (see section 2).

Leaves of a proof are axioms, and each of them is composed of a statement and a list of programs. A program is a representation of elementary components of the target programming language like assigning value to a variable, passing control, binding etc. These elements are different for each possible target programming language, therefore it is a good idea to pass this type as a parameter.

```
data Axiom prg
    = Axiom
    { axiomStatement  :: Statement
    , axiomProgram    :: [prg]
    }
```

An axiom ax states that axiomStatement ax is valid for any program that contains all elements of axiomProgram ax.

Now we can define a data structure representing the constructs for creating proofs.

```
data Proof prg
    = Step Statement (Proof prg)
    | Sequence [Proof prg]
    | Selection [(Formula,Proof prg)]
    | Call (Axiom prg)
    | ...
```

A step consists of a statement (a sub-goal for example) and its proof, a sequence is list of proof steps, a selection splits the current precondition in several cases and gives a proof for each case, while a call of an axiom completes a branch of the proof. We will shortly alter this data structure a little bit to add an induction alternative.

A theorem contains a statement and its proof.

```
data Theorem prg
    = Theorem
    { theoremStatement   :: Statement
    , theoremProof       :: Proof prg
    }
```

Induction and theorem parameters. Say, p is a predicate on integers with axioms stating that $p(0)$ holds as well as $p(n)$ implies $p(n + 1)$. By a simple inductive proof we can have $p(n)$ for all non-negative ns. This theorem is parametric, n being its parameter and its proof contains induction with parameter $n - 1$.

```
myTheorem :: Expression Int -> Theorem ()
myTheorem n =
    Theorem
    { theoremStatement =
        Statement
        { pre   = n >= 0
        , post  = p n
        , ...
        }
    , theoremProof =
        ...
        Induction (n-1)
        ...
    }
```

That is, we have to extend the `Proof` data structure with a new constructor:

```
data Proof prg param
    = ...
    | Induction param
```

As we have to bound the type variable `param`, the data type `Proof` gets a second type parameter. Consequently, the data type `Theorem` also needs this second type parameter.

The `validate` function checks if a given (parametric) theorem and its proof is sound or not. If `validate myTheorem` succeeds, the theorem is valid for any integer n, so passing anything of type `Expression Int` to myTheorem results in a valid theorem.

Note, that `validate` gets a function argument of type (`a -> Theorem prg a`). Let us call this argument the parametric theorem. First, a parameter p with unique identifier is generated (see section 3.3) and plugged into the parametric theorem. Then the proof of the resulting non-parametric theorem is checked. When an `Induction p'` leaf of this proof is encountered, the proof checker plugs the inductive parameter `p'` into the parametric theorem and uses its statement as inductive hypothesis.

The proof checking algorithm also enforces well-foundness of inductions. In order to achieve this, we restrict the `param` type parameter of `Theorem` and `Proof` such that the values of the type have to be linearly ordered and there has to be a zero element. This way, the proof checker can verify if the inductive parameter is non-negative ($p' \geq 0$) and less than the original one ($p' < p$) in order to enforce well-foundness.

As described in section 2.2, the `validate` function returns a list of elementary programs if the proof is valid. Its result is returned inside the IO monad, because of the need for unique identifiers. Using the IO monad is handy also for reporting errors. Thus, the type signature of the proof-checker function is the following:

```
validate :: (param -> Theorem prg param) -> IO [prg]
```

4   Frontend

In section 3 we discussed design decisions related to the representation of proofs as Haskell data structures. In order to make the embedding of the proof language complete, we have to create a frontend. It is a library consisting of functions that programmers can use to construct expressions, formulas and proofs.

As discussed earlier, in our case it is also important to completely hide the representation, so programmers can construct proofs using the frontend only, in order to avoid erroneous formulas like the one in section 3.3.

4.1   Frontend for Expressions and Formulas

Let us try to encode the formula $\forall p \exists q \; p + q = 0$ in our embedded language. If we use only the representation presented in the previous section, we get the following lengthy code.

```
Forall $ \p -> Exists $ \q -> Literal $
  Appl
    (Appl
      (Symbol "==")
      (Appl (Appl (Symbol "+") p) q))
    (Symbol "0")
```

The `Forall` constructor needs a function parameter from expressions to formulas. This function is the lambda expression `\p -> Exists ...`, where the argument of `Exists` is a similar function. However, in that function we need the `Literal` constructor to convert an expression to a formula. Functions have one argument in our representation. That is, functions like addition and equality are represented in a curried form, which is the reason for using the `Appl` constructor four times in the expression.

Instead of `Symbol "0"` we would like to write simply 0. In Haskell an integer literal can be of any type if that type is instance of the `Num` class. In order to make our `Expression` type an instance of this class, we have to define at least addition, multiplication, absolute value and signum functions for our data type, as well as the `fromInteger` function, which converts an integer to `Expression Int`. The latter function is straightforward to implement:

```
fromInteger i = Symbol $ show i
```

The `show` function used here converts an integer to string.

The mentioned arithmetic operations have to build compound expressions of their parameters instead of "doing computation", and their implementations are similar to each other. As an example, we present the definition of addition.

```
e1 + e2 = Appl (Appl (Symbol "+") e1) e2
```

The equality function is also used in our example formula. Haskell's standard equality returns a boolean value, but we need `Expression Bool` instead. This means that we should hide the standard (`==`) operator and define it similarly to addition.

The expression inside the literal can now be written conveniently. We can also make the quantifiers easier to use by removing the need for the explicit conversion from boolean expressions to formulas. We have achieved this by defining the class `ToFormula` providing the function `toFormula` which converts from a given type to `Formula`. It is easy to create instances of this class for the types `Expression Bool`[4] and `Formula`. In the former case `toFormula` is identity, in the latter case it is the `Literal` constructor. Given these instances, we can define the `exists` and `forall` functions such that they get parameters of type `Expression a -> t`, where `t` is a type that is instance of the `ToFormula` class.

```
exists :: (ToFormula t) => (Expression a -> t) -> Formula
exists f = Exists $ \p -> toFormula (f p)
```

---

[4] `Expression Bool` can only be instance of a class if the Haskell extension `FlexibleInstances` is enabled.

Using this frontend, we can encode the example formula much more conveniently:

```
forall $ \p -> exists $ \q -> p + q == 0
```

4.2 Frontend for Proofs

As an example let us consider the axiom stating the transitivity of equality.

```
eqTrans a b c =
   Axiom
   { axiomStatement =
       (Statement
           (a == b && b == c)
           (Literal $ a == c)
           []
       )
   , axiomProgram = []
   }
```

According to the semantics of axioms given in section 3.4, eqTrans states that the axiomStatement is valid for any program containing all elements of the axiomProgram list. As the statement expresses a mathematical property of equality, which is true regardless of the program being verified, the axiomProgram field of this axiom is an empty list.

To make statements more convenient to write, we have created a set of operators like the following one.

```
infix 0 =>.
(=>.) :: (ToFormula t, ToFormula u) => t -> u -> Statement
pre =>. post = Statement (toFormula pre) (toFormula post) []
```

The resulting "syntax" for axioms is then the following.

```
eqTrans a b c = Axiom
   (a == b && b == c =>. a == c)
   []
```

We can use this axiom to prove the following theorem.

```
myTheorem (a,b,c,d)
   = Theorem
       (Statement
           (a == b && b == c && c == d)
           (Literal $ a == d)
           []
       )
       (Sequence
           [ Call (eqTrans a b c)
           , Call (eqTrans a c d)
           ]
       )
```

First of all, the previously defined =>. operator can be used here too, to shorten the statement of the theorem. To make proof construction easier, we have defined the class ToProof with the function toProof that can turn different data structures to a proof. If we make an instance of this class for lists, we will be able to encode a sequence with a list. For selection and other constructs we need further instances.

This class can be implemented in an elegant way using the TypeFamilies extension of Haskell. This feature allows us to declare type functions for a class and define these types in each instance. In our case these type functions will give the two type parameters of the Proof data structure.

```
class ToProof t where
    type Prg t
    type Param t
    toProof :: t -> Proof (Prg t) (Param t)
```

First we need Proof prg param to be instance of this class. The type functions Prg and Param will return the prg and param type parameters, while toProof will be the identity function.

In our example, we will use the instance for lists.

```
instance ToProof t => ToProof [t] where
    type Prg [t] = Prg t
    type Param [t] = Param t
    toProof ps = Sequence $ map toProof ps
```

This instance requires that the elements of the list can also be transformed to proofs. The type parameters are that of the type parameters of the list elements, and the list is transformed to a sequence by applying the toProof function recursively to all elements of the list.

To complete our example, instead of the Theorem constructor, we need a function that can accept anything in its second parameter that can be transformed to a proof.

```
theorem :: ToProof t =>
    Statement -> t -> Theorem (Prg t) (Param t)
theorem s p = Theorem s $ toProof p
```

Note how the type functions of the ToProof class are used in the type signature of this function.

Having implemented these parts of the frontend, we can already write our example theorem in a much more comprehensible form.

```
myTheorem (a,b,c,d) = theorem
    (a == b && b == c && c == d =>. a == d)
    [ Call (eqTrans a b c)
    , Call (eqTrans a c d)
    ]
```

This theorem can be checked by the `validate` function. It confirms that the proof is sound and extracts an *empty program* from this proof, because this theorem is a purely mathematical one.

Of course, we have presented only a small subset of the frontend library, but these examples should give the general idea.

5   Summary and Discussion

5.1   Conclusions

An earlier implementation of our proof system was created as a standalone language using C++. During the work presented in this paper we experienced that using an advanced functional language with a smart type system enhanced the implementation of our proof system. The code became shorter and easier to maintain. We had the impression that development in C++ became more and more difficult as code complexity grew, while in Haskell the main effort was needed to create a suitable representation of expressions, formulas and proofs. Once the right design decisions were made, writing code became almost trivial.

The Haskell implementation yields shorter and less complex code because of the following reasons:

- In case of an embedded language, there is no need for lexer and parser.
- Type checking and scope analysis is done by the Haskell compiler due to the smart expression, formula and proof representation described in section 3.
- The proof checker backend can be implemented in a more elegant way using a declarative language compared to an imperative/object-oriented one.

Additionally, as a consequence of the embedding, Haskell itself became a meta language on top of the embedded one: One can use any feature of Haskell to write a function that generates a proof. This way we have got advanced tools for free to build tactics. These meta-language elements had to be implemented in the standalone version of our system, which is a task commensurable with the implementation of the proof language itself.

Only few problems were easier to solve using an imperative language. For example, a simple problem like the need for unique identifiers, which is trivial to solve in an imperative language, forced us to turn a part of the Haskell implementation monadic. Another issue is performance. Although we have not encountered problems concerning the speed or memory consumption of our system yet, it seems that it may be easier to optimize the imperative implementation. The Haskell version is much more abstract, but at the same time we are more dependent on the optimization technologies of the Haskell compiler.

The most tricky part of the embedding is clearly to define the "syntax" of the language by implementing the frontend library. Even if Haskell's own syntax is unobtrusive, it is sometimes harder to define convenient frontend functions than to invent own syntax and implement that with a context-free grammar.

5.2   Related Work

Proof systems for imperative languages usually take different approaches compared to our system. There are automatic provers like [23] and [8] which are limited by the fact that proving a program's soundness is not a decidable problem. Other educational [22] or industrial [6] projects include interactive theorem provers to verify a program already implemented. The philosophy of the B-method [5] is similar to that of our system: It can be used to derive programs from specifications. However, it includes own languages both for specification and program constructions, and proposes interactive theorem provers for discharging proof obligations.

For functional programs we can also find interactive provers, like *Sparkle* [9]. A common feature that this system shares with our one is, that it also uses a functional language (Clean) to express specifications. In fact, the prover only adds the equality as predicate, otherwise the theorems to prove can be composed of functions defined in Clean. The difference from our specification language is twofold: First, in our system it is possible to use functions which are axiomatized only and have no executable implementation. Secondly, expressions of Sparkle theorems are built of Clean expressions while in our case these are data structures because of deep embedding. The purpose of the two proof systems are also different: Sparkle can be used to verify properties of previously implemented Clean functions, while in our system one derives programs from specifications. An interesting common feature of the two systems is the support for temporal logic: There is an extension of Sparkle [15] that supports temporal operators.

Using the type system of functional languages to express specifications is another connected approach. This can be achieved by dependent type systems, used for example by *Epigram* [19] or *Agda* [21], and also using *subtype marks* [17]. In these cases the type signatures express a theorem and the function definitions are the proofs. In our case the program is generated from the proof, but the two entities do not coincide. Each approach has its advantages: Proofs, which are in fact programs, are executable and may also be easier for programmers to write, while in our case it is easier to add new target languages to the system. It is an interesting fact, that it is possible to simulate dependent typing using Haskell [18], although its type system does not support it directly.

As we pointed out in this paper, embedded language development requires less code to write and this makes it easier to experiment with different language constructs. Therefore embedding is a popular approach especially in case of domain specific languages (DSL). At the *languages* section of the *Hackage library database* [3], there are several embedded languages. We summarize here those dealing with similar implementation problems discussed in this paper and compare their solutions to ours.

- *Atom* is a DSL for embedded hard real-time applications. Expressions in Atom are typed similarly to our solution but there is a fixed set of functions and there is no lambda abstraction. The frontend of the language is monadic.
- *Feldspar* [1] is an embedded language for digital signal processing. It is also a deep embedding with typed expressions consisting of a fixed set of operations without lambda abstraction. Its frontend re-implements standard list

operations such that it performs fusion to optimize programs. Like in our case, unique identifiers are needed to build the internal representation. Here, this problem is solved by the technique called observable sharing [7]. Its implementation also uses Haskell's `Unique` type but this use of the IO monad is converted to a pure computation using the `unsafePerformIO` function.

- *ForSyDe* [2] is a library to design systems consisting of processes and communications channels carrying signals. Both types of embedding are applied in this project: The shallow one for simulation, the deep one for compilation with VHDL and GraphML backends.
- *HJavaScript* and *HJScript* are core and frontend libraries of deep embedding of JavaScript in Haskell. Typed expressions are similar to our ones but there is a fixed set of operations and lambda abstraction is not present. Variables have names of type `String` serving as unique identifiers.
- *LambdaCalculator* is a small library for working with lambda calculus. Expressions are embedded in a way we mentioned in section 3.1 to demonstrate deep embedding. This library demonstrates that using this technique one has to write transformations like β-reduction manually instead of reusing Haskell's runtime support.

All the packages at the Hackage database under the *theorem provers* section, contain deeply embedded formulas. As most of these projects (*Ivor*, *Logic-TPTP* and *Pesca*) include parsers and pretty printers instead of implementing embedded languages, the formulas are represented essentially with their syntax tree. The only library we found techniques similar to ours was *Dedukti*. This project uses the technique described in section 3.3 to encode application and λ-abstraction for untyped terms.

5.3   Future Work

We summarize here the most important ideas we would like to implement in the future in order to improve our proof system.

- Currently there is a list-based frontend for proof development. We would like to experiment with a monadic frontend which may be more convenient to use.
- As we discussed in this paper, by embedding our proof system to Haskell we get a powerful meta language. We would like to study these possibilities in more detail and implement a library that supports proof generation.
- In section 2 we pointed out that the refinement rules of our system are also suitable to develop purely functional programs. We plan to create more case studies to test this possibility and identify proof construction schemes for purely functional programs as we did earlier in case of imperative ones.

References

1. Home of Feldspar: `http://feldspar.sourceforge.net`
2. Home of ForSyDe, `http://www.ict.kth.se/forsyde`

3. Home of HackageDB, http://hackage.haskell.org
4. Home of LaCert, http://deva.web.elte.hu/LaCert
5. Abrial, J.-R.: The B-book: assigning programs to meanings. Cambridge University Press, New York (1996)
6. Beckert, B., Hähnle, R., Schmitt, P.H. (eds.): Verification of Object-Oriented Software. LNCS (LNAI), vol. 4334. Springer, Heidelberg (2007)
7. Claessen, K., Sands, D.: Observable sharing for functional circuit description. In: Thiagarajan, P.S., Yap, R.H.C. (eds.) ASIAN 1999. LNCS, vol. 1742, pp. 62–73. Springer, Heidelberg (1999)
8. Cok, D.R., Kiniry, J.R.: ESC/Java2: Uniting ESC/Java and JML. In: Barthe, G., Burdy, L., Huisman, M., Lanet, J.-L., Muntean, T. (eds.) CASSIS 2004. LNCS, vol. 3362, pp. 108–128. Springer, Heidelberg (2005)
9. de Mol, M., van Eekelen, M., Plasmeijer, R.: Theorem proving for functional programmers, Sparkle: A functional theorem prover. In: Arts, T., Mohnen, M. (eds.) IFL 2002. LNCS, vol. 2312, pp. 55–72. Springer, Heidelberg (2002)
10. Dévai, G.: Programming language elements for proof construction. In: Volume of abstracts of the 6th Joint Conference on Mathematics and Computer Science (2006)
11. Dévai, G.: Programming language elements for correctness proofs. Acta Cybernetica (accepted for publication 2007)
12. Dévai, G.: Meta programming on the proof level. Acta Universitatis Sapientiae, Informatica 1(1), 15–34 (2009)
13. Dévai, G., Csörnyei, Z.: Separation logic style reasoning in a refinement based language. In: Proceedings of the 7th International Conference on Applied Informatics (2007) (to appear)
14. Dévai, G., Pataki, N.: A tool for formally specifying the C++ standard template library. Annales Universitatis Scientiarum Budapestinensis de Rolando Eötvös Nominatae, Sectio Computatorica 31, 147–166 (2009)
15. Horváth, Z., Kozsik, T., Tejfel, M.: Extending the Sparkle core language with object abstraction. Acta Cybernetica 17, 419–445 (2005)
16. Peyton Jones, S., Vytiniotis, D., Weirich, S., Washburn, G.: Simple unification-based type inference for GADTs. In: ICFP 2006: Proceedings of the eleventh ACM SIGPLAN International Conference on Functional Programming, pp. 50–61. ACM Press, New York (2006)
17. Kozsik, T.: Proving Program Properties Specified with Subtype Marks. In: Horváth, Z., Zsók, V., Butterfield, A. (eds.) IFL 2006. LNCS, vol. 4449, pp. 163–180. Springer, Heidelberg (2007)
18. McBride, C.: Faking it: Simulating dependent types in Haskell. Journal of Functional Programming 12(5), 375–392 (2002)
19. McBride, C.: Epigram: Practical programming with dependent types. In: Advanced Functional Programming, pp. 130–170 (2004)
20. Morgan, C.: Programming from specifications, 2nd edn. Prentice Hall International (UK) Ltd. Englewood Cliffs (1994)
21. Norell, U.: Towards a practical programming language based on dependent type theory. PhD thesis, Chalmers University of Technology (2007)
22. Schreiner, W.: The RISC ProofNavigator: A proving assistant for program verification in the classroom. Formal Aspects of Computing 21(3) (2009)
23. Winkler, J.: The frege program prover FPP. Internationales Wissenschaftliches Kolloquium 42, 116–121 (1997)

Impact Analysis of Erlang Programs Using Behaviour Dependency Graphs*

Melinda Tóth, István Bozó, Zoltán Horváth, László Lövei,
Máté Tejfel, and Tamás Kozsik

Eötvös Loránd University, Budapest, Hungary
{toth_m,bozo_i,hz,lovei,matej,kto}@inf.elte.hu

Abstract. During the lifetime of a software product certain changes could be performed on its source code. After those changes a regression test should be performed, which is the most expensive part of the software development cycle. This paper focuses on programs written in a dynamic functional programming language Erlang, and discusses a mechanism that could select those test cases, which are affected by a change, i.e. altering the program on some point may have impact on the result/behaviour of those test cases. In the result of that analysis it is possible to reduce the number of necessary test cases, and after modifying the source code, just a subset of the test cases should be retested. The discussed approach introduces a behaviour dependency graph for Erlang programs to represent the dependencies in the source code. The impact of a change can be calculated by traversing the graph.

1 Introduction

Changes often happen in a software lifetime. These changes can be done manually by a programmer or using a refactoring tool. The phase "refactoring" [3] introduces a meaning preserving source code transformation, thus you change the structure of a program without altering its external behaviour. Refactoring could be done manually by a programmer or using a refactoring tool. The former case is tedious and error prone, the latter is safer and faster. A refactoring tool guarantees that the transformation does not change the meaning of the program and all the necessary changes will happen. However refactoring in Erlang [2] is not straightforward. The language is dynamically typed, so the syntactic and static semantic information sometimes may be not enough to guarantee a meaning preserving transformation, and the programmer want to test the behaviour of the transformed program. Since testing is a very expensive part of the software development process, we want to help the programmers to reduce the number of test cases which should be performed after a transformation or a sequence of transformations. Therefore we try to find the affected parts in the source code by analyzing the spread of the impact of performed changes. Assume we have found the affected code parts, then only a subset of test cases should be retested, those which are affected by the change.

---

* Supported by TECH_08_A2-SZOMIN08, ELTE IKKK, and Ericsson Hungary.

Z. Horváth, R. Plasmeijer, and V. Zsók (Eds.): CEFP 2009, LNCS 6299, pp. 372–390, 2010.

To find the affected parts we have to propagate the change of some data, therefore we introduce a behaviour dependency graph. During the generation of this graph we use static syntactic and semantic information based on the semantic program graph of the RefactorErl.

RefactorErl [6,5] is a refactoring tool for Erlang. To represent the source code the tool uses its own semantic program graph model, which contains lexical, syntactic and semantic information about the loaded Erlang programs. The graph is based on the AST. RefactorErl uses its own layout preserving parser to generate the syntax tree, then different semantic analyzers (function, variable, record, etc) extend the syntax tree to semantic program graph. The constructed program graph provides good interface for further source code analysis.

The rest of this paper is structured as follows. In Section 2 a motivating example is given. Section 3 introduces the used model of Erlang programs. Then the Section 4 introduces the behaviour dependency graph, the method of constructing the behaviour dependency edges and the way of retrieving dependency information from this graph. Section 5 presents related work, and Section 6 concludes the paper and discusses future work.

2   Motivating Example

For the sake of simplicity we demonstrate our mechanism in a more general example. We do not transform the source code by a refactoring and analyze its impact, rather we modify an element of a list (Figure 1 and 2) and then we estimate the impact of the data change to determine the test cases which should be retested.

Consider the following example (Figure 1), where we define the `tag_add/1` recursive function, which transforms the elements of the given list to a tagged tuple. We expect from this function, that it does not alter the length of the given list. The `test_tag_add/2` function is intended to describe this property of the `tag_add/2` function. The `len/1` function calculates and returns the length of the given list. In our example the `tag_list/0` function calls the `tag_add/2` function with a list containing two integers: [1,2].

Assume, that the programmer modify the first element of the list [1,2] in the body of `tag_list/0`. This value flows into the variable H1 (in `tag_add/2`) through the list construct. The result of the `tag_add/2` function is a list which spine does not depend on the value of H1 variable, however the elements of this result list depend on the value of H1. Therefore, we have to detect whether the elements of the resulted list are used elsewhere in the code. It can be used those point in the program where the `tag_add/2` function is called. The `test_tag_add/2` function calls the `tag_add/2` function, thus it uses its return value, so the elements of the resulted list may be used. The `test_tag_add/2` function passes the result of the `tag_add(L1, Tag)` function call as an argument for the `len/1` function and calculates the length of the resulted list with `len/1`, but during the calculation `len/1` does not use the value of the elements coming form its argument (in the body of `len/1` the values of the elements

```
tag_add([], _Tag) ->
    [];
tag_add([H1|T1], Tag)->
    [{Tag, H1} | tag_add(T1, Tag)].

tag_list() ->
    tag_add([1,2], integer).

test_tag_add(L1, Tag)->
    len(L1) == len(tag_add(L1, Tag)).

len([]) ->
    0;
len([_H | T]) ->
    1 + len(T).
```

Fig. 1. The definition of `tag_add/2`

(_H) of the parameter list are not used). Therefore the result of the `len(L1)` and `len(tag_add(L1))` function calls do not depend on the values of the elements coming from the L1 list and the return value of the `tag_add(L1)` function call. We can see, that changing any element of the list [1,2] under writing the program does not have any impact on the result of these function calls, thus does not have any impact on the return value and on the behaviour of the `test_tag_add/2` function, so we must not retest it.

However the elements of the list depend on the operation (a tuple constructor), in this case the structure of the list is independent of this operation. The change of one list element does not always has impact on the structure of the list or the context of the list usage.

In the second part of the example we give the definition of a similar function, but the behaviour of these functions are different. On Figure 2 we define the `tag_filter/2` recursive function, which filters the elements of the list with a given tag `Tag`. This function selects a sublist of the given list, it may throw out element from the list. Thus changing the elements of the parameter list may affect the spine of the resulted list. This function may keep or decrease the length of the list (depending on the given tag and the content of the given list), but it can never increase it. The `test_tag_filter/2` function is intended to describe this property of the `tag_filter/2` function. The `filter_list/0` function calls the `tag_filter/2` function to select the elements with key `integer` from the list [{integer, 1}, {atom, a}].

Assume, that the programmer change the first element of the list in the function call `tag_filter([{integer, 1}, {atom, a}], integer)`. The impact of this modification flows into the H2 variable, in the same way as in the first part of our example where the elements of the [1,2] list flows into the H1 variable, but after this point the difference between the `tag_add/2` and `tag_filter/2` functions shows up. The return value of the `tag_filter/2` function depends on the

```
tag_filter([], _Tag) ->
    [];
tag_filter([H2|T2], Tag) ->
    case H2 of
        {Tag, _Elem} -> [H2 | tag_filter(T2, Tag)];
        _        -> tag_filter(T2, Tag)
    end.

filter_list() ->
    tag_filter([{integer, 1}, {atom, a}], integer).

test_tag_filter(L2, Tag) ->
    len(L2) >= len(tag_filter(L2, Tag)).

len([]) ->
    0;
len([_H | T]) ->
    1 + len(T).
```

Fig. 2. The definition of `tag_filter/2`

elements passed as its arguments, because the case-expression depends on the result of the H2 expression, thus the return value of the `tag_filter/2`function depends on the elements of its parameter list (H2 gets its value from that list). The expression `len(tag_filter(L2, Tag))` comprehends a function call of `tag_filter/2`, which return value depends on the elements of its parameter list, thus the result of the entire expression depends transitively on the elements of the argument list. Therefore, any change on the elements of the input list may have an impact on the `test_tag_filter/2` function.

To detect these dependencies in an Erlang program, we have to define a dependency graph for Erlang. It should contain the data flow edges and behaviour dependency edges, too. The rules when the value or the behaviour of an expression has an impact on an other expression (for example, the case expression in the mentioned example depends on the expression H2) are defined in the following sections.

3   A Partial Model for Erlang Programs

In Section 4 we use the Erlang syntax shown in Figure 3. This syntax is a subset of the Erlang syntax presented in [4]. The symbol P denote the patterns can be used in Erlang, E represents guard expressions and expressions that can be defined in the language, and F denotes the named functions.

The presented syntax contains some simplification:

- Guard expressions are represented as expressions with some restrictions. Guard expressions can contain "guard" built-in function calls or type tests. The infix guard expressions are arithmetic or boolean expressions, or term comparisons. Guards can contain only bound variables.

V ::= variables (including _, the underscore pattern)
A ::= atoms
I ::= integers
K ::= $A \mid I \mid$ other constants (e.g. strings, floats)
P ::= $K \mid V \mid \{P,\dots,P\} \mid [P,\dots,P|P]$
E ::= $K \mid V \mid \{E,\dots,E\} \mid [E,\dots,E|E] \mid [E||P\text{<-}E] \mid P = E \mid$
      $E \circ E \mid (E) \mid E(E,\dots,E) \mid$
      case E **of**
          P **when** E **->** $E,\dots,E;$

          $\vdots$

          P **when** E **->** $E,\dots,E$
      end
F ::= $A(P,\dots,P)$ **when** E **->** $E,\dots,E;$

      $\vdots$

      $A(P,\dots,P)$ **when** E **->** $E,\dots,E.$

Fig. 3. The used Erlang syntax subset

- It does not contain those expression types which can be handled in the same way as one from the presented expressions. For example, the if and try construct can be handled similar as case expressions.
- Those language constructs which are not used to build the data dependency graph also left out from the model. For example, the attributes of an Erlang module do not hold relevant information in the meaning of data dependency.

4   Behaviour Dependency Graph

The most natural way to represent the impact of a change is a graph. To propagate dependency information we build a behaviour dependency graph (BDG).

4.1   The Representation of the Erlang Programs

To build the Erlang dependency graph we use the semantic program graph of RefactorErl. RefactorErl constructs the syntax tree representation of the source code and extends it with static semantic and lexical information. In RefactorErl each expression and pattern node is identified uniquely, we use these nodes as a base of the dependency graph, and the new edges represent the dependency information among them. While constructing the dependency graph we traverse the semantic graph, we take information from the graph, i.e. the structure of the syntax tree (expressions are attached to corresponding code parts), semantic information (the binding structure of the variables, the function calls are linked to the definition of the function, etc). Just those syntactic nodes (mainly the expressions) appear in the dependency graph which are relevant in dependency propagation.

4.2   Dependency Information

All the dependency information is represented in the behaviour dependency graph (BDG). The nodes of the graph are the expressions and patterns from the Erlang source code, the edges of the graph are representing dependency information. There are different kinds of dependency information, that is represented with labeled edges in the graph ($n_1 \overset{label}{\to} n_2$, where n_1 and n_2 are nodes of the graph). The different kinds of dependency edges are the followings:

Definition 1.

- **Data flow edges** – represent data flow between two nodes. There are different kinds of data flow information [7]:
  - Flow edges – $n_1 \overset{f}{\to} n_2$, represents that the result of n_2 can be a copy of the result of n_1. They value exactly the same, and changing the value of n_1 results the same change in the value of n_2.
  - Constructor edges – $n_1 \overset{c_i}{\to} n_2$, represents that the result of n_2 can be a compound value that contains n_1 as the ith element
  - Selector edges – $n_1 \overset{s_i}{\to} n_2$, represents that the result of n_2 can be the ith element of the n_1 compound data
- **Data dependency edges** – $n_1 \overset{d}{\to} n_2$, represents that the result of n_2 can directly depend on the result of n_1. Any change in n_1 may result a data or a behaviour change in n_2.
- **Behaviour dependency edges** – $n_1 \overset{b}{\to} n_2$, represents that the behaviour of n_2 can directly depend on the result of n_1. Any change in n_1 may result a behaviour change in n_2.

Note, that in case of constructing a list e is used as an element label, because we can not usually track their indexes([7]).

The change of a data has an impact on the behaviour of those expressions which depend on that data, thus each data dependency edge also represents behaviour dependency:

$$\frac{n_1 \overset{d}{\to} n_2}{n_1 \overset{b}{\to} n_2} \qquad \text{(d-b-rule)}$$

Similar, most of the flow edges propagate the change of the data, thus propagate dependency. Therefore there are nodes in the graph which are linked with multiply edges.

Examples. The following example demonstrate the differences among the edge types.

```
e:
  case X of
    {ok, Result} -> Result + 2;
    _ when is_list(X) -> X
  end
```

There are different kinds of flow edges in case of this case expression: e. The result of the variable X simply flows to the tuple pattern: X $\overset{f}{\rightarrow}$ {ok, Result}, then while this pattern is a selector, it selects the elements from the tuple: {ok, Result} $\overset{s_1}{\rightarrow}$ ok, {ok, Result} $\overset{s_2}{\rightarrow}$ Result. The result if this case expression is the result of the last expression in its branches, so the result of the last expressions flow into the case expression: Result+2 $\overset{f}{\rightarrow}$ e and X $\overset{f}{\rightarrow}$ e.

The result of the infix expression Result+2 depends on the value of its subexpressions: Result $\overset{d}{\rightarrow}$ Result+2 and 2 $\overset{d}{\rightarrow}$ Result+2.

This simple example also represent behaviour dependency information. The behaviour of the case expression is depend on the behaviour of its subexpressions. If the infix expression can not be evaluated then e also can not be evaluated: Result+2 $\overset{b}{\rightarrow}$ e.

4.3   Dependency Rules

As it is mentioned before, the dependency graph can be constructed based on the syntax tree and semantic information. The construction rules are summarized in Figures 4 and 5, and the major rules are described in the followings. The notation on the figures are: e is an expression (E), g is a guard expression (E), p is a pattern (P) and f is a function (F).

Variable. The only dependency among the variable bindings and the variable occurrences is the data flow (Figure 4: Variable). It does not hold data dependency, or behaviour dependency information.

Match expression. Figure 4: Match exp. shows that the match expression contains a various number of dependency. The value of the expression e simply copied to the pattern p and to the expression e_0, that represented by flow edges. Each expression depends on the behaviour of its subexpressions, thus the match expression also represents behaviour dependency. The expression $p = e$ binds the value of e to p. In case if the variable p is already bound, then the match expression fails if the value of the variable p and the value of e do not match, so the result of the match expression e_0 may depend on the value of e, thus the match expression contains data dependency.

Infix expressions. The infix expression does not propagate data flow information, rather propagates data dependency information (Figure 4: Infix exp.). The result of an infix expression depends on the result of its subexpressions. If one of the subexpressions can not be evaluated, the infix expression can not be evaluated, so it also propagate behaviour dependency information.

Compound data structures. Beside data flow (flow, constructor and selector edges) information compound data structures (tuples, lists) also hold behaviour dependency information (Figures 4: Tuple exp., List exp. and List gen.). The behaviour of a compound data structure depends on the behavior of its elements, i.e. the expression depends on the behaviour of its subexpression.

	Expressions	Graph edges
(Variable)	p is a binding n is a usage of the same variable	$p \xrightarrow{f} n$
(Match exp.)	e_0: $\quad p = e$	$e \xrightarrow{f} e_0, e \xrightarrow{d} e_0, e \xrightarrow{b} e_0$ $e \xrightarrow{f} p$
(Pattern)	p_0: $\quad p_1 = p_2$	$p_0 \xrightarrow{f} p_1$ $p_0 \xrightarrow{f} p_2$
(Infix exp.)	e_0: $\quad e_1 \circ e_2$	$e_1 \xrightarrow{d} e_0, e_1 \xrightarrow{b} e_0$ $e_2 \xrightarrow{d} e_0, e_2 \xrightarrow{b} e_0,$
(Parenthesis)	e_0: $\quad (e)$	$e \xrightarrow{f} e_0, e \xrightarrow{b} e_0$
(Tuple exp.)	e_0: $\quad \{e_1, \ldots, e_n\}$	$e_1 \xrightarrow{c_1} e_0, \ldots, e_n \xrightarrow{c_n} e_0$ $e_1 \xrightarrow{b} e_0, \ldots, e_n \xrightarrow{b} e_0$
(Tuple pat.)	p_0: $\quad \{p_1, \ldots, p_n\}$	$p_0 \xrightarrow{s_1} p_1, \ldots, p_0 \xrightarrow{s_n} p_n$
(List exp.)	e_0: $\quad [e_1, \ldots, e_n | e_{n+1}]$	$e_1 \xrightarrow{c_e} e_0, \ldots, e_n \xrightarrow{c_e} e_0, e_{n+1} \xrightarrow{f} e_0$ $e_1 \xrightarrow{b} e_0, \ldots, e_n \xrightarrow{b} e_0, e_{n+1} \xrightarrow{b} e_0$
(List gen.)	e_0: $\quad [e_1 \| p \leftarrow e_2]$	$e_1 \xrightarrow{c_e} e_0, e_2 \xrightarrow{s_e} p$ $e_1 \xrightarrow{b} e_0, e_2 \xrightarrow{b} e_0$
(List pat.)	p_0: $\quad [p_1, \ldots, p_n | p_{n+1}]$	$p_0 \xrightarrow{s_e} p_1, \ldots, p_0 \xrightarrow{s_e} p_n$ $p_0 \xrightarrow{f} p_{n+1}$
(BIF 1)	e_0: $\quad \mathsf{hd}(e_1)$	$e_1 \xrightarrow{s_e} e_0$ $e_1 \xrightarrow{b} e_0$
(BIF 2)	e_0: $\quad \mathsf{tl}(e_1)$	$e_1 \xrightarrow{f} e_0$ $e_1 \xrightarrow{b} e_0$
(BIF 3)	I is constant, e_0: $\quad \mathsf{element}(I, e_1)$	$e_1 \xrightarrow{s_I} e_0$ $e_1 \xrightarrow{b} e_0$

Fig. 4. Static behaviour dependency graph generation rules

Conditional expressions. The behaviour of a conditional expression, like each complex expression, depends on its subexpressions. Thus each subexpression is linked to the expression with a behaviour dependency edge (Figure 4: Case exp.). For example, the case-expression depends on the behaviour of the expressions of its clauses, because an exception in these expressions propagate an exception into the case-expression.

Function calls. A function call similar to complex expressions, depends on its arguments, but it also depends on the body of the referred function (Figure 5: Fun. call 1). An exception from the body of the function has an impact on the function call expression, too. The result of an actual parameter flows into the corresponding formal parameter of the function, and the return value of the

	Expressions	Graph edges

(Case exp.)	e_0:
	
	    case e of
	        p_1 when $g_1 \to e_1^1, \ldots, e_{l_1}^1$;
	        $\vdots$
	        p_n when $g_n \to e_1^n, \ldots, e_{l_n}^n$
	    end
		$e \xrightarrow{f} p_1, \ldots, e \xrightarrow{f} p_n$
		$e_{l_1}^1 \xrightarrow{f} e_0, \ldots, e_{l_n}^n \xrightarrow{f} e_0$
		$e \xrightarrow{d} e_0, e \xrightarrow{b} e_0$
		$e_1^1 \xrightarrow{b} e_0, \ldots, e_{l_1}^1 \xrightarrow{b} e_0$
		$\vdots$
		$e_1^n \xrightarrow{b} e_0, \ldots, e_{l_n}^n \xrightarrow{b} e_0$
		$g_1 \xrightarrow{b} e_0, \ldots, g_n \xrightarrow{b} e_0$

(Fun. call 1)	e_0:
	    $f(e_1, \ldots, e_n)$
	
	f/n:
	    $f(p_1^1, \ldots, p_n^1)$ when $g_1 \to$
	        $e_1^1, \ldots, e_{l_1}^1$;
	    $\vdots$
	    $f(p_1^m, \ldots, p_n^m)$ when $g_m \to$
	        $e_1^m, \ldots, e_{l_m}^m$.
		$e_1 \xrightarrow{b} e_0, \ldots, e_n \xrightarrow{b} e_0$
		$e_{l_1}^1 \xrightarrow{f} e_0, \ldots, e_{l_m}^m \xrightarrow{f} e_0$
		$e_1 \xrightarrow{f} p_1^1, \ldots, e_1 \xrightarrow{f} p_1^m$
		$\vdots$
		$e_n \xrightarrow{f} p_n^1, \ldots, e_n \xrightarrow{f} p_n^m$
		$e_1^1 \xrightarrow{b} e_0, \ldots, e_{l_1}^1 \xrightarrow{b} e_0$
		$\vdots$
		$e_1^m \xrightarrow{b} e_0, \ldots, e_{l_m}^m \xrightarrow{b} e_0$
		$g_1 \xrightarrow{b} e_0, \ldots, g_m \xrightarrow{b} e_0$

(Fun. call 2)	e_0: $e(e_1, \ldots, e_n)$ e is not constant, or e/n undefined	$e_1 \xrightarrow{d} e_0, \ldots, e_n \xrightarrow{d} e_0, e \xrightarrow{d} e_0$ $e_1 \xrightarrow{b} e_0, \ldots, e_n \xrightarrow{b} e_0, e \xrightarrow{b} e_0$

Fig. 5. Static behaviour dependency graph generation rules (cont.)

function (the result of the last expression of the function clause) flows back into the function call expression.

$e(e_1, \ldots, e_n)$ is an Erlang function call. In case when e is not a constant, we can not create dependency edges between the application and the function definition. The same situation occurs when the function is not defined in our graph – it is not added to the database(Figure 5: Fun. call 2). We handle that case as a worst case scenario, and we generate data dependency edges among the function call and its subexpressions, because we do not know anything about the body of the function and the way how it uses and transforms the value of its parameters.

Built in functions (BIF). There are some built in function in Erlang which operate similar to the data selectors (Figure 4: BIF). For example the `hd/1` function selects the first elements of the list, or the `element/2` function selects the I-th element of a tuple. In these cases we add selector edges to the graph.

When the first parameter of the `element/2` function (I) is not a constant, the Function call 2 rule is applied.

4.4 Deriving Dependency Information

To determine the impact of a modification we need indirect/deeper dependency knowledge, thus we should calculate the transitive closure of the graph and traverse that graph. Each edge in the graph represent a dependency in the program, therefore when we want to determine the impact of a change, we have to traverse the graph using the corresponding defined edges.

A dependency relation between two graph nodes ($n_1 \rightsquigarrow n_2$) means the behaviour of n_2 depends on the result/behaviour of n_1, so the change of the value of n_1 may have an impact on n_2. This relation can be computed using the data flow, data dependency and the behaviour dependency edges.

The informal definition of the dependency relation $n_1 \rightsquigarrow n_2$ is that n_2 is an expression in the graph which could be affected by changing the value of n_1. Those nodes from the graph which could be a copy of n_1 are affected by changing the value of n_1, so modifying n_1 could have an impact on them. Therefore the data flow propagate the changes (data-rule).

Consider the following expression: 1+2. Changing the expression 1 to atom results that the expression 1+2 could not be evaluated and that results a runtime error. Then each expression which behaviour depend on the value of 1+2 also could not be evaluated. Therefore when there is data dependency connection between two nodes ($n_1 \overset{d}{\rightarrow} n_2$), changing the data in n_1 could have an impact on the behaviour of n_2, and those node which behaviour may depend from n_2, also could alter behaviour from the same data change (b-dep-rule). Data flow and the behaviour dependency edges ($\overset{b}{\rightarrow}$) also propagates behaviour dependency among expressions (d-rule, b-rule).

In the followings we formalize the mentioned behaviour dependency relation.

Definition 2. The data flow relation $\overset{d}{\rightsquigarrow}$ is defined as the minimal that satisfies the following rules [7]:

$$n \overset{d}{\rightsquigarrow} n \qquad \text{(reflexive)}$$

$$\frac{n_1 \overset{f}{\rightarrow} n_2}{n_1 \overset{d}{\rightsquigarrow} n_2} \qquad \text{(f-rule)}$$

$$\frac{n_1 \overset{c_i}{\rightarrow} n_2, \ n_2 \overset{d}{\rightsquigarrow} n_3, \ n_3 \overset{s_i}{\rightarrow} n_4}{n_1 \overset{d}{\rightsquigarrow} n_4} \qquad \text{(c-s-rule)}$$

$$\frac{n_1 \overset{d}{\rightsquigarrow} n_2, \ n_2 \overset{d}{\rightsquigarrow} n_3}{n_1 \overset{d}{\rightsquigarrow} n_3} \qquad \text{(transitive)}$$

Definition 3. The behaviour dependency relation $\overset{b}{\rightsquigarrow}$ is defined as the minimal relation that satisfies the following rules:

$$\frac{n_1 \overset{d}{\rightsquigarrow} n_2}{n_1 \overset{b}{\rightsquigarrow} n_2} \qquad \text{(d-rule)}$$

$$\frac{n_1 \overset{b}{\rightsquigarrow} n_2, \ n_2 \overset{b}{\rightarrow} n_3, \ n_3 \overset{b}{\rightsquigarrow} n_4}{n_1 \overset{b}{\rightsquigarrow} n_4} \qquad \text{(b-rule)}$$

Definition 4. The dependency relation $\rightsquigarrow$ is defined as the minimal relation that satisfies the following rules:

$$\frac{n_1 \overset{d}{\rightsquigarrow} n_2}{n_1 \rightsquigarrow n_2} \qquad \text{(data-rule)}$$

$$\frac{n_1 \overset{d}{\rightsquigarrow} n_2, \ n_2 \overset{d}{\rightarrow} n_3, \ n_3 \overset{b}{\rightsquigarrow} n_4}{n_1 \rightsquigarrow n_4} \qquad \text{(b-dep-rule)}$$

4.5   Lemmas

In this section some lemmas about the properties of relations $\overset{b}{\rightsquigarrow}$ and $\rightsquigarrow$ are introduced. The detailed proofs of the lemmas are presented in appendix A.

Lemma 1 ($\overset{b}{\rightsquigarrow}$ reflexive)

$n \overset{b}{\rightsquigarrow} n$

Proof. Applying the rules (reflexive) and (d-rule).

Lemma 2 ($\overset{b}{\rightsquigarrow}$ transitive)

$n_1 \overset{b}{\rightsquigarrow} n_2, \ n_2 \overset{b}{\rightsquigarrow} n_3 \Rightarrow n_1 \overset{b}{\rightsquigarrow} n_3$

Proof. Applying structural induction on $n_1 \overset{b}{\rightsquigarrow} n_2$ and then structural induction on $n_2 \overset{b}{\rightsquigarrow} n_3$.

Lemma 3 ($\rightsquigarrow$ reflexive)

$n \rightsquigarrow n$

Proof. Applying the rules (reflexive) and (data-rule).

Lemma 4 ($\rightsquigarrow$ transitive)

$n_1 \rightsquigarrow n_2, \ n_2 \rightsquigarrow n_3 \Rightarrow n_1 \rightsquigarrow n_3$

Proof. Applying case distinction on $n_1 \rightsquigarrow n_2$ and then case distinction on $n_2 \rightsquigarrow n_3$.

Lemma 5 (generalized b-dep-rule)

$n_1 \overset{d}{\rightsquigarrow} n_2, \ n_2 \overset{d}{\rightarrow} n_3, \ n_3 \rightsquigarrow n_4 \Rightarrow n_1 \rightsquigarrow n_4$

Proof. Applying case distinction on $n_3 \rightsquigarrow n_4$.

Lemma 6 ($\overset{b}{\rightsquigarrow}$ is not symmetrical and is not anti-symmetrical)

Proof. See the counterexamples in appendix A.

4.6   Example

Figures 6 and 7 shows the relevant part of the dependency graphs for the motivation examples.

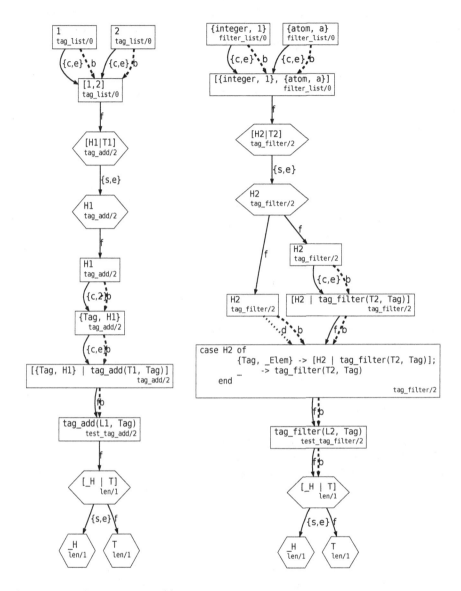

Fig. 6. Dependencies in tag_add   **Fig. 7.** Dependencies in tag_filter

The main difference between them is the H2 $\xrightarrow{d}$ case H2 of ... end edge, which describes that the result and the behaviour of the case-expression depends on H2.

On the left hand side figure, the value 1 simply flows (as a meaning of data flow) into the variable _H (in len/1). The len/1 function does not use the value of _H, so its return value does not depend on it. On the other figure the value of the tuple {integer, 1} flows into the variable H2 (in tag_filter/2). The case-expression depends on the value of H2, the value of the case-expression copied to the result of tag(L1, Tag) (in len/1), so the change of the tuple may have an impact on the len/1 function.

In summary, if we modify the integer 1 we must not the test_tag_add/2 test case, but if we modify the tuple {integer, 1}, we should run test case test_tag_filter/2.

5 Related Work

A methodology for regression test selection in object oriented designs have been already presented in [1]. That methodology represents the designs using the Unified Modeling Language, and gives a formal mapping between design changes and a classification of regression test cases (reusable, retestable, obsolete).

Our model tries to find affected test cases using a graph traversal on the BDG. The BDG adds behaviour edges according to the semantics of the Erlang language to a 0-th order Data Flow Graph (0DFG). Most of the data flow and the behaviour flow edges are specific for Erlang (some of them are discussed in Section 4.3) which do not appears in other languages. Specially, the behaviour edges manly refers to exceptions (that can arise during the evaluation after a data change) in our model. In the analysis of other languages this kind of edges usually do not appear with a data flow graph, rather just the exception handling constructs are handled in a control flow graph [9]. Our model could be applicable to other strict functional languages to detect the spread of a data change, however when applying it to a lazy language further analysis could be useful.

Estimating the impact of a change in functional programming languages is not really widespread yet, however control flow analysis have been already studied by Shivers [8], but this work applied for optimizing compilers. Data flow analysis already defined for Erlang [7] and successfully applied to module interface upgrade. For Erlang the Control flow analysis successfully applied for improving testing [10].

6 Conclusions and Future Work

In this paper we present a dependency graph to calculate the impact of some modification in an Erlang source code. The base idea behind this is to support the programmers to reduce the number of test cases which should be performed after a refactoring transformations. Therefore we have to propagate the change made by the transformation in a behaviour dependency graph. This graph contains the relevant expression nodes from the syntax tree and data flow, data dependency and behaviour dependency edges. The result of the dependency graph has been illustrated in the motivating example.

The size of the presented graph is linear to the size of the syntax tree. If there are n expression nodes in the syntax tree, the size of the graph is $O(n)$, the size of its transitive closure is maximum $O(n^2)$.

This paper shows a structural algorithm to construct the BDG and a relation to calculate the dependency in that graph. The DFG is already implemented in the RefactorErl system, thus we should add the behaviour edges to that graph and implement the dependency relation. Then we could examine the efficiency of our model.

We can improve the presented solution in different ways. The presented model does not make a distinction among the different calls of a function, and the return value of the function is linked to each function call. The problem with that approach is that when we call the function, we reach the result of other function calls, too. To solve this problem we should store context information about the source, i.e. where is the function called. Therefore, more accurate graph could be generated using 1CFA-s [8] or nCFA-s, as the behaviour dependency edges could be generalized according to the order of the analysis, so labeled edges could be used in our BDG to represent the context information. We note, that our model based on a 0DFG and adds behaviour edges to that graph, and it results less test case subset in our example, but using 1DFG-s could also result less test case subset than using 0DFG-s.

When we generate a BDG, it could grow fast, and could be unnecessary huge. Therefore, we should trim the irrelevant parts from the graph. A possible solution should be to combine the control flow with the result of a call graph. First we can create a call graph part from the change, and then we can should create the data flow and the control flow using the affected functions from the call graph. We can build the whole dependency graph and then trim it (for example with slicing), or just build the smaller graph. Thus we can calculate other analysis and iterative algorithms on smaller graphs.

References

1. Briand, L., Labiche, Y., Soccar, G.: Automating impact analysis and regression test selection based on uml designs. In: 18th IEEE International Conference on Software Maintenance, ICSM 2002 (2002)
2. Ericsson, AB, Erlang Reference Manual,
   http://www.erlang.org/doc/reference_manual/part_frame.html
3. Fowler, M., Beck, K., Brant, J., Opdyke, W., Roberts, D.: Refactoring: Improving the Design of Existing Code. Addison-Wesley, Reading (1999)
4. Fredlund, L.-A.: A Framework for Reasoning about ERLANG code. PhD thesis, Royal Institute of Technology, Stockholm, Sweden (2001)
5. Horváth, Z., Lövei, L., Kozsik, T., Kitlei, R., Tóth, M., Bozó, I., Király, R.: Modeling semantic knowledge in Erlang for refactoring. In: Knowledge Engineering: Principles and Techniques, Proceedings of the International Conference on Knowledge Engineering, Principles and Techniques, KEPT 2009, Cluj-Napoca, Romania, Sp. Issue of Studia Universitatis Babe-Bolyai, Series Informatica, vol. 54, pp. 7–16 (July 2009)
6. Horváth, Z., Lövei, L., Kozsik, T., Kitlei, R., Víg, A.N., Nagy, T., Tóth, M., Király, R.: Building a refactoring tool for erlang. In: Workshop on Advanced Software Development Tools and Techniques, WASDETT 2008, Paphos, Cyprus (July 2008)

7. Lövei, L.: Automated module interface upgrade. In: Erlang 2009: Proceedings of the 8th ACM SIGPLAN workshop on Erlang, pp. 11–22. ACM, New York (2009)
8. Shivers, O.: Control-Flow Analysis of Higher-Order Languages. PhD thesis, Carnegie Mellon University (1991)
9. Sinha, S., Harrold, M.J.: Control-flow analysis of programs with exception-handling constructs. Technical Report (1998)
10. Widera, M.: Flow graphs for testing sequential erlang programs. In: Proceedings of the ACM SIGPLAN 2004 Erlang Workshop, pp. 48–53 (2004)

A   The Detailed Proofs of Lemmas.

Lemma 1 ($\overset{b}{\rightsquigarrow}$ reflexive)

$n \overset{b}{\rightsquigarrow} n$

Proof

$$\frac{n \overset{d}{\rightsquigarrow} n \text{ (reflexive)}}{n \overset{b}{\rightsquigarrow} n} \text{ (d-rule)}$$

$\square$

Lemma 2 ($\overset{b}{\rightsquigarrow}$ transitive)

$n_1 \overset{b}{\rightsquigarrow} n_2, \; n_2 \overset{b}{\rightsquigarrow} n_3 \Rightarrow n_1 \overset{b}{\rightsquigarrow} n_3$

Proof. structural induction on $n_1 \overset{b}{\rightsquigarrow} n_2$

a) (base step) $n_1 \overset{d}{\rightsquigarrow} n_2, \; n_2 \overset{b}{\rightsquigarrow} n_3 \Rightarrow n_1 \overset{b}{\rightsquigarrow} n_3$

   structural induction on $n_2 \overset{b}{\rightsquigarrow} n_3$

   i) (base step) $n_1 \overset{d}{\rightsquigarrow} n_2, \; n_2 \overset{d}{\rightsquigarrow} n_3 \Rightarrow n_1 \overset{b}{\rightsquigarrow} n_3$

$$\frac{\dfrac{n_1 \overset{d}{\rightsquigarrow} n_2, \; n_2 \overset{d}{\rightsquigarrow} n_3}{n_1 \overset{d}{\rightsquigarrow} n_3} \text{ (transitive)}}{n_1 \overset{b}{\rightsquigarrow} n_3} \text{ (d-rule)}$$

   ii) (induction step) $n_1 \overset{d}{\rightsquigarrow} n_2, \; n_2 \overset{b}{\rightsquigarrow} n_4, \; n_4 \overset{b}{\rightarrow} n_5, \; n_5 \overset{b}{\rightsquigarrow} n_3 \Rightarrow n_1 \overset{b}{\rightsquigarrow} n_3$

$$\frac{\dfrac{n_1 \overset{d}{\rightsquigarrow} n_2, \; n_2 \overset{b}{\rightsquigarrow} n_4, \; n_4 \overset{b}{\rightarrow} n_5, \; n_5 \overset{b}{\rightsquigarrow} n_3}{n_1 \overset{b}{\rightsquigarrow} n_4, \; n_4 \overset{b}{\rightarrow} n_5, \; n_5 \overset{b}{\rightsquigarrow} n_3} \text{ (induction hypothesis)}}{n_1 \overset{b}{\rightsquigarrow} n_3} \text{ (b-rule)}$$

b) (induction step) $n_1 \overset{b}{\leadsto} n_4, \; n_4 \overset{b}{\to} n_5, \; n_5 \overset{b}{\leadsto} n_2, \; n_2 \overset{b}{\leadsto} n_3 \Rightarrow n_1 \overset{b}{\leadsto} n_3$

$$\frac{n_1 \overset{b}{\leadsto} n_4, \; n_4 \overset{b}{\to} n_5, \; n_5 \overset{b}{\leadsto} n_2, \; n_2 \overset{b}{\leadsto} n_3}{\frac{n_1 \overset{b}{\leadsto} n_4, \; n_4 \overset{b}{\to} n_5, \; n_5 \overset{b}{\leadsto} n_3}{n_1 \overset{b}{\leadsto} n_3} \text{ (b-rule)}} \text{ (induction hypothesis)}$$

$\square$

Lemma 3 ($\leadsto$ reflexive)

$n \leadsto n$

Proof

$$\frac{n \overset{d}{\leadsto} n \text{ (reflexive)}}{n \leadsto n} \text{ (data-rule)}$$

$\square$

Lemma 4 ($\leadsto$ transitive)

$n_1 \leadsto n_2, \; n_2 \leadsto n_3 \Rightarrow n_1 \leadsto n_3$

Proof
case distinction on $n_1 \leadsto n_2$

a) $n_1 \overset{d}{\leadsto} n_2, \; n_2 \leadsto n_3 \Rightarrow n_1 \leadsto n_3$
   case distinction on $n_2 \leadsto n_3$
   i) $n_1 \overset{d}{\leadsto} n_2, \; n_2 \overset{d}{\leadsto} n_3 \Rightarrow n_1 \leadsto n_3$

$$\frac{n_1 \overset{d}{\leadsto} n_2, \; n_2 \overset{d}{\leadsto} n_3}{\frac{n_1 \overset{d}{\leadsto} n_3}{n_1 \leadsto n_3} \text{ (data-rule)}} \text{ (transitive)}$$

   ii) $n_1 \overset{d}{\leadsto} n_2, \; n_2 \overset{d}{\leadsto} n_4, \; n_4 \overset{d}{\to} n_5, \; n_5 \overset{b}{\leadsto} n_3 \Rightarrow n_1 \leadsto n_3$

$$\frac{n_1 \overset{d}{\leadsto} n_2, \; n_2 \overset{d}{\leadsto} n_4, \; n_4 \overset{d}{\to} n_5, \; n_5 \overset{b}{\leadsto} n_3}{\frac{n_1 \overset{d}{\leadsto} n_4, \; n_4 \overset{d}{\to} n_5, \; n_5 \overset{b}{\leadsto} n_3}{n_1 \leadsto n_3} \text{ (b-dep-rule)}} \text{ (transitive)}$$

b) $n_1 \overset{d}{\leadsto} n_4, \; n_4 \overset{d}{\to} n_5, \; n_5 \overset{b}{\leadsto} n_2, \; n_2 \leadsto n_3 \Rightarrow n_1 \leadsto n_3$
   case distinction on $n_2 \leadsto n_3$

i) $n_1 \overset{d}{\leadsto} n_4, \ n_4 \overset{d}{\to} n_5, \ n_5 \overset{b}{\leadsto} n_2, \ n_2 \overset{d}{\leadsto} n_3 \Rightarrow n_1 \leadsto n_3$

$$\frac{n_1 \overset{d}{\leadsto} n_4, \ n_4 \overset{d}{\to} n_5, \ n_5 \overset{b}{\leadsto} n_2, \ n_2 \overset{d}{\leadsto} n_3}{\vDash\!=} \text{(d-rule)}$$

$$\frac{n_1 \overset{d}{\leadsto} n_4, \ n_4 \overset{d}{\to} n_5, \ n_5 \overset{b}{\leadsto} n_2, \ n_2 \overset{b}{\leadsto} n_3}{\vDash\!=} (\overset{b}{\leadsto} \text{ transitive})$$

$$\frac{n_1 \overset{d}{\leadsto} n_4, \ n_4 \overset{d}{\to} n_5, \ n_5 \overset{b}{\leadsto} n_3}{\vDash\!=\!=\!=\!=\!=\!=\!=\!=\!=\!=\!=\!=\!=\!=\!=\!=\!=\!=} \text{(b-dep-rule)}$$
$$n_1 \leadsto n_3$$

ii) $n_1 \overset{d}{\leadsto} n_4, \ n_4 \overset{d}{\to} n_5, \ n_5 \overset{b}{\leadsto} n_2, \ n_2 \overset{d}{\leadsto} n_6, \ n_6 \overset{d}{\to} n_7, \ n_7 \overset{b}{\leadsto} n_3$
$\Rightarrow n_1 \leadsto n_3$

$$\frac{\begin{array}{c} n_1 \overset{d}{\leadsto} n_4, \ n_4 \overset{d}{\to} n_5, \ n_5 \overset{b}{\leadsto} n_2, \\ n_2 \overset{d}{\leadsto} n_6, \ n_6 \overset{d}{\to} n_7, \ n_7 \overset{b}{\leadsto} n_3 \end{array}}{\vDash\!=\!=\!=\!=\!=\!=\!=\!=\!=\!=\!=\!=\!=\!=\!=\!=\!=\!=} \text{(d-rule)}$$

$$\frac{\begin{array}{c} n_1 \overset{d}{\leadsto} n_4, \ n_4 \overset{d}{\to} n_5, \ n_5 \overset{b}{\leadsto} n_2, \\ n_2 \overset{b}{\leadsto} n_6, \ n_6 \overset{d}{\to} n_7, \ n_7 \overset{b}{\leadsto} n_3 \end{array}}{\vDash\!=\!=\!=\!=\!=\!=\!=\!=\!=\!=\!=\!=\!=\!=\!=\!=\!=\!=} (\overset{b}{\leadsto} \text{ transitive})$$

$$\frac{\begin{array}{c} n_1 \overset{d}{\leadsto} n_4, \ n_4 \overset{d}{\to} n_5, \\ n_5 \overset{b}{\leadsto} n_6, \ n_6 \overset{d}{\to} n_7, \ n_7 \overset{b}{\leadsto} n_3 \end{array}}{\vDash\!=\!=\!=\!=\!=\!=\!=\!=\!=\!=\!=\!=\!=\!=\!=\!=\!=\!=} \text{(d-b-rule)}$$

$$\frac{\begin{array}{c} n_1 \overset{d}{\leadsto} n_4, \ n_4 \overset{d}{\to} n_5, \\ n_5 \overset{b}{\leadsto} n_6, \ n_6 \overset{b}{\to} n_7, \ n_7 \overset{b}{\leadsto} n_3 \end{array}}{\vDash\!=\!=\!=\!=\!=\!=\!=\!=\!=\!=\!=\!=\!=\!=\!=\!=\!=\!=} \text{(b-rule)}$$

$$\frac{n_1 \overset{d}{\leadsto} n_4, \ n_4 \overset{d}{\to} n_5, \ n_5 \overset{b}{\leadsto} n_3}{\vDash\!=\!=\!=\!=\!=\!=\!=\!=\!=\!=\!=\!=\!=\!=\!=\!=\!=\!=} \text{(b-dep-rule)}$$
$$n_1 \leadsto n_3$$

□

Lemma 5 (generalized b-dep-rule)
$n_1 \overset{d}{\leadsto} n_2, \ n_2 \overset{d}{\to} n_3, \ n_3 \leadsto n_4 \Rightarrow n_1 \leadsto n_4$

Proof
case distinction on $n_3 \leadsto n_4$

a) $n_1 \overset{d}{\leadsto} n_2, \ n_2 \overset{d}{\to} n_3, \ n_3 \overset{d}{\leadsto} n_4 \Rightarrow n_1 \leadsto n_4$

$$\frac{n_1 \overset{d}{\leadsto} n_2, \ n_2 \overset{d}{\to} n_3, \ n_3 \overset{d}{\leadsto} n_4}{\vDash\!=\!=\!=\!=\!=\!=\!=\!=\!=\!=\!=\!=\!=\!=\!=\!=\!=\!=} \text{(b-rule)}$$

$$\frac{n_1 \overset{d}{\leadsto} n_2, \ n_2 \overset{d}{\to} n_3, \ n_3 \overset{b}{\leadsto} n_4}{\vDash\!=\!=\!=\!=\!=\!=\!=\!=\!=\!=\!=\!=\!=\!=\!=\!=\!=\!=} \text{(b-dep-rule)}$$
$$n_1 \leadsto n_4$$

b) $n_1 \overset{d}{\rightsquigarrow} n_2$, $n_2 \overset{d}{\rightarrow} n_3$, $n_3 \overset{d}{\rightsquigarrow} n_5$, $n_5 \overset{d}{\rightarrow} n_6$, $n_6 \overset{b}{\rightsquigarrow} n_4 \Rightarrow n_1 \rightsquigarrow n_4$

$$\frac{n_1 \overset{d}{\rightsquigarrow} n_2, \; n_2 \overset{d}{\rightarrow} n_3, \; n_3 \overset{d}{\rightsquigarrow} n_5, \; n_5 \overset{d}{\rightarrow} n_6, \; n_6 \overset{b}{\rightsquigarrow} n_4}{} \quad \text{(d-b-rule)}$$

$$\frac{n_1 \overset{d}{\rightsquigarrow} n_2, \; n_2 \overset{d}{\rightarrow} n_3, \; n_3 \overset{d}{\rightsquigarrow} n_5, \; n_5 \overset{b}{\rightarrow} n_6, \; n_6 \overset{b}{\rightsquigarrow} n_4}{} \quad \text{(d-rule)}$$

$$\frac{n_1 \overset{d}{\rightsquigarrow} n_2, \; n_2 \overset{d}{\rightarrow} n_3, \; n_3 \overset{b}{\rightsquigarrow} n_5, \; n_5 \overset{b}{\rightarrow} n_6, \; n_6 \overset{b}{\rightsquigarrow} n_4}{} \quad \text{(b-rule)}$$

$$\frac{n_1 \overset{d}{\rightsquigarrow} n_2, \; n_2 \overset{d}{\rightarrow} n_3, \; n_3 \overset{b}{\rightsquigarrow} n_4}{n_1 \rightsquigarrow n_4} \quad \text{(b-dep-rule)}$$

□

Lemma 6 ($\overset{b}{\rightsquigarrow}$ is not symmetrical and is not anti-symmetrical)

Proof. Lets consider the following examples:

Example 1

```
ten()-> 10.
add_ten(X) -> X + ten().
```

$\overset{b}{\rightsquigarrow}$ is not symmetrical if exist two expression in the graph n_1 and n_2 where $n_1 \overset{b}{\rightsquigarrow} n_2$ but *not* $n_2 \overset{b}{\rightsquigarrow} n_1$. If n_1 is the integer 10 from the body of `ten/0` and n_2 is the function call `ten()` in the body of `add_ten/1` then:

$$\frac{n_1 \overset{b}{\rightsquigarrow} n_1, \; n_1 \overset{b}{\rightarrow} n_2, \; n_2 \overset{b}{\rightsquigarrow} n_2}{n_1 \overset{b}{\rightsquigarrow} n_2} \quad \text{(b-rule)}$$

Based on the behaviour dependency graph building rules (Figures 4. and 5.), only two edges start from n_2: a $\overset{b}{\rightarrow}$ and a $\overset{d}{\rightarrow}$ edge, both to the direction of the infix expression `X + ten()`. There is now direct edges or graph paths starting from the expression `X + ten()`, thus does not exist any path from n_2 to n_1, so *not* $n_2 \overset{b}{\rightsquigarrow} n_1$.

Example 2

```
f(0) -> 0;
f(A) when A > 0 -> f(A) - 1.
```

$\overset{b}{\rightsquigarrow}$ is not anti-symmetrical if exist two expression in the graph n_1 and n_2 where $n_1 \overset{b}{\rightsquigarrow} n_2$ and $n_2 \overset{b}{\rightsquigarrow} n_1$. If n_1 is the infix expression `f(A)-10` and n_2 is the function call `f(A)` then both $n_1 \overset{b}{\rightsquigarrow} n_2$ and $n_2 \overset{b}{\rightsquigarrow} n_1$ are true:

$$\frac{n_1 \overset{f}{\rightarrow} n_2}{\models======== \quad \text{(f-rule)}}{n_1 \overset{d}{\rightsquigarrow} n_2}$$

$$\frac{n_1 \overset{d}{\rightsquigarrow} n_2}{\models======== \quad \text{(d-rule)}}{n_1 \overset{b}{\rightsquigarrow} n_2}$$

$$\frac{n_2 \overset{b}{\rightsquigarrow} n_2 \ (\overset{b}{\rightsquigarrow} reflexive), \ n_2 \overset{b}{\rightarrow} n_1, \ n_1 \overset{b}{\rightsquigarrow} n_1 \ (\overset{b}{\rightsquigarrow} reflexive)}{\models================================= \quad \text{(b-rule)}}{n_2 \overset{b}{\rightsquigarrow} n_1}$$

$n_1 \overset{f}{\rightarrow} n_2$ is based on the rule *Fun call 1.* and $n_2 \overset{b}{\rightarrow} n_1$ is based on the rule *Infix exp.*

$\square$

Author Index

Achten, Peter   224

Bergstrom, Lars   94
Bozó, István   372

Cesarini, Francesco   19

Dévai, Gergely   354
Diviánszky, Péter   146

Fluet, Matthew   94
Ford, Nic   94

Granicz, Adam   1

Hinze, Ralf   42
Horváth, Zoltán   372
Hughes, John   183

Kennedy, Andrew   268
Koopman, Pieter   224
Kozsik, Tamás   372

Lövei, László   372

Plasmeijer, Rinus   224
Porkoláb, Zoltán   306

Rainey, Mike   94
Reppy, John   94

Shaw, Adam   94

Tejfel, Máté   372
Thompson, Simon   19
Tóth, Melinda   372

Xiao, Yingqi   94

Printed in the United States
By Bookmasters